"The controversy over the serious flaws in the 1619 Project's accounts of American history began with the WSWS's interviews of numerous highly distinguished liberal and left scholars. Th̲... e critiques and others met with no re̲... the project's overseers. Even now, des̲... ̲g, glaring factual errors remain in the̲... vindicates W. E. B. Du Bois's conde̲... ̲ as history."

— Sean Wilentz, Princeton University, Bancroft Prize-winning author of
The Rise of American Democracy: Jefferson to Lincoln

"This is a conscientious collection of criticisms of the *New York Times'* 1619 Project. It includes interviews with eminent historians; especially valuable is that of Richard Carwardine, who provides a perspective from overseas. The documents expose the shortcomings in the Project and the extent to which the *Times* has withdrawn and minimized the most exaggerated aspects of the 1619 Project. The collection would be even more valuable if it included documents from the New York Times as well as from its critics."

— Daniel Walker Howe, University of California, Los Angeles,
Pulitzer Prize-winning author of *What Hath God Wrought*

"Although not everyone will agree with all of its arguments, this volume presents a powerful critique of the *New York Times'* 1619 Project and deserves a wide readership. The contributors to that Project incorrectly maintain that slavery was a uniquely American evil, that a principal motive of those who engaged in the American Revolution was to defend slavery, that virtually no white Americans opposed slavery, and—ignoring the extensive attention of scholars during the past half century—that slavery and antiblack racism represent the 'suppressed history' of the United States. The Project's authors essentialize race, arguing that throughout American history virtually all white Americans have displayed an unchanging antiblack racism that 'runs in the very DNA of this country.' In essays first published on the World Socialist Web Site, and in interviews with several prominent historians, these arguments receive convincing refutation."

— Peter Kolchin, University of Delaware, Bancroft Prize-winning author of
Unfree Labor: American Slavery and Russian Serfdom

"Fears of association with Trump and his white-supremacist allies can inhibit leftist criticism of the 1619 Project. But from a bold socialist-revolutionary perspective, Mackaman's and North's volume argues cogently that the 1619 Project misinterprets historical causes and effects by positing eternal and immutable cultural or 'racial' identities that deny past—and preclude present and future—collective action against capitalist and imperial power."

— Kerby Miller, University of Missouri, Pulitzer Prize finalist author of
   Emigrants and Exiles: Ireland and the Irish Exodus to North America

"The breadth and lucidity of its arguments, paired to its intelligent defense of the great revolutionary and democratic traditions of the United States, should commend this book to the broadest readership in ordinary times. But the publication of this extraordinary volume in today's climate of accelerating crisis signals, at last, the beginning of a struggle against the complacent, racialist, disingenuously 'intersectional,' and unalloyedly reactionary conceptions dominating academia and the broader political discourse."

— Emanuele Saccarelli, San Diego State University, author of *Gramsci and Trotsky in
   the Shadow of Stalinism: The Political Theory and Practice of Opposition*

"The publication of the 1619 Project has prompted a robust conversation about the relationship between slavery, racism, and the American founding. David North and Thomas Mackaman have been important players in this conversation. They have gathered an impressive array of American historians to critique the 1619 Project, making this book essential reading for anyone interested in a nuanced and informed take on an issue that is central to our democratic life."

— John Fea, Messiah University, author of
   Why Study History: Reflecting on the Importance of the Past

"*The New York Times' 1619 Project and the Racialist Falsification of History* is a brave and necessary response to the errors in fact and interpretation that characterize the 1619 Project. It may be that the survival of the historical profession as a legitimate enterprise depends on this critique being heard."

— William E. Weeks, San Diego State University, author of *Building the Continental
   Empire: American Expansion from the Revolution to the Civil War*

"[A] frank, refreshing, and unrelenting critique of the 1619 Project. In the age of cancel culture, identity politics, Twitterstars, and the toxic Trump nightmare, much of academia has fallen silent as the 1619 Project wrenched the American Revolution and the institution of slavery from their global historical context, dismissed Abraham Lincoln as a run-of-the-mill racist, and skipped like a river rock over the abolitionist movement, Civil War, and more than fifty years of historiography. The spell that the 1619 Project cast on academia makes the publication of this book all the more timely and important."

— Gregg Andrews, Department of History, Texas State University, author *of Thyra J. Edwards: Black Activist in the Global Freedom Struggle*

"You don't have to agree with the historical interpretations of Leon Trotsky's old Fourth International to respect and benefit from the institutional stance it has taken—almost alone—against the false statements printed, and sensationalized, by the *New York Times* in the introduction to its '1619' series. All who care about this nation's history of slavery and racism, and all who reject the efforts of powerful institutions to falsify that history, should read the interviews of eight reputable scholars reprinted here. Those eight interviews—along with public statements made elsewhere by historians Leslie Harris and Peter Coclanis—call the *New York Times* to account for its dishonesty. They show that we can still rely on some academic professionals—if only these ten—to demand and defend the truth about our racist past. The historians' profession as a whole declined to hold 'the' *Times* responsible for its falsehoods—even as that once distinguished paper began to hype its false mythology as a pre-fab curriculum for unsuspecting public schools. '1619' boosters are still offering the curriculum as a magical way for schools to inoculate themselves against charges of racism.

Most of the historical profession continues to temporize, prevaricate, or remain conspicuously off the record. Thus the profession enables the Trump administration's equal and opposite mythology, '1776,' to occupy the only alternative space in the broad public view of our mass-mediated world. The alleged paper of record could have discreetly retracted its mistakes, in time-honored fashion, and moved on. Instead, it insisted it had nothing to apologize for. It presents itself, almost unchallenged, as the authority best equipped to reform America's history curriculum and, more hilariously, as the vanguard of a new mass movement of opposition to racism. This book contains enough material to show that honest students of the American past, and honest journalists, can do better. Interested readers can get the honesty they deserve, if they are willing to demand it. I'm dropping my subscription to the *NY Times* long enough to pay for this book."

— David Chappell, University of Oklahoma,
  author of *A Stone of Hope* and *Waking from the Dream*

"This book is essential in two ways: it helps you realize how historically inaccurate the 1619 Project is and how fundamentally reactionary its politics are. Everyone interested in understanding what actually happened then and what's actually happening now needs to read it."

— Walter Benn Michaels, Department of English, University of Illinois Chicago, author
  of *The Trouble with Diversity: How We Learned to Love Identity and Ignore Inequality*

The New York Times' 1619 Project and the Racialist Falsification of History

The New York Times' 1619 Project and the Racialist Falsification of History

Essays and Interviews

Edited by David North
and Thomas Mackaman

Mehring Books
Oak Park, Michigan
2021

Library of Congress Cataloging-in-Publication Data
Names: North, David, 1950– editor. | Mackaman, Thomas, 1975– editor.
Title: The New York Times' 1619 Project and the racialist falsification of history:
    essays and interviews edited by David North, and Thomas Mackaman.
Description: Oak Park, Michigan : Mehring Books, 2021. | Includes bibliographical
    references and index. | Summary: "The New York Times' 1619 Project, launched in
    August 2019, mobilized vast editorial and financial resources to portray racial conflict as
    the central driving force of American history. By denigrating the democratic content of
    the American Revolution and of the Civil War, it sought to erode democratic
    consciousness and to undermine the common struggle of the working class of all ethnic
    backgrounds against staggering social inequality. The book includes the World Socialist
    Web Site refutation of the 1619 Project, interviews with eight leading historians, a lecture
    series on American history, and a record of the controversy"—Provided by publisher.
Identifiers: LCCN 2021005130 | ISBN 9781893638938 (paperback) |
    ISBN 9781893638945 (kindle edition) | ISBN 9781893638952 (epub)
Subjects: LCSH: 1619 Project. | Slavery—United States—History. |
    United States—History—Study and teaching. | United States—Historiography. |
    Critical pedagogy.
Classification: LCC E441 .N57 2021 | DDC 306.3/620973—dc23
LC record available at https://lccn.loc.gov/2021005130

Cover design: Kevin Reed

Contents

III   Polemics

IV   Historical Commentary

V   The Crisis of the *New York Times'* 1619 Project

Contents

Contributors

Thomas Mackaman is associate professor of history at King's College in Wilkes-Barre, Pennsylvania. He is the author of *New Immigrants and the Radicalization of American Labor, 1914–1924*, and writes on historical topics for the World Socialist Web Site (WSWS).

David North has played a leading role in the international Trotskyist movement for nearly a half century. He is chairman of the International Editorial Board of the WSWS and national chairman of the Socialist Equality Party (SEP) in the US. He is the author of numerous books on history and Marxist theory, including *The Heritage We Defend: A Contribution to the History of the Fourth International*; *In Defense of Leon Trotsky*; *The Russian Revolution and the Unfinished Twentieth Century*; *The Frankfurt School, Postmodernism and the Politics of the Pseudo-left: A Marxist Critique*; *The Crisis of American Democracy*; and *A Quarter Century of War: The US Drive for Global Hegemony 1990–2016*.

Niles Niemuth is managing editor of the WSWS; in 2018, he ran as the SEP candidate to represent Michigan's Twelfth Congressional District in the US House. Niemuth earned an MA in history at the University of Wisconsin, Milwaukee.

Eric London is a writer for the WSWS. He is the author of the book *Agents: The FBI and GPU Infiltration of the Trotskyist Movement*.

Joseph Kishore is national secretary of the SEP in the US and was its candidate for president in 2020.

Bill Van Auken, who has played a leading role in the Trotskyist movement since the 1970s, is the international foreign affairs editor of the WSWS.

Tom Peters and John Braddock are members of the Socialist Equality Group in New Zealand and contributors to the WSWS.

Renae Cassimeda is a writer for the WSWS.

Trévon Austin is a writer for the WSWS.

Tom Carter is a writer for the WSWS.

Foreword

I should respectfully suggest that although the oppressed may need history for identity and inspiration, they need it above all for the truth of what the world has made of them and of what they have helped make of the world. This knowledge alone can produce that sense of identity which ought to be sufficient for inspiration; and those who look to history to provide glorious moments and heroes invariably are betrayed into making catastrophic errors of political judgment.
—Eugene Genovese[1]

Both ideological and historical myths are a product of immediate class interests. ... These myths may be refuted by restoring historical truth—the honest presentation of actual facts and tendencies of the past.
—Vadim Z. Rogovin[2]

On August 14, 2019, the *New York Times* unveiled the 1619 Project. Timed to coincide with the four-hundredth anniversary of the arrival of the first slaves in colonial Virginia, the 100-page special edition of the *New York Times Magazine* consisted of a series of essays that present American history as an unyielding racial struggle, in which black Americans have waged a solitary fight to redeem democracy against white racism.

The *Times* mobilized vast editorial and financial resources behind the 1619 Project. With backing from the corporate-endowed Pulitzer Center on Crisis

---

1. "The Nat Turner Case," in the *New York Review of Books,* September 12, 1968.
2. Vadim Z. Rogovin, *Bolsheviks Against Stalinism 1928–1933: Leon Trotsky and the Left Opposition* (Oak Park: Mehring Books, 2019), p. 2.

Reporting, hundreds of thousands of copies were sent to schools. The 1619 Project fanned out to other media formats. Plans were even announced for films and television programming, backed by billionaire media personality Oprah Winfrey.

As a business venture the 1619 Project clambers on, but as an effort at historical revision it has been, to a great extent, discredited. This outcome is owed in large measure to the intervention of the World Socialist Web Site, with the support of a number of distinguished and courageous historians, which exposed the 1619 Project for what it is: a combination of shoddy journalism, careless and dishonest research, and a false, politically-motivated narrative that makes racism and racial conflict the central driving forces of American history.

In support of its claim that American history can be understood only when viewed through the prism of racial conflict, the 1619 Project sought to discredit American history's two foundational events: the Revolution of 1775–83 and the Civil War of 1861–65. This could only be achieved by a series of distortions, omissions, half-truths, and false statements—deceptions that are catalogued and refuted in this book.

The *New York Times* is no stranger to scandals produced by dishonest and unprincipled journalism. Its long and checkered history includes such episodes as its endorsement of the Moscow frame-up trials of 1936–38 by the Pulitzer Prize-winning correspondent Walter Duranty and, during World War II, its unconscionable decision to treat the murder of millions of European Jews as "a relatively unimportant story" that did not require extensive and systematic coverage.[3] More recently, the *Times* was implicated, through the reporting of Judith Miller and the columns of Thomas Friedman, in the peddling of government misinformation about "weapons of mass destruction" that served to legitimize the 2003 invasion of Iraq. Many other examples of flagrant violations even of the generally lax standards of journalistic ethics could be cited, especially during the past decade, as the *New York Times*—listed on the New York Stock Exchange with a market capitalization of $7.5 billion—acquired increasingly the character of a media empire.

The "financialization" of the *Times* has proceeded alongside another critical determinant of the newspaper's selection of issues to be publicized and promoted: that is, its central role in the formulation and aggressive marketing of the policies of the Democratic Party. This process has served to obliterate the always tenuous boundary lines between objective reporting and sheer propa-

---

3. Laurel Leff, *Buried by the Times: The Holocaust and America's Most Important Newspaper* (Cambridge: Cambridge University Press, 2005), p. 5.

ganda. The consequences of the *Times'* financial and political evolution have found a particularly reactionary expression in the 1619 Project. Led by Nikole Hannah-Jones and *New York Times Magazine* editor Jake Silverstein, the 1619 Project was developed for the purpose of providing the Democratic Party with a historical narrative that legitimized its efforts to develop an electoral constituency based on the promotion of racial politics. Assisting the Democratic Party's decades-long efforts to disassociate itself from its identification with the era of social welfare liberalism, from the New Deal to the Great Society, the 1619 Project, by prioritizing racial conflict, marginalizes, and even eliminates, class conflict as a notable factor in history and politics.

The shift from class struggle to racial conflict did not develop within a vacuum. The *New York Times*, as we shall explain, is drawing upon and exploiting reactionary intellectual tendencies that have been fermenting within substantial sections of middle-class academia for several decades.

The political interests and related ideological considerations that motivated the 1619 Project determined the unprincipled and dishonest methods employed by the *Times* in its creation. The *Times* was well aware of the fact that it was promoting a race-based narrative of American history that could not withstand critical evaluation by leading scholars of the Revolution and Civil War. The *New York Times Magazine's* editor deliberately rejected consultation with the most respected and authoritative historians.

Moreover, when one of the *Times'* fact-checkers identified false statements that were utilized to support the central arguments of the 1619 Project, her findings were ignored. And as the false claims and factual errors were exposed, the *Times* surreptitiously edited key phrases in 1619 Project material posted online. The knowledge and expertise of historians of the stature of Gordon Wood and James McPherson were of no use to the *Times*. Its editors knew they would object to the central thesis of the 1619 Project, promoted by lead essayist Hannah-Jones: that the American Revolution was launched as a conspiracy to defend slavery against pending British emancipation.

Hannah-Jones had asserted:

> Conveniently left out of our founding mythology is the fact that one of the primary reasons the colonists decided to declare their independence from Britain was because they wanted to protect the institution of slavery. By 1776, Britain had grown deeply conflicted over its role in the barbaric institution that had reshaped the Western Hemisphere. In London, there were growing calls

to abolish the slave trade. ... Some might argue that this nation
was founded not as a democracy but as a slavocracy.[4]

This claim—that the American Revolution was not a revolution at all,
but a counterrevolution waged to defend slavery—is freighted with enormous
implications for American and world history. The denunciation of the
American Revolution legitimizes the rejection of all historical narratives
that attribute any progressive content to the overthrow of British rule over
the colonies and, therefore, to the wave of democratic revolutions that it
inspired throughout the world. If the establishment of the United States was a
counterrevolution, the founding document of this event—the Declaration of
Independence, which proclaimed the equality of man—merits only contempt
as an exemplar of the basest hypocrisy.

How, then, can one explain the explosive global impact of the American
Revolution upon the thought and politics of its immediate contemporaries
and of the generations that followed?

The philosopher Denis Diderot—among the greatest of all Enlightenment
thinkers—responded ecstatically to the American Revolution:

> After centuries of general oppression, may the revolution which
> has just occurred across the seas, by offering all the inhabitants of
> Europe an asylum against fanaticism and tyranny, instruct those
> who govern men on the legitimate use of their authority! May
> these brave Americans, who would rather see their wives raped,
> their children murdered, their dwellings destroyed, their fields
> ravaged, their villages burned, and rather shed their blood and
> die than lose the slightest portion of their freedom, prevent the
> enormous accumulation and unequal distribution of wealth, lux-
> ury, effeminacy, and corruption of manners, and may they pro-
> vide for the maintenance of their freedom and the survival of
> their government![5]

Voltaire, in February 1778, only months before his death, arranged a
public meeting with Benjamin Franklin, the much-celebrated envoy of the
American Revolution. The aged *philosophe* related in a letter that his embrace

---

4. *New York Times Magazine*, August 18, 2019, p. 18.
5. Quoted in Peter Gay, *The Enlightenment: The Science of Freedom* (New York and London:
W. W. Norton, 1996), pp. 556–57.

of Franklin was witnessed by twenty spectators who were moved to "tender tears."[6]

Marx was correct when he wrote, in his 1867 preface to the first edition of *Das Kapital*, that "the American War of Independence sounded the tocsin for the European middle class," inspiring the uprisings that were to sweep away the feudal rubbish, accumulated over centuries, of the *Ancien Régime.*[7]

As the historian Peter Gay noted in his celebrated study of Enlightenment culture and politics, "The liberty that the Americans had won and were guarding was not merely an exhilarating performance that delighted European spectators and gave them grounds for optimism about man; it was also proving a realistic ideal worthy of imitation."[8]

R. R. Palmer, among the most erudite of mid-twentieth-century historians, defined the American Revolution as a critical moment in the evolution of Western civilization, the beginning of a forty-year era of democratic revolutions. Palmer wrote:

> The American and the French Revolutions, the two chief actual revolutions of the period, with all due allowance for the great differences between them, nevertheless shared a great deal in common, and that what they shared was shared also at the same time by various people and movements in other countries, notably in England, Ireland, Holland, Belgium, Switzerland, and Italy, but also in Germany, Hungary, and Poland, and by scattered individuals in places like Spain and Russia.[9]

More recently, Jonathan Israel, historian and author of several volumes on the radical Enlightenment, argues that the American Revolution

> formed part of a wider transatlantic revolutionary sequence, a series of revolutions in France, Italy, Holland, Switzerland, Germany, Ireland, Haiti, Poland, Spain, Greece, and Spanish America. ... The endeavors of the Founding Fathers and their followings abroad prove the deep interaction of the American Revolution and its principles with the other revolutions,

---

6. Ibid, p. 557.
7. Karl Marx, "Capital, Volume 1" *Marx & Engels Collected Works*, Vol. 35 (London: Lawrence & Wishart, 1996), p. 9.
8. Gay, *The Enlightenment: The Science of Freedom,* p. 558.
9. R. R. Palmer, *The Age of Democratic Revolution: A Political History of Europe and America, 1760–1800* (Princeton: Princeton University Press, 1959), p. 5.

substantiating the Revolution's global role less as a directly intervening force than inspirational motor, the primary model, for universal change.[10]

Marxists have never viewed either the American or French Revolutions through rose-tinted glasses. In examining world-historical events, Friedrich Engels rejected simplistic pragmatic interpretations that explain and judge "everything according to the motives of the action," which divides "men who act in history into noble and ignoble and then finds that as a rule the noble are defrauded and the ignoble are victorious." Personal motives, Engels insisted, are only of a "secondary importance." The critical questions that historians must ask are: "What driving forces in turn stand behind these motives? What are the historical causes which transform themselves into these motives in the minds of the actors?"[11]

Whatever the personal motives and individual limitations of those who led the struggle for independence, the revolution waged by the American colonies against the British Crown was rooted in objective socioeconomic processes associated with the rise of capitalism as a world system. Slavery had existed for several thousand years, but the specific form that it assumed between the sixteenth and nineteenth centuries was bound up with the development and expansion of capitalism. As Marx explained:

> The discovery of gold and silver in America, the extirpation, enslavement and entombment in mines of the aboriginal population, the beginning of the conquest and looting of the East Indies, the turning of Africa into a warren for the commercial hunting of black-skins, signalised the rosy dawn of the era of capitalist production. These idyllic proceedings are the chief momenta of the era of capitalist accumulation.[12]

Marx and Engels insisted upon the historically progressive character of the American Revolution, an appraisal that was validated by the Civil War. Marx wrote to Lincoln in 1865 that it was in the American Revolution that "the idea of one great Democratic Republic had first sprung up, whence the first

---

10. Jonathan Israel, *The Expanding Blaze: How the American Revolution Ignited the World, 1775–1848* (Princeton: Princeton University Press, 2017), pp. 17–18.

11. Friedrich Engels, "Ludwig Feuerbach and the Outcome of Classical German Philosophy," *Marx & Engels Collected Works*, Vol. 26 (London: Lawrence & Wishart, 2010), p. 388.

12. Karl Marx, "Capital, Volume 1," *Marx & Engels Collected Works*, Vol. 35 (New York: International Publishers, 1984), p. 739.

Declaration of the Rights of Man was issued, and the first impulse given to the European revolution of the eighteenth century."[13]

Nothing in Hannah-Jones's essay indicates that she has thought through, or is even aware of the implications, from the standpoint of world history, of the 1619 Project's denunciation of the American Revolution. In fact, the 1619 Project was concocted without consulting the works of the preeminent historians of the Revolution and Civil War. This was not an oversight, but rather, the outcome of a deliberate decision by the *New York Times* to bar, to the greatest extent possible, the participation of "white" scholars in the development and writing of the essays. In an article titled "How the 1619 Project Came Together," published on August 18, 2019, the *Times* informed its readers, "Almost every contributor in the magazine and special section—writers, photographers and artists—is black, a nonnegotiable aspect of the project that helps underscore its thesis. ..."[14]

In fact, despite the color barrier favored by Hannah-Jones, essays included in the 1619 Project were written by "whites." These efforts—by sociologist Matthew Desmond and historian Kevin Kruse—are no better than the rest. This only goes to prove that the racialist viewpoint is rooted not in the racial identity of the author, but rather, in his or her class position and ideological orientation.

In any event, even if the *Times* had to bend its own rules, the "nonnegotiable" and racist insistence that the 1619 Project be produced almost exclusively by blacks was justified with the false claim that white historians had largely ignored the subject of American slavery. And on the rare occasions when white historians acknowledged slavery's existence, they either downplayed its significance or lied about it. Therefore, only black writers could "tell our story truthfully." The 1619 Project's race-based narrative would place "the consequences of slavery and the contributions of black Americans at the very center of the story we tell ourselves about who we are."[15]

The 1619 Project was a falsification not only of history, but of historiography. It ignored the work of American historians, dating back to the 1950s. The authors and editors of the 1619 Project had consulted no serious scholarship on slavery, the American Revolution, the abolitionist movement, the

13. Karl Marx, "To Abraham Lincoln, President of the United States," *Marx & Engels Collected Works*, Vol. 20 (New York: International Publishers, 1984), p. 19.

14. "How the 1619 Project Came Together." Accessed on 12/3/2020: https://www.nytimes.com/2019/08/18/reader-center/1619-project-slavery-jamestown.html

15. *New York Times Magazine*, August 18, 2019, p. 5

Civil War, or Jim Crow segregation. There is no evidence that Hannah-Jones's study of American history extended beyond the reading of a single book, written in the early 1960s, by the late black nationalist writer, Lerone Bennett Jr., *Before the Mayflower*.[16] Her "reframing" of American history, to be sent out to the schools as the foundation of a new curriculum, did not even bother with a bibliography.

Hannah-Jones and Silverstein argued that they were creating "a new narrative," to replace the supposedly "white narrative" that had existed before. In one of her countless Twitter tirades, Hannah-Jones declared that "the 1619 Project is not a history." It is, rather, "about who gets to control the national narrative, and, therefore, the nation's shared memory of itself." In this remark, Hannah-Jones explicitly extols the separation of historical research from the effort to truthfully reconstruct the past. The purpose of history is declared to be nothing more than the creation of a serviceable narrative for the realization of one or another political agenda. The truth or untruth of the narrative is not a matter of concern.

Nationalist myth-making has, for a long period, played a significant political role in promoting the interests of aggrieved middle-class strata that are striving to secure a more privileged place in the existing power structures. As Eric Hobsbawm laconically observed, "The socialists ... who rarely used the word 'nationalism' without the prefix 'petty-bourgeois,' knew what they were talking about."[17]

Despite the claims that Hannah-Jones was forging a new path for the study and understanding of American history, the 1619 Project's insistence on a race-centered history of America, authored by African American historians, revived the racial arguments promoted by black nationalists in the 1960s. For all the militant posturing, the underlying agenda, as subsequent events were to demonstrate, was to carve out special career niches for the benefit of a segment of the African American middle class. In the academic world, this agenda advanced the demand that subject matter pertaining to the historical experience of the black population should be allocated exclusively to African Americans. Thus, in the ensuing fight for the distribution of privilege and status, leading historians who had made major contributions to the study of slavery were denounced for intruding, as whites, into a subject that could be

---

16. Lerone Bennett Jr., *Before the Mayflower: A History of the Negro in America, 1619–1964* (Penguin Books, 1970).

17. E. J. Hobsbawm, *Nations and Nationalism Since 1780: Program, Myth, Reality* (London: Cambridge University Press, 1991), p. 117.

understood and explained only by black historians. Peter Novick, in his book *That Noble Dream*, recalled the impact of black nationalist racism on the writing of American history:

> Kenneth Stampp was told by militants that, as a white man, he had no right to write *The Peculiar Institution*. Herbert Gutman, presenting a paper to the Association for the Study of Negro Life and History, was shouted down. A white colleague who was present (and had the same experience), reported that Gutman was "shattered." Gutman pleaded to no avail that he was "extremely supportive of the black liberation movement—if people would just forget that I am white and hear what I am saying ... [it] would lend support to the movement." Among the most dramatic incidents of this sort was the treatment accorded Robert Starobin, a young leftist supporter of the Black Panthers, who delivered a paper on slavery at a Wayne State University conference in 1969, an incident which devastated Starobin at the time, and was rendered the more poignant by his suicide the following year.[18]

Despite these attacks, white historians continued to write major studies on American slavery, the Civil War, and Reconstruction. Rude attempts to introduce a racial qualification in judging a historian's "right" to deal with slavery met with vigorous opposition. The historian Eugene Genovese (1930–2012), author of such notable works as *The Political Economy of Slavery* and *The World the Slaveholders Made*, wrote:

> Every historian of the United States and especially the South cannot avoid making estimates of the black experience, for without them he cannot make estimates of anything else. When, therefore, I am asked, in the fashion of our inane times, what right I, as a white man, have to write about black people, I am forced to reply in four-letter words.[19]

This passage was written more than a half century ago. Since the late 1960s, the efforts to racialize scholarly work, against which Genovese rightly polemi-

---

18. Peter Novick, *That Noble Dream: The "Objectivity Question" and the American Historical Profession* (Cambridge: Cambridge University Press, 1988), p. 475.
19. Eugene D. Genovese, *In Red and Black: Marxian Explorations in Southern and Afro-American History* (New York: Random House, 1968), p. viii.

cized, have assumed such vast proportions that they cannot be adequately described as merely "inane." Under the influence of postmodernism and its offspring, "critical race theory," the doors of American universities have been flung wide open for the propagation of deeply reactionary conceptions. Racial identity has replaced social class and related economic processes as the principal and essential analytic category.

"Whiteness" theory, the latest rage, is now utilized to deny historical progress, reject objective truth, and interpret all events and facets of culture through the prism of alleged racial self-interest. On this basis, the sheerest nonsense can be spouted with the guarantee that all objections grounded on facts and science will be dismissed as a manifestation of "white fragility" or some other form of hidden racism. In this degraded environment, Ibram X. Kendi can write the following absurd passage, without fear of contradiction, in his *Stamped from the Beginning*:

> For Enlightenment intellectuals, the metaphor of light typically had a double meaning. Europeans had rediscovered learning after a thousand years in religious darkness, and their bright continental beacon of insight existed in the midst of a "dark"world not yet touched by light. Light, then, became a metaphor for Europeanness, and therefore Whiteness, a notion that Benjamin Franklin and his philosophical society eagerly embraced and imported to the colonies. ... Enlightenment ideas gave legitimacy to this long-held racist "partiality," the connection between lightness and Whiteness and reason, on the one hand, and between darkness and Blackness and ignorance, on the other.[20]

This is a ridiculous concoction that attributes to the word "Enlightenment" a racial significance that has absolutely no foundation in etymology, let alone history. The word employed by the philosopher Immanuel Kant in 1784 to describe this period of scientific advance was *Aufklärung*, which may be translated from the German as "clarification" or "clearing up," connoting an intellectual awakening. The English translation of *Aufklärung* as *Enlightenment* dates from 1865, seventy-five years after the death of Benjamin Franklin, whom Kendi references in support of his racial argument.[21]

---

20. Ibram X. Kendi, *Stamped from the Beginning: The Definitive History of Racist Ideas in America* (New York: Bold Type Books, 2017), p. 80.
21. Online Etymology Dictionary, https://www.etymonline.com/search?q=enlightenment

Another term used by English-speaking people to describe the seventeenth and eighteenth centuries has been "The Age of Reason," which was employed by Thomas Paine in his scathing assault on religion and all forms of superstition. Kendi's attempt to root the Enlightenment in a white racist impulse is based on nothing but empty juggling with words. In point of fact, modern racism is connected historically and intellectually to the Anti-Enlightenment, whose most significant nineteenth-century representative, Count Gobineau, wrote *The Inequality of the Human Races.* But actual history plays no role in the formulation of the pseudo-intellectual fabrications of Kendi. His work is stamped with ignorance.

History is not the only discipline assaulted by the race specialists. In an essay titled "Music Theory and the White Racial Frame," Professor Philip A. Ewell of Hunter College in New York declares, "I posit that there exists a 'white racial frame' in music theory that is structural and institutionalized, and that only through a reframing of this white racial frame will we begin to see positive racial changes in music theory."[22]

This degradation of music theory divests the discipline of its scientific and historically developed character. The complex principles and elements of composition, counterpoint, tonality, consonance, dissonance, timbre, rhythm, notation, etc. are derived, Ewell claims, from racial characteristics. Professor Ewell is loitering in the ideological territory of the Third Reich. There is more than a passing resemblance between his call for the liberation of music from "whiteness" and the efforts of Nazi academics in the Germany of the 1930s and 1940s to liberate music from "Jewishness." The Nazis denounced Mendelssohn as a mediocrity whose popularity was the insidious manifestation of Jewish efforts to dominate Aryan culture. In similar fashion, Ewell proclaims that Beethoven was merely "above average as a composer," and that he "occupies the place he does because he has been propped up by whiteness and maleness for two hundred years."[23]

Academic journals covering virtually every field of study are exploding with ignorant rubbish of this sort. Even physics has not escaped the onslaught of racial theorizing. In a recent essay, Chanda Prescod-Weinstein, assistant physics professor at the University of New Hampshire, proclaims that "race and ethnic-

---

22. "Music Theory and the White Racial Frame," in *MTO,* Volume 26, Number 2, September 2020.
23. "Beethoven Was an Above Average Composer—Let's Leave It at That," April 24, 2020. Accessed on 12/3/2020: https://musictheoryswhiteracialframe.wordpress.com/2020/04/24/beethoven-was-an-above-average-composer-lets-leave-it-at-that/

ity impact epistemic outcomes in physics," and introduces the concept of *"white empiricism"* (italics in the original), which "comes to dominate empirical discourse in physics because whiteness powerfully shapes the predominant arbiters of who is a valid observer of physical and social phenomena."[24]

Prescod-Weinstein asserts that "knowledge production in physics is contingent on the ascribed identities of the physicists," that the racial and gender background of scientists affects the way scientific research is conducted, and, therefore, that the observations and experiments conducted by African American and female physicists will produce results different than those conducted by white males. Prescod-Weinstein identifies with the contingentists who "challenge any assumption that scientific decision making is purely objective."[25]

The assumption of objectivity is, she claims, a major problem. Scientists, Prescod-Weinstein complains, are "typically monists—believers in the idea that there is only one science. ... This monist approach to science typically forecloses a closer investigation *of how identity and epistemic outcomes intermix.* Yet white empiricism undermines a significant theory of twentieth century physics: General Relativity" (emphasis added).[26]

Prescod-Weinstein's attack on the objectivity of scientific knowledge is buttressed with a distortion of Einstein's theory:

> Albert Einstein's monumental contribution to our empirical understanding of gravity is rooted in the principal of covariance, which is the simple idea that there is no single objective frame of reference that is more objective than any other. *All frames of reference, all observers, are equally competent and capable of observing the universal laws that underlie the workings of our physical universe* [emphasis added].[27]

In fact, general relativity's statement about covariance posits a fundamental symmetry in the universe, so that the laws of nature are the same for all observers. Einstein's great (though hardly "simple") initial insight, studying Maxwell's equations on electromagnetism involving the speed of light in a vacuum, was that these equations were true in all reference frames. The fact that

---

24. "Making Black Women Scientists under White Empiricism: The Racialization of Epistemology in Physics," in *Signs: Journal of Women in Culture and Society*, 2020, Vol. 45, No. 2, p. 421.
25. Ibid., p. 422.
26. Ibid.
27. Ibid.

two observers measure a third light particle in space as traveling at the same speed, even if they are in motion relative to each other, led Einstein to a profound theoretical redefinition of how matter exists in space and time. These theories were confirmed by experiment, a result that will not be refuted by changing the race or gender of those conducting the experiment.

Mass, space, time, and other quantities turned out to be varying and relative, depending on one's reference frame. But this variation is lawful, not subjective—let alone racially determined. It bears out the monist conception. There are no such things as distinct "racially superior," "black female," or "white empiricist" statements or reference frames on physical reality. There is an ascertainable objective truth, genuinely independent of consciousness, about the material world.

Furthermore, "all observers," regardless of their education and expertise, are not "equally competent and capable" of observing, let alone discovering, the universal laws that govern the universe. Physicists, whatever their personal identities, must be properly educated, and this education, hopefully, will not be marred by the type of ideological rubbish propagated by race and gender theorists.

There is, of course, an audience for the anti-scientific nonsense propounded by Prescod-Weinstein. Underlying much of contemporary racial and gender theorizing is frustration and anger over the allocation of positions within the academy. Prescod-Weinstein's essay is a brief on behalf of all those who believe that their professional careers have been hindered by "white empiricism." She attempts to cover over her falsification of science with broad and unsubstantiated claims that racism is ubiquitous among white physicists, who, she alleges, simply refuse to accept the legitimacy of research conducted by black female scientists.

It is possible that a very small number of physicists are racists. But this possibility does not lend legitimacy to her efforts to ascribe to racial identity an epistemological significance that affects the outcome of research. Along these lines, Prescod-Weinstein asserts that the claims to objective truth made by "white empiricism" rest on force. This is a variant of the postmodernist dogma that what is termed "objective truth" is nothing more than a manifestation of the power relations between conflicting social forces. She writes:

> White empiricism is the practice of allowing social discourse to insert itself into empirical reasoning about physics, and it actively harms the development of comprehensive understandings of the natural world by precluding putting provincial European ideas about science—*which have become dominant through colonial*

force—into conversation with ideas that are more strongly associated with "indigeneity," whether it is African indigeneity or another [emphasis added].[28]

The prevalence and legitimization of racialist theorizing is a manifestation of a deep intellectual, social, and cultural crisis of contemporary capitalist society. As in the late nineteenth and early twentieth centuries, race theory is acquiring an audience among disoriented sections of middle-class intellectuals. While most, if not all, of the academics who promote a racial agenda may sincerely believe that they are combating race-based prejudice, they are, nevertheless, propagating anti-scientific and irrationalist ideas which, whatever their personal intentions, serve reactionary ends.

The interaction of racialist ideology as it has developed over several decades in the academy and the political agenda of the Democratic Party is the motivating force behind the 1619 Project. Particularly under conditions of extreme social polarization, in which there is growing interest in and support for socialism, the Democratic Party—as a political instrument of the capitalist class—is anxious to shift the focus of political discussion away from issues that raise the specter of social inequality and class conflict. This is the function of a reinterpretation of history that places race at the center of its narrative.

The 1619 Project did not emerge overnight. For several years, corresponding to the growing role played by various forms of identity politics in the electoral strategy of the Democratic Party, the *Times* has become fixated, to an extent that can be legitimately described as obsessive, on race. It often appears that the main purpose of the news coverage and commentary of the *Times* is to reveal the racial essence of any given event or issue.

A search of the archive of the *New York Times* shows that the term "white privilege" appeared in only four articles in 2010. In 2013, the term appeared in twenty-two articles. By 2015, the *Times* published fifty-two articles in which the term is referenced. In 2020, as of December 1, the *Times* had published 257 articles in which there is a reference to "white privilege."

The word "whiteness" appeared in only fifteen *Times* articles in 2000. By 2018, the number of articles in which the word appeared had grown to 222. By December 1, 2020, "whiteness" was referenced in 280 articles.

The *Times*' unrelenting focus on race during the past year, even in its obituary section, has been clearly related to the 2020 electoral strategy of the Democratic Party. The 1619 Project was conceived of as a critical element of this strat-

---

28. Ibid., p. 439.

egy. This was explicitly stated by the *Times'* executive editor, Dean Baquet, in a meeting on August 12, 2019 with the newspaper's staff:

> Race and understanding of race should be a part of how we cover the American story. ... One reason we all signed off on the 1619 Project and made it so ambitious and expansive was to teach our readers to think a little bit more like that. Race in the next year—and I think this is, to be frank, what I hope you come away from this discussion with—race in the next year is going to be a huge part of the American story.[29]

The *New York Times'* effort to "teach" its readers "to think a little bit more" about race assumed the form of a falsification of American history, aimed at discrediting the revolutionary struggles that gave rise to the founding of the United States in 1776 and the ultimate destruction of slavery during the Civil War. This falsification could only contribute to the erosion of democratic consciousness, legitimize a racialized view of American history and society, and undermine the unity of the broad mass of Americans in their common struggle against conditions of social inequality and exploitation.

The racialist campaign of the *New York Times* has unfolded against the backdrop of a pandemic ravaging working-class communities, regardless of race and ethnicity, throughout the United States and the world. The global death toll has already surpassed 1.5 million. Within the United States, the number of COVID-19 deaths will surpass 300,000 before the end of the year. The pandemic has also brought economic devastation to millions of Americans. The unemployment rate is approaching Great Depression levels. Countless millions of people are without any source of income and depend upon food banks for their daily sustenance.

And while the pandemic rages, the structures of American democracy are breaking down beneath the weight of the social contradictions produced by a staggering level of wealth concentration in a small fraction of the population. The 2020 presidential campaign was conducted amid fascistic conspiracies, orchestrated from within the White House, to establish a dictatorship. The old adage, "It Can't Happen Here," coined in the 1930s during the ascent of fascism in Europe, has been refuted by events. "It is happening here" is a correct description of the American reality.

---

29. "The New York Times Unites vs. Twitter," *Slate* magazine, August 15, 2019. Accessed on 12/3/2020:
https://slate.com/news-and-politics/2019/08/new-york-times-meeting-transcript.html

In the midst of this unprecedented social and political catastrophe, requiring a united response by all sections of the working class, the *New York Times* has devoted its energies to promoting a false narrative that portrays American history as a perpetual war between the races. In this grotesque distortion, there is no place for the working class or for the class struggle, which has been the dominant factor in American social history for the past 150 years, and in which African American workers have fought heroically alongside their white brothers and sisters. The extreme social crisis triggered by the pandemic and the desperate conditions that confront tens of millions of working people of all racial and ethnic backgrounds constitute an unanswerable indictment of the reactionary premises of the 1619 Project.

*   *   *   *   *

This volume contains lectures, essays, and interviews originally posted in the World Socialist Web Site in 2019 and 2020. It is organized in five sections.

Essays and lectures in the first section, "Historical Critique of the 1619 Project," respond to the *New York Times*' racialist and factually inaccurate narrative of the American Revolution and the Civil War.

The second section features interviews conducted by the WSWS with leading historians of the Revolutionary War, Civil War, and civil rights era.

The third section, "Polemics," includes responses to efforts by the *New York Times* and the *American Historical Review* to defend the 1619 Project and discredit its critics.

Section four, "Historical Commentary," examines the consequences of the racialist distortion of American history, such as the pulling down of monuments that honor the memory of leaders of the American Revolution and Civil War. The essay "Martin Luther King Jr. and the Fight for Social Equality" reviews the influence of socialist thought on the civil rights leader. An obituary of Bernard Bailyn examines the contribution of this major American historian to the study of the Revolution.

The final section, "The Crisis of the *New York Times*' 1619 Project," documents the intellectually unprincipled response of editors and writers of the *New York Times* to the exposure of the 1619 Project's inaccuracies and deliberate falsifications.

David North
Detroit
December 3, 2020

An Afterword examines Trump's "1776 Project."

Part I

Historical Critique of the 1619 Project

The *New York Times*' 1619 Project: A Racialist Falsification of American and World History

"The 1619 Project," published by the *New York Times* as a special one-hundred-page edition of its Sunday magazine on August 19, 2019, presents and interprets American history entirely through the prism of race and racial conflict. The occasion for this publication is the four-hundredth anniversary of the initial arrival of twenty African slaves at Point Comfort in Virginia, a British colony in North America. On the very next day, the slaves were traded for food.

The Project, according to the *Times*, intends to "reframe the country's history, understanding 1619 as our true founding, and placing the consequences of slavery and the contributions of black Americans at the very center of the story we tell ourselves about who we are."[1]

Despite the pretense of establishing the United States' "true" foundation, the 1619 Project is a politically motivated falsification of history. Its aim is to create a historical narrative that legitimizes the effort of the Democratic Party to construct an electoral coalition based on the prioritizing of personal "identities"—i.e., gender, sexual orientation, ethnicity, and, above all, race.

The *Times* is promoting the project with an unprecedented and lavishly financed publicity blitz. It is working with the Pulitzer Center on Crisis Reporting, which has developed a teaching curriculum that will be sent to schools for teachers to use in their classes. Hundreds of thousands of extra copies of

---

Niles Niemuth, Thomas Mackaman, and David North, "The New York Times' 1619 Project: A racialist falsification of American and world history," September 3, 2019.

1. The *New York Times Magazine* online edition, August 18, 2019, https://www.nytimes.com/interactive/2019/08/14/magazine/1619-america-slavery.html

the magazine and a special supplement have been printed for free distribution at schools, libraries, and museums across the country. Nikole Hannah-Jones, the staff writer and New America Foundation fellow who first pitched the idea for the project, oversaw its production, and authored the introduction, will be sent on a national lecture tour of schools.

The essays featured in the magazine are organized around the central premise that all of American history is rooted in race hatred—specifically, the uncontrollable hatred of "black people" by "white people." Hannah-Jones writes in the series' introduction: "Anti-black racism runs in the very DNA of this country."

This is a false and dangerous conception. DNA is a chemical molecule that contains the genetic code of living organisms and determines their physical characteristics and development. The transfer of this critical biological term to the study of a country—even if meant only in a metaphorical sense—leads to bad history and reactionary politics. Countries do not have DNA, they have historically formed economic structures, antagonistic classes, and complex political relationships. These do not exist apart from a certain level of technological development, nor independently of a more or less developed network of global economic interconnections.

The methodology that underlies the 1619 Project is idealist (i.e., it derives social being from thought, rather than the other way around) and, in the most fundamental sense of the word, irrationalist. All of history is to be explained from the existence of a suprahistorical emotional impulse. Slavery is viewed and analyzed not as a specific economically rooted form of the exploitation of labor but, rather, as the manifestation of white racism. But where does this racism come from? It is embedded, claims Hannah-Jones, in the historical DNA of American "white people." Thus, it must persist independently of any change in political or economic conditions.

Hannah-Jones's reference to DNA is part of a growing tendency to derive racial antagonisms from innate biological processes. Democratic Party politician Stacey Abrams, in an essay published recently in *Foreign Affairs*, claims that whites and African Americans are separated by an "intrinsic difference."[2]

---

2. Stacey Y. Abrams, Michael Tesler, Lynn Vavreck, John Sides, Jennifer A. Richeson, and Francis Fukuyama, "E Pluribus Unum?," *Foreign Affairs*, November 22, 2020. https://www.foreignaffairs.com/articles/2019-02-01/stacey-abrams-response-to-francis-fukuyama-identity-politics-article.

This irrational and scientifically absurd claim serves to legitimize the reactionary view—entirely compatible with the political perspective of fascism—that blacks and whites are hostile and incompatible species.

In yet another article, published in the current edition of *Foreign Affairs*, the neurologist Robert Sapolsky argues that the antagonism between human groups is rooted in biology. Extrapolating from bloody territorial conflicts between chimpanzees, with whom humans "share more than 98 percent of their DNA," Sapolsky asserts that understanding "the dynamics of human group identity, including the resurgence of nationalism—that potentially most destructive form of in-group bias—requires grasping the biological and cognitive underpinnings that shape them."[3]

Sapolsky's simplistic dissolution of history into biology recalls not only the reactionary invocation of "social Darwinism" to legitimize imperialist conquest by the late nineteenth- and early twentieth-century imperialists, but also the efforts of German geneticists to provide a pseudo-scientific justification for Nazi anti-Semitism and racism.

Dangerous and reactionary ideas are wafting about in bourgeois academic and political circles. No doubt, the authors of the 1619 Project essays would deny that they are predicting race war, let alone justifying fascism. But ideas have a logic, and authors bear responsibility for the political conclusions and consequences of their false and misguided arguments.

American slavery is a monumental subject with vast and enduring historical and political significance. The events of 1619 are part of that history. But what occurred at Port Comfort is one episode in the global history of slavery, which extends back into the ancient world, and of the origins and development of the world capitalist system. There is a vast body of literature dealing with the widespread practice of slavery outside the Americas. As Professor G. Ogo Nwokeji of the Department of African American Studies at the University of California, Berkeley, has explained, slavery was practiced by African societies. It existed in West Africa "well before the fifteenth century, when the Europeans arrived there via the Atlantic Ocean."[4]

Historian Rudolph T. Ware III of the University of Michigan writes, "Between the beginning of the fifteenth century and the end of the eighteenth, mil-

---

3. Robert Sapolsky, "This Is Your Brain on Nationalism," *Foreign Affairs*, March/April 2019. https://www.foreignaffairs.com/articles/2019-02-12/your-brain-nationalism

4. G. Ogo Nwokeji, *The Cambridge World History of Slavery, Vol. 3, AD 1420–AD 1804*, David Eltis and Stanley L. Engerman eds. (Cambridge: Cambridge University Press, 2011), p. 81.

lions lived and died as slaves in African Muslim societies."[5] Among the most important of contemporary scholarly works on the subject is *Transformations in Slavery: A History of Slavery in Africa*, originally published in 1983, by the Canadian historian Paul E. Lovejoy. He explained:

> Slavery has been an important phenomenon throughout history. It has been found in many places, from classical antiquity to very recent times. Africa has been intimately connected with this history, both as a major source of slaves for ancient civilizations, the Islamic world, India, and the Americas, and as one of the principal areas where slavery was common. Indeed, in Africa slavery lasted well into the twentieth century—notably longer than in the Americas. Such antiquity and persistence require explanation, both to understand the historical development of slavery in Africa in its own right and to evaluate the relative importance of the slave trade to this development. Broadly speaking, slavery expanded in at least three stages—1350 to 1600, 1600 to 1800, and 1800 to 1900—by which time slavery had become a fundamental feature of the African political economy.[6]

Professor Lovejoy remarked, in the preface to the third edition of his now-classic study, that one of his aims in undertaking his research "was to confront the reality that there was slavery in the history of Africa, at a time when some romantic visionaries and hopeful nationalists wanted to deny the clear facts."[7]

In relation to the New World, the phenomenon of slavery in modern history cannot be understood apart from its role in the economic development of capitalism in the sixteenth and seventeenth centuries. As Karl Marx explained in the chapter titled "The Genesis of the Industrial Capitalist" in Volume One of *Das Kapital*:

> The discovery of gold and silver in America, the extirpation, enslavement and entombment in mines of the aboriginal population, the beginning of the conquest and looting of the East Indies, the turning of Africa into a warren for the commercial hunting of black-skins, signalised the rosy dawn of the era of capitalist

---

5. Rudolph T. Ware, ibid., p. 47.
6. Paul E. Lovejoy, *Transformations in Slavery* (Cambridge: Cambridge University Press, 2012), p. 1.
7. Ibid., p. xxiii.

production. These idyllic proceedings are the chief momenta of primitive accumulation. On their heels treads the commercial war of the European nations, with the globe for a theatre. It begins with the revolt of the Netherlands from Spain, assumes giant dimensions in England's Anti-Jacobin War, and is still going on in the opium wars against China, &c.[8]

Marx's analysis inspired the critical insight of the brilliant West Indian historian Eric Williams, who wrote in his pioneering study *Capitalism and Slavery*, published in 1944:

> Slavery in the Caribbean has been too narrowly identified with the Negro. A racial twist has thereby been given to what is basically an economic phenomenon. Slavery was not born of racism: rather, racism was the consequence of slavery. Unfree labor in the New World was brown, white, black, and yellow; Catholic, Protestant and pagan.[9]

The formation and development of the United States cannot be understood apart from the international economic and political processes that gave rise to capitalism and the New World. Slavery was an international economic institution that stretched from the heart of Africa to the shipyards of Britain, the banking houses of Amsterdam, and the plantations of South Carolina, Brazil, and the Caribbean. Every colonial power was involved, from the Dutch who operated slave trading posts in West Africa to the Portuguese who imported millions of slaves to Brazil. An estimated 15 million to 20 million Africans were forcibly sent to the Americas throughout the entire period of the trans-Atlantic slave trade. Of these, 400,000 ended up in the thirteen British colonies/United States.

Slavery was the inescapable and politically tragic legacy of the global foundation of the United States. It is not difficult to recognize the contradiction between the ideals proclaimed by the leaders of the American Revolution—which were expressed with extraordinary force by Thomas Jefferson in the Declaration of Independence—and the existence of slavery in the newly formed United States.

---

8. Karl Marx, "Capital Volume 1," *Marx & Engels Collected Works*, Vol. 35 (Lawrence & Wishart, 1996), p. 739.

9. Eric Williams, *Capitalism and Slavery* (Chapel Hill: University of N. Carolina Press, 1944), p. 7.

But history is not a morality tale. The efforts to discredit the Revolution by focusing on the alleged hypocrisy of Jefferson and other founders contribute nothing to an understanding of history. The American Revolution cannot be understood as the sum of the subjective intentions and moral limitations of those who led it. The world-historical significance of the Revolution is best understood through an examination of its objective causes and consequences.

The analysis provided by Williams refutes the scurrilous attempt by the 1619 Project to portray the Revolution as a sinister attempt to uphold the slave system. Apart from the massive political impact of Jefferson's Declaration and the subsequent overthrow of British rule, Williams stressed the objective impact of the Revolution on the economic viability of slavery. He wrote:

> "When in the course of human events, it becomes necessary for one people to dissolve the political bands which have connected them with another. ..." Jefferson wrote only part of the truth. It was economic, not political, bands that were being dissolved. A new age had begun. The year 1776 marked the Declaration of Independence and the publication of the *Wealth of Nations*. Far from accentuating the value of the sugar islands [in the Caribbean], American independence marked the beginning of their uninterrupted decline, and it was a current saying at the time that the British ministry had lost not only thirteen colonies but eight islands as well.[10]

It was not an accident that the victorious conclusion of the revolutionary war in 1783 was followed just four years later by the famous call of English abolitionist William Wilberforce for the ending of Britain's slave trade.

In examining the emergence of British opposition to the slave trade, Williams made a fundamental point about the study of history that serves as an indictment of the subjective and antihistorical method employed by the 1619 Project. He wrote:

> *The decisive forces in the period of history we have discussed are the developing economic forces.*
>
> These economic changes are gradual, imperceptible, but they have an irresistible cumulative effect. Men, pursuing their interests, are rarely aware of the ultimate results of their activity. The commercial capitalism of the eighteenth century developed the

---

10. Ibid., p. 120.

wealth of Europe by means of slavery and monopoly. But in so doing it helped to create the industrial capitalism of the nineteenth century, which turned round and destroyed the power of commercial capitalism, slavery, and all its works. Without a grasp of these economic changes the history of the period is meaningless.[11]

The victory of the American Revolution and the establishment of the United States did not solve the problem of slavery. The economic and political conditions for its abolition had not sufficiently matured. But the economic development of the United States—the simultaneous development of industry in the North and the noxious growth of the cotton-based plantation system in the South (as a consequence of the invention of the cotton gin in 1793)—intensified the contradictions between two increasingly incompatible economic systems—one based on wage labor and the other on slavery.

The United States heaved from crisis to crisis in the seven decades that separated the adoption of the Constitution and the election of President George Washington in 1789 from Abraham Lincoln's inauguration and the outbreak of the Civil War in 1861. None of the repeated compromises which sought to balance the country between slave and free states, from the Missouri Compromise of 1820 to the Kansas-Nebraska Act in 1854, were ever able to finally settle the issue.

It is worth bearing in mind that the eighty-seven years of history invoked by Lincoln when he spoke at Gettysburg in 1863 is the same span of time that separates our present day from the election of Franklin Delano Roosevelt in 1932. The explosive socioeconomic tendencies which would do away with the entire economic system of slavery developed and erupted in this relatively concentrated period of time.

The founding of the United States set into motion a crisis which resulted in the Civil War, the second American Revolution, in which hundreds of thousands of whites gave their lives to finally put an end to slavery. It must be stressed that this was not an accidental, let alone unconscious, outcome of the Civil War. In the end, the war resulted in the greatest expropriation of private property in world history, not equaled until the Russian Revolution in 1917, when the working class, led by the Bolshevik Party, took state power for the first and, so far, only time in world history.

---

11. Ibid., p. 210.

Hannah-Jones does not view Lincoln as "the Great Emancipator," as the freed slaves called him in the 1860s, but as a garden-variety racist who held "black people [as] the obstacle to national unity."[12] The author simply disregards Lincoln's own words—for example, the Gettysburg Address and the magisterial Second Inaugural Address—as well as the books written by historians such as Eric Foner, James McPherson, Allen Guelzo, David Donald, Ronald C. White, Stephen Oates, Richard Carwardine, and many others that demonstrate Lincoln's emergence as a revolutionary leader fully committed to the destruction of slavery.

But an honest portrayal of Lincoln would contradict Hannah-Jones's claims that "black Americans fought back alone" to "make America a democracy." So, too, would a single solitary mention, anywhere in the magazine, of the 2.2 million Union soldiers who fought, and the 365,000 who died, to end slavery.

Likewise, the interracial character of the abolitionist movement is blotted out. The names William Lloyd Garrison, Wendell Phillips, Elijah Lovejoy, John Brown, Thaddeus Stevens, and Harriet Beecher Stowe, among others, do not appear in her essay. A couple of abolitionists are selectively quoted for their criticism of the Constitution, but Hannah-Jones dares not mention that for the antislavery movement Jefferson's Declaration of Independence was, in the words of the late historian David Brion Davis, their "touchstone, the sacred scripture."[13]

Hannah-Jones and the other 1619 Project contributors—claiming that slavery was the unique "original sin" of the United States, and discrediting the American Revolution and the Civil War as elaborate conspiracies to perpetuate white racism—have little to add for the rest of American history. Nothing ever changed. Slavery was simply replaced by Jim Crow segregation, and this in turn has given way to the permanent condition of racism that is the inescapable fate of being a "white American." It all goes back to 1619 and "the root of the *endemic* racism that we still *cannot purge* from this nation to this day" (emphasis added).[14]

This is not simply a "reframing" of history. It is an attack and falsification that ignores more than a half century of scholarship. There is not the slightest indication that Hannah-Jones (or any of her coessayists) have even heard

---

12. The *New York Times Magazine*, August 18, 2019, p. 21.
13. David Brion Davis, *From Homicide to Slavery: Studies in American Culture* (Oxford University Press, 1988), p. 301.
14. Ibid., p. 19.

of, let alone read, the work on slavery carried out by Eric Williams, David Brion Davis, or Peter Kolchin; on the American Revolution by Bernard Bailyn and Gordon Wood; on the political conceptions that motivated Union soldiers by James McPherson; on Reconstruction by Eric Foner; on segregation by C. Vann Woodward; or on the Great Migration by James N. Gregory or Joe William Trotter.

What is left out of the *Times'* racialist morality tale is breathtaking, even from the vantage point of African American scholarship. The invocation of "white racism" takes the place of any concrete examination of the economic, political, and social history of the country.

There is no examination of the historical context, foremost the development of the class struggle, within which the struggle of the African American population developed in the century that followed the Civil War. And there is no reference to the transformation of the United States into an industrial colossus and the most powerful imperialist country between 1865 and 1917, the year of its entry into World War I.

While the 1619 Project and its stable of well-to-do authors find in the labor exploitation of slavery a talisman to explain all of history, they pass over in deafening silence the exploitation inherent in wage labor.

A reader of the 1619 Project would not know that the struggle against slave labor gave way to a violent struggle against wage slavery, in which countless workers were killed. There is no reference to the Great Railroad Strike of 1877, which spread like wildfire along the railways from Baltimore to St. Louis, and was only suppressed by the deployment of federal troops, nor to the emergence of the Knights of Labor, the Haymarket Massacre of 1886 and the fight for the eight-hour day, the Homestead Steel Strike of 1892, the Pullman strike of 1894, the formation of the American Federation of Labor (AFL), the founding of the Socialist Party, the emergence of the Industrial Workers of the World (IWW), the Ludlow Massacre of 1914, the Great Steel Strike of 1919, the countless other labor struggles that followed World War I, and finally the emergence of the Congress of Industrial Organizations (CIO) and the massive industrial struggles of the 1930s.

In short, there is no class struggle and, therefore, there is no real history of the events that shaped a population of freed slaves into a critical section of the working class. Replacing real history with a mythic racial narrative, the 1619 Project ignores the actual social development of the African American population over the last 150 years.

Nowhere do any of the authors discuss the Great Migration between 1916 and 1970, in which millions of blacks—and whites—uprooted from the rural South and flocked to take jobs in urban areas across the US, particularly in the industrialized North. James P. Cannon, the founder of American Trotskyism, captured the revolutionary implications of this process, for both African American and white workers, in his inimitable prose:

> American capitalism took hundreds of thousands of Negroes from the South, and exploiting their ignorance, and their poverty, and their fears, and their individual helplessness, herded them into the steel mills as strike-breakers in the steel strike of 1919. And in the brief space of one generation, by its mistreatment, abuse and exploitation of these innocent and ignorant Negro strike-breakers, this same capitalism succeeded in transforming them and their sons into one of the most militant and reliable detachments of the great victorious steel strike of 1946.
>
> This same capitalism took tens of thousands and hundreds of thousands of prejudiced hill-billies from the South, many of them members and sympathizers of the Ku Klux Klan; and thinking to use them, with their ignorance and their prejudices, as a barrier against unionism, sucked them into the auto and rubber factories of Detroit, Akron and other industrial centers. There it sweated them, humiliated them and drove and exploited them until it finally changed them and made new men out of them. In that harsh school the imported Southerners learned to exchange the insignia of the K.K.K. for the union button of the C.I.O., and to turn the Klansman's fiery cross into a bonfire to warm pickets at the factory gate.[15]

As late as 1910, nearly 90 percent of African Americans lived in the former slave states, overwhelmingly in conditions of rural isolation. By the 1970s, they were highly urbanized and proletarianized. Black workers had gone through the experiences of the great industrial strikes alongside whites in cities like Detroit, Pittsburgh, and Chicago. It is no historical accident that the civil rights

---

15. James P. Cannon, "The Coming American Revolution," Speech delivered at the Twelfth National Convention of the Socialist Workers Party, 1946 (New York: Pioneer Publishers, 1947), pp. 28–29.

movement emerged in the South in Birmingham, Alabama, a center of the steel industry and the locus of the actions of communist workers, black and white.

The struggle of wage labor against capital at the point of production united workers across racial boundaries. And so, in the fevered rhetoric of the Jim Crow politician, the civil rights movement was equated with communism and the fear of "race-mixing"—that is, that the working masses, black and white, might be united around their common interests.

Just as it leaves out the history of the working class, the 1619 Project fails to provide political history. There is no accounting for the role played in stoking up race hatred by the Democratic Party, a union of Northern industrialists and machine politicians wed to Southern slave masters before the Civil War and Jim Crow politicians after it.

In the numerous articles which make up the 1619 Project, the name of Martin Luther King Jr. appears just once, and then only in a photo caption. The reason for this is that King's political outlook was opposed to the racialist narrative advanced by the *Times*. King did not condemn the American Revolution and the Civil War. He did not believe that racism was a permanent characteristic of "whiteness." He called for the integration of blacks and whites, and set as his goal the ultimate dissolution of race itself. Targeted and harassed as a "communist" by the FBI, King was murdered after launching the interracial Poor People's Campaign and announcing his opposition to the Vietnam War.

King encouraged the involvement of white civil rights activists, several of whom lost their lives in the South, including Viola Liuzzo, the wife of a Teamsters union organizer from Detroit. His statement following the murders of the three young civil rights workers in 1964, Michael Schwerner, James Chaney, and Andrew Goodman (two of whom were white), was an impassioned condemnation of racism and segregation. King clearly does not fit into Hannah-Jones's narrative.

But, in its most significant and telling omission, the 1619 Project says nothing about the event that had the greatest impact on the social condition of African Americans—the Russian Revolution of 1917. Not only did this arouse and inspire broad sections of the African American population—including countless black intellectuals, writers, and artists, among them W. E. B. Du Bois, Claude McKay, Langston Hughes, Ralph Ellison, Richard Wright, Paul Robeson, and Lorraine Hansberry—but the Revolution also undermined the political foundations of American racial apartheid.

Given the 1619 Project's black nationalist narrative, it may appear surprising that nowhere in the issue do the names Malcolm X or Black Panthers appear. Unlike the black nationalists of the 1960s, Hannah-Jones does not condemn American imperialism. She boasts that "we [i.e., African Americans] are the most likely of all racial groups to serve in the United States military," and celebrates the fact that "we" have fought "in every war this nation has waged."[16] Hannah-Jones does not note this fact in a manner that is at all critical. She does not condemn the creation of a "volunteer" army whose recruiters prey on poverty-stricken minority youth. There is no indication that Hannah-Jones opposes the "War on Terror" and the brutal interventions in Iraq, Libya, Yemen, Somalia, and Syria—all supported by the *Times*—that have killed and made homeless upwards of twenty million people. On this issue, Hannah-Jones is remarkably "color-blind." She is unaware of, or simply indifferent to, the millions of "people of color" butchered and made refugees by the American war machine in the Middle East, Central Asia, and Africa.

The toxic identity politics that underlies this indifference does not serve the interests of the working class in the United States or anywhere else, which is dependent for its very survival on unifying across racial and national boundaries. It does, however, serve the class interests of privileged sections of the American upper-middle class.

In a revealing passage at the end of her essay, Hannah-Jones declares that, since the 1960s, "black Americans have made astounding progress, not only for ourselves but also for all Americans." She is speaking here not for her "race" but for a tiny layer of the African American elite, beneficiaries of affirmative action policies, who came to political maturity in the years leading up to and through the administration of Barack Obama, the United States' first black president.

A 2017 analysis of economic data found extreme levels of wealth inequality within racial groupings. Among those who identify as African American, the richest 10 percent controlled 75 percent of all wealth; during Obama's tenure, the wealthiest 1 percent increased their share of wealth among all African Americans from 19.4 percent to 40.5 percent. Meanwhile, it is estimated that the bottom half of African American households have zero or negative wealth.

While a very narrow layer of black millionaires and billionaires has been deliberately cultivated in response to the mass unrest of the 1960s and 1970s, the conditions for working-class African Americans are worse than they were forty years ago. This has been the period of deindustrialization, which saw the

---

16. The *New York Times Magazine*, August 18, 2019, p. 16.

systematic shutdown of auto, steel, and other factories across the United States, devastating working-class cities such as Detroit, Milwaukee, and Youngstown, Ohio.

The major social gains won by workers in the bitter struggles of the twentieth century have been rolled back so that an immense amount of wealth could be transferred from the bottom 90 percent of the population to the top. Poverty, declining life expectancy, deaths of despair, and other forms of social misery are drawing together workers of all racial and national backgrounds.

It is no coincidence that the promotion of this racial narrative of American history by the *Times*, the mouthpiece of the Democratic Party and the privileged upper-middle-class layers it represents, comes amid the growth of class struggle in the US and around the world.

Earlier in 2019, auto parts workers in Matamoros, Mexico, called on their American counterparts, white and black, to join them in wildcat strikes. Across the South, black, white, and Hispanic workers took strike action together against telecommunications giant AT&T. In Tennessee, black and white neighbors defended an immigrant working-class family against deportation. Now, the multiracial and multiethnic American auto industry labor force finds itself entering a pitched battle against the global auto giants and the corrupt unions.

At the same time, opinion polls demonstrate growing support in the population for socialism—that is, the conscious political unity of the working class across all boundaries and divisions imposed on it. Under these conditions the American capitalist elite, Democrats and Republican alike, are terrified of social revolution. They are joining with their ruling-class counterparts around the world in deploying sectarian politics, be it based on race, religion, nationality, ethnicity, or language to block this development.

The 1619 Project is one component of a deliberate effort to inject racial politics into the heart of the 2020 elections and foment divisions among the working class. The Democrats think it will be beneficial to shift their focus for the time being from the reactionary, militarist, anti-Russia campaign to equally reactionary racial politics.

The *Times'* executive editor, Dean Baquet, was explicit in this regard, telling staffers in a taped meeting in August 2019 that the narrative upon which the paper was focused would change from "being a story about whether the Trump campaign had colluded with Russia and obstruction of justice to being a more head-on story about the president's character." As a result, reporters will be directed to "write more deeply about the country, race, and other divisions."

Baquet declared:

> Race and understanding of race should be a part of how we cover the American story. ... One reason we all signed off on the 1619 Project and made it so ambitious and expansive was to teach our readers to think a little bit more like that. Race in the next year—and I think this is, to be frank, what I would hope you come away from this discussion with—race in the next year is going to be a huge part of the American story.[17]

This focus on race is a mirror image of Trump's own racial politics, and it bears a disturbing resemblance to the race-based world view of the Nazis. The central role of race in the politics of fascism was explained concisely in Leon Trotsky's analysis of the ideology of German fascism:

> In order to raise it above history, the nation is given the support of the race. History is viewed as the emanation of the race. The qualities of the race are construed without relation to changing social conditions. Rejecting "economic thought" as base, National Socialism descends a stage lower: from economic materialism it appeals to zoologic materialism.[18]

There are many scholars, students, and workers who know that the 1619 Project makes a travesty of history. It is their responsibility to take a stand and reject the coordinated attempt, spearheaded by the *Times*, to dredge up and rehabilitate a reactionary race-based falsification of American and world history.

Above all, the working class must reject any such effort to divide it, efforts which will become ever more ferocious and pernicious as the class struggle develops. The great issue of this epoch is the fight for the international unity of the working class against all forms of racism, nationalism, and related forms of identity politics.

---

17. "The New York Times Unites vs. Twitter," *Slate*, August 15, 2019, https://slate.com/news-and-politics/2019/08/new-york-times-meeting-transcript.html
18. Leon Trotsky, "What Is National Socialism?" https://www.marxists.org/archive/trotsky/germany/1933/330610.htm

Slavery and the American Revolution

Thank you to the University of Michigan Chapter of the International Youth and Students for Social Equality for inviting me. The IYSSE, together with the World Socialist Web Site, is organizing similar lectures at colleges across the country.

These are important meetings. Their purpose is to answer the *New York Times'* 1619 Project, which seeks to impose a new narrative of American history, in which all is to be explained by white racism. In its own words, the project "aims to reframe the country's history, understanding 1619 [the year the first slaves were brought to colonial Virginia] as our true founding."[1] The lavishly funded campaign includes a glossy magazine that is being distributed by the hundreds of thousands, free of charge, to museums, libraries, and schools, including, so far, every high school in Buffalo, Washington D.C., Winston-Salem, and Chicago, where the public school workers went out on strike last week.

In a more fundamental sense, this series of meetings are motivated by the need to build an international movement of the working class and youth

---

Thomas Mackaman, "Slavery and the American Revolution: A Response to the New York Times 1619 Project," World Socialist Web Site, November 1, 2019. The lecture series "Race, Class, and Socialism" was organized by the Socialist Equality Party (SEP) and the International Youth and Students for Social Equality (IYSSE). Professor Thomas Mackaman gave the first lecture at the University of Michigan on October 22, 2019.

1. This phrase initially appeared on the *New York Times Magazine* website of the 1619 Project on August 18, 2019. It is no longer available. The *Magazine*'s editor, Jake Silverstein, defended the change on October 16, 2020 (https://www.nytimes.com/2020/10/16/magazine/criticism-1619-project.html).

against war, the destruction of living standards, police-state repression and the threat of dictatorship, and ecological catastrophe. The Socialist Equality Party, together with the IYSSE, insists that the basic division of society is class, not race. Class is defined by an individual's relationship to the means of production. Working-class people, regardless of their skin color, gender, or whether they live in the United States, Mexico, China, or anywhere else, sell their labor power in order to survive. This unifies them against capitalist owners and their governments. The task of socialists is to make this objective reality, and the tasks arising from it, consciously understood.

This is not just wishful thinking. In the past year, mass opposition and working class movements have erupted in France, Puerto Rico, Hong Kong, Egypt, Iraq, Ecuador, and now Chile, among other places. The global nature of the auto industry has been revealed by strikes in Mexico, South Korea, Romania, India, and now among American auto workers at General Motors and Mack Volvo, struggles that the United Auto Workers bureaucracy is attempting to sabotage. Some 2,000 miners in Arizona and Texas and more than 20,000 teachers in Chicago are also currently on strike.

Every attempt will be made to divert and divide this movement of the working class. Donald Trump appeals openly to xenophobia, racism, anti-Semitism, and anticommunism, and threatens political violence on opponents, the deployment of the military to crush domestic opposition, and the suspension of all constitutional norms. The emergence of an openly authoritarian government and the development of a fascist movement whipped up from the White House pose the gravest of threats.

However, Trump is not the creator, but rather the product of a diseased ruling class. The pursuit of American imperialism's aims abroad and at home through war has proceeded for decades under Democratic and Republican administrations alike, through massive military and police spending, attacks on democratic rights, the rollback of workers' wages and benefits, tax cuts for the rich, and the evisceration of all forms of social spending.

There is also agreement between Trump and his ruling-class opponents that the working class should be divided. For the Democratic Party, this entails the promotion of various forms of identity, including gender, sexuality, and, above all, race, as the decisive social category.

This is the political essence of the 1619 Project. *Times* reporter Nikole Hannah-Jones sets the tone in the project's lead essay. She insists that "anti-black racism *runs in the very DNA* of this country," that slavery is its "original sin" and "the root of the *endemic* racism that we still *cannot purge* from this nation to this day," and that "the inhumanity visited on black people by *every generation of white America* justified the inhumanity of the past." Against all of this, "black Americans fought back alone" [emphases added].[2]

What are the political implications of this approach to history? If we grant as true that "white America" can never overcome its racism, it follows that there exists no possibility for political cooperation and genuine solidarity among working-class people and youth in America, let alone the world, to confront the crises that threaten all of humanity. Black workers and youth should subordinate themselves to the African American wealthy and upper-middle class, people like Hannah-Jones, and organize as an identity group inside the Democratic Party—for which, of course, the *New York Times* is a primary mouthpiece.

There is nothing progressive about this in the slightest. Indeed, in its insistence that *race*—which has no basis in science—is the determinative category of both the present and past, the 1619 Project shares the most basic premise of the white supremacists and fascists who are being set into motion by the Trump administration.

This is dangerous politics, and very bad history. Hannah-Jones mixes antihistorical metaphors pertaining to biological determinism (that racism is printed in a "national DNA") and to religious obscurantism (that slavery is the uniquely American "original sin"). But whether ordained by God or genetic code, racism by whites against blacks serves, for the 1619 Project, as history's *deus ex machina*. There is no need to consider questions long placed at the center of historical inquiry: cause and effect, contingency and conflict, human agency, and change over time. History is simply a morality tale written backward from 2019.

To answer all that the 1619 Project falsifies and all that it leaves out would require far more than the time we have this evening. Another lecture here at the University of Michigan, by World Socialist Web Site reporter Eric London, will deal with the sectional conflict between North and South and the Civil War. A final lecture, by Socialist Equality Party National Secretary Joseph Kishore, will address the development of the African American population as a critical component of the working class and the impact of the Russian Revolution on American class and race relations. Collectively, these lectures will show that race and racism are not immutable, but emerge out of material and political interests. They will demonstrate the crucial role of revolution—the

---

2. This and other quotes from Hannah-Jones come from the *New York Times Magazine*, August 18, 2019, unless otherwise noted.

American, the Civil War, and the Russian, and finally, the fight for socialism today, in advancing human equality.

My task this evening is to address the 1619 Project's attack on the American Revolution and its principles, which Hannah-Jones contemptuously refers to as a "founding mythology" and "lies." If one knew nothing more than what the 1619 Project teaches about American history, he or she would be left to assume that slavery was a uniquely American affair, and that the American Revolution was waged by greedy slaveowners trying to stop the benevolent King George III from freeing the slaves!

Thus, Hannah-Jones tells us, "One of the primary reasons the colonists decided to declare their independence from Britain was because they wanted to protect the institution of slavery," and that, at the time of the American Revolution, "one-fifth of the population within the thirteen colonies struggled under a brutal system of slavery unlike anything that had existed in the world before."

But this is the "founding mythology" of the 1619 Project, not the American Revolution. In answering, I will address the origins of the chattel slave system and its vast development in the Atlantic world from the fifteenth through the eighteenth centuries, and then the origins of the American Revolution and its impact on slavery.

As a system of forced labor and subordinate social status, slavery was not at all unique to the thirteen colonies. It reached back to antiquity—including Babylonia, Egypt, Greece, and Rome—and arose also in the New World before Columbus in the Aztec, Mayan, and other empires. Slavery was a source of surplus value in ancient agricultural societies, and, as a form of legal property, was closely associated with domesticated animals. It is noteworthy that the word *chattel* has a common origin with *cattle* and *capital* in the old Latin *capitale*.

In Europe, the Middle East, North Africa, and East Africa, the slave networks developed in ancient times survived the fall of Rome. Long before the Atlantic slave trade, people were deported into slavery from among the many peoples and cultural groups of Central and Western Africa across the Sahara, and for a thousand years the African rim of the Indian Ocean bustled with slave ships. The captors of slaves in Africa were other Africans. They maintained slavery in their own societies, and sold their slaves to Arabs and Persians, and later to Europeans.

Nor was slavery confined to Africans. The term "slave" is itself derived from the Latin word for "Slav," *sclavus*. The word took on its modern meaning as the pagan Slavic populations of Eastern Europe were subjected to servile labor after military defeat; the word's "transferred sense is clearly evidenced in documents of the 9th century," comments the *Oxford English Dictionary*.

What Americans would today call "white people" continued to be subjected to slavery right on up until the 1800s. Between about 1500 and 1700, some 2.5 million slaves from the Black Sea, overwhelmingly Eastern Europeans, passed through Istanbul. Further west in the Mediterranean world, according to Ohio State University historian Robert Davis, as many as 1.25 million Europeans were captured by Arab corsairs and taken into slavery in North Africa between 1500 and 1800—precisely the same centuries as the rise of the trans-Atlantic African slave trade. Entire villages in locations as far away as Iceland were depopulated. Europeans themselves also enslaved people who today would be called "white." Until 1453, the Italian city-states dominated the Black Sea slave trade, sending Bulgarians and others to labor on the sugar plantations of the Mediterranean.

Thus, when the first European merchants made their way to Africa's west coast and began purchasing slaves in significant numbers in the late fifteenth century, they tapped into longstanding networks of slavery that existed in both Africa and Europe. Gradually over the ensuing three centuries, the ancient system of slavery, transplanted to the New World, became bound up with the vast development of key agricultural commodities: tobacco, sugar, rice, indigo, and finally cotton, in the period of history Marx defined as primitive capitalist accumulation.

As we stated in the World Socialist Web Site in our reply to the 1619 Project, far from being a phenomenon unique to the colonies that would become the United States:

> Slavery was an international economic institution that stretched from the heart of Africa to the shipyards of Britain, the banking houses of Amsterdam, and the plantations of South Carolina, Brazil, and the Caribbean. Every colonial power was involved, from the Dutch who operated slave trading posts in West Africa to the Portuguese who imported millions of slaves to Brazil.[3]

The mind reels at the horrors of the slave trade—the forced marches from villages in Africa; the dungeons where slaves awaited the "middle passage;" the slave ships in which an appalling number died; the auction block; and then a

---

3. "The New York Times' 1619 Project: A racialist falsification of American and world history," World Socialist Web Site, September 3, 2019, https://www.wsws.org/en/articles/2019/09/03/proj-a03.html

life of forced labor, degradation, and the routine and at times horrific violence that ensued.

However, the 1619 Project's assertion, put forward by both Hannah-Jones and Princeton sociologist Matthew Desmond, that the cruelty of slavery was unique to the thirteen colonies, does not survive even an elementary examination of the slave trade. The British North American colonies received only 6.5 percent of the 9 million to 15 million slaves taken across the Atlantic, whereas the vast subtropical and tropical zone stretching from the Caribbean and the Gulf of Mexico to Brazil took some 90 percent. Yet by 1830 the American slave states accounted for roughly 30 percent of all people of African descent in the Western Hemisphere. The only way to explain this staggering statistical disparity is that, horrible as slavery in the American colonies (and then states) certainly was, the survival rate was much higher than in the massive plantations of the Caribbean and Brazil, where a great many were literally worked to death, to be replaced by a steady stream of new arrivals.

Because slavery in the New World ultimately became confined overwhelmingly to Africans and their descendants, it is a deceptively easy step to imagine, as the 1619 Project does, that it was a system of racial oppression and deny that it was first, and always foremost, a system of labor exploitation. As the great West Indian historian Eric Williams pointed out:

> A racial twist has thereby been given to what is basically an economic phenomenon. Slavery was not born of racism: rather, racism was the consequence of slavery. Unfree labor in the New World was brown, white, black, and yellow; Catholic, Protestant and pagan.[4]

In fact, historians have searched in vain for any sort of racial justification for slavery in colonial Virginia. They have found neither that, nor even an original legal justification. To the extent that there was any ideological rationale for slavery, it was first religious, not racial. By custom of both Christian and Muslim societies, slavery was reserved for infidels. Muslims enslaved Christians, and Christians enslaved Muslims, and both enslaved those they viewed to be pagans, including the sub-Saharan Africans. In other words, slavery's longstanding existence and its religious sanction appears to have been all that was needed to set it afoot around Chesapeake Bay.

The 1619 Project would have us believe that John Rolfe's observation of the arrival of "20-odd Negroes" aboard the *White Lion*, an English pirate ship

---

4. Eric Williams, *Capitalism and Slavery* (University of North Carolina Press, 1944) p. 7.

flying under a Dutch flag—whose cargo of Angolans was stolen from a Portuguese slave vessel bound for Veracruz in New Spain!—was a world-altering event. As the first recorded moment when African slaves arrived in the American colonies, it is highly symbolic, but only symbolic. In fact, there were already people of African descent in Virginia, and it would take nearly a century before slavery became entrenched in the colonies. And not until the final decades before the Civil War did a fully developed system of racist ideology exist to justify slavery.

The slaves taken ashore in Virginia found an, as yet, sparsely populated colony that was remarkable for its lack of sharp definition regarding slavery *or* race. As Edmund S. Morgan and other historians have shown, slavery shaded imperceptibly into indentured servitude—a system of nonremunerated labor under which people could also be bought, sold, whipped, and separated from family, but which lacked the inheritable status of slavery. For most of the seventeenth century, indentured servitude was the leading form of labor in colonial Virginia and Maryland, and it continued to be so further to the north in Pennsylvania until after the American Revolution.

When viewed next to indentured servitude, chattel slavery appears to have been, as put by historian Gordon Wood, "the most base and degraded status in a society of several degrees of unfreedom." Another eminent historian, Bernard Bailyn, describes the lot of many indentured servants caught up in a Transatlantic journey strikingly similar to slavery:

> It was a brutal traffic ... [that] developed into an organized system with safe houses for confining victims until shipping could be arranged. ... Week after week, month after month, children, male and female, were snatched from the streets of London for shipment and sale "for a slave" in Virginia.[5]

Not only was slavery as a form of labor similar to indentured servitude in Colonial Virginia, it was socially proximate as well. Some African slaves were treated as indentured servants and gained their freedom. Some free Africans became landowners, and perhaps even themselves slaveowners. There were numerous marriages that would later be defined as "interracial" between African men and European women, and vice versa. There is even some evidence of political solidarity, most notably in Bacon's Rebellion against the William Berke-

---

5. Bernard Bailyn, *The Barbarous Years: The Peopling of British North America—The Conflict of Civilizations 1600–1675* (New York: Vintage Books, 2013), p. 167.

ley faction of the Virginia gentry, waged in 1676, which included Africans and Englishmen, slaves and indentured servants.

African slavery eclipsed indentured servitude in the Southern colonies for a variety of reasons, including the British seizure from the Dutch of the slave trade after the commercial war of 1654–1656 and the Great Fire of London in 1666, which dried up the supply of indentured servants. But it took many decades, until the first years of the eighteenth century, for a legal code governing slavery to develop. Among the laws that emerged was one that included the elimination of conversion to Christianity as a means of gaining freedom and the establishment of *partus sequitur ventrem*, that the condition of the mother, slave or free, determined the condition of the child.

Born into this world of masters and slaves as the sons and inheritors of slaveholding tobacco planters was the generation of Virginians who would lead the American Revolution—George Washington in 1732, Patrick Henry in 1736, Thomas Jefferson in 1743, and James Madison in 1751. In a clear example of bad history (and logical fallacy), the 1619 Project argues that, because the American Revolution did not achieve the destruction of slavery, it must therefore have been waged to preserve it. "We may never have revolted against Britain if the founders had not understood that slavery empowered them to do so; nor if they had not believed that independence was required in order to ensure that slavery would continue," as Hannah-Jones speculates. "Some might argue that this nation was founded not as a democracy but as a slavocracy."

There is nothing to support this contention. As we explained in our reply, "the world-historical significance of the Revolution is best understood through an examination of its objective causes and consequences." But what was the American Revolution?

Like other great revolutions—including the French Revolution of 1789 that it helped inspire, and later, the Russian Revolution of 1917—the American Revolution fused the most advanced political thought with economic conditions that had reached sufficient maturity to make the overthrow of an old order both possible and, from an objective standpoint, historically necessary.

The rapid growth of the colonies in the mid-eighteenth century—economic, demographic, and cultural—increasingly challenged the bands of aristocratic-feudal control imposed on them by Great Britain. King George and Parliament responded to these changes by attempting to prop up the mercantile-capitalist economic order and the old power structures through a series of taxes and acts, which were once well known to all students of American history. The Colonists, in turn, responded by asserting, increasingly forcefully, their own rights in the language of Enlightenment natural law and reason. The revolutionary implications of this, what historians call the imperial crisis, were well described by John Adams in an 1815 letter to Thomas Jefferson:

> As to the history of the Revolution, my Ideas may be peculiar, perhaps Singular. What do We mean by the Revolution? The War? That was no part of the Revolution. It was only an Effect and Consequence of it. The Revolution was in the Minds of the People, and this was effected, from 1760 to 1775, in the course of fifteen Years before a drop of blood was drawn at Lexington.[6]

The American Revolution was, in its time, a radical event. Never before had a colonial people, who lived on what was then viewed as the fringe of the civilized world, risen up and thrown off an imperial power. Not only did the Revolution dispose of the King and parliament, it established a new government whose founding document, Jefferson's Declaration of Independence, proclaimed universal human equality and the right to revolution when any government fails in its duty to protect basic rights.

It established a written constitution which asserted that the people are the ultimate repository of power. And it established a Bill of Rights, much under attack these days, that guaranteed basic democratic rights—the freedom of speech, of the press, of assembly; the right to be secure from government searches; the prohibition of torture. A republican revolution, it shattered the aristocratic principle, feudal economic structures such as primogeniture and entail, and drove out of the colonies the courtiers, King's favorites, and Loyalists, and in this way was a revolution "not just over home rule, but who would rule at home," as one historian put it long ago.

The American Revolution made incarnate the thought of the Enlightenment, the period of intellectual rebirth that undermined the divinely sanctioned feudal order of the Middle Ages, and that grew in tandem with the incipient capitalist economy. Just as scientists—natural philosophers as they were then called—such as Copernicus, Galileo, and Newton challenged the feudal-religious conception of the natural world, so Enlightenment political philosophers began to raise questions about the political world, but not the social, which was only dimly understood prior to Marx. Why did kings rule?

---

6. John Adams to Thomas Jefferson, August 24, 1815, https://founders.archives.gov/documents/Jefferson/03-08-02-0560

What was the purpose of government? What were the rights of man? Ultimately, in answer to these questions, the Enlightenment established that there existed natural rights—that is, rights that preceded government, or that exist in a state of nature.

One natural right identified was the right to private property. Another was the right to freedom, or self-ownership. However, the right to property, as James Oakes has pointed out, was increasingly viewed to be the outcome of self-ownership and the right to dispose of one's own labor. "The property which every man has in his own labour, as it is the original foundation of all other property, so it is the most sacred and inviolable," Adam Smith wrote in the *Wealth of Nations*.

Smith's book, the foundation of capitalist political economy and an attack on the mercantilist capitalist system, was published in 1776, the same year as the Declaration of Independence. Their simultaneity was not accidental.

Again, Eric Williams:

> The decisive forces in the period of history we have discussed are the developing economic forces. These economic changes are gradual, imperceptible, but they have an irresistible cumulative effect. Men, pursuing their interests, are rarely aware of the ultimate results of their activity. The commercial capitalism of the eighteenth century developed the wealth of Europe by means of slavery and monopoly. But in so doing it helped to create the industrial capitalism of the nineteenth century, which turned round and destroyed the power of commercial capitalism, slavery, and all its works. Without a grasp of these economic changes the history of the period is meaningless.[7]

Adam Smith's argument had been anticipated by the *Somerset* ruling of 1772, in which Lord Mansfield, the chief justice of the Court of King's Bench, ruled that there was no natural right to slavery, or property in man. It could only be established by positive law, which did not exist in England, where, as Somerset's barrister argued, the "air [was] too pure for slaves to breathe in."[8] The founding fathers were of course aware of the famous Somerset case. Yet they established no positive slave law in the Constitution, and in fact carefully excluded the word entirely, referring to it only obliquely in the three-fifths clause on representation.

---

7. Williams, *Capitalism and Slavery*, p. 210.
8. Capel Lofft, *Reports*, p. 2. Margrave's Argument. (May 14, 1772)

They were acutely aware of the contradiction between their espousal of equality and the existence of slavery. Patrick Henry called slavery a "Practice so totally repugnant to the first Impression of right and wrong." Washington hoped for a "plan adopted for its abolition." Madison worried that "Where slavery exists the republican Theory becomes still more fallacious." And Jefferson perceived a change

> since the origin of the present revolution. The spirit of the master is abating, that of the slave rising from the dust, his condition mollifying, the way, I hope preparing, under the auspices of heaven, for a total emancipation; and that this is disposed, in the order of events, to be with the consent of the masters, rather than by their extirpation.[9]

Jefferson's hope was not realized. The masters were extirpated, as a class, in the American Civil War. Yet that later event, the Second American Revolution, is inconceivable without the first.

The generation of 1776 were not mere hypocrites. They took certain measures toward the gradual ending of slavery. Jefferson authored the Northwest Ordinance in 1787, banning slavery in the states that would later become Ohio, Michigan, Indiana, Illinois, Wisconsin, and Minnesota. Under the second Jefferson administration, the United States banned the trans-Atlantic slave trade in 1808, the earliest year made possible by the Constitution and one year after the trade was banned by Britain.

The first state to enter the American union after the Revolution, Vermont, became in 1777 the first place in the Western Hemisphere to ban slavery by law. The Northern states set into motion plans for gradual abolition that ended slavery there in the antebellum, and, among Virginia and Maryland slaveowners, the Revolution instigated a manumission movement that substantially increased the number of free people of African descent in the United States. As noted, the American Revolution inspired the French Revolution of 1789 and the Haitian Revolution of 1791, which resulted in the first abolition of slavery in the Caribbean.

In the US, slavery might have withered away peacefully, as the founders hoped, had it not been for the invention of the cotton gin by Eli Whitney in 1793. Cotton production expanded from a minuscule amount in 1790 to 750,000 bales in 1830, to 2.85 million bales in 1850. By 1860 the US South

---

9. Thomas Jefferson, Notes on the state of Virginia, http://tjrs.monticello.org/letter/2218

was providing 80 percent of Great Britain's cotton. By the 1830s, cotton, a single commodity, generated more than half of all US export dollars. With the growth of the Cotton Kingdom, the number of slaves rose from 700,000 in 1790 to around 3.2 million in 1850.

The entrenchment of slavery in the American South is the subject of the next lecture, by Eric London. However, the question remains: In the scale of history, did the American Revolution signify the founding of a slavocracy, as the 1619 Project claims, or did it represent a progressive world-historical event?

The abolitionists had no doubts on this question. For them, the Declaration of Independence, in the words of the late David Brion Davis, was "the touchstone, the sacred scripture." For Frederick Douglass, who like Martin Luther King Jr. is passed over in silence by the 1619 Project, the Declaration was "the ring-bolt to the chain of destiny." Indeed, in her condemnation of Jefferson and the founders as so many liars, Hannah-Jones, ironically, finds herself in league with the fire-eating advocates of slavery, including John Calhoun, who called Jefferson's claim of human equality "the most false and dangerous of all political errors."

The American Revolution, and the Enlightenment, gave a powerful ideological impulse to the idea of human equality and to the conception of the dignity of labor. First in Great Britain, where the development of industrial capitalism and the working class emerged far earlier, then in the United States, it created the conditions for an antislavery movement that placed the institution of chattel slavery on a collision course with destruction. The struggle between the two principles of right—the right of private property up to and including ownership of man and the right of self-ownership—was ultimately decided in the Civil War, which, as Marx observed, set the stage for a great advancement in the class struggle.

The "Irrepressible Conflict": Slavery, the Civil War, and America's Second Revolution

The 1619 Project is a politically motivated attack on historical truth. Through this initiative, the Democratic Party seeks to present race, and not class, as the essential dividing line in American and world society.

This historical falsification has a clear political value for the American financial aristocracy. In the US, the wealthiest 1 percent of households now owns 40 percent of the wealth. The next 9 percent owns another 30 percent, meaning the top 10 percent owns 70 percent of all wealth. The bottom 50 percent—160 million people—owns less than 2 percent. That's less than the 3 percent owned by the richest 400 Americans.

Only an oligarchic society such as this one could produce a figure like Donald Trump, who epitomizes in his reactionary politics and personal depravity all the characteristics of the degenerate financial aristocracy.

In a country of 320 million people, roughly 285 million—the bottom 90 percent—constitute the working class. Of those, roughly 40 million are identified as black, 170 million are identified as white, 50 million are Hispanic, 17 million are Asian, and 4 million are Native American. Of all categories, roughly 40 million are foreign born, while another 35 million are second-generation immigrants. And, of course, within each category there are younger and older workers and women and men. Within this diverse working class, there exist various levels of stratification—from highly skilled workers with higher incomes to those living below or at the very fringes of solvency.

Eric London, "The 'Irrepressible Conflict': Slavery, the Civil War and America's Second Revolution," World Socialist Web Site, November 9, 2019. Eric London delivered this lecture on November 5, 2019.

29

These are just the figures for the working class in America. Across the world the working class comes from all different national and cultural backgrounds. The workers' position in society, however, is determined not by the color of their skin, their religion, their language, or their gender, but by their class—by the fact that they sell their labor power in order to survive. The task of socialists is to break down the racial myths, clarify the historical record, and bring workers of all the backgrounds together in a common, united struggle for social equality.

Historical falsification and identity politics are strategic weapons in the hands of the ruling class, which deliberately employs these tools to weaken the objective position of the working class by pitting workers against each other and thereby suppressing the class struggle. Trump opts for the openly fascistic method, scapegoating immigrants, excoriating socialism, and appealing to the most openly racist elements of American society.

But this lecture will address the Democratic Party and its history, its use of racial politics—today and in the decades leading up to the Civil War. Today, this brand of racialism is in no way a progressive alternative to the fascism of Trump. In fact, as an ideology, the Democratic Party's identity politics shares much in common with the party's racist roots and with fascist racial and irrationalist theories of the early twentieth century. It is an extremely dangerous and right-wing ideology and it must be opposed.

This critique will focus on two articles in the 1619 Project, the first by journalist and *New York Times* staff writer Nikole Hannah-Jones, the originator of the project, titled "Our founding ideals of liberty and equality were false when they were written. Black Americans fought to make them true," and the second, by Princeton sociologist Matthew Desmond, titled "In order to understand the brutality of American capitalism, you have to start on the plantation."

Both Hannah-Jones and Desmond argue that slavery was the fault of all white people, who are fundamentally predisposed to be racist. Key to the argument of Hannah-Jones is the claim that even Abraham Lincoln's Emancipation Proclamation had no relation to any progressive political struggle for equality. In her words, Lincoln "was blaming them [black people] for the [civil] war." The decision to free the slaves was merely a question of winning the war. She writes, "Anti-black racism runs in the very DNA of this country, as does the belief, so well articulated by Lincoln, that black people are the obstacle to national unity." We will return to Mr. Lincoln momentarily.

The *Times* asserts that the entire white population, poor and rich alike, supported and benefited from slavery and violently opposed postwar Reconstruction. Desmond claims:

> Witnessing the horrors of slavery drilled into poor white workers that things could be worse. So they generally accepted their lot, and American freedom became broadly defined as the opposite of bondage. It was a freedom that understood what it was against but not what it was for; a malnourished and mean kind of freedom that kept you out of chains but did not provide bread or shelter. It was a freedom far too easily pleased.[1]

Referencing the period following the Civil War, Hannah-Jones similarly states, "The many gains of Reconstruction were met with fierce white resistance throughout the South, including unthinkable violence against the formerly enslaved, wide-scale voter suppression, electoral fraud and even, in some extreme cases, the overthrow of democratically elected biracial governments."

And further: "White Southerners of all economic classes, on the other hand, thanks in significant part to the progressive policies and laws black people had championed, experienced substantial improvement in their lives even as they forced black people back into a quasi slavery."

How convenient for the capitalist class and the multi-millionaire editors of the *New York Times* that the 1619 authors conclude that the historic levels of inequality and exploitation in America today are not the fault of today's ruling class, but of ... the "DNA" of the country in general, and "white people" of "all economic classes" in particular.

Having introduced the positions of the *Times*, let's address the real historical record, starting with the Great Emancipator, Abraham Lincoln.

Lincoln the attorney would have pointed out that since Hannah-Jones and Desmond have impeached his political character by claiming that he "blamed blacks" for the Civil War and have presented the abolition of slavery as a reluctant act of last resort, we are entitled to introduce evidence to rehabilitate him and, in so doing, address the *Times'* underlying falsifications of the whole historical period.

As a preliminary issue, one feels the need to remind these people of the small matter that Lincoln did, in fact, carry out one of the most revolutionary acts of the nineteenth century—freeing the slaves—an accomplishment for

---

1. This and other quotes from Hannah-Jones and Matthew Desmond come from the *New York Times* Magazine of August 18, 2019, unless otherwise stated.

which he was assassinated. It was a world dominated by kings and tsars, with Europe mired in reaction following the defeats of the revolutions of 1848. In the Russian Empire, millions of peasants lived under serfdom, a form of unfree labor. The English crown was pumping China with opium and robbing the country blind. France invaded Mexico and established an emperor to collect its debts. Millions more risked their lives traveling on disease-ridden ships to throw off the weight of feudal reaction and make it in America. Fifteen years after Cavaignac in 1848 suppressed the Paris workers in blood and eight years before Thiers in 1871 would do the same to the Commune, Abraham Lincoln sat at his desk and wrote that four million human beings—with a market price of billions of dollars in today's money—were "Thenceforth and forever free."

Lincoln is an absolutely unique figure in American history. His own life is indissolubly connected to the American Revolution, which Thomas Mackaman addressed in the first of this lecture series. Lincoln was born on February 12, 1809, with three weeks remaining in the second term of President Thomas Jefferson, author of the Declaration of Independence.

In his biography of Lincoln, Sidney Blumenthal summarizes Lincoln's young career in relation to the question of slavery:

> Lincoln's deepening understanding of slavery in its full complexity as a moral, political, and constitutional dilemma began in his childhood among the Primitive Baptist antislavery dissidents in backwoods Kentucky and Indiana, whose churches his parents attended. As a boy he rode down the Mississippi River to New Orleans, where the open-air emporium of slaves on gaudy display shocked him. His development was hardly a straight line, but he was caught up in the currents of the time. His self-education, which started with his immersion in the Bible, Shakespeare, and the freethinking works of Thomas Paine and French philosophes, was the intellectual foundation for his profoundly felt condemnation of Southern Christian pro-slavery theology.[2]

Lincoln's hatred for slavery was in part personal. Blumenthal explains that at a campaign event, Lincoln, "the man who had been extraordinarily reluctant about discussing his past, sensitive about his social inferiority, blurted out a startling confession":

---

2. Sidney Blumenthal, *The Self-Made Man: The Political Life of Abraham Lincoln, Vol 1, 1809-1849* (New York: Simon and Schuster, 2016) p. 17.

"I used to be a slave," said Lincoln. He did not explain what prompted him to make this incredible statement, why he branded himself as belonging to the most oppressed, stigmatized, and untouchable caste, far worse than being accused of being an abolitionist. Illinois, while a free state, had a draconian Black Code. Why would Lincoln announce that he was a former "slave?" The bare facts he did not disclose to his audience were these: Until he was twenty-one years old, Lincoln's father had rented him out to neighbors in rural Indiana at a price of ten to thirty-one cents a day, to labor as a rail splitter, farmhand, hog butcher, and ferry operator. The father collected the son's wages. Lincoln was in effect an indentured servant, a slave. He regarded his semiliterate father as domineering and himself without rights.[3]

Lincoln's political career was dedicated to opposing the domination of the interests of the Southern slave owners on American political life, a domination they exercised after the conclusion of the so-called "Era of Good Feelings" [1815–1825, eds.] through the newly formed Democratic Party. From the 1830s, Lincoln was attracted to and active within the Whig Party, led by Henry Clay of Kentucky, a vicious opponent of Andrew Jackson and the Democrats and an advocate of national economic development—a specter the Democratic Party and the slaveholders opposed on the grounds that economic modernization would undercut the backward slave system.

A word about the Democratic Party's ignoble roots and its long strategy of inflaming racial divisions to maintain social stability and protect private property. The Democratic Party is one of the oldest bourgeois political parties in the world, formally founded in 1828. It was consciously conceived of by Southern slave owners and Northern Tammany Hall politicians as an alliance to protect the interests of the slave owners and preserve social stability in both South and North. The ideological glue of this alliance was an obsessive focus on race and identity, directed first and foremost against blacks, indigenous people, and, later, the Chinese.

Two figures stand out in the enunciation of this strategy: John C. Calhoun and Martin Van Buren.

Democrat John C. Calhoun, South Carolina senator and vice president during the presidencies of John Quincy Adams and Andrew Jackson, was an

---

3. Ibid., p. 3.

extremely class-conscious slave owner, aware that slavery could not politically survive on the basis of sectionalism alone. In 1828, he appealed to wealthy Northerners and said: "After we [the planters] are exhausted, the contest will be between the capitalist and operatives [workers]; for into these two classes it must, ultimately, divide society. The issue of the struggle here must be the same as it has been in Europe."

The historian Richard Hofstadter labeled Calhoun the "Marx of the Master Class," writing:

> Calhoun proposed that no revolution should be allowed to take place. To forestall it he suggested consistently—over a period of years—what Richard Current has called "planter-capitalist collaboration against the class enemy." In such a collaboration the South, with its superior social stability, had much to offer as a conservative force. In return, the conservative elements in the North should be willing to hold down abolitionist agitation; and they would do well to realize that an overthrow of slavery in the South would prepare the ground for social revolution in the North.[4]

Calhoun said in the Senate:

> There is and always has been in an advanced stage of wealth and civilization, a conflict between labor and capital. The condition of society in the South exempts us from the disorders and dangers resulting from this conflict; and which explains why it is that the political condition of the slaveholding states has been so much more stable and quiet than that of the North. ... The experience of the next generation will fully test how vastly more favorable our condition of society is to that of other sections for free and stable institutions, provided we are not disturbed by the interference of others, or shall ... resist promptly and successfully such interference.[5]

Calhoun's alliance was forged in no small part through the political talent of New York's Martin Van Buren, known as the "little magician" and "the Red Fox of Kinderhook." He headed the Democratic ticket after Jackson's second term, becoming president for one term from 1837 to 1841.

---

4. Richard Hofstadter, *The American Political Tradition, and the Men Who Made it* (Vintage Books, New York, 1989) p. 105.
5. Ibid., pp. 106–107.

Van Buren was a master politician who, well before he became president, understood that growing Northern cities would become centers of class struggle and that the ruling class needed a strategy to maintain social order. The historian Daniel Walker Howe describes Van Buren's own class-conscious political motives for forging the Democratic alliance:

> Leaders preoccupied with sovereignty and authority sensed a very real problem in America: the danger of anarchy. Significantly, when Martin Van Buren was in England at the time of the Great Reform Bill of 1832, his comments on it had to do not with improving the quality of representative government but with his fears for maintaining order.[6]

Such concerns among Northern elites led Calhoun to comment that those elites feared "the needy and corrupt in their own section. They begin to feel what I have long foreseen, that they have more to fear from their own people than we from our slaves."[7]

Through the Jackson administration and afterward, fanning racial hatred of the slaves and freed blacks became the Democrats' ideological mechanism for tying the Northern political machines to the political interests of the Southern slave owners. In both cases this racial politics had equal utility, maintaining slavery in the South and maintaining profits for the urban Northern industrialists. Poor whites and arriving immigrants were informed by the Democrats that it was not their class, but their race that determined their social position. They should fear a race war if the slaves were ever freed. This became the glue that held together the Democratic Party's cross-regional alliance—solidified by efforts to twist Northern workers' organic hatred of the new capitalist exploitation by idealizing slavery as the lesser evil.

There was another tradition that arose in opposition to the slave owners' conspiracy to dominate the entire political system, North, South, East and, in particular, West. Trailblazing abolitionists like publisher William Lloyd Garrison characterized the heroic spirit of these radical iconoclasts in his letter "To the Public" in the first edition of the abolitionist *The Liberator* on January 1, 1831, three decades before the war, published when Lincoln was a young man:

> I determined, at every hazard, to lift up the standard of emancipation in the eyes of the nation, *within sight of Bunker Hill and in*

---

6. Daniel Walker Howe, *What Hath God Wrought: The Transformation of America, 1815–1848* (Oxford: Oxford University Press, 2007), p. 438.
7. Hofstadter, *The American Political Tradition*, p. 96.

the birth place of liberty. That standard is now unfurled; and long may it float, unhurt by the spoliations of time or the missiles of a desperate foe—yea, till every chain be broken, and every bondman set free! Let Southern oppressors tremble—let their secret abettors tremble—let their northern apologists tremble—let all the enemies of the persecuted blacks tremble [emphasis added].[8]

Lincoln, though not an abolitionist, spent his young career opposing the Democratic Party, at first as a leader of the Whigs in Illinois. While Lincoln was active in the Whig Party, first in the state legislature and then as a representative in Congress, the US conquered new territory and forced its way westward—both through robbing Mexico of half its territory in the Mexican-American War of 1846–1848 and through the extermination and forced removal of Native Americans. The question of slavery was addressed in numerous "compromises" regarding the extension of slavery, orchestrated by the Whigs and by Clay himself. The American population, though not overwhelmingly or explicitly abolitionist in its political sentiments, came to view the expansionist aims of the slave owners with increasing hostility. Garrison's isolation of the 1830s shifted greatly during the following quarter-century, as the public turned against slavery.

By the early 1850s, Lincoln—and millions more—grew weary of the Whig Party's incessant compromises with the Slave Power, which had shifted the framework of American politics to the right and more tightly under the control of the slaveowning minority. Lincoln's former law partner, William Herndon, wrote:

> The warriors [of the Whig Party], young and old, removed their armor from the walls, and began preparations for the impending conflict. Lincoln had made a few speeches in aid of [Whig candidate Winfield] Scott during the campaign of 1852, but they were efforts entirely unworthy of the man. Now, however, a live issue was presented to him. No one realized this sooner than he. In the office discussions he grew bolder in his utterances. He insisted that the social and political difference between slavery and freedom was becoming more marked; that one must overcome the other; and that postponing the struggle between them

---

8. *The Liberator*, January 1, 1831, https://courses.lumenlearning.com/ushistory1os/chapter/primary-source-the-liberator-1831/

would only make it the more deadly in the end. "The day of compromise," he still contended, "has passed. These two great ideas have been kept apart only by the most artful means. They are like two wild beasts in sight of each other, but chained and held apart. Someday these deadly antagonists will one or the other break their bonds, and then the question will be settled."[9]

Antislavery sentiment continued to grow throughout the 1850s, in particular as antislavery forces conducted a campaign against the Kansas-Nebraska Act of 1854, a reactionary measure orchestrated by Democrat Stephen A. Douglas that repealed the Compromise of 1850 and allowed slavery's expansion to the Kansas and Nebraska territories through "popular sovereignty." By the mid-1850s, abolitionism had acquired an unprecedented degree of popularity, and abolitionists formed a key constituency in the founding of the Republican Party on explicitly antislavery principles.

Lincoln left the Whigs in 1854 and joined the new Republican Party. The domination of the slave owners over the Supreme Court, the Congress, and the presidency came more and more to be viewed as a conspiracy against the interests of the entire population, free and slave. Lincoln's attitude on slavery is well documented. Dozens of letters, speeches, and memoranda could be cited, not the least of which in terms of historical import was the Emancipation Proclamation.

But to give a sense of Lincoln's own attitude toward slavery, here is an excerpt from a diary entry, not meant for public consumption, written in 1858, the year after the Supreme Court's notorious decision in *Dred Scott v. Sanford*, which exploded the Missouri Compromise and held that people of African descent were not citizens and had no rights no matter where they were—North or South. Lincoln wrote:

> I have never professed an indifference to the honors of official station; and were I to do so now, I should only make myself ridiculous. Yet I have never failed—do not now fail—to remember that in the republican cause there is a higher aim than that of mere office. I have not allowed myself to forget that the abolition of the Slave-trade by Great Brittain [sic], was agitated a hundred years before it was a final success; that the measure had its open fire-eating opponents; its stealthy "don't care" opponents; its dollars

---

9. William H. Herndon and Jesse W. Weik, *Herndon's Life of Lincoln* (World Publishing Co., 1949), p. 295.

and cent opponents; its inferior race opponents; its negro equality opponents; and its religion and good order opponents; that all these opponents got offices, and their adversaries got none. But I have also remembered that though they blazed, like tallow-candles for a century, at last they flickered in the socket, died out, stank in the dark for a brief season, and were remembered no more, even by the smell. School-boys know that Wilbe[r]force, and Granville Sharpe, [sic] helped that cause forward; but who can now name a single man who labored to retard it? Remembering these things I can not but regard it as possible that the higher object of this contest may not be completely attained within the term of my natural life. But I can not doubt either that it will come in due time. Even in this view, I am proud, in my passing speck of time, to contribute an humble mite to that glorious consummation, which my own poor eyes may not last to see.[10]

It does not undercut the unparalleled hardship and hatred for slavery felt by enslaved blacks, nor reduce the historic significance of the slave rebellions of the eighteenth and nineteenth centuries, to point out the courage and sacrifice of white abolitionists. The *Times'* presentation of the category of "white people" as unified in support of slavery is an insult to the heroism of many who gave their lives for the cause of abolition. In October 1859, an abolitionist veteran of the crisis of Bleeding Kansas, John Brown, was captured by a military deployment commanded by then-US Army Colonel Robert E. Lee at Harper's Ferry, Virginia, after attempting to capture an arms depot and trigger a slave rebellion in the central Piedmont. He was executed for the crime of treason on December 2, 1859, at the age of 59.

One final point on Lincoln. Lincoln's assassination, less than a week after the surrender of the Confederacy, on April 9, 1865, shocked the country and the world. He was, of course, not a Marxist. But Karl Marx recognized the historical significance of Lincoln's life for the poor and oppressed of the world, writing in mid-May 1865:

> The demon of the "peculiar institution," for the supremacy of which the South rose in arms, would not allow his worshippers to honorably succumb on the open field. What he had begun in treason, he must needs end in infamy. ...

---

10. *Collected Works of Abraham Lincoln*, Vol. 2, Fragment on the Struggle Against Slavery, c. July 1858. https://quod.lib.umich.edu/l/lincoln/lincoln2/1:521?rgn=div1;view=fulltext

It is not our part to call words of sorrow and horror, while the heart of two worlds heaves with emotion. Even the sycophants who, year after year, and day by day, stuck to their Sisyphus work of morally assassinating Abraham Lincoln and the great republic he headed stand now aghast at this universal outburst of popular feeling, and rival with each other to strew rhetorical flowers on his open grave. They have now at last found out that he was a man neither to be browbeaten by adversity nor intoxicated by success, inflexibly pressing on to his great goal, never compromising it by blind haste, slowly maturing his steps, never retracing them, carried away by no surge of popular favor, disheartened by no slackening of the popular pulse, tempering stern acts by the gleams of a kind heart, illuminating scenes dark with passion by the smile of humor, doing his titanic work as humbly and homely as heaven-born rulers do little things with the grandiloquence of pomp and state; in one word, one of the rare men who succeed in becoming great without ceasing to be good.[11]

Beneath the change in political attitudes that had been taking place over these critical decades, major transformations were taking place in America, especially in the North and Northwest. From 1820 to 1850, the urban population increased from 7 to 18 percent of the national total. In 1820, there were just five cities with a population over 25,000. By 1850, there were twenty-six cities of more than 25,000 and six of more than 100,000. Mass migration from 1820 to the end of the 1830s drew approximately 667,000 overseas immigrants, not including slaves. From 1840 through the 1850s, another 4.2 million immigrants came to the US from Europe and Asia.

This period was also marked by the growth of social inequality and the changing character of work. In the largest American cities of the 1840s, the richest 5 percent of free males owned 70 percent of the real and personal property. The visibility of a small group of superrich is attested by the invention of the word "millionaire" around 1840. The historian Howe writes: "Instead of owning his tools and selling what he made with them, the mechanic now feared being left with nothing to sell but his labor. A lifetime as a wage-earner seemed a gloomy prospect to men who had imbibed the political outlook of

---

11. Karl Marx, "Address of the International Workingmen's Association to President Johnson, May 13, 1865," *Marx & Engels, Letters to Americans 1848–1895* (International Publishers, 1953), pp. 71–72.

Old Republicanism, who identified themselves with independent farmers or shopkeepers and looked upon wage labor as a form of dependency."[12]

This new system was incompatible with the slave system. Slavery is a mode of production, a term that encompasses both the productive forces—how products are made, including the actual instruments and the labor involved—as well as the objective material and social relations that arise on the basis of the productive forces and exist independently of human consciousness. These were the objective forces beneath the changing attitudes on slavery which exploded in violent conflict.

The 1619 Project presents slavery as a purely racial and racist institution from which all whites benefited in the South. But such a view of slavery in the American South is not only wrong, it actually minimizes the thoroughly reactionary character of the social order which arose on the rotten foundations of human bondage and, in a strange way, idealizes it. According to the *Times*, slavery was bad for the slaves but improved the lives of the majority of people in the South. To put it bluntly, the *Times* is regurgitating the argument of the slaveholders.

In her 2017 book *Masterless Men: Poor Whites and Slavery in the Antebellum South*, the scholar Keri Leigh Merritt sheds critical light on the reactionary essence of slavery as an economic system. The vast majority of whites did not derive any social, political, or economic benefits from the system of slavery. On the contrary, Merritt explains:

> Under capitalism, labor power was the commodity of the laborer. Conversely, under feudalism, as well as under slavery, the ruling classes owned, either completely or partially, the labor power of the working classes. The system was predicated on elites coercing individuals to work, often by violent means. In the slave South, where white laborers were in competition with brutalized, enslaved labor, the laborers, whether legally free or not, had little to no control over their labor power. The profitability and profusion of plantation slave labor consistently reduced the demand for free workers, lowered their wages, and rendered their bargaining power ineffective, indeed generally (except in the case of specialized skills) worthless. In essence, they were not truly "free"

---

12. Howe, *What Hath God Wrought?*, p. 539.

laborers, especially when they could be arrested and forced to labor, for the state or for individuals.[13]

In the first half of the nineteenth century, an oligarchy basing itself on slavery and aristocratic privilege enforced its rule through vigilante terror and police-state dictatorship aimed at the whole non-slaveholding population, black and white alike.

This slaveholding class, enriching itself through trade with the ruling classes of aristocratic Europe, threatened to destroy the egalitarian and democratic principles of the American Revolution. Secession, which the oligarchy carried out in the face of broad opposition among poor whites, was not a popular movement from below. It was a counterrevolutionary rebellion from above against the principle enshrined in the Declaration of Independence that "all men are created equal."

What were conditions for the majority of whites under slavery?

The antebellum South was defined by extreme inequality, not only between slaveholders and their human "property," but also among whites. In 1850, one thousand cotton-state families received $50 million per year in income, as compared to $60 million per year for the remaining 66,000 families. A study of Louisiana found that 43 percent of whites lived in urban areas in 1860, and that of these city dwellers, 80 percent were semiskilled or unskilled workers. Meanwhile, half of rural white families were landless, and half of those who owned land tilled less than fifty acres. Poor whites comprised the vast majority of the free population, and only about 14 percent of Louisiana's whites could be classified as middle class.

In 1860, 56 percent of personal wealth in the United States was concentrated in the South. In that region's cotton belt, wealth in slaves accounted for 60 percent of all wealth, greater even than the value of the land itself. As the price of slaves rose in the final decade before the Civil War, from $82,000 per slave in 1850 to $120,000 in 1860 (in 2011 dollars), the concentration of slave ownership at the top of Southern society increased dramatically. Slave ownership was far beyond the economic reach of even most landowning whites.

Whites lived in one-room shacks made of logs and mud, normally without windows. They had difficulty traveling from place to place, often in carts pulled by dogs. Without shoes, hookworm was a constant concern, and starvation was a threat. "Not having enough to eat was a constant worry for a sizable

---

13. Keri Leigh Merritt, *Masterless Men: Poor Whites and Slavery in the Antebellum South* (Cambridge University Press, 2017), p. 23.

percentage of the white population," Merritt writes, citing one slave who said, "We had more to eat than them." Of their white neighbors, the slave noted, "They were sorry folk."[14]

Merritt cites historian Avery Craven, who "identified several similarities between the material lives of poor whites and slaves. Their cabins differed 'little in size or comfort,' he wrote, as both were constructed from chinked logs and generally had only one room. Furthermore, these two underclasses 'dressed in homespuns, [and] went barefoot in season. ... The women of both classes toiled in the fields or carried the burden of other manual labor and the children of both early reached the age of industrial accountability.' Even the food they prepared and ate, Craven concluded, 'was strikingly similar.'"[15]

White men often spent months apart from their families as they walked through the country looking for work. "In contrast to the low divorce rates of the upper class," Merritt writes, "poor whites' relationships were similar to slaves' in some respects" due to this lack of economic stability.[16]

Alcoholism and illiteracy were widespread. The Southern antislavery advocate Hinton Helper explained that among Southern whites, "Thousands of them die at an advanced age, as ignorant of the common alphabet as if it had never been invented."[17] While a widespread system of "common school" public education had taken root in the North, there were hardly any schools in the antebellum South. Curtailing access to public education was a deliberate measure to socially control whites who were natural opponents of slavery. As Merritt explains:

> Whether the means involved disenfranchising poor whites, keeping them uneducated and illiterate, heavily policing them and monitoring their behaviors, or simply leaving them to wallow in cyclical poverty, the ends were always the same: the South's master class continued to lord over the region, attempting to control an increasingly unwieldy hierarchy. Slaveholders' worst fears were coming to pass as the ranks of disaffected poor whites grew. As one editorial out of South Carolina contended, the biggest danger to southern society was neither northern abolitionists nor black slaves. Instead, the owners of flesh needed to concern themselves with the masterless men and women in their own neigh-

14. Ibid., pp. 118–119.
15. Ibid., p. 118.
16. Ibid., p. 132.
17. Ibid., p. 145.

borhoods—this "servile class of mechanics and laborers, unfit for self-government, and yet clothed with the attributes and powers of citizens."[18]

To maintain order under conditions of extreme social inequality, an entire legal code was established to police non-slaveholding whites. The South's first police forces and prison systems were established "to impose social and racial conformity," with police "jailing individuals for the most benign behavioral infractions. Indeed, the rise of professional law enforcement changed the entire system of criminal justice."[19] In the antebellum South it was whites who filled the new jails, since black property was too valuable to remove from labor through incarceration. White convicts were subjected to brutal acts of public whipping and even water torture. Slave owners illegalized trade between poor whites and slaves and arrested whites suspected of befriending or engaging in sexual relationships with slaves.

Slaveowners established vigilante groups, especially following the devastating Panic of 1837, "in an effort to force the population into acquiescence." They were not, as the *Times* claims, comprised merely of "white people," but rather of wealthy white people.

Merritt explains that these vigilante groups were:

> Essentially bands of slave- and property-holders who monitored both the behaviors and beliefs of less affluent whites. [Historian Charles] Bolton described the targeted whites as those "whose poverty or indolence made them undesirable." Slaveless whites increasingly found themselves inhabiting a world in which they had to censor every utterance and defend every action.[20]

Under the direction of this oligarchic terror:

> Local mobs lynching and killing poorer whites abounded in the late antebellum period. The majority of those brutalized were accused of abolitionism of some sort—whether they were distributing reading materials, talking to other non-slaveholders about workers' rights, or simply seemed too friendly with African Americans.[21]

---

18. Ibid., p. 161.
19. Ibid., p. 227.
20. Ibid., p. 276.
21. Ibid., p. 278.

This contradicts a claim made by the *Times'* 1619 project that "slave patrols throughout the nation were created by white people who were fearful of rebellion," and showed "our nation's unflinching willingness to use violence on nonwhite people."

Far from gaining political privilege as a result of slavery, poor whites' supposed rights existed at the mercy of the masters. They could be jailed without charge, arrested for "vagrancy," and even executed for committing property crimes like burglary and forgery. As Merritt notes, "For all intents and purposes, due process was nullified."[22]

Nor is it true, as the *Times* claims, that whites failed to oppose slavery in the South. Within the South, these class tensions made it impossible—politically, economically, and militarily—for the Confederacy to continue fighting the war. The *Times'* falsification is aimed at eliminating the role of class and economic divisions from any study of US history. It is attempting to create a new "narrative" to abolish the class struggle from history to serve its reactionary contemporary aims.

Professor David Williams, author of the 2008 book *Bitterly Divided: The South's Inner Civil War*, writes: "Instead of the united front that has been passed down in Southern mythology, the South was in fact fighting two civil wars—an external one that we know so much about and an internal one about which there is scant literature and virtually no public awareness."[23]

Secession was held to statewide votes across the South and was roundly opposed by poor whites. Williams notes:

"The balloting for state convention delegates [preceding the war] makes clear that the Deep South was badly divided. It also suggests that those divisions were largely class related."[24]

Williams explains that non-slaveholding whites in Louisiana saw "the whole secession movement as an effort simply to maintain 'the peculiar rights of a privileged class,'" and that poor counties in Alabama, for example, voted to elect antisecessionist delegates by margins of up to 90 percent.[25]

Anti-Confederate rebellions broke out as early as 1861. In Winston County, Alabama, several union leaders organized mass meetings of unionists and declared the "Free State of Winston," while poor whites did the same

---

22. Ibid., p. 224.
23. David Williams, *Bitterly Divided: The South's Inner Civil War* (New York: The New Press, 2008), back cover.
24. Ibid., p. 47.
25. Ibid.

in areas across the South. A similar rebellion took place in Jones County, Mississippi, as described in Victoria Bynum's critical work *The Free State of Jones: Mississippi's Longest Civil War.*

In April 1862, the Confederate legislature passed the first conscription act, followed in October by the "Twenty Slaves Act," which exempted slave owners from military service.

It is estimated that up to two-thirds of all Southern soldiers deserted from the army during the war. What's more, 300,000 Southerners fled the South at the onset of the war to fight for the Union army. This number nearly equals the total number of Union soldiers killed throughout the course of the war.

The Confederate government sought to provide for the army by stealing from the poor through a process called "impressment," depicted skillfully in the film *Free State of Jones*, based on the book by Bynum. Indeed, thousands of poor Southern whites opposed attempts by the Confederacy to steal their property. Industrial accidents were also extremely common as Southern industrialists cut costs to feed the war machine. Factory explosions killed hundreds in places like Jackson, Mississippi. In Virginia, a cartridge-manufacturing plant exploded, "scattering workers like confetti." Child labor was especially common. Wrote one mother to Jefferson Davis in 1862:

"It is folly for a poor mother to call on the rich people about here. There [sic] hearts are of steel. They would sooner throw what they have to spare to their dogs than give it to a starving child."[26]

Strikes broke out from the onset of the war, beginning with a strike of iron-workers at Richmond, Virginia's Tredegar Iron Works. In retaliation, the Confederacy's Conscription Act of 1862 included a provision requiring conscription for striking workers.

The inner civil war deepened in 1863. On the war front, high desertion rates contributed greatly to the Southern losses at Vicksburg and Gettysburg in July. On the home front, the enmity of the poor toward the big planters threatened to take on political forms.

In several cities throughout the South, white workers organized Mechanics' and Working Men's Tickets to challenge the planter class's control of the Confederate legislature and state legislatures. One South Carolina planter wrote, "The poor hate the rich & make war on them everywhere & here especially with universal suffrage."[27] Planters devised the idea of a poll tax to limit class opposition from finding reflection during the 1863 elections.

---

26. Ibid., p. 116.
27. Ibid., p. 131.

Bread riots spread in 1863 as well. Shops were ransacked, planters' stores of tobacco and cotton were burned, and soldiers were sent to attack and jail demonstrators. A Mobile, Alabama, newspaper noted in April 1863 that an "army of women" with "axes, hatchets, hammers and brooms," swept through the town with banners that read "Bread or Blood" and "Bread and Peace." According to a local merchant, "The military was withdrawn from the field as soon as possible—for there were unmistakable signs of fraternizing with the mob."[28]

As the war dragged on, opposition to the Confederacy took on increasingly insurrectionary forms, especially guerrilla warfare. Pro-Union groups, often composed of blacks and whites, numbered in the tens, if not hundreds of thousands. They constructed their own lines of communication, supply chains, and fortifications and attacked Confederate soldiers. A network of safe houses was set up for deserters and abolitionists from Alabama through Chattanooga, the Sequatchie Valley, and Possum Creek, Kentucky, leading to Union territory.

By 1864, wide sections of the South began to initiate popular votes to end the war or secede from the Confederacy.

The profound anger over the war that was boiling over by 1865 was expressed by one poor Southerner, who wrote a letter directed to the wealthy in a local newspaper:

> That is right. Pile up wealth—no matter whether bread be drawn from the mouth of the soldier's orphan or the one-armed, one limbed hero who hungry walks your streets—take every dollar you can, pay out as little as possible, deprive your noble warriors of every comfort and luxury, increase in every way the necessaries of life, make everybody but yourself and non-producers bear the taxes of the war; but be very careful to parade everything you give before the public—talk boldly on the street corners of your love of country, be a grand home general—and, when the war is over, point to your princely palace and its magnificent surroundings and exclaim with pompous swell, "these are the results of my patriotism."[29]

Among Northern soldiers, the war which began as a fight for national unity began to be viewed by millions—including hundreds of thousands of sol-

---

28. Ibid., p. 143.
29. Ibid., p. 392.

diers—as a war for abolition. As James McPherson writes in his book *What They Fought For*, the Union Army was a highly political army, where soldiers were "eagerly snapping up newspapers that were sometimes available in camp only a day or two after publication." McPherson quotes letters from several soldiers: One said he "Spent a good portion of my time reading the news and arguing politics," another referenced "Considerable excitement on politics in camp," a third: "politics the principal topic of the day," and so on.[30]

But even those many soldiers who held racial prejudices and previously opposed a war to free the slaves came to view abolition as a military necessity and the Emancipation Proclamation as a blow against the Southern slave owners, whose armies they were fighting. Many Union soldiers also interacted—most for the first time—with "contraband" slaves who had escaped to Northern lines. In the course of this revolutionary cultural experience, the masses of people underwent a remarkable political transformation.

"It is astonishing how things has changed in reference to freeing the Negros," wrote one Illinois farmer and Union soldier. "It allwais has been plane to me that this rase must be freed befor god would recognize us ... we bost liberty and we Should not be Selfish in it as god gives us chanes will Soon be bursted ... now I belive we are on gods side ... now I can fight with a good heart."[31]

A Michigan soldier wrote: "The more I learn of the cursed institution of Slavery, the more I feel willing to endure, for its final destruction. ... After this war is over, this whole country will undergo a change for the better ... abolishing slavery will dignify labor; that fact of itself will revolutionize everything."[32]

It would require an additional lecture to address another critical fact: that the reactionary governments of Britain and France were prevented from intervening militarily on the side of the South by the overwhelming support among British and French workers for the cause of abolition.

Beneath the surface of the Civil War, profound changes had been taking place, both in class relations and the development of the means of production. In *The Republic for Which It Stands*, Richard White explains that the Civil War saw the replacement of the small "shop" by the "factory" as the central workplace. "Factories did differ from shops," White writes. "They were not just

---

30. James McPherson, *What They Fought For* (Baton Rouge: Louisiana State University Press, 1994), pp. 4–5.
31. Ibid., p. 67.
32. Ibid.

larger, but they also imposed a distance between the owner, who no longer worked alongside his men and who often did not know them by name."[33]

White notes that by the early 1870s:

> The number of factories in the United States, most of them in the Northeast, New England, and parts of the Midwest, had nearly doubled in the ten years since 1860. These factories vastly increased the number of workers involved in manufacturing. New York City alone had 130,000 manufacturing workers by 1873. ...
>
> Industry was becoming more capital-intensive, and the trend was accelerating in the 1870s as manufacturers switched to coal and steam, added machines, and built larger factories.[34]

As a result of this growth, for example: "Between 1863 and 1867 nineteen new unions arose in Chicago. These unions were multiethnic, and their members considered themselves part of a permanent working class. They no longer anticipated, as Lincoln had, that wage labor formed a transitory stage in their lives."[35]

A leading labor publication, the *Boston Daily Evening Voice*, expressed the feeling of many workingmen at the end of the Civil War: "All this talk about Republican equality and the rights of man is as water spilled upon sand, if the right of the laboring man to govern those affairs which pertain to his political, social, and moral standing in society be denied him."[36]

The Civil War and its major achievements—the abolition of slavery, the Fourteenth and Fifteenth Amendments, and the first federal Civil Rights Act—represented a dramatic step forward for all workers.

However, the war accomplished bourgeois tasks and the Republican Party was a capitalist party. Having carried out emancipation, the largest seizure of private property in world history prior to the Russian Revolution, it proved to be far more assertive in representing the interests of private property and the railroad corporations than in defending the interests and rights of the freed slaves.

The former slaveowning class, deprived of their human property but not of their land, viewed forced racial division as necessary for maintaining social or-

---

33. Richard White, *The Republic for Which It Stands: The United States during Reconstruction and the Gilded Age, 1865–1896* (Oxford University Press, 2017), p. 235.
34. Ibid., pp. 235–236.
35. Ibid., p. 243.
36. Ibid., p. 240.

der and defending extreme levels of social inequality. The political mechanism through which this was achieved was, as before, the Democratic Party, this time overseeing a political monopoly based on Jim Crow segregation—whose aim was the total division of black workers from white.

For millions of Southern blacks, the initial celebration of freedom soon transformed into a realization that sharecropping and wage labor marked a new type of exploitation.

Following the end of Reconstruction in 1877, thousands of blacks were lynched, tens of thousands more thrown in jail, and blacks as an entire segment of Southern society were forced into legal and social second-class citizenship in what was a racial caste system.

Skin color made a qualitative difference in the life of a Southern person living under Jim Crow. Sharecroppers and agricultural workers were attacked and killed for seeking to organize. The cultivation of racism as a political program was a response to efforts by reformers like the Populist Party to unite black and white farmers in a common movement against the railroad companies and big landowners.

But segregation did not provide poor whites with positive political or social benefits that would lead to an improvement of their living standards. In economic and political terms, racial segregation drove wages down for all races, it reduced social spending on schools, hospitals, and other social services, and entrenched the backward political and cultural climate that dominated the South.

In a larger sense, regardless of what an individual poor white person thought (and racism was not the sole property of the rich), the Jim Crow system did not provide the majority of whites with "privilege" because segregation ultimately blocked the development of a united movement from below, which was the only thing that could have improved the living conditions of all workers and farmers.

American politics and the development of the war and its aftermath were followed closely by Karl Marx and Friedrich Engels, who recognized that the explosive growth of American capitalism was transforming world history and the dynamics of the class struggle on an international scale. Before the conclusion of the Civil War, in a letter to the Marxist Union General Joseph Weydemeyer on November 24, 1864, Friedrich Engels made the following point:

> Your war over there is one of the most imposing experiences one
> can ever live through. ... A people's war of this sort, on both sides,

is unprecedented ever since the establishment of powerful states; its outcome will doubtless determine the future of America for hundreds of years to come. As soon as slavery—that greatest of obstacles to the political and social development of the United States—has been smashed, the country will experience a boom that will very soon assure it an altogether different place in the history of the world.[37]

In Marx's address to the National Labor Union of the US, published on May 12, 1869, four years after the war, Marx wrote: "And the successful close of the war against slavery has indeed inaugurated a new era in the annals of the working class. In the United States itself an independent labor movement has since arisen which the old parties and the professional politicians view with distrust."[38]

Engels emphasized the critical importance of the struggles of the American working class for the success of the world revolution. In 1886, he wrote, "What the downbreak of Russian Czarism would be for the great military monarchies of Europe—the snapping of their mainstay—that is for the bourgeois of the whole world the breaking out of class war in America."[39]

At the same time, Engels was acutely aware of the challenges Marxists would confront in fighting for the political unity of the working class of all races in America.

The ruling class "divides the workers into two groups: the native-born and the foreigners, and the latter in turn into (1) the Irish, (2) the Germans, (3) the many small groups, each of which understands only itself: Czechs, Poles, Italians, Scandinavians, etc. And then the Negroes. To form a single party out of these requires quite unusually powerful incentives."[40]

Elsewhere he wrote, "Your bourgeoisie knows much better even than the Austrian government how to play off one nationality against the other: Jews, Italians, Bohemians, etc., against Germans and Irish, and each one against the other, so that differences in workers' standards of living exist, I believe, in New York to an extent unheard of elsewhere."[41]

But an amendment to these prescient words by Engels is required. The Democratic Party and *New York Times'* campaign to falsify history is more

---

37. *Marx & Engels, Letters to Americans 1848–1895*, p. 63.
38. Ibid., p. 76.
39. Ibid., p. 157.
40. Ibid., p. 258.
41. Ibid., p. 242.

than a tactic to divide the working class. That it is, but the initiative has far more dangerous implications.

Today's bourgeoisie is repudiating any association with anything progressive in its own past. By denouncing the revolutions it led—the bourgeois revolutions of 1775–1783 and 1861–1865—today's ruling class is signaling its hostility to the Declaration of Independence, to the principle of equality before the law, to the Constitution, to the Enlightenment and rationalist thought, and to the fundamental principle that the people are endowed with certain inalienable rights.

In an era of skyrocketing social inequality, these principles—those "truths" the bourgeoisie once held to be "self-evident"—are now too dangerous to remain embedded in the popular consciousness. To prepare for future wars and attacks on living standards and to maintain the unbridled profits of American corporations, the democratic traditions of the country must be undermined. To accomplish this, history must be falsified. Lincoln must become a racist. Jefferson must become a racist. Race—not reason—must become the guiding principle for the study of history.

The ruling class is admitting that the progressive development of mankind is dependent upon removing it from power and transforming the world through socialist revolution.

Race, Class, and Socialism

"The most indubitable feature of a revolution," Trotsky wrote in his *History of the Russian Revolution*, "is the direct interference of the masses in historic events. In ordinary times the state, be it monarchical or democratic, elevates itself above the nation, and history is made by specialists in that line of business—kings, ministers, bureaucrats, parliamentarians, journalists. But at those crucial moments when the old order becomes no longer endurable to the masses, they break over the barriers excluding them from the political arena, sweep aside their traditional representatives, and create by their own interference the initial groundwork for a new régime."[1]

Such is the period we are now entering. In a recent commentary published by the Center for Strategic & International Studies, a leading geostrategic think tank, Samuel Brannen, the director of the "Risk and Foresight Group," defines the present period as "The Age of Leaderless Revolution." He points to the mass uprisings and protests in recent weeks in Lebanon, Iraq, Chile, Spain, Hong Kong, Ecuador, Honduras, Haiti, Egypt, and Algeria.[2]

Brannen does not mention, but one should add, the significant growth of the class struggle here in the United States, including major strikes over the past month by General Motors autoworkers and Chicago teachers. Polls show,

Joseph Kishore, "Perspectives for the coming revolution in America: Race, class and the fight for socialism," World Socialist Web Site, December 2, 2019. Joseph Kishore delivered this lecture in November 2019.

1. Leon Trotsky, *History of the Russian Revolution* (London: Pluto Press, 1977), p. 17.
2. Samuel Brannen, "The Age of Leaderless Revolution," CSIS, https://www.csis.org/analysis/age-leaderless-revolution

particularly among young people, a sharp shift to the left and growing interest in socialism and hostility to capitalism.

"The world is experiencing," Brannen writes, "the volatility of what my late colleague Zbigniew Brzezinski identified in 2008 as a 'global political awakening'—a sweeping revolution the likes of which we had never before seen." This "awakening" is fueled by the connectivity of the world's population in a way that is unprecedented. "The ability for individuals to connect, to inspire and coordinate millions onto the streets, is without precedent."[3]

Brannen warns: "The risks and implications are mounting for governments, businesses, and organizations of every type. It is a question of when, not if, the digital flash mob comes for those in power."[4]

Brannen defines these revolutions as "leaderless," however, and holds out the hope that they "can be co-opted for ... good," by which he means channeled in a way that does not threaten the interests of the ruling elite.

The question of leadership is indeed the central issue. As Trotsky stressed in 1938, "The historical crisis of mankind is reduced to the crisis of the revolutionary leadership." Building a leadership, developing within the working class and youth a political movement conscious of its aims, is a complicated process. It requires a protracted struggle against all those who would seek to pollute consciousness, to "co-opt" and divert social anger and opposition.

It is within this context that the Socialist Equality Party and the International Youth and Students for Social Equality decided to hold a series of meetings on the *New York Times'* 1619 Project. Understanding and combating the conceptions advanced in this "project," which is being aggressively promoted at schools and campuses throughout the country, is of immense importance for the working class and youth.

What is involved is a form of historical revisionism and contemporary politics aimed at elevating race as the central social and political category—indeed, at promoting racial conflicts. At the very point that masses of workers and youth all over the world are entering into struggle over issues of class, there is a conscious effort to divide and disorient.

One must state at the outset: There is nothing left-wing about this campaign. It shares more in common with the fascistic reaction of Donald Trump than anything traditionally associated with progressive politics.

The argument of the *Times* is that the central problem in the United States, in its history and in its present, the "root," is the "racism that we still cannot

---

3. Ibid.
4. Ibid.

purge from this nation to this day," in the words of Nikole Hannah-Jones, the lead author in the *Times* project. "Anti-black racism runs in the very DNA of this country," she writes.

This "original sin" of American society is "endemic"—that is, it is a disease embedded in a particular people that cannot be purged. At a meeting at New York University on November 18, Hannah-Jones declared that racism among white people is a "psychosis," presumably embedded deep in the irrational mind of white people.

It is not just that racism exists, but that the conflict between races is *the* basic and enduring issue. For the *Times*, the history of the United States is a history of the struggle between races, between "white people," who have all benefited from the oppression of "black people," first through slavery, then through segregation and now through "white supremacy," and their black victims. History is defined in terms of the conflict between races, with common interests shared only by individuals who are categorized by their race.

It is not possible in the course of a single meeting to review all the historical falsifications that flow from this analysis. We have already published on the World Socialist Web Site detailed replies to the *Times*' account of the American Revolution and the Civil War, two monumental events in world history that initiated and completed the bourgeois democratic revolution in America. We have also published three excellent interviews with American historians James McPherson, James Oakes and Victoria Bynum that address these themes.

One element of the *Times*' attitude toward these revolutions is important to underscore in relation to the themes of this lecture—namely, the hostility that this interpretation of history displays toward the Enlightenment. The Enlightenment is the intellectual and political revolution in thought, arising out of immense advances in science during the sixteenth and seventeenth centuries, that emphasized the ability of humans to understand the world through reason and reconstruct it on rational foundations. The two figures in the history of bourgeois politics in the United States most closely associated with the Enlightenment—Thomas Jefferson and Abraham Lincoln—are the two particular targets of the *Times*' historical falsification.

Ibram X. Kendi, in his book *Stamped from the Beginning: The Definitive History of Racist Ideas in America*, a major inspiration for the 1619 Project, denigrates the Enlightenment as a "metaphor for Europeanness, and therefore Whiteness. ... Enlightenment ideas gave legitimacy to this long-held racist 'partiality,' the connection between lightness and Whiteness and reason, on the one hand, and between darkness and Blackness and ignorance, on the other."[5]

This hostility to the Enlightenment is the provenance of the far right, not the left, but it is connected to a contempt for rationality and democratic principles that characterizes the modern pseudo-left, a theme to which I will return.

To carry forward the *Times'* narrative of history into the latter portion of the nineteenth century and the twentieth century requires that the *Times* completely ignore and cover up the profound social and political developments that transformed the freed slaves into a critical section of the working class. It is necessary to wash away from history the history of the class struggle, and therefore the history of the African American working class.

In the *Times'* account, there simply is no working class. The word "class" does not make an appearance in the entire introductory historical essay by Hannah-Jones. The term "White Americans" appears fifteen times, "White people" nineteen times, "Black Americans" twenty-eight times, and "Black people" forty-three times. Yet "working class" appears zero times.

If one were to base a curriculum on the *Times* account, as schools and colleges throughout the country are being urged to do, this new "narrative" of American history would remove all reference to the insurrectionary and violent class battles that have characterized American capitalism since it emerged fully in the decades following the Civil War. The purpose is as much about cutting workers and youth off from these traditions of class struggle as it is about establishing an alternative narrative of enduring and unending racial conflict.

Absent from the *Times* account is any mention of the Populist movement in the South, which sought in the decades following the Civil War to unite freed blacks with poor whites. The *Times* cannot, therefore, account for the origins of Jim Crow segregation and the Ku Klux Klan (KKK), the conscious response of the ruling class to the threat of an alliance of blacks and whites. There is no mention of Tom Watson, the leader of the Populist movement, who early in his career addressed his appeal to both races:

> You are made to hate each other because upon that hatred is rested the keystone of the arch of financial despotism which enslaves you both. You are deceived and blinded that you may

---

5. Ibram X. Kendi, *Stamped from the Beginning* (Bold Type Books, 2016), pp. 80–81. For an analysis of this passage, see the Foreword to this book.

not see how this race antagonism perpetuates a monetary system that beggars you both.[6]

The Populist Party did not, and could not, given its class heterogeneity, overcome the imposition of Jim Crow. This failure was expressed tragically in the personal fate of Watson, who became a racist and anti-Semite and ended his career as a Democrat.

Nonetheless, the farmers' insurgency supplied important lessons. The historian of the South C. Vann Woodward noted in his essential account of the origins and development of Jim Crow segregation, *The Strange Career of*, that the emergence and development of the Populist movement demonstrated that the policies of segregation and racism were not a product of "the immutable 'folkways' of the South," and "the belief that they are immutable and unchangeable is not supported by history."[7]

The deliberate and systematic promotion of racial divisions, including the use of the Ku Klux Klan as the militant arm of the Southern reactionaries in the Democratic Party, was rooted in both the fear of social unrest and the emergence of American imperialism toward the end of the nineteenth century. The militarist adventures that marked this emergence, beginning with the Spanish-American War of 1898, Woodward explained, "suddenly brought under the jurisdiction of the United States some eight million people of the colored races, 'a varied assortment of inferior races,' as the *Nation* described them, 'which of course could not be allowed to vote. ...'"[8]

> At the very time that imperialism was sweeping the country, the doctrine of racism reached a crest of acceptability and popularity among respectable scholarly and intellectual circles. At home and abroad biologists, sociologists, anthropologists, and historians, as well as journalists and novelists, gave support to the doctrine that races were discrete entities and that "Anglo-Saxon" or "Caucasian" was the superior of them all.[9]

To refer to any of the monumental class struggles that emerged in the aftermath of the Civil War, beginning with the Great Railroad Strike of 1877

---

6. Quoted in C. Vann Woodward, *The Strange Career of Jim Crow* (New York: Oxford University Press, 2002), p. 63.
7. Ibid., p. 65.
8. Ibid., p. 72.
9. Ibid., p. 74.

through to the sit-down strikes of the 1930s, would require that the *Times* acknowledge that the fight against social inequality—and the fight against racism—became centered in the struggle to unify the working class against the corporations and against capitalism.

The *Times* makes no mention of the Industrial Workers of the World (IWW), which was established in 1905 and organized a series of militant industrial struggles and strikes in the early part of the twentieth century. At its founding convention in June of 1905, Big Bill Haywood called the organization of the IWW, in a historical reference to the American Revolution, the "Continental Congress of the working class."

"The American Federation of Labor," Haywood declared, "which presumes to be the labor movement of this country, is not a working class movement. It does not represent the working class. There are organizations that are affiliated, but loosely affiliated with the A.F. of L., which in their constitution and by-laws prohibit the initiation of or conferring the obligation on a colored man; that prohibit the conferring of the obligation on foreigners. What we want to establish at this time is a labor organization that will open wide its doors to every man that earns his livelihood either by his brain or his muscle."[10]

The *Times* makes no mention of the founding of the Socialist Party of America in 1901, or its leader Eugene Debs, who refused to speak before segregated audiences. Debs declared in 1903: "I have said and say again that, properly speaking, there is no Negro question outside of the labor question—the working class struggle. ... Our position as Socialists and as a party is perfectly plain. We have simply to say: 'The class struggle is colorless.' The capitalists, white, black and other shades, are on one side and the workers, white, black and all other colors, on the other side."[11]

Yet it was the Russian Revolution that made the decisive contribution to the struggle for equality in the US—in both its class and racial dimensions. Debs' belief in the equality of all the "toiling masses" expressed the most advanced American thought of the time. But his contention that the Socialist Party has "nothing special to offer the Negro" evaded the racism that saturated

10. "Opening Convention of the IWW"
https://www.marxists.org/history/usa/unions/iww/1905/convention/ch01.htm
11. Eugene V. Debs, "The Negro in the Class Struggle," *International Socialist Review*, Vol. 4, No. 5, November 1903, p. 259. https://www.marxists.org/history/usa/pubs/isr/v04n05-nov-1903-ISR-gog-Princ.pdf

the AFL, and even a prominent wing of the Socialist Party itself, led by Milwaukee's Victor Berger.

As James P. Cannon later recalled, "Everything new on the Negro question came from Moscow—after the Russian Revolution began to thunder its demand throughout the world for freedom and equality for all national minorities, all subject peoples and all races—for all the despised and rejected of the earth." Immediately, the Comintern under Lenin and Trotsky called on the American comrades with "the harsh, insistent demand that they shake off their own unspoken prejudices, pay attention to the special problems and grievances of the American Negroes, go to work among them and champion their cause in the white community."[12]

The Russian Revolution—also unmentioned by the *Times*—profoundly influenced a layer of black intellectuals, artists, and militants in the 1920s, associated with "the Harlem Renaissance." The agitation of the communists in the South in the 1920s and 1930s, for example the defense of the Scottsboro Boys falsely accused of rape in 1931, laid the groundwork for the later civil rights movement. In the North it paid dividends by the 1930s, when for the first time in the history of the American labor movement black workers won citizenship rights in the industrial unions of the Congress of Industrial Organizations (CIO). A layer of liberals followed in the wake of the fight for racial equality lead by the socialists, among them C. Vann Woodward. As for the Democratic Party, it remained the bastion of Jim Crow white supremacy.

None of this can be mentioned because it cuts across the claim that the United States is riven by irreconcilable racial antagonisms, that the workers who are white are irredeemably racist.

To understand the origins and political function of the conceptions promoted by the *Times*, it is necessary to understand the way in which the ruling class, and, in particular, the Democratic Party, responded to the threat of social revolution that emerged in the twentieth century. In the 1930s, with the example of the Russian Revolution fresh in their minds and amid a growing working-class insurgency within the United States, American liberalism, under the Democratic Party administration of Franklin Roosevelt, fashioned the "New Deal," a reform agenda that implemented restraints on the power of big business.

Trotsky explained at the time, "America's wealth permits Roosevelt his experiments."

---

12. James P. Cannon, "The Russian Revolution and the American Negro Movement," *International Socialist Review*, Summer 1959, p. 81, p. 79.

Already by the mid-1940s, however, under the impact of the Second World War, liberalism began its retreat. Alan Brinkley, in his book *The End of Reform*, notes that by 1945, the policies of the Democratic Party began to shift "from a preoccupation with 'reform' (with a set of essentially class-based issues centered around confronting the problem of monopoly and economic disorder) and toward a preoccupation with 'rights' (a commitment to the liberties and entitlements of individuals and thus to the liberation of oppressed people and groups). 'Rights-based' liberalism was in some respects part of a retreat from a broad range of economic issues involving the structure of the industrial economy and the distribution of wealth and power within it."[13]

However, ruling-class policy following the Second World War still maintained significant redistributive measures, including high taxes on the wealthy. The top marginal tax rate for the wealthiest Americans was 90 percent under presidents Harry Truman and Dwight Eisenhower. In 1964, President Lyndon Johnson announced that the fight against poverty "would prove the success of our system," that is capitalism, which was followed by the introduction of Medicare, Medicaid, and food stamps.

This, in fact, proved to be the last gasp of American liberalism. By the late 1960s, the postwar boom had begun to unravel and the policies of the Democratic Party and the ruling class as a whole underwent a further lurch to the right. The "Great Society" and the "War on Poverty" were shipwrecked by the Vietnam War and the protracted decline in the global position of American capitalism. The period of significant social reform proved to be very short-lived.

The move toward a policy of social counterrevolution coincided with a deliberate strategy aimed at elevating sections of the middle class within minority populations into the institutions of class rule.

Here it is critical to understand the significance of the transformation that took place in the 1960s and 1970s, from the civil rights movement to identity politics. The civil rights movement was part of a broader wave of social unrest in the United States in the 1960s, including major strike action by the working class, the Vietnam antiwar protest movement, and the ghetto uprisings in major cities throughout the US.

It is a striking fact that, in an essay supposedly dedicated to the history of race relations in the United States, Hannah-Jones hardly mentions the civil

---

13. Alan Brinkley, *The End of Reform: New Deal Liberalism in Recession and War* (New York: Alfred A. Knopf, 1995), p. 170.

rights movement. The name Martin Luther King Jr. does not appear in her essay, nor that of Malcolm X.

This is for good reason. King's own writings during this period are themselves a refutation of the racialist narrative of the *Times*, which places all "white Americans" and "white people" on the side of racist reaction and bigotry, benefiting and supporting the lynching of blacks.

In a speech before a convention of the AFL-CIO in 1961, King attacked those who insist on the "intrinsic differences" between the races. "There is no intrinsic difference, as I have tried to demonstrate. Differences have been contrived by outsiders who seek to impose disunity by dividing brothers because the color of their skin has a different shade."[14]

Writing in 1964, King noted that a majority of whites in the US supported voting rights, housing, and integrated schools and restaurants throughout the country. He proposed that same year a "Bill of Rights for the Disadvantaged." He argued: "The moral justification for special measures for Negroes is rooted in the robberies inherent in the institution of slavery. Many poor whites, however, were the derivative victims of slavery [again, contrary to the *Times*]. As long as labor was cheapened by the involuntary servitude of the black man, the freedom of white labor, especially in the South, was little more than a myth. ... To this day the white poor also suffer deprivation and the humiliation of poverty if not of color. They are chained by the weight of discrimination, though its badge of degradation does not mark them."[15]

The Poor People's Campaign of 1968 specifically sought to embrace white workers in the South and in Appalachia. At the same time, King came out ever more forcefully in opposition to the Vietnam War. He was assassinated on April 4, 1968.

King was a social democrat and not a Marxist. He expressed the view that guaranteed employment and basic social rights for all workers, regardless of race, was possible in the "richest nation on earth" through capitalist reforms. By the late 1960s, however, the relative position of American capitalism had already begun its protracted decline. Three years after King's assassination, the Nixon administration ended dollar-gold convertibility, the cornerstone of the Bretton Woods monetary system set up in the aftermath of the Second World War.

---

14. Martin Luther King, speech before the Fourth Constitutional Convention of the American Federation of Labor-Congress of Industrial Organizations, Bal Harbour, Florida, December 11, 1961. http://www.substancenews.net/articles.php?page=4740

15. Martin Luther King, *Why We Can't Wait* (Signet Classic, 2000), pp. 128–29.

As the ruling class shifted to the offensive, beginning the process of tearing up all the gains won by workers in an earlier period, it very consciously adopted a policy of integrating and elevating a privileged section of the upper-middle class into positions of power.

The policy was announced by none other than Richard Nixon, who declared in response to the urban rebellions of the late 1960s: "Black Americans, no more than white Americans, they do not want more government programs which perpetuate dependency. ... They want the pride, and the self-respect, and the dignity that can only come if they have an equal chance to own their own homes, to own their own businesses, to be managers and executives as well as workers, to have a piece of the action in the exciting ventures of private enterprise."[16]

The *New York Times*, expressing the consensus that was developing within the ruling class, declared that Nixon's position "on the need for the development of black capitalism and ownership in the ghetto could prove to be more constructive than anything yet said by other presidential candidates on the crisis of the cities."

Thus began the policies of affirmative action and racial quotas, of the promotion of a layer of black businessmen and politicians to preside over an immense increase of social inequality. Nixon expressed the view that "we sooner or later must bring those who threaten [domestic peace] back within the system." Through an executive order, he established the Office of Minority Business Enterprise for this purpose. Over the next several years, a layer of the black middle class was brought into positions of political power, including Coleman Young, who became mayor of Detroit and, over the next twenty years, oversaw a massive deindustrialization of the city.

A decade after Nixon's election in 1968, the Supreme Court upheld affirmative action policies for the first time, in the 1978 case of *California v. Bakke*. Supreme Court Justice Thurgood Marshall argued in his opinion, "It is because of a legacy of unequal treatment that we now must permit the institutions of this society to give consideration to race in making decisions about who will hold positions of influence, affluence and prestige in America."[17]

---

16. Richard M. Nixon, speech accepting the Republican Party nomination, August 8, 1968. https://www.presidency.ucsb.edu/documents/address-accepting-the-presidential-nomination-the-republican-national-convention-miami

17. "Excerpts From Opinions by Supreme Court Justices in the Allan P. Bakke Case (Published 1978)," *The New York Times*, June 29, 1978, https://www.nytimes.com/1978/06/29/archives/excerpts-from-opinions-by-supreme-court-justices-in-the-allan-p.html

That is, not social equality, but the equal distribution of positions of power and "affluence" among races and minority groups. Not programs to uplift all poor people, or to improve the conditions of the entire working class, but the selective elevation of a small minority to preside over deindustrialization and the destruction of the living conditions of the vast majority.

This was an international phenomenon. In an analysis of Affirmative Action measures in the US, India, and South Africa, University of Michigan economist Thomas Weisskopf noted: "The most important purpose that can be served by ethnicity-based [positive discrimination] in admissions to [higher educational institutions] is not to redistribute educational opportunities from the rich to the poor. Instead it is to reduce identity-based differentials in access to the upper strata of a society, that is, to integrate the societal elite."[18]

Already by the late 1970s, the impact of these and other measures adopted by the ruling class had produced a significant growth of social inequality among African Americans.

The noted sociologist William Julius Wilson, who is African American, pointed as early as 1978, the same year as the *Bakke* decision and a decade after the assassination of King, to the development of "a deepening economic schism ... in the black community, with the poor blacks falling further and further behind middle- and upper-income blacks. ... Class has become more important than race in determining black life-chances."[19]

Such conceptions continue to be at the center of Democratic Party politics today. Democratic Party candidate Cory Booker put it bluntly in an interview with *Democracy Now!* last week, when he criticized "a lot of people [who] want to talk to you about the wealth gap, the wealth gap, the wealth gap. Look, there are a lot of people in my community that want to be entrepreneurs, that want to be millionaires. And so, I always talk about the wealth gap, yeah, but what we really need to be talking about is the opportunity gap and to make sure that everybody has equal opportunity to start a business, to be innovators, to

---

18. Randall Kennedy, "Rethinking affirmative action in Admissions to Higher Educational Institutions," quoted in *For Discrimination: Race, affirmative action, and the Law* (Vintage Books, 2015), p. 86.

19. Richard Polenberg, "The Declining Significance of Race: Blacks and Changing American Institutions," quoted in *One Nation Divisible: Class, Race and Ethnicity in the United States Since 1938* (Penguin, 1980), p. 273.

participate in the new job booms of the future and the new businesses of the future."[20]

The shift in ruling-class policy from reform to social counterrevolution coincided with and was integral to a rightward movement within sections of the upper-middle class of all races. The promotion of a politics based on racial and gender identity became the hallmark of pseudo-left and ex-Marxist intellectuals, whose response to the wave of social upheavals and class struggles between 1968 and 1975 was to repudiate any association with working-class politics.

Herein lie the origins of "intersectionality theory," "critical race theory," "identity politics," "whiteness studies," and associated schools. The theoretical foundation of these tendencies is rooted in an idealist rejection of Marxism.

The great advance of Marxism was the materialist conception of history, the understanding that at the foundation of society are definite forms of production, and that to the phases in the development of these forms of production correspond definite social, that is, class relations. In particular, modern capitalist society is characterized by private ownership of the means of production, which are in the hands primarily of the owners of the banks and giant corporations.

The working class, as a class, is united in its relationship to this process of production. It is that class of people, today the majority of the world's population, that must sell its labor power on the market for a wage. The fundamental unity of the working class, across nationalities, races, ethnicities, genders, or any other category, is defined by this relationship.

The politics of race and identity begins not with the process of production and the objective interests, independent of thought, that are determined by this production process, but by racial divisions. Where does racism itself come from? It is "endemic," the "original sin," embodied in the "DNA" of white people, per the *Times*. History is not the transition from one form of social organization to another—from slavery to feudalism, then capitalism and finally to socialism—but merely different forms in the eternal persistence of racial antagonisms.

An important document marking the repudiation by middle-class groups of Marxism and an orientation to the working class is the statement of the so-called Combahee River Collective, a black lesbian feminist organization formed in 1974 and led by Barbara Smith, Demita Frazier, and Beverly

---

20. "Sen. Cory Booker on Environmental Justice, Nuclear Power & 'Savage Racial Disparities' in the U.S." November 15, 2020. Democracy Now! https://www.democracynow.org/2019/11/15/cory_booker_presidential_forum_environmental_justice

Smith. The statement, published in April 1977, a year before the *Bakke* decision, claimed to be an extension of Marxist theory, but was in fact a direct repudiation of all its fundamental conceptions.

To this day, the Combahee statement, which contains the first use of the term "identity politics," is regularly cited by organizations of the pseudo-left as a major turning point. It was published as the centerpiece of a 2017 book, *How We Get Free*, by Keeanga-Yamahtta Taylor, a tenured professor at Princeton and at that time a leading member of the International Socialist Organization, which dissolved itself into the Democratic Party earlier in 2019. The various caucuses of the Democratic Socialists of America that are centered on issues of race and gender cite the statement as a key document.

The purpose of the collective, the authors wrote, was to develop an "integrated analysis and practice based upon the fact that the major systems of oppression are interlocking." The most significant "oppressions," however, were those based on race and gender. "Black women's extremely negative relationship to the American political system (a system of white male rule) has always been determined by our membership in two oppressed racial and sexual castes. ... Black women have always embodied, if only in their physical manifestation, an adversary stance to white male rule."[21]

Underscoring the self-obsessed character of the new politics of the upper-middle class, the authors wrote: "This focusing upon our own oppression is embodied in the concept of identity politics. We believe that the most profound and potentially most radical politics come directly out of our own identity, as opposed to working to end somebody else's oppression."[22]

The aim was not social equality and the liberation of all mankind, but one's own personal advancement, leveraging various categories of identity to achieve positions of power and privilege. There is an analogy to the social motivations behind the rise of the Stalinist bureaucracy and its attacks on the program and perspective of permanent revolution. "Not everything for world revolution," Trotsky said of the thinking of the petty Soviet official, "Something for me too."

Robin Morgan writes, "I haven't the faintest notion what possible revolutionary role white heterosexual men could fulfill, since they are the very embodiment of reactionary-vested-interest power."[23] Poor whites, and particularly

---

21. The Combahee River Collective Statement (1977) https://combaheerivercollective.weebly.com/
22. Ibid.
23. Quoted in ibid.

white men, were categorized by the Combahee Collective under the general heading of "white male rule."

Consider the period in which this was being written. The Combahee Collective was formed in 1974, the year of the largest strike movement in the United States since the 1950s, including a twenty-eight-day strike of coal miners in West Virginia and other states. The statement was written less than one year before the 1977–78 coal miners' strike, waged in defiance of the invocation of the Taft-Hartley Act by the Democratic Party administration of Jimmy Carter. The workers involved in these struggles and many others were in their majority white men. Were they not then part of "reactionary-vested-interest power?" Was their effort to maintain their jobs and living conditions an expression of a longing for "white privilege"?

The rejection of a politics based on class, and with it an ever more direct opposition among sections of the so-called left to the theoretical conceptions of Marxism, was an international phenomenon. The rise to prominence of figures like Michel Foucault in France, a major inspiration for intersectionality and critical race theory, was part of a broader turn away from Marxism.

Foucault, a pupil of the Stalinist Louis Althusser and once a member of the French Communist Party, developed in the 1960s and 1970s a theoretical framework that rejected the primacy of class conflict in favor of the "multiplicity of force relations immanent in the sphere in which they operate."[24] Foucault rejected the notion of an objective truth existing outside of language and "discourse." Truth and power are constructed through language, through ideas, rather than existing in the material relations of production.

"Force relations" based on race or other categories, conditioned by thought, are no less fundamental—indeed are more fundamental—than the exploitation inherent in the capitalist system, which in any case cannot be said to exist outside of language and "discourse." He considered talk of the objective interests of a class to be invalid, since there are no "force relations" that exist outside of our construction of them through language.

Such conceptions were part of a broader rejection of a politics rooted in class. To the extent that "socialism" meant anything, it was to be divorced from the class struggle, from the interests of the working class. Ernesto Laclau and Chantal Mouffe, in their influential 1985 book *Hegemony and Socialist Strategy*, wrote, "What is now in crisis is a whole conception of socialism which rests upon the ontological centrality of the working class, upon the role of Rev-

---

24. Michel Foucault, *The Order of Things* (Taylor and Francis, 2018), p. 1.

olution, with a capital 'r', as the founding moment in the transition from one type of society to another. ..."[25]

The theoretical conceptions developed by the new proponents of racial and gender politics became anchored to definite social interests, the interests of a privileged layer of the upper-middle class, including, but not limited to, the tenured professors who populate the humanities departments of the major universities, where anti-Marxism has become a requirement of the profession.

The past four decades have seen a massive redistribution of wealth from the working class of all races to the rich. Since 1980, the share of the national income going to the bottom 50 percent of the population has fallen from 20 percent to 12 percent, while the income share of the top 1 percent has risen from 12 percent to 20 percent.

However, the perpetual rise in the stock markets and the intensification in the exploitation of the working class have benefited more than the superrich. A layer of the upper-middle class, the "next 9 percent," that is, the top 10 percent excluding the top 1 percent, has also benefited. This layer, with income over about $150,000 a year, has seen its share of national income increase from 23 percent in 1970 to nearly 28 percent today.[26]

The growth of inequality within minority populations is particularly significant. The richest 10 percent of African Americans owns 75.3 percent of the wealth owned by all African Americans, and the top 1 percent owns 40.5 percent. The bottom 60 percent combined have zero net wealth. This is a massive increase since the early 1990s, when the share of wealth going to the top 1 percent of African Americans was less than 25 percent.[27]

Toward the end of her essay, Hannah-Jones declares that over the past half century, "black Americans have made astounding progress, not only for ourselves but also for all Americans." The vast majority of "black Americans," as with the vast majority of the working class as a whole, have, in fact, suffered a historic retrogression in their conditions of life. A small section, however, has made significant "progress."

---

25. Ernesto Laclau and Chantal Mouffe, *Hegemony and Socialist Strategy* (Vintage Press, 1994), p. 2.

26. "Changes in Family Finances from 2013 to 2016: Evidence from the Survey of Consumer Finances," US Federal Reserve Bulletin, Vol. 103 No. 3, September 2017, https://www.federalreserve.gov/publications/files/scf17.pdf

27. Lisa J. Dettling, Joanne W. Hsu, Lindsay Jacobs, Kevin B. Moore, and Jeffrey P. Thompson, "Recent Trends in Wealth-Holding by Race and Ethnicity: Evidence from the Survey of Consumer Finances," US Federal Reserve, September 27, 2017. https://doi.org/10.17016/2380-7172.2083

In 1957, sociologist E. Franklin Frazier wrote of the "black bourgeoisie," an initial analysis of the emerging layer of middle-class and upper-middle-class blacks. The conditions of life for the black elite have risen to levels that massively eclipse those that prevailed in the time of Frazier. The outlook of this "black bourgeoisie" is expressed by individuals like Ta-Nehisi Coates, whose *We Were Eight Years in Power* is a celebration of the Obama administration, which oversaw the largest transfer of wealth from the working class to the rich in American history.

The politics of racial, gender, and other forms of identity is the politics of the upper-middle class, of all races and genders. It is a mechanism for dividing the working class, subordinating it to the right-wing, prowar politics of the Democratic Party, and a mechanism for carrying out bitter struggles within the top 10 percent for access to positions in academia, corporate boardrooms, and the state.

In the aftermath of the dissolution of the Soviet Union, this layer of the upper-middle class moved further to the right, openly repudiating any association with socialism and opposition to imperialism. The *Times'* reframing of American history along racial lines is entirely compatible with its absolute support for the military and the CIA.

The theoretical and political conceptions promoted by this layer have absolutely nothing to do with "left" politics. Indeed, the irrationalist, anti-Enlightenment, anti-Marxist, and anti-working-class perspective developed over the past half century has brought the pseudo-left into increasing alignment with the conceptions and politics of the far right. The obsession with race, the interpretation of history in terms of the conflict of races, the categorization of society into "white America" and "black America," "white people" and "black people"—this is not the language of the left, of progressive social reform, let alone socialist revolution.

It was the French aristocrat Arthur de Gobineau, who exercised enormous influence on Hitler and the Nazi ideologists, who most consistently developed, in the mid-nineteenth century, the racialist theory of history. The historian Richard Wolin, in a book analyzing the postmodernists' "intellectual romance with fascism," notes that "Gobineau's ingenious strategy was to reestablish the Counter-Enlightenment worldview on pseudoscientific foundations by employing the concept of *race* as a universal key to historical development. Racially based taxonomies of human types were already widely used by anthropologists and natural historians. But Gobineau was the first to apply race systematically to the study of history as a type of hidden master code."[28]

And what is the *Times'* 1619 Project if not an effort to "apply race systematically to the study of history?" Wolin also notes that the theoreticians of the "New Right" have adapted themselves to the language and style of the pseudo-left. The New Right in France, he writes, has

> shifted its emphasis from the concept of "race" to that of "culture." Abandoning outmoded arguments for biological racism, it moved in the direction of what might be called a cultural racism. ... Sounding like a liberal's liberal, [New Right theorist Alain] de Benoist embraced what one might [sic] be best described as a nonhierarchical, "differentialist racism." No culture was intrinsically better than any other. Instead, they were all "different," and these differences should be respected and preserved. Practically speaking, this meant that the place where Algerians should enjoy civil liberties was Algeria. "France for the French"—an old racist slogan from the Dreyfus Affair (and resurrected during the 1930s)—Europe for the Europeans, and so on. As de Benoist explained in the early 1980s, "The truth is that the people must preserve and cultivate their differences. ... Immigration merits condemnation because it strikes a blow at the identity of the host culture as well as the immigrants' identity."[29]

What separates such a conception from the position of Stacey Abrams, a rising star in the Democratic Party, who wrote in a defense of identity politics published in *Foreign Affairs* earlier this year that racial groups have "intrinsic differences?" This is not to say that the Democratic Party is a fascist organization. However, ideas have consequences, or, rather, political ideas reflect the movement of social forces. And the social forces behind the politics of racial division are right-wing.

The insistence on the unbridgeable chasm between blacks and whites does not reflect reality. While racism exists, attitudes toward race have been transformed enormously over the past half century. Globalization has integrated the working class of the entire world into a single process of production. The masses of workers and youth who are being driven into struggle throughout

---

28. Richard Wolin, *The Seduction of Unreason: The Intellectual Romance with Fascism, from Nietzsche to Postmodernism* (Princeton University Press, 2004), pp. 289–290.
29. Ibid., p. 268.

the world are not motivated by issues centered on race, gender, age, sexual orientation, or any other identity, but by issues of class. The obsessive focus on race and racial division by the *Times* and the Democratic Party will only play into the hands of Donald Trump and his fascistic advisers.

The world situation is fraught with immense danger, but also immense possibilities. The Trump administration is part of the rise of far-right and fascistic forces throughout the world. In the face of growing social unrest, the ruling elites are resorting ever more openly to authoritarian methods of rule, resurrecting all the political filth of the twentieth century. Geopolitical antagonisms are mounting, and the ruling elites of all the major capitalist countries are remilitarizing in preparation for world war.

Another social force, however, is emerging—the working class. In the fight against social inequality, war, and authoritarianism, the working class and youth cannot allow themselves to be subordinated to any faction of the ruling elite. The working class cannot allow itself to be divided along national or racial lines. It must reject the chauvinism of Trump as well as the racial politics of the Democrats.

Part II

Interviews

Victoria Bynum

Victoria Bynum

Victoria E. Bynum is Distinguished Professor Emeritus of History at Texas State University, San Marcos. She is author of *The Free State of Jones: Mississippi's Longest Civil War* and *Unruly Women: The Politics of Social and Sexual Control in the Old South.*

WSWS: Hello, Victoria, it is a pleasure to speak to you. The *New York Times* writes that slavery is "America's national sin," implying that the whole of American society was responsible for the crime of slavery.

But Lincoln said in his second inaugural address in 1865 that the Civil War was being fought "until every drop of blood drawn with the lash shall be paid by another drawn with the sword." What was the attitude of the subjects of your study toward slavery? Is it possible to separate those attitudes from the economic grievances that many white farmers and poor people harbored against the Confederate government of the slavocracy?

Victoria Bynum: Direct comments about the injustice of slavery are rare among plain Southern farmers who left few written records. Knowing this at the outset of my research, I was delighted to find clear and strong objections to slavery expressed by the Wesleyan Methodist families of Montgomery County, North Carolina, which I highlighted in my first book, *Unruly Women*. In 1852, members of the Lovejoy Methodist Church invited the Rev. Adam Crooks, a well-known abolitionist, to address their church. Crooks' presence incited violent protests from several slaveholders of the community,

Eric London, "Historian Victoria Bynum on the inaccuracies of the New York Times 1619 Project," World Socialist Web Site, October 30, 2019.

while those who invited him protected him from physical harm. Shortly before the Civil War, the same church members were arrested for distributing Hinton Rowan Helper's forbidden 1857 abolitionist tract, *The Impending Crisis of the South*. Some of these families, all of whom supported the Union during the war, may personally have known Helper, who was raised in the same North Carolina "Quaker Belt" that the Wesleyan Methodist community inhabited.

In Jones County, Mississippi, antislavery views were not so evident, yet are still discernible. The county's leading Unionists came from five interrelated families, of which the Collins family was most prominent. The Collinses were prosperous landowners who chose not to own slaves, participated in local politics, and who rallied local citizens to oppose secession. In 1863, three Collins brothers and several of their sons joined Newt Knight's band of pro-Union guerrillas. Jasper Collins, Newt's first sergeant, was interviewed shortly before his death in 1913. At age eighty-five, Jasper expressed pride in his Civil War support for US forces, noting that the "Twenty Negro Law" had enabled wealthy slaveholders to escape the battlefield, as well as that he was unwilling to fight a cause dedicated to keeping blacks enslaved. To make such statements in Mississippi during the era of "Lost Cause" orthodoxy was remarkable to say the least. Furthermore, the Collins family's Unionism extended into East Texas, where a branch of the family migrated around 1852. There, three additional Collins brothers formed their own pro-Union guerrilla band headed by Warren J. Collins. In a 1949 family memoir, Warren's son, Texas Senator Vinson Collins, remarked that the Collinses "were all opposed to slavery and to concession [sic]."

Similarly, Newt Knight's likely mixed-race daughter, Anna Knight, remarked in her 1951 autobiography that her childhood home had been headed by a man [Newt] who did not believe in slavery. Certainly, the openly interracial family and neighborhood that Newt founded in 1870 suggests as much.

Given such evidence—and there are many more examples—I would answer "no" to your question of whether it is "possible to separate those attitudes from the economic grievances they harbored against the Confederate government." Research into the military, county, and family records left by Unionist families in North Carolina, Mississippi, and Texas reveals a class-based yeoman ideology grounded in republican principles of representative government, civic duty, and economic independence. Though we cannot assume that individual Unionists were antislavery, their aggregate words and actions indicate that many—especially their leaders—at the very least connected slavery to their own economic plight in the Civil War era.

WSWS: In the 1619 Project, Matthew Desmond writes that the slave system "allowed [white workers] to roam freely and feel a sense of entitlement." Desmond then acknowledges that slavery led to the oppression of all whites. Can you reconcile this contradiction? What were the economic and social circumstances driving men like Newton Knight to resist the confederacy?

VB: It's difficult to reconcile Desmond's above statement with his words that follow, which echo the works of historians such as Keri Leigh Merritt and Charles C. Bolton: "Slavery pulled down all workers' wages. Both in the cities and countryside, employers had access to a large and flexible labor pool made up of enslaved and free people ... day laborers during slavery's reign often lived under conditions of scarcity and uncertainty, and jobs meant to be worked for a few months were worked for lifetimes. Labor power had little chance when the bosses could choose between buying people, renting them, contracting indentured servants, taking on apprentices or hiring children and prisoners."[1]

In 1998, Bolton and Scott P. Culclasure co-edited *The Confessions of Edward Isham*, a terrific volume that features several essays (one authored by myself) that analyze the rare autobiography of an illiterate poor white man. Edward Isham dictated his life's story, one grounded in the class and labor relations of the Old South, to his lawyer on the eve of his execution for murder. Bolton's essay highlights the typical aspects of Isham's life as a male wage earner—his constant search for menial, low-paying jobs such as ditching, rail-splitting, land clearing, and mining—which reflected the extent to which poor white laborers in the South functioned as a "supplemental labor force" to slavery. Significantly, the man that Isham murdered was an employer who refused to pay him his wages. More broadly, the essays in this volume reveal that the old stereotype repeated by Desmond, that poor white Southerners "roamed freely," in fact reflected their need to be mobile and flexible simply to make a living. Sporadic short-term work contributed to an unstable, violent world in which such men literally fought over menial jobs or headed West in an elusive search for prosperity. Poor white women labored under similar circumstances, but with far fewer paying jobs available. Time and again, they settled for common-law relationships that promised greater economic security, but which often resulted in their abandonment. As for apprenticeship, my work in *Unruly Women* and Karen Zipf's book, *Forced Apprenticeship in North Car-*

---

1. The *New York Times Magazine*, August 18, 2019, p. 36.

olina, reveal how the children of free women of color and indigent white mothers were routinely apprenticed to propertied white men, where their labor was appropriated in a manner similar to slavery.

The forces that drove men like Newt Knight to reject the Confederacy involved three classes of Southern whites—slaveholders, non-slaveholders (the yeomanry), and the propertyless (poor whites). Proslavery leaders defused issues of inequality among whites by placing free blacks below poor whites and regularly touting the superiority of all whites over blacks on account of Southern slavery. To a large degree, the white yeoman class bought into this, priding itself on its superiority to both blacks and poor whites, particularly since white elites blamed the poverty of poor whites on their degradation and inferior heritage. At the same time, however, a sizable slice of the yeomanry developed a keen sense of class consciousness as slavery expanded and became ever more concentrated in the hands of wealthy elites. These were the conditions that led Hinton Rowan Helper, who emerged from the yeoman class of North Carolina, and his followers to condemn slavery and advocate its abolition.

Just as the followers of Helper recognized the secession movement as a scheme to protect and expand slavery, so too did the yeomanry of Piney Woods, Mississippi, who armed themselves against the Confederacy under the leadership of Newton Knight and declared their county to be the "Free State of Jones." Throughout the South, as historians Margaret Storey and David Williams have shown for Alabama and Georgia, similar yeoman communities organized themselves into guerrilla bands that temporarily collaborated with poor whites, slaves, and free people of color in common cause against the Confederacy. More broadly, Jarret Ruminski's study of Civil War Mississippi locates the stark limits of white Confederate loyalty in the greater devotion of common people to family, farm, and community.

WSWS: Do you see parallels between the *New York Times'* references to genetics (the historic "DNA" of the United States) and the argument, advanced by the slavocracy, that "one drop" of black "blood" was enough to count a light-skinned person in the expanded pool of slave labor. Can you expand on this?

VB: The frequent correlation of identity with ancestral DNA continues to mask the historical economic forces and shifting constructions of class, race, and gender that have far more relevance to one's identity than one's DNA can ever reveal. Historically, race-based slavery required legal definitions of whiteness and blackness that upheld the fiction that British/US slavery was reserved for Africans whom the institution "civilized." From the earliest days of colonization, however, both forced and consensual sexual relations created slaveholding and non-slaveholding households that were neither "black" nor "white," but rather were mixed-race. The frequent rape of enslaved women by slaveholders produced multitudes of such children, but so also were many mixed-race children born to whites and free blacks. Slave law dictated that the child of an enslaved woman was also a slave—and therefore "black"—regardless of who fathered the child. Conversely, deciding the race of children born to free women who crossed the color line was not so easy, and became even more difficult after slavery was abolished. In the segregated South, where one's ability to work, live, love, travel, and enjoy the full benefits of American citizenship depended on one's perceived race, such questions might end up in court, as was the case in 1946 for Newt Knight's mixed-race great-grandson, Davis Knight, after he married a white woman. While custom dictated that Davis Knight was "black" based on his great-grandmother Rachel's mixed-race status, state laws required more precise evidence. Under Mississippi law, unless one was proved to have at least one-fourth African ancestry, one was legally—though not socially—white. On this basis, Davis Knight went free.

The crux of the matter is that people of European, American Indian, and African ancestry have long been referred to as "black," regardless of their physiognomy, and still are today. All that is required, regardless of one's appearance, is "one drop" of African "blood." As historian Daniel Sharfstein and others have noted, however, the one-drop rule of race historically has been inconsistently applied, and, as in the case of Davis Knight, rarely upheld by the law. Still, the custom of defining anyone suspected or known to have an African ancestor as a "person of color," served to justify slavery, segregation, and the violent treatment inherent to both institutions. Importantly, creating a biracial society has also historically enabled those in power to destroy interracial class alliances among oppressed peoples. Whether it be Bacon's Rebellion in 1676, Reconstruction during the 1870s, labor struggles in the 1930s, or the civil rights movement of the 1950s, interracial alliances have been crushed time and again through the exploitation of racism.

Despite this history, and although denying people civil rights according to their race is no longer legal, socially, the one-drop rule is still very much alive. Many Americans, including liberals who politically reject racism, routinely define white people who have black ancestors as "passing" for white. The same Americans would find it absurd to accuse a black person who has white ancestors of "passing" for black, since the one-drop rule is based on hypodescent—i.e., the belief that African "blood" overwhelms all others. Sadly, folks who employ the term "passing" seem unaware that they are repeating two centuries of essentialist pseudoscience developed by white supremacists to justify slavery and segregation.

WSWS: One of the arguments implied in the 1619 Project is that anyone living in the mid-1800s who harbored racial prejudice was responsible for slavery, regardless of their political views or activity. What do you make of this argument? What was ultimately the source of racial backwardness in the period you studied?

VB: This is a specious argument that ignores the historical context in which North American racism emerged, as well as the complicated place of race relations within both class and gender relations. With Africa supplying the demand for ever more slaves for the mines and plantations of the Americas, New World chattel slavery became increasingly race-based. Elaborate racist theories enabled the builders of empire to argue as "good Christians" that slavery was part of a God-decreed "natural" order. Historian Ibram X. Kendi and others cite plenty of evidence that European racism preceded the rise of the trans-Atlantic slave trade, but it's also clear that New World slavery elevated racism by fueling Europe's commercial revolution and justifying the brutal labor demands of colonial plantation agriculture. As Eric Williams argued in *Capitalism and Slavery* (1944), slavery underwrote early capitalism.

Compared to Spain and France, slavery in British North America grew relatively slowly despite slaves' noted arrival in 1619. The labor needs of British colonizers were originally met by various means that either failed or proved inadequate: conquered Indians were enslaved on grounds of their "Godless" savagery; lower-class whites from European nations were indentured on grounds of their degradation and burdensome presence in home countries. Edmund Morgan argued that African slaves were initially too expensive an investment in the death trap of North America. That changed when unruly servants began to live long enough to claim freedom dues; replacing temporary unfree labor with chattel slavery helped to defuse class conflict.

By the nineteenth century, racist dogma was deeply entrenched and practiced with special urgency among elite Southerners whose wealth and leisure depended on slavery. Beliefs in white superiority resonated as well among non-slaveholding whites who defined their freedom from chattel slavery on the basis of being part of the "superior" race. Still, regardless of how successful slaveholders were in inculcating the common people with racism, the idea that anyone "that harbored racial prejudice was a priori historically responsible for slavery," appears to be a rhetorical device aimed at rendering racism timeless and immutable.

WSWS: What was the experience of people like Newton Knight in the Reconstruction Era? What did they think about the changes that took place in Southern society following the war? Did they have any relationship to the Populist movement, for example?

VB: Alongside Northern Carpetbagger Republicans, Scalawag Unionists celebrated their victory over Confederate forces. In Jones County, as elsewhere, Unionists such as Newton Knight and Jasper Collins eagerly sought and received political appointments. Newt was appointed relief commissioner by Republican Governor William Sharkey in 1865 and, in 1872, Governor Adelbert Ames appointed him deputy marshal of the Southern District of Mississippi. As a Reconstruction Republican, Newt fought election fraud and protected the rights of freedmen. In 1870, he optimistically applied to the US government for financial compensation for himself and the band of fifty-four men who had "held out true" to the Union cause during the Civil War.

Newt Knight's optimism was doomed to defeat. With crucial aid from the Ku Klux Klan and other white supremacist groups, defeated Confederates waged a counterrevolution against Reconstruction that succeeded in less than a decade. The Republican Party proved inadequate to the task of winning the postwar battle to reform the South in the name of racial justice and expanded democracy. In the Compromise of 1876, Republicans agreed to remove troops from the South in return for Democrats granting the disputed US presidential election to Rutherford B. Hayes. The Republican Party thus promoted its own narrow interests in the name of national prosperity and civility by accepting a "New South" led by former slaveholders. This move facilitated the rapid industrialization of the nation while simultaneously handing the fate of freed people and pro-Union whites to their oppressors. Republicans' abandonment of Reconstruction ushered in a dark, violent period in which people of color faced segregation, poverty, and the constant threat of lynchings, while former Unionists were vilified and some even murdered. Working the land often meant sharecropping for blacks and tenant farming for whites rather than owning one's own plot. The poorest people scrambled for day labor jobs, just as they had before the war.

The tentative Civil War alliances between whites and blacks were destroyed by shrill white supremacist campaigns backed up by segregationist laws. In time, wartime Unionism was virtually erased from Southern history and literature, replaced by Lost Cause dogma that insisted the "noble" Confederate cause had been spurred by devotion to Constitutional principles rather than slavery.

Despite the devastating defeat of Reconstruction, Newton Knight applied for federal compensation until 1900, when his claims were denied once and for all from a federal government no longer interested in Southern Unionists. After leaving politics and retreating to his interracial community, an embittered Newt told one interviewer that the non-slaveholding farmers of the South should have just risen up and killed the slaveholders rather than fighting for the Union side. His old ally, Jasper Collins, took a different path. During the 1870s, Jasper left his pro-Confederate Baptist church and joined a newly established Universalist Church. During the 1890s, he became active in the Populist Party, and in 1895, founded Jones County's only Populist newspaper. Several of Jasper's descendants took his rejection of the two-party system even further by running for local offices on a Socialist ticket around the time of his death in 1913. Likewise, in East Texas, Jasper's brother, pro-Union guerrilla Warren J. Collins, ran for office as a Socialist in 1910. For white Southerners who'd fought against the Confederacy during the Civil War in hopes of achieving a democratic revolution, the Republican Party's betrayal of Reconstruction was a bitter pill to swallow.

James McPherson

James McPherson

James M. McPherson is the George Henry Davis '86 Professor Emeritus of United States History at Princeton University. He was awarded the Pulitzer Prize in history for *Battle Cry of Freedom: The Civil War Era*, the Lincoln Prize for *For Cause and Comrades: Why Men Fought in the Civil War*, and the Anisfield-Wolf Book Award for *The Struggle for Equality: Abolitionists and the Negro in the Civil War and Reconstruction*. McPherson served as president of the American Historical Association in 2003.

WSWS: What was your initial reaction to the 1619 Project?

James McPherson: Well, I didn't know anything about it until I got my Sunday paper, with the magazine section entirely devoted to the 1619 Project. Because this is a subject I've long been interested in, I sat down and started to read some of the essays. I'd say that, almost from the outset, I was disturbed by what seemed like a very unbalanced, one-sided account, which lacked context and perspective on the complexity of slavery, which was clearly, obviously, not an exclusively American institution, but existed throughout history. And slavery in the United States was only a small part of a larger world process that unfolded over many centuries. And in the United States, too, there was not only slavery but also an antislavery movement. So I thought the account, which emphasized American racism—which is obviously a major part of the history, no question about it—but it focused so narrowly on that part of the story that it left most of the history out.

Thomas Mackaman, "An interview with historian James McPherson on the *New York Times*' 1619 Project," World Socialist Web Site, November 14, 2019.

So I read a few of the essays and skimmed the rest, but didn't pursue much more about it because it seemed to me that I wasn't learning very much new. And I was a little bit unhappy with the idea that people who did not have a good knowledge of the subject would be influenced by this and would then have a biased or narrow view.

WSWS: Are you aware that the glossy magazine is being distributed to schools across the country, and the Chicago public school district has already announced that it will be part of the curriculum?

JM: I knew that its purpose was for education, but I haven't heard many of the details of that, including what you've just mentioned.

WSWS: When you look at the way the historiography on the Civil War and on slavery has changed over the generations—and I know you've made this point in the past—it's been influenced by contemporary politics. Why do you think the 1619 Project is happening now, and being so heavily promoted?

JM: I think it's partly an outgrowth of broader social and political developments of the past twenty years or so. Just as the civil rights movement of the 1950s and 1960s influenced a lot of new scholarship on slavery, the abolitionists, the radical Republicans, the Civil War, and Reconstruction—including my own introduction to those subjects in the 1950s and 1960s—I think that the current events, and contemporary matters, are going to influence something like the 1619 Project. That is, apart from the four-hundredth anniversary, which is the convenient hook on which this is hanging.

WSWS: It seems to me, however, that the mass civil rights movement transmitted really healthy impulses to the scholarship ...

JM: ... Absolutely, I think so. Up until that time, the perspective on slavery and the abolitionists was very much a Southern perspective—that's oversimplifying it, but it was there—and a kind of right-of-center perspective. And the scholarship that emerged with the civil rights movement—to oversimplify it again—moved in a leftward, and Northern liberal perspective.

WSWS: You were a student of C. Vann Woodward, if I am not mistaken. Could you tell us something about him?

JM: Back in the 1930s, he, like many intellectuals and artists, flirted with socialism, even the Communist Party. As a young man in the early 1930s he went to the Soviet Union. He never made the complete trip over to the Communist

Party, but he was very much on the left wing of academics. And his interpretation of the Southern Populists and Tom Watson grew out of that.

Over time, like most people I suppose, he became more conservative, moving toward a sort of Southern liberal ideology, in his interpretation of segregation in *The Strange Career of Jim Crow*, which Martin Luther King publicly called a kind of Bible of the civil rights movement. He was very much in that mode in the 1950s. He was one of the academics that did the research for the plaintiffs in *Brown v. Board of Education* in the early 1950s. I studied with him at Johns Hopkins from 1958 to 1962, when, I think, he was gradually moving a little bit toward the right.

He was bothered by the countercultural aspects of liberalism that emerged in the later 1960s.

But his sympathies and his perspective were with the civil rights movement—even while maintaining a Southern perspective, there's no question about that. He remained interested in the South and wanted to find a Southern liberal tradition, and even a radical tradition, which was the underlying motive of his interest in the Southern Populists and Tom Watson, portraying them as potential racial egalitarians until the 1890s when things went sour for them, and they themselves went sour.

But he continued to pursue that through the 1950s and 1960s, and I think that influenced me as much as anything in my graduate work. Other influences on me were being in Baltimore during the civil rights movement, and sit-ins and demonstrations in a border city. And the Freedom Rides that started in 1961 when I was still in graduate school. While I don't know entirely what Woodward thought of some of these things, certainly his basic underlying attitude was sympathetic to these changes. And he played a role in bringing them about.

WSWS: You mentioned that you were totally surprised when you found the 1619 Project in your Sunday paper. You are one of the leading historians of the Civil War and slavery. And the *Times* did not approach you?

JM: No, they didn't, no.

WSWS: We've spoken to a lot of historians, leading scholars in the fields of slavery, the Civil War, the American Revolution, and we're finding that none of them were approached. Although the *Times* doesn't list its sources, what do you think, in terms of scholarship, this 1619 Project is basing itself on?

JM: I don't really know. One of the people they approached is Kevin Kruse, who wrote about Atlanta. He's a colleague, a professor here at Princeton. He doesn't quite fit the mold of the other writers. But I don't know who advised them, and what motivated them to choose the people they did choose.

WSWS: Nikole Hannah-Jones, the lead writer and leader of the 1619 Project, includes a statement in her essay—and I would say that this is the thesis of the project—that "anti-black racism runs in the very DNA of this country."

JM: Yes, I saw that too. It does not make very much sense to me. I suppose she's using DNA metaphorically. She argues that racism is the central theme of American history. It is certainly part of the history. But again, I think it lacks context, lacks perspective on the entire course of slavery and how slavery began, and how slavery in the United States was hardly unique. And racial convictions, or "anti-other" convictions, have been central to many societies.

But the idea that racism is a permanent condition, well that's just not true. And it also doesn't account for the countervailing tendencies in American history as well. Because opposition to slavery, and opposition to racism, has also been an important theme in American history.

WSWS: Could you speak on this a little bit more? Because elsewhere in her essay, Hannah-Jones writes that "black Americans have fought back alone" to make America a democracy.

JM: From the Quakers in the eighteenth century, on through the abolitionists in the antebellum, to the radical Republicans in the Civil War and Reconstruction, to the NAACP which was an interracial organization founded in 1909, down through the civil rights movement in the 1950s and 1960s, there have been a lot of whites who have fought against slavery and racial discrimination, and against racism. Almost from the beginning of American history that's been true. And that's what's missing from this perspective.

WSWS: Could you speak specifically on what motivated Union soldiers in the Civil War? I know you've written on this question.

JM: Attitudes in the Union Army ranged from extreme racism to a kind of radical idealism and antislavery. I think that any one statement about "the soldiers" in the Union Army would not make any sense. I read the letters and diaries of well over one thousand of them, and their attitudes on this question ranged all the way from a racist, proslavery position to a kind of radical egalitarian perspective. I tried to quantify these things, but it's hard to make a generalization about two and a half million soldiers.

WSWS: The motivations are complex, and the major political perspectives of the time are bound up with the soldiers' motivations, whether it was a war to preserve the Union or a war to end slavery, or a combination of the two ...

JM: ... Well, the initial motivation was revenge for the attack on the flag. The response in the North, and especially among the men who signed up—and they were all volunteers for the first two years of the Civil War, and they were mostly volunteers throughout—viewed it at first as an unprovoked attack on the flag. And that broadened into an idea of not only revenging the flag, and the ideas that it stood for, but of taking revenge against what they were increasingly calling "the Slave Power." So, almost from the beginning, there was not really a sharp division between fighting for the integrity of the United States, and against the institution that had attacked it.

So, while the official motivation was preservation of the Union, that increasingly became merged with the destruction of slavery, which had launched the attack on the flag in the first place. And so I don't think you can really separate those two motives. While the emphasis originally was on fighting for the Union, fighting for the United States, fighting to defend the flag, increasingly that became bound up with a conviction that the only way the North was going to win the war, preserve the Union, and prevent further, future rebellions against the Union, was to destroy slavery, which had brought the war on in the first place.

WSWS: The analysis you've just given fits with the very good histories of the era, which acknowledge the complexities and contradictory character of the politics, and the way that that interacted with the movement of many, many people. It seems to me that much of that complexity finds manifestation in the figure of Abraham Lincoln.

JM: Oh, absolutely.

WSWS: Maybe you could speak on Lincoln. Nikole Hannah-Jones refers to Lincoln as viewing African Americans as "an obstacle to national unity." And then she moves on. I think that that's a vast oversimplification.

JM: It is a vast oversimplification. Lincoln became increasingly convinced, as many of the Union soldiers did, that that the Union could not be preserved if that disturbing factor—slavery—remained. And Lincoln's frequently quoted statement, in his famous letter to Horace Greeley, that, "my paramount object is to preserve the Union. If I could do that without freeing the slaves, I would do that. But if I could do it by freeing the slaves, I would do that." He'd in fact already made up his mind when he wrote that letter. He had already drafted the Emancipation Proclamation, and he was preparing the way for it. He had become convinced by the summer of 1862 that he could never achieve his primary goal—the preservation of the Union—without getting rid of slavery. And this was the first step toward doing that.

WSWS: Is it correct to say that by the end of his life Lincoln had drawn to a position proximate to that of the Radical Republicans?

JM: He was moving in that direction. In his last speech—it turned out to be his last speech—he came out in favor of qualified suffrage for freed slaves, those who could pass a literacy test, and those who were veterans of the Union Army.

WSWS: Another element implicit in the 1619 Project is that all white people in the South were unified behind slavery.

JM: George Frederickson came up with the idea of "Herrenvolk democracy." He was a historian at Stanford University who wrote on the ideology of white supremacy in the US, and comparatively with South Africa. I think it gets at a powerful element in the Southern ideology in the antebellum. That even though two-thirds to three-quarters of Southern whites did not own slaves, they all owned the white skin. So with the slave system, as Senator Hammond of South Carolina put it, the slaves are the "mudsill" of the society, and all whites were above that mudsill because they were white. And that's a good definition of white privilege.

It did exist, at least in theory. Whether it existed in practical relations is another matter. But it existed in the ideology of the proslavery argument.

WSWS: I think in *Battle Cry of Freedom* you refer to this as "holding the line" in the South—in the context of the war in which the Confederacy has to muster all these soldiers into the ranks. But it's not so simple, as it turns out.

JM: Yes. In the parts of the South where slavery was a minimal factor—in the Appalachian Mountain chain for example, in western Virginia, and in eastern Tennessee, where there are very few slaves and very few slaveholders, a lot of the whites did not want to fight for the Confederacy, to risk their lives for what they saw as a slaveholders' war. So you had strong currents of Unionism in those parts of the South. In fact, West Virginia becomes a Union state—one-third of the state of Virginia—in the Civil War.

The Herrenvolk idea was an ideological effort to undercut class conflict among whites in the South by saying that all whites are superior to all blacks, all whites are in the same category, they are not of different classes. You may not be a slaveholder, and you may not have much money, but you are white. Well, not every white Southerner bought that argument. And that's especially true in parts of the South where slavery was marginal to the social order: western Virginia, eastern Tennessee, western North Carolina.

WSWS: Part of the Republican critique of slavery that emerges in the 1850s is the idea that slavery degraded all labor.

JM: That was a part of the "free labor ideology" that fifty years ago Eric Foner wrote about so effectively. Slavery undermined the concept of the dignity of labor and held down the white working man because labor was identified in the South with slavery. Hinton Rowan Helper made that a theme of his famous book.

WSWS: Can you explain who Hinton Helper was?

JM: He was a sort of middle-class resident of western North Carolina who became in the 1850s increasingly resentful of the control of Southern society, of the suppression of the non-slaveholders by the slaveholding elite that held them back, as he saw it. And he wrote a book in 1857 called *The Impending Crisis of the South*, in which he attacked the slaveholders and the Slave Power controlling society in their interest, and using this argument of Herrenvolk democracy to keep down, to mitigate, class resentment and class conflict among whites in the South. And Republicans in the North seized on that as part of their free labor ideology.

WSWS: Another argument frequently made, and that is at least implicit in the 1619 Project, is that the Civil War didn't accomplish all that much, that what followed it in the South—Jim Crow—was simply slavery by another name.

JM: The Civil War accomplished three things. First, it preserved the United States as one nation. Second, it abolished the institution of slavery. Those two were, in effect, permanent achievements. The United States is still a single nation. Slavery doesn't exist anymore. The third thing the Civil War accomplished was a potential, and partial, transformation, in the status of the freed slaves, who with the Fourteenth and Fifteenth Amendments achieved, on paper at least, civil and political equality. But the struggle ever since 1870, when the Fifteenth Amendment was ratified, has been how to transform this achievement on paper into real achievement in the society.

The people you're talking about claim that it's never gone beyond slavery, or that something almost as bad as slavery replaced slavery. The way I see it, while the bottle is not full, it is half full. I acknowledge that it is half empty. But it's also half full. So with the abolition of slavery you have at least the partial achievement of a substantive freedom for the freed slaves.

Even though Jim Crow segregation, disenfranchisement, lynching, all of these things became blots on the United States in the later nineteenth century, and well into the twentieth, at least children couldn't be sold apart from their parents, wives couldn't be sold apart from their husbands, and marriage was now a legal institution for freedpeople. That's a significant step beyond slavery as it existed before 1865. It's the ancient question about whether the glass is half full or half empty. It's both. And this is what the people who say the Civil War didn't accomplish anything are missing. The Civil War did fill up half the bottle.

WSWS: Let me ask you a counterfactual question. Suppose the South had won the Civil War. What would have happened with the slavery institution?

JM: I get asked this question a lot. Nobody knows for sure. It's like the question of what would have happened had Lincoln not been assassinated. I think slavery would have continued for another generation. It did continue to exist in Brazil and Cuba for another generation, and it might not have come to an end as it did in those two countries had it not already been abolished in the United States. So another generation of black people would have been slaves, another generation of children being sold apart from their parents, and so on. Clearly that would have gone on. We can't say for sure when slavery would have come to an end, and under what conditions it would have come to an end, but clearly there would have been no Fourteenth and Fifteenth Amendments for a long time, if ever.

WSWS: Yet another argument that's made is that the Civil War, and emancipation in the United States, came late, compared to Great Britain where it came in 1833, and it's argued, "Look, the British did it voluntarily without a great civil war."

JM: Well antislavery in Great Britain emerged in the late eighteenth century, with Wilberforce and Buxton and so on, and became focused early on the abolition of slavery everywhere. In the British constitution Parliament is all-powerful. And there's nothing like the protections for the institution of slavery that exist in the American Constitution in the British political order. If you gain a majority in Parliament, which the antislavery forces in Britain did in the early 1830s, you can pass legislation banning slavery, which is exactly what happened. And the slaveholders in the Caribbean, who obviously opposed this, had very little power in Parliament.

Meanwhile, the slaveholders in the United States actually controlled the government through their domination of the Democratic Party, right through the 1850s. In fact, the principal reason for secession in 1861 was because they had lost control of the United States government for the first time ever.

WSWS: This relates to your concept of the "counterrevolution of 1861." Can you explain that?

JM: I called it a "preemptive counterrevolution." This is a concept I borrowed shamelessly from my colleague here at Princeton, Arno Mayer, who wrote on preemptive counterrevolution in Europe in the twentieth century. The slaveholders saw the triumph of the Republicans in 1860 as a potential revolution that would abolish slavery. That's how the Republicans got votes in 1860. They saw Abraham Lincoln and his Republican Party as just as bad as the abolitionists. In order to preempt that revolution that would have overthrown slavery in the South, they undertook what I called, and borrowing this from Arno Mayer, a preemptive counterrevolution, which was secession. But secession, ironically, brought on the very revolution that it attempted to preempt, through the war: the abolition of slavery.

WSWS: Have you read Karl Marx's writings on the Civil War?

JM: Yes, I have.

WSWS: What do you think of them?

JM: Well, I think they have a lot of very good insight into what was going on in the American Civil War. Marx certainly saw the abolition of slavery as a kind of bourgeois revolution that paved the way for the proletarian revolution that he hoped would come in another generation or so. It was a crucial step on the way to the eventual proletarian revolution, as Marx perceived it.

WSWS: Have you had a chance to review any of the literature on slavery and capitalism, by for example Sven Beckert, Ed Baptist, and Walter Johnson?[1]

JM: It's been some time since I've read it.

WSWS: It looks like that literature informs the 1619 Project, especially the essay by Matthew Desmond. I find it problematic. These authors draw an equal sign between what they perceive to be a fully developed capitalist South, and the North. I don't think that any serious historian ever denied that the South was bound up with the global capitalist system. But this scholarship is going further with the argument.

JM: Yes, that's right. That part of it—that the South is as capitalist as the North, or Great Britain—is unpersuasive to me. Certainly, they were part of a capitalist world order. There's no question about that. Cotton and sugar were central. But the idea that the ideology of the planter class in the South was a capitalist ideology, there I've always been a little bit more on the side of Eugene Genovese,[2] who sees the Southern ideology as seigneurial.

WSWS: It seems to me that all of these books jump over the Civil War. One of the problems they run into is that, if it's the case that everyone agreed …

JM: … Then why was there a war?

WSWS: Exactly. Let me ask you about the American Revolution, even though I know this was not your research field. The 1619 Project also attacks it as founding a slavocracy. There is a historian, Gerald Horne, who has recently argued that it was waged as a slaveholders' counterrevolution, to protect their property rights.

JM: Well, the American Revolution was first and foremost a war for independence. But there was also a more social dimension to the American Revolution, and a movement toward greater democracy, though they didn't like to use that term. And it coincided with, and partially caused, the abolition of slavery in half of the states, the Northern states, as well as a manumission movement among Virginia slaveholders. It was not a revolution in the sense of the French Revolution, which followed it by a decade, or the Soviet Revolution of 1917, but that doesn't mean it didn't accomplish anything. Its accomplishments were

---

1. Beckert (*Empire of Cotton*) is at Harvard University. Baptist (*The Half Has Never Been Told*) is at Cornell University. Johnson (*River of Dark Dreams*) is also at Harvard.
2. Eugene Genovese (1930–2012). His most noted work was *Roll, Jordan, Roll: The World the Slaves Made.*

more political than social and economic, but nevertheless there were some social and economic dimensions to it, progressive dimensions I would say.

Out of the Revolution came an antislavery ethos, which never disappeared, even though the period from the 1790s to the 1830s was a quiet period in the antislavery movement—though there was the Missouri Compromise of 1820. Nevertheless, the antislavery ethos that did come out of the Revolution was a subterranean movement that erupted in the 1830s and shaped American political discourse.

WSWS: David Brion Davis says that the abolitionists viewed the Declaration of Independence as sacred scripture …

JM: … So did Lincoln. It was basic to the Republican Party.

WSWS: Do you recommend any recent books on the subjects we've discussed today?

JM: I thought that Eric Foner's biography of Lincoln was excellent. *The Fiery Trial: Abraham Lincoln and Slavery.*

James Oakes

James Oakes

James Oakes is Distinguished Professor of History and Graduate School Humanities Professor at the Graduate Center of the City University of New York. He is a two-time winner of the Lincoln Prize for his books *The Radical and the Republican: Frederick Douglass, Abraham Lincoln, and the Triumph of Antislavery Politics*, and *Freedom National: The Destruction of Slavery in the United States, 1861–1865*.

WSWS: Can you discuss some of the recent literature on slavery and capitalism, which argues that chattel slavery was, and is, the decisive feature of capitalism, especially American capitalism? I am thinking in particular of the recent books by Sven Beckert, Ed Baptist, and Walter Johnson. This seems to inform the contribution to the 1619 Project by Matthew Desmond.

James Oakes: Collectively their work has prompted some very strong criticism from scholars in the field. My concern is that by avoiding some of the basic analytical questions, most of the scholars have backed into a neoliberal economic interpretation of slavery, though I think I'd exempt Sven Beckert somewhat from that, because I think he's come to do something somewhat different theoretically.

What you really have with this literature is a marriage of neoliberalism and liberal guilt. When you marry those two things, neoliberal politics and liberal guilt, this is what you get. You get the *New York Times*, you get the literature on slavery and capitalism.

Thomas Mackaman, "An interview with historian James Oakes on the New York Times' 1619 Project," World Socialist Web Site, November 18, 2019.

WSWS: And Matthew Desmond's argument that all of the horrors of contemporary American capitalism are rooted in slavery.

JO: There's been a kind of standard bourgeois-liberal way of arguing that goes all the way back to the eighteenth century, that whenever you are talking about some form of oppression, or whenever you yourself are oppressed, you instinctively go to the analogy of slavery. At least since the eighteenth century in our society, in Western liberal societies, slavery has been the gold standard of oppression. The colonists, in the imperial crisis, complained that they were the "slaves" of Great Britain. It was the same thing all the way through the nineteenth century. The leaders of the first women's movement would sometimes liken the position of a woman in a Northern household to that of a slave on a Southern plantation. The first workers' movement, coming out of the culture of republican independence, attacked wage labor as wage slavery. Civil War soldiers would complain that they were treated like slaves.

Desmond, following the lead of the scholars he's citing, basically relies on the same analogy. They're saying, "Look at the ways capitalism is just like slavery, and that's because capitalism came from slavery." But there's no actual critique of capitalism in any of it. They're saying: "Oh my God! Slavery looks just like capitalism. They had highly developed management techniques just like we do!" Slaveholders were greedy, just like capitalists. Slavery was violent, just like our society is. So there's a critique of violence and a critique of greed. But greed and violence are everywhere in human history, not just in capitalist societies. So there's no actual critique of capitalism as such, at least as I read it.

There's this famous book on the crop lien system and debt peonage in the late nineteenth-century South called *Slavery by Another Name* [Douglas Blackmon, 2008]. It wasn't slavery. But it was a horrible system and naturally you want to attack it so you liken it to slavery. So that's the basic conceptual thrust of what we're now reading.

One of the things that Desmond does in his piece, and he did in the podcast as well, is to leap from the inequality of wealth in slavery to enormous claims about capitalism. He will say that the value of all the slaves in the South was equal to the value of all the securities, factories, and railroads, and then he'll say, "So you see, slavery was the driving force of American capitalism." But there's no obvious connection between the two. Does he want to say that gross inequalities of wealth are conducive to robust economic development? If so, we should be in one of the greatest economic expansions of all time right now, now that the maldistribution of wealth has reached grotesque levels.

This ignores a large and impressive body of scholarship produced a generation ago by historians of the capitalist transformation of the North, all of it pointing to the Northern countryside as the seedbed of the Industrial Revolution. Christopher Clark, Jeanne Boydston, John Faragher, Jonathan Prude, and others—these were and are outstanding scholars, and anyone interested in the origins of American capitalism must come to terms with them. Some of them, like Amy Dru Stanley and Christopher Tomlins, launched sophisticated criticisms of capitalism. The "New Historians of Capitalism," reflected in the 1619 Project, ignore that scholarship and revert instead to standard neoliberal economics. There's nothing remotely radical about it.

WSWS: And a point we made in our response to the 1619 Project, is that it dovetails also with the major political thrust of the Democratic Party, identity politics. And the claim that is made, and I think it's almost become a commonplace, is that slavery is the uniquely American "original sin."

JO: Yes. "Original sin," that's one of them. The other is that slavery or racism is built into the DNA of America. These are really dangerous tropes. They're not only ahistorical, they're actually antihistorical. The function of those tropes is to deny change over time. It goes back to those analogies. They say: "Look at how terribly black people were treated under slavery. And look at the incarceration rate for black people today. It's the same thing." Nothing changes. There has been no industrialization. There has been no Great Migration. We're all in the same boat we were back then. And that's what original sin is. It's passed down. Every single generation is born with the same original sin. And the worst thing about it is that it leads to political paralysis. It's always been here. There's nothing we can do to get out of it. If it's the DNA, there's nothing you can do. What do you do? Alter your DNA?

WSWS: You have a very good analysis of the literature on slavery and capitalism that Desmond is drawing on, in the journal *International Labor and Working Class History*. And one of the very important points you make is that this literature is just jumping over the Civil War, as if nothing really happened.

JO: From our perspective, for someone who thinks about societies in terms of the basic underlying social relations of production or social property relations, the radical overthrow of the largest and wealthiest slave society in the world is a revolutionary transformation. An old colleague of mine at Princeton, Lawrence Stone, used to say, when he was arguing with the revisionists about the English Civil War, that "big events have big causes."

The Civil War was a major conflict between the North and South over whether or not a society based on free labor, and ultimately wage labor, was morally, politically, economically, and socially superior to a society based on slave labor. That was the issue. And it seems to me that the attempt to focus on the financial linkages between these two systems, or the common aspects of their exchange relations, masks the fundamental conflict over the underlying relations of production between these two ultimately incompatible systems of social organization, these political economies.

By focusing on the similar *commercial* aspects of the slave economy of the South and the industrializing economy of the North, the "New Historians of Capitalism" effectively erase the fundamental differences between the two systems. This makes the Civil War incomprehensible. They practically boast about this.

WSWS: It seems that they're inviting in through the back door the old argument about the Civil War being the "war between brothers." But now it's the war between capitalist brothers. It begs the question, what was the dispute about then?

JO: They don't have an explanation. In the introduction to *Slavery's Capitalism*[1] they write something like, "This raises some serious questions about the Civil War." Well, for you it does, because of how you've framed it. But there's plenty of evidence even in that book to indicate that they're playing around with their own evidence.

For example, there's a very fine book, *Accounting for Slavery*,[2] published by an economic historian out of Berkeley named Caitlin Rosenthal, and Matt Desmond cites it. She also has a piece in *Slavery's Capitalism*. It's a history of those plantation management techniques that Desmond emphasizes. But Rosenthal comes to this subject as a historian of accounting practices. She's looking for *best* practices, not *typical* practices, and she discovered that the most sophisticated version of plantation account books were more sophisticated than anything to be found in the North at the time. In the North you don't get that level of sophistication—taking into account depreciation and the like—until the late nineteenth century.

---

1. Sven Beckert and Seth Rockman, *Slavery's Capitalism: A New History of American Economic Development* (University of Pennsylvania Press, 2018).
2. Caitlin Rosenthal, *Accounting for Slavery: Masters and Management* (Cambridge: Harvard University Press, 2018).

But what Rosenthal also says in fact is that—this one planter's account book, that everyone is citing, that Desmond is citing, this Thomas Affleck's account book—that these account books were used by maybe a quarter of the planters, and many of them didn't even bother filling them out. There's a quotation in her article from James Henry Hammond, a huge South Carolina planter, who wrote to Affleck and said something like, "I can't get my overseers to use these books." So Rosenthal's article in *Slavery's Capitalism* shows that keeping minute records of the daily rates of cotton picking was not a uniform way of organizing labor in the slave South. And moreover she shows the kind of incentives the planters used to increase productivity—or at least the incentives they used to get slaves to pick more cotton during the picking season. Sometimes planters gave slaves gifts, sometimes they withheld Christmas gifts; they used as many devices as they could during the cotton-picking season.

The New Historians pick out the most highly rationalized systems of plantations management because, once again, they *look* like highly-regimented capitalist bureaucracies. But a capitalist bureaucracy is regimented 365 days a year, and it doesn't speed up for the weather. You could just as easily focus on the vast *differences* between the yearly cycle of work on a slave plantation and the repetitive daily conditions in an auto factory. Moreover, the auto workers go home after the shift with their wages and live in an entirely different world of consumption patterns, voluntary contracts, etc. You can't cherry-pick one aspect of plantation agriculture, one part of it, and make it the whole thing in order to make it look like industrial capitalism.

WSWS: You mentioned the ahistorical character of some of this work, and it seems to me that they also have to overlook a lot of what people back then said and thought about these divergent systems. Planters imagined that they were defending a feudal-patriarchal world. But if you consider a figure like Frederick Douglass, who worked as a slave and as a wage laborer in the North, he and others like him were convinced that the Northern economy was more dynamic.

JO: Certainly, the antislavery position is that the free labor economy of the North is more dynamic than the slave labor economy of the South. In the 1850s this was not an unreasonable position to take. But the sectional crisis didn't happen because all of a sudden Northerners became antislavery. The problem was that the antislavery North gradually became a lot more powerful. It became a lot more powerful because the capitalist economy was proving to be far more dynamic and wealthy than the slave economy. The slave economies of the New World were basically extractive economies whose function was to provide commodities and raw materials to the more developed economies of the metropole. Specifically, the Southern cotton economy was the creature of British industrial development, and industrial development in the North. It came into existence to feed that increasingly dynamic system.

British and Northern textile manufacturers wanted cotton, but they didn't much care where it came from. Merchant capitalism has always been amoral that way. It didn't care what system it engaged for trade. The merchant capitalist of the Atlantic world engaged with all sorts of systems—a revived feudalism in Eastern Europe; a completely different set of social relationships in Africa, free labor systems in the US North; slave labor systems and plantation economies elsewhere. Merchant capitalists don't care what form of social organization they are engaging in trade with. To the extent the trade relationship is successful and profitable, it will make profitable all of those systems. But the dynamic force behind this is really the capitalist world that is developing in the North Atlantic, particularly Great Britain and the United States.

WSWS: Let me ask you about Lincoln. He's not discussed much in Hannah-Jones's article ...

JO: ... Yes, she does the famous 1862 meeting Lincoln had in the White House on colonization ...

WSWS: ... Lincoln is presented as a garden-variety racist ...

JO: ... Yes, and she also says somewhere else that he issued the Emancipation Proclamation simply as a military tactic ...

WSWS: ... Could you comment on that?

JO: It's ridiculous. Most of what Abraham Lincoln had to say about African Americans was antiracist, from the first major speech he gives on slavery in 1854, when he says, "If the negro is a man, why then my ancient faith teaches me that 'all men are created equal'; and that there can be no moral right in connection with one man's making a slave of another." Lincoln says, can't we stop talking about this race and that race being equal or inferior and go back to the principle that all men are created equal? And he says this so many times and in so many ways. By the late 1850s he was vehemently denouncing Stephen Douglas and his Northern Democrats for their racist demagoguery, which Lincoln complained was designed to accustom the American people to the idea that slavery was the permanent, natural condition of black people. His speeches were becoming, quite literally, antiracist.

Now, he grew up in Indiana and he lived as an adult in Illinois, and Illinois had some of the harshest discriminatory laws in the North. That is to say, he inhabited a world in which it's almost unimaginable to him that white people will ever allow black people to live as equals. So on the one hand he denounces racism and is committed to emancipation, to the overthrow of slavery, gradually or however it would take place. But on the other hand he believes white people will never allow blacks equality. So he advocates voluntary colonization. Find a place somewhere where blacks can enjoy the full fruits of liberty that all human beings are entitled to. It's a very pessimistic view about the possibilities of racial equality. Ironically, it's not all that far from Lincoln's critics today who say that racism is built into the American DNA. At least Lincoln got over it and came to the conclusion that we're going to have to live as equals here.

The statement he makes on colonization was framed as an unflinching attack on the colonizationists who were motivated by their hatred of blacks, who wanted free blacks expelled from the country simply because they were black. It's a vehement attack on the racist justification of colonization. So Lincoln favors colonization, but he abandons it with the Emancipation Proclamation once it no longer serves the political function of promoting state abolition, and once he comes to accept that America was going to have to be a multiracial nation.

Still, that meeting with African Americans in the summer of 1862 was terrible. As I said in a previous book, it was a low point in his presidency. But although Lincoln at that point was still sincerely committed to colonization, he was also a politician and it was also a strategic meeting. He was sitting on the Emancipation Proclamation. He knew that Northern racists were going to be annoyed because they'd been saying from the start that they didn't want the Civil War to be about freeing the slaves, they wanted it to be about nothing more than restoring the Union. So Lincoln is throwing them a sop by behaving in a disgraceful, condescending manner toward a group of African American leaders in the most conspicuous, public way.

WSWS: Yes, context is important, and it reminds me of his letter to the *New-York Tribune* ...

JO: ... To Greeley. Exactly. It's the same month. It's the same summer. And it's doing exactly the same thing. It's strategic.

WSWS: It reads differently if you know that he has the Emancipation Proclamation in pocket ...

JO: ... In the Greeley letter Lincoln says that if he could restore the Union without freeing a single slave he would. But he's already signed the Washington D.C. emancipation bill. He's already signed the bill banning slavery from the Western territories. And he's already ordered the Union soldiers to emancipate all the slaves coming to their lines in the war. So option one is already off the table. He can't, in fact, restore the Union without freeing any slaves. Then he says in the same letter to Horace Greeley that if he could restore the Union by freeing all the slaves, he would. But he can't do that either, because as he said many times, that the only emancipating power he had under the Constitution derived from the war powers to suppress a rebellion. He can't do that in Maryland, because it's not in rebellion, or in Delaware, Kentucky, and Missouri, because those states were not formally in rebellion. So option two is out: He can't restore the Union by freeing all the slaves. That leaves option three: If he could restore the Union while freeing some slaves, he would. So when Lincoln says to Greeley he has these three options, he doesn't really have three options. He is simply saying he is going to restore the Union. That's what I'm supposed to do. That's the only thing I can do. The Constitution doesn't let me fight a war for the purpose of abolishing slavery. But if I need to free some—actually most—of the slaves to restore the Union, I will. Lots of Northerners denied that Lincoln needed to free any slaves to restore the Union. And this is the critical point: The only people who viewed emancipation as a military necessity were the people who hated slavery. And Lincoln was one of them.

WSWS: I assume that you are familiar with Marx's writings on the Civil War, and it seems to me that he had a very good handle on it.

JO: He did. He had a very good handle on it. He did. Did you ever read the letter from the Workingmen's Association to Lincoln?

WSWS: Yes. In another instance he criticized the unremarkable prose of the Emancipation Proclamation, writing that it was like a summons from a country lawyer.

JO: Right. But plenty of Lincoln's rhetoric about slavery is emotive. There are many examples. "If slavery isn't wrong, nothing is wrong," he says. Again, though, he needs to maintain a coalition of Northerners—some of whom are not antislavery—and to keep them in that coalition against the slaveholders' rebellion, he has to find ways of justifying emancipation, basically not to lose the support of the racist members of that coalition, mainly the Northern Democrats. They can accept an argument for the restoration of the Union, and maybe they can accept an argument for military necessity, but they can't accept an argument such as, "I'm doing this because I hate slavery." Constitutionally, he could not have justified such a claim.

WSWS: As an aside, I'm always struck when I hear people saying that the United States today is just as racist as it has always been. It's as if they know nothing about the level of racism that prevailed in a state like Illinois before the Civil War.

JO: Yes, they're not familiar with Stephen Douglas ...

WSWS: For example, I believe that Illinois forbade blacks from settling in its borders.

JO: They passed these laws that antislavery people viewed to be unconstitutional, that said no black person can enter Illinois who is not also a citizen of the United States. They often had to keep the citizenship provision in, because at the time of the Missouri Compromise—there were in fact two debates about Missouri. Missouri, having been allowed to enter as a slave state, submitted a constitution banning blacks from settling. The antislavery people said you can't do that. In the Constitution the privileges and immunities granted to citizenship are very real, and the least of them is the privilege to move from one state to another. And black people are citizens. So the racial restriction laws tended to say a black person can't come in who is not a citizen. By and large, by saying that a black person cannot come in who is not a citizen of another state, they are trying to keep fugitive slaves out, because slaves are not citizens. It's a fugitive slave enforcement statute essentially.

Not all the exclusion statutes were so careful, however, and all of them were intensely racist. The Northern states passed all sorts of racially discriminatory legislation. They segregate blacks in schools. They segregate street cars. But they are also starting, in the 1840s, as antislavery builds up, to repeal those laws. There is a famous repeal in Ohio in 1849, there is a repeal in Rhode Island as a consequence of the Dorr Rebellion. Massachusetts repeals its school segregation law, repeals its streetcar segregation laws. There's a major book coming out by Kate Masur on this subject.

WSWS: You have this provocative quote in *Scorpion's Sting*, in which you write, "Scratch beneath the surface of any debate about 'race' in American history and sooner or later you're bound to discover a struggle for power—ultimately political power."[3] Can you elaborate on that?

JO: Barbara Fields once said that plantation owners didn't enslave Africans because they didn't like black people. They enslaved Africans because they wanted to produce cotton. I'm making a similar point about using racial appeals to achieve political power.

Before the Civil War the Democratic Party in the North is tied, inextricably, to a Southern Democratic Party that is increasingly and aggressively proslavery. The Northern Democrats cannot go before their own voters and say: "The proslavery argument is correct. Slaves are constitutionally protected property." They can't because that position is unacceptable in virtually all of the North. So when they can't go where the proslavery wing of their party wants them to go, the only way they can cling to power—without losing the Southern base—is through increasingly extreme, demagogic racism. It's what they need to maintain their dominant position in Northern politics. It's not that they don't believe what they're saying. I'm sure they believe what they're saying. And it's atrocious. But they're saying it for a reason. And it's becoming increasingly extreme in the 1850s because they're actually losing their grip on power because of the emergence of this antislavery party. So their racism is closely related to their desire to cling to political power.

Historians have made very similar arguments about the rise of Jim Crow in the late nineteenth century. The threat that emerges in the late 1880s, with one million or more black farmers joining the Colored Farmers Alliance, along with another one million or more white farmers in the Farmers Alliance, that turns into a very real Populist threat. It is met with this incredible upsurge of racist demagoguery, laws proliferate, blacks are disenfranchised. So the racist backlash of the 1890s is very closely related to the need to push down this emerging threat, the possibility of a white-black alliance. Of course they're racist, and I'm sure they believe everything in their own racism. But there's a reason they're saying it and a reason they're doing what they're doing. And it has to do with maintaining the political power of the landlord-merchant class.

WSWS: The formulation that behind debates over race are struggles over power struck me in relationship to the present as well, and in particular the promotion by the 1619 Project of racialist politics, which is certainly once again a cornerstone of the Democratic Party.

---

3. James Oakes, *The Scorpion's Sting: Antislavery and the Coming of the Civil War* (New York: W. W. Norton, 2014), p. 85.

JO: Here I agree with my friend Adolph Reed. Identity is very much the ideology of the professional-managerial class. They prefer to talk about identity over capitalism and the inequities of capitalism. We have an atrocious wealth gap in this country. It's not a black-white wealth gap. It's a wealth gap. But if you keep rephrasing it as black-white, and shift it off to a racial argument, you undermine the possibility of building a working-class coalition, which by definition would be disproportionately black, disproportionately female, disproportionately Latino, and still probably majority white. That's the kind of working-class coalition that identity politics tends to erase.

WSWS: Another point that you make in *Scorpion's Sting* is that Lincoln and the Republicans didn't really want to talk about race. They wanted to talk about slavery.

JO: Right. They want to defend the Northern system of labor, a capitalist system, free labor, over and against what they viewed as a backward system, slavery, a system that gave rise to a powerful slaveholding class that was becoming more and more aggressive in its demand. And the Northern Democrats the Republicans are facing keep on focusing on the race issue. It's quite clear that the Democrats are using the race issue to avoid talking about slavery. Republicans don't want to talk about race, but they are confronting this racism and they have to face it.

A lot of historians have pointed out that Lincoln is cagey in the way he talks about racial equality. The most famous example is the Charleston debate of 1858—everybody quotes it—where he says that he has never declared himself to be in favor of blacks voting, blacks serving on juries. He says, "I have never advocated those things." But notice, he does not say whether or not he himself supports them. He is just saying he has never publicly advocated for them. He is being cagey because he is being pushed. It doesn't make his deference to racism acceptable, but the context surely matters.

And it changes. The more Northerners become committed to antislavery politics, the more their racist tendencies subside. When antislavery was peaking in the late eighteenth century, when the Northern states one after another were abolishing slavery, there was also an antiracist aspect to that. The antislavery people then assumed that once the slaves were emancipated, they would be on the path to full citizenship. But once that movement fades, because no more states are going to abolish slavery, and then the second party system comes along and suppresses antislavery, you get a bulge in American racism. And when antislavery comes back, starting with the abolitionists in the 1830s, culminating in a mass party, the Republicans—the first really successful mass antislavery party—then those people tend to moderate their racism.

And Lincoln is part of that. He never much thought about race. In the 1830s in the Illinois legislature, he advocated discrimination in voting. But by the 1850s, he's increasingly required, by the political situation he's in, to emphasize the fundamental premises of antislavery, which are the principles in the Declaration of Independence—all men are created equal—that in the right to earn her bread from the sweat of her brow the black woman is my equal and the equal of every living man. There's a way in which that capitalist logic, in the context of nineteenth century liberalism, pushes racism to the side. So as antislavery peaks, so does that push back against racism. As Eric Foner says, Lincoln always hated slavery, but he grows on questions of race. There's real growth there. So that by the end, the last speech he gives, he's publicly advocating the right to vote for some of the freedmen, the first president ever to advocate such a thing. His thinking on race changes as his commitment to antislavery and then abolition deepens.

WSWS: Right. He's pulled in the direction of the Radical Republicans.

JO: Yes. They're the standard bearers. They set the tone.

WSWS: Central to the argument of the 1619 Project is not just that there is white racism, but a permanent state of white privilege. That can be answered in the present with data, but I'm curious how, as a historical question, you approach that claim, for example when you look at the antebellum South, where you have a lot of white households who own no slaves.

JO: The slaveholders dominated the legislatures in polities that were formally democratic, where property qualifications for voting were disappearing, and where the overriding need of that planter class is to protect slavery. They can't go to the electorate and say: "I'm superior to you. You're inferior to me. Vote for me." It's not going to work. They have to conform to the requirements of a formally democratic polity. And they claim that "any man who wants to can rise up and become a slaveholder." But that's increasingly tenuous. The steeply rising price of slaves makes that harder and harder. And so the slaveholders resort to white supremacy. They try to use white supremacy to maintain the loyalty of the non-slaveholders.

But how well it's going to work in any situation is not so clear. A substantial number of non-slaveholders were not interested in seceding. Ultimately one of the major factors in the collapse of the Confederacy is the collapse in support from the non-slaveholders. The slave states that have the largest share of non-slaveholders—Maryland, Kentucky, Delaware, and Missouri—don't secede. The slaveholders in those states are themselves divided and may want to join the Confederacy, but they can't get majorities to support secession.

Did you know that more Missisippians fought against the Confederacy than for it, when you add the blacks and the whites? So there's this collapse of internal support. And then there's this fear all through Reconstruction, that the goal of Republicans is to get poor whites and blacks together based on shared interests. That's the frightening thing to the landed class. So it's something that they try to impress on the poor whites. But it doesn't always work.

Sometimes people act on their interests. If their kids are dying in the opioid epidemic, their towns are ravaged by deindustrialization, they're closing one factory after another, and there's poison coming out of the water faucets, telling them to feel good about being white isn't going to mean much.

WSWS: It seems to me that there are two aspects to the argument. One is that poor whites in the South allegedly derive some sort of psychological wage from being white. But as you've discussed, that is actually a political argument, and its authors are the planters. But then there's also an allegation that poor whites derive an economic benefit from slavery, whether or not they own slaves. Have you looked in your research at any of the data on wages in the antebellum South?

JO: There's dispute about that, and it's not so clear as it used to be that wages are depressed by slavery. But what's clear, to me at least, is that the slave economy inhibits the kind of development that Northern farmers are engaged in. So that the average wealth of a non-slaveholding farmer in the South is half the wealth of a Northern farmer.

This is one of the things I find so disturbing about the argument that slavery is the basis of capitalism. Slavery made the slaveholders rich. But it made the South poor. And it didn't make the North rich. The wealth of the North was based on the emerging, capitalist internal market that allowed the North to win the Civil War. It's true that cotton dominated the export market. But it's only something like 5 percent of GDP. It's really the wealth of the internal Northern market that's decisive. That depends on a fairly widespread distribution of wealth, and that doesn't exist in the South. There's a lot of evidence from western Virginia, for example, that non-slaveholders were angry at the slaveholders for blocking the railroads and things like that that would allow them to take advantage of the internal market. So the legacy of slavery is poverty, not wealth. The slave societies of the New World were comparatively impoverished. To say things like, the entire wealth of "the white world" is based on slavery seems to me to ignore the enormous levels of poverty among whites as well as blacks.

WSWS: One of the points you make in one of your earlier books, and raise again in *Scorpion's Sting*, is the relationship between the concept of self-ownership and private property, which you trace back to the English Civil War. Could you elaborate on this?

JO: Well, earlier you mentioned Eugene Genovese's *Roll, Jordan, Roll*, and I actually disagree with his concept of paternalism. In the United States these people are operating inside liberal constitutional structures, no monarchy, no titled aristocracy, no entail or primogeniture, and they are also operating in a global market that forces them to be competitive, to be aware of the productivity of their plantations. Forced to defend their way of life against a rising tide of antislavery politics, they move away from paternalism, if by paternalism you mean the defense of organically unified hierarchy on the model of the patriarchal family, a defense that transcends racism. Nope.

The primary defense of slavery was always, always, the defense of private property: slaves are our property and you can't take our property away from us. You can say, and slaveholders do say, that our material interest in the value of slave property leads us to take good care of these valuable human beings. You can say that as a result we treat our slaves kindly. But Genovese was clear that by paternalism he did not mean benevolence. I actually think paternalism was a much more powerful element in antislavery ideology, which emphasized slavery selling apart wives and children from fathers. When the Republicans in 1856 compare slavery and polygamy as the twin relics of barbarism, it's part of an attack on the Slave South—that it doesn't recognize the legitimacy of slave families, their familial bonds.

So my argument is that the centrality of property rights is something the slaveholders are always going back to, basing themselves on liberal theorists, that the function of a state is to protect private property. And in that sense, it's coming out of the same liberal tradition that produces an antislavery ideology based on the premise that property rights themselves initiate in self-ownership. What C. B. Macpherson called the "political theory of possessive individualism," produces ultimately a defense of slavery—based on the possessive individualism of the slaveholders—but also an antislavery argument based on the premise that my rights of property begin with my ownership of myself, and that is incompatible with being owned by someone else. Liberalism is the lingua franca of the debate over slavery.

WSWS: Can you address the role of identity politics on the campus? How is it to try to do so serious work under these conditions?

JO: Well, my sense is that among graduate students the identitarians stay away from me, and they badger the students who are interested in political and economic history. They have a sense of their own superiority. The political historians tend to feel besieged.

The reflection of identity politics in the curriculum is the primacy of cultural history. There was a time, a long, long time ago, when a "diverse history faculty" meant that you had an economic historian, a political historian, a social historian, a historian of the American Revolution, of the Civil War, and so on. And now a diverse history faculty means a women's historian, a gay historian, a Chinese American historian, a Latino historian. So it's a completely different kind of diversity.

On a global scale the benefit of this has been tremendous. We have more—and we should have more—African history, Latin American history, Asian history, than we ever have. Within US history it has produced narrow faculties in which everybody is basically writing the same thing. And so you don't bump into the economic historian at the mailbox and say, "Is it true that all the wealth came from slavery?" and have them say, "That's ridiculous," and explain why it can't be true.

WSWS: Another aspect of the way the 1619 Project presents history is to imply that it is a uniquely American phenomenon, leaving out the long history of chattel slavery, the history of slavery in the Caribbean.

JO: And they erase Africa from the African slave trade. They claim that Africans were stolen and kidnapped from Africa. Well, they were purchased by these kidnappers in Africa. Everybody's hands were dirty. And this is another aspect of the tendency to reify race because you're attempting to isolate a racial group that was also complicit. This is conspicuous only because the obsession with complicity is so overwhelming in the political culture right now, but also as reflected in the 1619 Project. Hypocrisy and complicity are basically the two great attacks. Again, not a critique of capitalism. It's a critique of hypocrisy and complicity. Here I agree with Genovese, who once said that "hypocrites are a dime a dozen." Hypocrisy doesn't interest me as a critique, nor does complicity.

WSWS: And their treatment of the American Revolution?

JO: I don't like "great man history." Not many professional historians do. So I'm sympathetic with my colleagues who complain about "Founders Chic." (I have the same problem in my field: Lincoln is great, but he didn't free the slave with the stroke of his pen.) But that's different from erasing the American Revolution, which amounts to erasing the conflict. What you're doing by erasing abolitionism, antislavery politics, antiracism, is you're erasing the conflict. And if you erase the conflict, you have no way of explaining anything that happens, and then you wind up with these terrible genetic metaphors—everything is built into the DNA and nothing changes. It's not just ahistorical. It's antihistorical.

WSWS: What are you working on now?

JO: I am finishing a book on Abraham Lincoln and the antislavery Constitution, which I never expected to write. That's almost finished. But the big project I'm working on is the history of the Civil War. I published a review recently in the *Nation* on a new book on the Civil War, and that's my first outing on how I'm going to approach this. The project is, how do you build an antislavery politics and sustain it over four years of a very brutal war, to come to the conclusion that it comes to. And, by contrast, how does the Confederacy fail to build and sustain such a coalition.

Notwithstanding the claim that we don't have class in this country, antislavery politics is a politics whose dominant framework, as far as the Republicans were concerned, was that this was a war between slaveholder and nonslaveholders. They framed it as a class war. And if you don't understand that going in, then the increasing tendency of the war to become a more and more radical assault on slavery, to the point that they rewrite the Constitution—if you don't understand where they're coming from before the war—then you're just going to say the radicalism is an accidental byproduct of it.

WSWS: I'm looking forward to it. Are there other scholars we should be looking out for?

JO: There's a lot of good work. There's a historian named Van Gosse coming out with a book on African American voting between the American Revolution and the Civil War that will show there's a lot more voting than Leon Litwack's book would have let you believe. It's very important. Kate Masur has a book coming out, that I mentioned before. There's a bright young historian at Penn named Sarah Gronningsater, writing on the children of emancipation.

There are several good books recently on the fugitive slave issue and its role in the origins of the Civil War. There's a book by one of my former students, just about to come out, Paul Polgar at the University of Mississippi, on emancipation in the mid-Atlantic states showing that the first emancipations were driven by people who were also antiracist.

Gordon Wood

Gordon Wood

Gordon S. Wood is Alva O. Way University Professor and Professor of History Emeritus at Brown University. His book *The Creation of the American Republic, 1776–1787* won the Bancroft Prize. *The Radicalism of the American Revolution* was awarded the Pulitzer in History, and *Empire of Liberty: A History of the Early Republic, 1789–1815* was a Pulitzer finalist. Wood was awarded the National Humanities Medal by Barack Obama in 2010.

WSWS: Let me begin by asking you your initial reaction to the 1619 Project. When did you learn about it?

Gordon Wood: Well, I was surprised when I opened my Sunday *New York Times* in August and found the magazine containing the project. I had no warning about this. I read the first essay by Nikole Hannah-Jones, which alleges that the Revolution occurred primarily because of the Americans' desire to save their slaves. She claims the British were on the warpath against the slave trade and slavery and that rebellion was the only hope for American slavery. This made the American Revolution out to be like the Civil War, where the South seceded to save and protect slavery, and that the Americans seventy years earlier revolted to protect their institution of slavery. I just couldn't believe this.

I was surprised, as many other people were, by the scope of this thing, especially since it's going to become the basis for high school education and has the

Thomas Mackaman, "An interview with historian Gordon Wood on the New York Times' 1619 Project," World Socialist Web Site, November 28, 2019.

authority of the *New York Times* behind it, and yet it is so wrong in so many ways.

WSWS: I want to return to the question of slavery and the American Revolution, but first I wanted to follow up, because you said you were not approached. Yet you are certainly one of the foremost authorities on the American Revolution, which the 1619 Project trains much of its fire on.

GW: Yes, no one ever approached me. None of the leading scholars of the whole period from the Revolution to the Civil War, as far I know, have been consulted. I read the Jim McPherson interview and he was just as surprised as I was.

WSWS: Can you discuss the relationship between the American Revolution and the institution of slavery?

GW: One of the things that I have emphasized in my writing is how many Southerners and Northerners in 1776 thought slavery was on its last legs and that it would naturally die away. You can find quotation after quotation from people seriously thinking that slavery was going to wither away in several decades. Now we know they couldn't have been more wrong. But they lived with illusions, and were so wrong about so many things. We may be living with illusions too. One of the big lessons of history is to realize how the past doesn't know its future. We know how the story turned out, and we somehow assume they should know what we know, but they don't, of course. They don't know their future any more than we know our future, and so many of them thought that slavery would die away, and at first there was considerable evidence that that was indeed the case.

At the time of the Revolution, the Virginians had more slaves than they knew what to do with, so they were eager to end the international slave trade. But the Georgians and the South Carolinians weren't ready to do that yet. That was one of the compromises that came out of the Constitutional Convention. The Deep South was given twenty years to import more slaves, but most Americans were confident that the despicable trans-Atlantic slave trade was definitely going to end in 1808.

WSWS: Under the Jefferson administration?

GW: Yes, it was set in the Constitution at twenty years, but everyone knew this would be ended because nearly everyone knew that this was a barbaric thing, importing people and so on. Many thought that ending the slave trade would set slavery itself on the road to extinction. Of course, they were wrong.

I think the important point to make about slavery is that it had existed for thousands of years without substantial criticism, and it existed all over the New World. It also existed elsewhere in the world. Western Europe had already more or less done away with slavery. Perhaps there was nothing elsewhere comparable to the plantation slavery that existed in the New World, but slavery was widely prevalent in Africa and Asia. There is still slavery today in the world.

And it existed in all of these places without substantial criticism. Then suddenly in the middle of the eighteenth century you begin to get some isolated Quakers coming out against it. But it's the American Revolution that makes it a problem for the world. And the first real antislavery movement takes place in North America. So this is what's missed by these essays in the 1619 Project.

WSWS: The claim made by Nikole Hannah-Jones in the 1619 Project that the Revolution was really about founding a slavocracy seems to be coming from arguments made elsewhere that it was really Great Britain that was the progressive contestant in the conflict, and that the American Revolution was, in fact, a counterrevolution, basically a conspiracy to defend slavery.

GW: It's been argued by some historians, people other than Hannah-Jones, that some planters in colonial Virginia were worried about what the British might do about slavery. Certainly, Dunmore's proclamation in 1775, which promised the slaves freedom if they joined the Crown's cause, provoked many hesitant Virginia planters to become patriots. There may have been individuals who were worried about their slaves in 1776, but to see the whole Revolution in those terms is to miss the complexity.

In 1776, Britain, despite the Somerset decision, was certainly not the great champion of antislavery that the 1619 Project suggests. Indeed, it is the Northern states in 1776 that are the world's leaders in the antislavery cause. The first antislavery meeting in the history of the world takes place in Philadelphia in 1775. That coincidence I think is important. I would have liked to have asked Hannah-Jones how would she explain the fact that in 1791 in Virginia at the College of William and Mary, the Board of Visitors, the Board of Trustees, who were big slaveholding planters, awarded an honorary degree to Granville Sharp, who was the leading British abolitionist of the day. That's the kind of question that should provoke historical curiosity. You ask yourself what were these slaveholding planters thinking? It's the kind of question, the kind of seeming anomaly, that should provoke a historian into research.

The idea that the Revolution occurred as a means of protecting slavery—I just don't think there is much evidence for it, and in fact the contrary is more true to what happened. The Revolution unleashed antislavery sentiments that led to the first abolition movements in the history of the world.

WSWS: In fact, those who claim that the American Revolution was a counterrevolution to protect slavery focus on the timing of the Somerset ruling of 1772, which held that slavery wasn't supported by English common law, and Dunmore's promise to free slaves who escape their masters.

GW: To go from these few facts to create such an enormous argument is a problem. The Somerset decision was limited to England, where there were very few slaves, and it didn't apply to the Caribbean. The British don't get around to freeing the slaves in the West Indies until 1833, and if the Revolution hadn't occurred, might never have done so then, because all of the Southern colonies would have been opposed. So supposing the Americans hadn't broken away, there would have been a larger number of slaveholders in the greater British world who might have been able to prolong slavery longer than 1833. The West Indies planters were too weak in the end to resist abolition. They did try to, but if they had had all those planters in the South still being part of the British Empire with them, that would have made it more difficult for the British Parliament to move toward abolition.

WSWS: Hannah-Jones refers to America's founding documents as its founding myths ...

GW: ... Of course, there are great ironies in our history, but the men and the documents transcend their time. That Jefferson, a slaveholding aristocrat, has been—until recently—our spokesman for democracy, declaring that all men are created equal, is probably the greatest irony in American history. But the document he wrote and his confidence in the capacities of ordinary people are real, and not myths.

Jefferson was a very complicated figure. He took a stand against slavery as a young man in Virginia. He spoke out against it. He couldn't get his colleagues to go along, but he was certainly courageous in voicing his opposition to slavery. Despite his outspokenness on slavery and other enlightened matters, his colleagues respected him enough to keep elevating him to positions in the state. His colleagues could have, as we say today, "canceled" him if they didn't have some sympathy for what he was saying.

WSWS: And after the Revolution?

GW: American leaders think slavery is dying, but they couldn't have been more wrong. Slavery grows stronger after the Revolution, but it's concentrated in the South. North of the Mason-Dixon line, in every Northern state by 1804, slavery is legally put on the road to extinction. Now, there's certain "grandfathering in," and so you do have slaves in New Jersey as late as the eve of the Civil War. But in the Northern states, the massive movement against slavery was unprecedented in the history of the world. So to somehow turn this around and make the Revolution a means of preserving slavery is strange and contrary to the evidence.

As a result of the Revolution, slavery is confined to the South, and that puts the Southern planters on the defensive. For the first time they have to defend the institution. If you go into the colonial records and look at the writings and diary of someone like William Byrd, who's a very distinguished and learned person—he's a member of the Royal Society—you'll find no expressions of guilt whatsoever about slavery. He took his slaveholding for granted. But after the Revolution that's no longer true. Southerners began to feel this antislavery pressure now. They react to it by trying to give a positive defense of slavery. They had no need to defend slavery earlier because it was taken for granted as a natural part of a hierarchical society.

We should understand that slavery in the colonial period seemed to be simply the most base status in a whole hierarchy of dependencies and degrees of unfreedom. Indentured servitude was prevalent everywhere. Half the population that came to the colonies in the eighteenth century came as bonded servants. Servitude, of course, was not slavery, but it was a form of dependency and unfreedom that tended to obscure the uniqueness of racial slavery. Servants were bound over to masters for five or seven years. They couldn't marry. They couldn't own property. They belonged to their masters, who could sell them. Servitude was not lifetime and was not racially based, but it was a form of dependency and unfreedom. The Revolution attacked bonded servitude and by 1800 it scarcely existed anywhere in the US.

The elimination of servitude suddenly made slavery more conspicuous than it had been in a world of degrees of unfreedom. The antislavery movements arose out of these circumstances. As far as most Northerners were concerned, this most base and despicable form of unfreedom must be eliminated along with all the other forms of unfreedom. These dependencies were simply incompatible with the meaning of the Revolution.

After the Revolution, Virginia had no vested interest in the international slave trade. Quite the contrary. Virginians began to grow wheat in place of tobacco. Washington does this, and he comes to see himself as more a farmer than a planter. He and other farmers begin renting out their slaves to people in Norfolk and Richmond, where they are paid wages. And many people thought that this might be the first step toward the eventual elimination of slavery. These anti-slave sentiments don't last long in Virginia, but for a moment it seemed that Virginia, which dominated the country as no other state ever has, might abolish slavery as the Northern states were doing. In fact, there were lots of manumissions and other anti-slave moves in Virginia in the 1780s.

But the black rebellion in Saint-Domingue—the Haitian Revolution—scares the bejesus out of the Southerners. Many of the white Frenchmen fled to North America—to Louisiana, to Charleston, and they brought their fears of slave uprisings with them. Then, with Gabriel's Rebellion in Virginia in 1800, most of the optimism that Virginians had in 1776–90 is gone.

Of course, I think the ultimate turning point for both sections is the Missouri crisis of 1819–20. Up to that point, both sections lived with illusions. The Missouri crisis causes the scales to fall away from the eyes of both Northerners and Southerners. Northerners come to realize that the South really intended to perpetuate slavery and extend it into the West. And Southerners come to realize that the North is so opposed to slavery that it will attempt to block them from extending it into the West. From that moment on I think the Civil War became inevitable.

WSWS: There's the famous quote from Jefferson that the Missouri crisis awakened him like a fire bell in the night and that in it he perceived the death of the Union ...

GW: ... Right. He's absolutely panicked by what's happening, and these last years of his life leading up to 1826 are really quite sad, because he's saying these things. Reading his writings between 1819 and his death in 1826 makes you wince because he so often sounds like a Southern fire-eater of the 1850s. Whereas his friend Madison has a much more balanced view of things, Jefferson becomes a furious and frightened defender of the South. He sees a catastrophe in the works, and he can't do anything about it.

His friend Adams was, of course, opposed to slavery from the beginning, and this is something that Hannah-Jones should have been aware of. John Adams is the leading advocate in the Continental Congress for independence. He's never been a slaveowner. He hates slavery and he has no vested interest in it. By 1819–20, however, he more or less takes the view that the Virginians have a serious problem with slavery and they are going to have to work it out for themselves. He's not going to preach to them. That's essentially what he says to Jefferson.

By the early nineteenth century, Jefferson had what Annette Gordon-Reed calls "New England envy." His granddaughter marries a New Englander and moves there, and she tells him how everything's flourishing in Connecticut. The farms are all neat, clean, and green, and there are no slaves. He envies the town meetings of New England, those little ward republics. And he just yearns for something like that for Virginia.

WSWS: How is it that the American Revolution raises the dignity of labor? Because it seems to me that this concept certainly becomes a burning issue by the time of the Civil War.

GW: It's a good question. Central to the middle-class revolution was an unprecedented celebration of work, especially manual labor, including the working for money. For centuries, going back to the ancient Greeks, work with one's hands had been held in contempt. Aristotle had said that those who worked with their hands, and especially those who worked for money, lacked the capacity for virtue. This remained the common view until the American Revolution changed everything.

The Northern celebration of work made the slaveholding South seem even more anomalous than it was. Assuming that work was despicable and mean was what justified slavery. Scorn for work and slavery were two sides of the same coin. Now the middle-class Northerners—clerks, petty merchants, farmers, etc.—began attacking the leisured gentry as parasites living off the work of others. That was the gist of the writings of William Manning, the obscure Massachusetts farmer, writing in the 1790s. This celebration of work, of course, forced the slaveholding planters to be even more defensive and they began celebrating leisure as the source of high culture in contrast with the money-grubbing North.

Slavery required a culture that held labor in contempt. The North, with its celebration of labor, especially working for money, became even more different from the lazy, slaveholding South. By the 1850s, the two sections, though both American, possessed two different cultures.

WSWS: In my discussion with James Oakes, he made the point about the emergence of the Democratic Party in the 1820s, that in the North it can't do what the Southern slave owners really want it to do, which is to say slaves are property, but what they do instead is to begin to promote racism.

GW: That's right. When you have a republican society, it's based on equality of all citizens, and now many whites found that difficult to accept. And they had to justify the segregation and the inferior status of the freed blacks by saying blacks were an inferior race. As I said earlier, in the Colonial period, whites didn't have to mount any racist arguments to justify the lowly status of blacks. In a hierarchical society with many degrees of unfreedom, you don't bother with trying to explain or justify slavery or the unequal treatment of anyone. Someone like William Byrd never tries to justify slavery. He never argues that blacks are inferior. He doesn't need to do that because he takes his whole world of inequality and hierarchy for granted. Racism develops in the decades following the Revolution because in a free republican society, whites needed a new justification for keeping blacks in an inferior and segregated place. And it became even more complicated when freed blacks with the suffrage tended to vote for the doomed parties of the Federalists and the Whigs.

WSWS: The 1619 Project claims basically that nothing has ever gotten any better. That it's as bad now as it was during slavery, and instead what you're describing is a very changed world.

GW: Imagine the inequalities that existed before the Revolution. Not just in wealth—I mean, we have that now—but in the way in which people were treated. Consider the huge number of people who were servants of some kind. I just think that people need to know just how bad the *Ancien Régime* was. In France, we always had this Charles Dickens *Tale of Two Cities* view of the society, with a nobleman riding through the village and running over children, and so on. But similar kinds of brutalities and cruelties existed in the English-speaking world in the way common people were treated. In England, there must have been two hundred capital crimes on the books. Consequently, juries became somewhat reluctant to convict to hanging a person for stealing a handkerchief. So the convict was sent as a bonded servant to the colonies, fifty thousand of them. And then when the American Revolution occurs, Australia becomes the replacement.

I don't think people realize just what a cruel and brutal world existed in the *Ancien Régime*, in the premodern societies of the West, not just for slaves, but for lots of people who were considered the mean or lowly sort. And they don't appreciate what a radical message is involved in declaring that all men are created equal and what that message means for our obsession with education, and the implications of that for our society.

WSWS: You spoke of the "consensus school" on American history before, from the 1950s, that saw the Revolution, I think, as essentially a conservative event. And one of the things that they stressed was that there was no aristocracy, no native aristocracy, in America, but you find, if I recall your argument in *The Radicalism of the American Revolution*, that though aristocracy was not strong, it was something that was still a powerful factor.

GW: There's no European-type aristocracy, the kind of rich, hereditary aristocracy of the sort that existed in England—great landholders living off the rents of their tenants. But we had an aristocracy of sorts. The Southern slaveholding planters certainly came closest to the English model, but even in the more egalitarian North there was an aristocracy of sorts. Men of wealth and distinction that we would label elites sought to make the title of gentleman equal some kind of aristocracy. "Gentleman" was a legal distinction, and such gentlemen were treated differently in the society because of that distinction. With the Revolution, all this came under assault.

It's interesting to look at the debates that occur in the New York ratifying convention in 1788. The leading Anti-Federalist, Melancton Smith, a very smart guy but a middling sort and with no college graduate degree, gives the highly educated Alexander Hamilton and Robert Livingston a run for their money. He calls Hamilton and Livingston aristocrats, and charges that the proposed Constitution was designed to give more power to the likes of them. Hamilton, who certainly felt superior to Smith, denied he was an aristocrat. There were no aristocrats in America, he said; they existed only in Europe. That kind of concession was multiplied ten-thousand-fold in the following decades in the North, and this denial of obvious social superiority in the face of middling criticism is denied even today. You see politicians wanting to play down their distinctiveness, their elite status. "I can have a beer with Joe Six-pack," they say, denying their social superiority. That was already present in the late 1780s. That's what I mean by radicalism. It's a middle-class revolution, and it is essentially confined to the North.

WSWS: You were speaking earlier of the despair of Madison, Adams, and Jefferson late in life. And it just occurred to me that they lived to see Martin Van Buren.

GW: That's right. Van Buren is probably the first real politician in America elected to the presidency. Unlike his predecessors, he never did anything great; he never made a great speech, he never wrote a great document, he never won a great battle. He simply was the most politically astute operator that the United

States had ever seen. He organized a party in New York that was the basis of his success.

Van Buren regarded the founding fathers as passé. He told his fellow Americans, look, we don't need to pay too much attention to those guys. They were aristocrats, he said. We're Democrats—meaning both small "d" and also capital "D." Those aristocrats don't have much to say to us.

Did you know that the "founding fathers" in the antebellum period are not Jefferson and Madison and Washington and Hamilton? In the antebellum period when most Americans referred to the "founders," they meant John Smith, William Penn, William Bradford, John Winthrop, and so on, the founders of the seventeenth century. There's a good book on this subject by Wesley Frank Craven [*The Legend of the Founding Fathers* (1956)].

It's Lincoln who rescues the eighteenth-century founders for us. From the Civil War on, the "founders" become the ones we celebrate today, the revolutionary leaders. Lincoln makes Jefferson the great hero of America. "All honor to Jefferson," he says. Only because of the Declaration of Independence. Jefferson didn't have anything to do with the Constitution, and so Lincoln makes the Declaration the most important document in American history, which I think is true.

WSWS: Could you discuss something of the world-historical significance of the Revolution? Of course, we are under no illusion that it represented a socialist transformation. Yet it was a powerful revolution in its time.

GW: It was very important that the American colonial crisis, the imperial crisis, occurred right at the height of what we call the Enlightenment, where Western Europe was full of new ideas and was confident that culture—what people believed and thought—was man-made and thus could be changed. The Old World, the *Ancien Régime*, could be transformed and made anew. It was an age of revolution, and it's not surprising that the French Revolution and other revolutions occur in in the wake of the American Revolution.

The notion of equality was really crucial. When the Declaration says that all men are created equal, that is no myth. It is the most powerful statement ever made in our history, and it lies behind almost everything we Americans believe in and attempt to do. What that statement meant is that we are all born equal and all the differences that we see among us as adults are due solely to our differing educations, differing upbringings, and differing environments. The Declaration is an Enlightenment document because it repudiated the *Ancien Régime* assumption that all men are created unequal and that nothing much could be done about it. That's what it meant to be a subject in the old society. You were born a patrician or a plebeian and that was your fate.

WSWS: One of the ironies of the 1619 Project is that they are saying the same things about the Declaration of Independence as the fire-eating proponents of slavery said—that it's a fraud. Meanwhile, abolitionists like Frederick Douglass upheld it and said we're going to make this "all men are created equal" real.

GW: That points up the problem with the whole project. It's too bad that it's going out into the schools with the authority of the *New York Times* behind it. That's sad because it will color the views of all these youngsters who will receive the message of the 1619 Project.

Adolph Reed Jr.

Adolph Reed Jr.

Adolph Reed Jr. is Professor Emeritus of Political Science at the University of Pennsylvania. He is author of *W. E. B. Du Bois and American Political Thought: Fabianism and the Color Line* and *Stirrings in the Jug: Black Politics in the Post-Segregation Era*. Reed has contributed to popular publications including the *New Republic*, *Harper's*, and the *Nation*.

WSWS: Could you say something about your background and what you view to be the main thrust of your career?

Adolph Reed: I'm one of those people who was largely formed through the social movements of the 1960s. The only modification to that was that I came out of a left-wing household, and so I was kind of looking to be formed and was always more attentive to politics than anybody in my cohort. One of the reasons I made the decision to go to graduate school when I did, in the 1970s, was that I could feel that the Movement was kind of drying up around us. The opportunities that there seemed to have been for left interventions were disappearing, especially within black politics, because that was the domain I was operating in after I left college in 1969. The challenge as I saw it when I went to grad school in 1972 was to figure out how we've gotten outflanked by petty-bourgeois politicians and how to do it better next time. So, I went to graduate school without a sense that there was a clear boundary between my political concerns and interests, and my intellectual concerns and interests.

Thomas Mackaman, "An interview with political scientist Adolph Reed Jr. on the New York Times' 1619 Project," World Socialist Web Site, December 20, 2019.

One of the reasons I think it is kind of hard to look back on that now is that something quite different has happened over the last thirty years, and that's been the cultural turn in academia. One of its ironic entailments is this notion that doing cultural work in academia itself is a form of political practice, and that advancing certain programmatic and intellectual interests within the Academy or in bourgeois public discourse is simultaneously a political practice and an intellectual practice.

That mindset brings to mind Marx's critique of Proudhon, where he pointed out that in Germany, where they didn't know political economy, Proudhon presented himself as a political economist, and in France, where they didn't know philosophy, he presented himself as a philosopher. It's like a character from *Amos and Andy* or *The Life of Riley*, where the character's expertise is always in another place. But this is also a marker of the extent to which academia is one of the last strongholds of the professional and managerial class.

What I've strived for throughout my career is to provide a historical-materialist account of race and class, and American society. One of the major problems I combat is the idea of class as culture. Looking back at the first two decades after World War II, one of the most meaningful but damaging interventions that American social scientists made during that period is rendering class invisible by reconstructing it as a category of culture.

WSWS: Let me ask a little bit about your initial reaction to the 1619 Project. I have spoken to several historians who concentrated their criticism on Nikole Hannah-Jones's lead essay, which is meant to frame the whole thing, and also Matthew Desmond's claim that American capitalism is basically the direct descendent of chattel slavery. Maybe you can help us to understand the rest of the magazine, which is being pushed as a curriculum for school children. It seems to me that what the rest of the essays do is focus on a particular social problem—traffic jams in Atlanta, lack of national health care, high sugar in the American diet, and so on—and argue by implication that that's all coming out of slavery. The dominant tendency in academia is to attribute all social problems to race, or to other forms of identity, but the 1619 Project goes farther still, saying that they are all rooted in slavery.

AR: I didn't know about the 1619 Project until it came out, and frankly when I learned about it my reaction was a big sigh. But again, the relation to history has passed to the appropriation of the past in support of whatever kind of "just-so" stories about the present are desired. This approach has taken root within the Academy. It's like all bets are off.

Merlin Chowkwanyun[1] and I did an article a few years ago in the *Socialist Register* that's a critique of disparitarianism in the social sciences, by which this or that disparity has replaced the study of inequality and its effects. As Walter Benn Michaels[2] said, and as I have said time and time again, if antidisparitarianism is your ideology, then for you a society qualifies as being just if 1 percent of the population controls 90 percent of the wealth so long as that within that 1 percent 12 percent or so are black, etc., reflecting their share of the national population. This is the ideal of social justice for neoliberalism. There's no question of actual redistribution.

What are the stakes that people imagine to be bound up with demonstrating that capitalism in this country emerged from slavery and racism, which are treated as two different labels for the same pathology? Ultimately, it's a race reductionist argument. What the Afro-pessimist types or black nationalist types get out of it is an insistence that we can't ever talk about anything except race. And that's partly because talking about race is the things they have to sell.

If you follow through the logic of disparities discourse, and watch the studies and follow the citations, what you get is a sort of bold announcement of findings, but findings that anybody who has been reading a newspaper over the last fifty or seventy years would assume from the outset: blacks have it worse, and women have it worse, and so on.

It's in part an expression of a generic pathology of sociology, the most banal expression of academic life. You follow the safe path. You replicate the findings. But it's not just supposed to be a matter of finding a disparity in and of itself, like differences in the number of days of sunshine in a year. It's supposed to be a promise that in finding or confirming the disparity in this or that domain that it will bring some kind of mediation of the problem. But the work never calls for that.

WSWS: You make important points about the way social problems are approached. As an example, we have a scourge of police violence in this country. Over 1,000 Americans are killed each year by police. And the common knowledge, so to speak, is that this is a racial problem. The reality is that the largest number of those killed are white, but blacks are disproportionately killed. But

1. Merlin Chowkwanyun is an Assistant Professor of Sociomedical Sciences at Columbia University.
2. Walter Benn Michaels is a Professor of English at the University of Illinois Chicago and author of *The Trouble with Diversity: How We Learned to Love Identity and Ignore Inequality.*

if the position is that this is simply a racial problem, there is no real solution on offer. We have a militarized police force operating under conditions of extreme social inequality, with lots of guns on the streets, with soldiers coming back from serving in neocolonial wars abroad becoming police officers. And all of this is excised in the racialist argument, which, if taken at face value, boils down to allegations about racial attitudes among police.

AR: Cedric Johnson[3] has made good points on this and I've spoken with him at considerable length about the criminal justice system. To overdraw the point, a black Yale graduate who works on Wall Street is no doubt several times more likely to be jacked up by the police on the platform of Metro-North than his white counterpart, out of mistaken identity. And that mistaken identity is what we might call racism. But it's a shorthand. He's still less likely to be jacked up by the police than the broke white guy in northeast Philadelphia or west Baltimore.

The point of this stress on policing is containing those working-class and poor populations and protecting property holders downtown, and in making shows of force in doing so. I mean the emergence of, or the intensification of, militarized policing in the 1990s and 2000s was directly connected with an increased focus on urban redevelopment directed toward turning central cities into havens for play and leisure. To do this, you have to accomplish a couple of things, as Saskia Sassen[4] pointed out almost thirty years ago, in the reconfiguration of the urban political economy in ways that create a basis for upscale consumption, and an industrial reserve army who will work for little enough to make that culture of upscale consumption profitable. Then you have to have the police to protect all of this. It's really like a tourist economy.

So that's kind of natural enough and you don't need to have a devil theory like the crack epidemic to explain it—all of this pointless back-and-forth about how the cultural and political authorities are responding to the opioid crisis compared to how they responded to the crack epidemic. I mean, it's all beside the point.

WSWS: I was remembering your response to Hurricane Katrina. New Orleans is your hometown, right?

AR: Yes.

---

3. Cedric Johnson is an Associate Professor of African American Studies and Political Science at the University of Illinois-Chicago.
4. Saskia Sassen is a Dutch-American scholar of urban sociology.

WSWS: Maybe you could say something about that because I think you made a strong critique of identity politics in the context of that disaster.

AR: First of all, the narrative that only black people lived in the most flood-prone areas was false. The Lakeview section of the city, which was built on reclaimed marshland on the lakefront when I was too small to remember, in the first decades after World War II, was every bit as much below sea level as the Lower Ninth Ward and flooded as completely.

I guess we owe something to Anderson Cooper and Soledad O'Brien for when they began to recoil from, and then eventually to rebel against, the victim-blaming in the aftermath of the hurricane. But what was unfortunate about that moment was that, even though they were moved by it, the power of the iconography, of the disproportionate representation of poor black people on the overpasses in the Convention Center and the Superdome, fed this idea that "nothing has changed," that there is this insoluble race problem.

Well the first question is, where do you think that the people who brought you those tropical drinks and turned down your bed in the hotel lived? I mean how do you think they lived? Did it never occur to you to wonder what their wages were or anything like that?

Of course it's a poor city. But it turns out that, proportionally, blacks weren't displaced at a higher rate than whites. It's just that there are a lot more blacks in the city. And also, blacks actually didn't die at a higher rate than whites. But the best predictor, or a better predictor than race, of who was able to evacuate first of all, who was able to survive the period of evacuation under relatively decent circumstances, and who was able to come back to the city afterwards—every step along the way, class was a better predictor than race. Class as in a sociological sense, class as access to resources—both monetary and other resources; your lack of dependence on a job, your access to social networks. But it didn't appear to be that way so there becomes this narrative that the story of Katrina's displacement proves the continuing significance, or new significance, of race.

Well, it turns out that the concrete version of the story is that it shows the power of class and the impact of neoliberalism. Before Mitch Landrieu was elected mayor in 2010 there hadn't been a white mayor since his father left office in 1977. So you had a black government all the way through. But now, even with them coming back to the city, for a year or two afterwards, when you'd drive around the city—and granted this is informal observation, but I did it on every trip there, and kept tabs—but following the recovery, it's not only that the more affluent neighborhoods recovered without regard to race, but that even within the better-off neighborhoods and more affluent blocks, the bigger houses came back first.

But where it really gets corrosive is this narrative that the city was being de-populated of blacks so that whites could take it back. And the first few weeks after the inundation you could certainly find people saying: "We'll get rid of the crime. Let it all go to Houston." But it was also pretty clear after a few weeks that the governing elite didn't really have any interest in altering the po-litical regime. Now post-Katrina, and this is a big irony given the race line of arguing, if anything the ruling class in the city is now more seamlessly interra-cial and biracial than it had been previously.

WSWS: I think identity politics makes for some strange bedfellows. There's some agreement between the likes of Hannah-Jones and the far right, for ex-ample, the neo-Confederates you were mentioning when we sat down, who oppose the concept of equality. But she, in the 1619 Project, also calls the Dec-laration of Independence a "founding myth."

AR: Every state is going to have its founding myths, if you think of them as ide-als. But what is so important about Jim Oakes' book, *Scorpion's Sting*, is that you can see this tension about human equality that was rooted in the found-ing documents and debates. It's especially ironic to consider, for instance, the three-fifths compromise to the Constitution, which was an expression of ex-actly the opposite political value that the people who invoke it as part of an Afro-pessimist discourse claim. These people are kind of just making it up as they go, or reinventing the past to suit the purposes of the present.

Right from the outset. Those first twenty people weren't slaves. There wasn't chattel slavery yet in British North America. But the 1619 Project as-sumes, in whatever way, that slavery was the natural condition of Africans. And that's where the Afro-pessimist types wind up sharing a cup of tea with the likes of James Henry Hammond.[5]

WSWS: Let me ask you about what in academia is called "critical race theory," and how you see it at work in the 1619 Project.

AR: It's another expression of reductionism. On the most pedestrian level it's an observation that what you see is a function of where you stand. At that level there's nothing in it that wasn't in Marx's early writings, or in Mannheim. But

---

5. James Henry Hammond was a Democratic Party Senator from South Carolina (1857–1860) and leading proponent of slavery in the lead-up to the Civil War.

then you get an appropriation of the standpoint theory for identity that says for example, all blacks think the same way. It's taxonomic, a reification. So the retort to that critique has been "intersectionality." Yes, there's a black perspective, but what you do is fragment it, so there are multiple black perspectives, because each potential—or each sacralized—social position becomes discrete. That's what gives you intersectionality.

But listening to how people talk about intersectionality, it just seems like dissociative personality disorder. How do you carve out when your male is talking, and your black is talking, and when your steelworker is talking? It seems like the kind of perspective that can work only at a level of abstraction at which no one ever asks to see something concrete. Herbert Butterfield, in *The Whig Interpretation of History*, back in 1931, had this great criticism of what he calls concepts that are incapable of concrete visualization. But we have this world of theory where big cultural abstractions kind of cross-pollinate and relieve the theorists of historical work.

WSWS: We've spoken to a number of leading historians, including James McPherson, James Oakes, Gordon Wood, and Victoria Bynum, and Hannah-Jones launched into a Twitter tirade against them, dismissing them as "white historians." She is not a historian, but she is the recipient of a MacArthur Foundation "Genius Grant," just like Ta-Nehisi Coates and Ibram X. Kendi have been in recent years.

AR: I have spent most of my adult life trying to avoid the kind of old-fashioned Stalinist conspiracy theory, but it's getting hard. My dad used to say that in one sense ideology is the mechanism that harmonizes the principles that you want to believe with what advances your material interest.

And so I understand that the people of MacArthur, for instance, think they're doing something quite different. But when they look for voices, the voices that they look for are the voices that say ultimately: "Well it's a tragedy that's hopeless. We have to atone as individuals. Do whatever you can do to confront disparity."

I've been joking for a number of years that here at Penn the university administration has three core values: Building the endowment, already at $16 billion. Buying up as much of the real estate as they can on both sides of the Schuylkill River. And diversity. And they're genuinely committed to all three of those because they think that part of their mission is to make the ruling class look like the photo of America.

I made a reference once to Coates being an autodidact, and what I meant by that was that he did not know history, that he's not a historian. Kendi's book, I don't know anyone who has actually read it.

WSWS: *Stamped from the Beginning* is the title. There couldn't be a more anti-historical title. In just four words it mixes biblical and genetic metaphors. He's now on a national speaking tour.

AR: It's a career path. A number of years ago Ken Warren at the University of Chicago and I ran a seminar, and what we noticed is that a lot of students of color were applying to PhD programs saying that they wanted to get a credential to help them become public intellectuals. And it's only gotten more and more normalized. I mean at this point, if you look at faculty home pages, or even graduate student pages, they read like they're prepared by the William Morris Agency, for example assistant professors claiming fifteen subfields of expertise. It's like the bios are written for MSNBC.

WSWS: I think one element of it is that there's this presumption that it's somehow all "left." But then you look, and well, it's funded by the MacArthur Foundation, and the *New York Times* loves it, and the Ivy League boards of trustees love it, so how left can it be? How could it possibly be radical?

AR: I've seen some students take umbrage to describing slavery as a labor system, that that is somehow demeaning. I don't know if you remember this, but there was a controversy a few years ago, where this textbook made a reference to the trans-Atlantic slave trade, and then, in the context of the trans-Atlantic slave trade, made a statement that Africans were brought to the New World to work, or were brought as workers. There was a big to-do about this. But the simple structure of the paragraph makes clear that whoever wrote this text was not claiming that African workers weren't slaves, since they were brought here through the trans-Atlantic slave trade. My son, Touré Reed, who is a historian at Illinois State University, puts it this way, "There is a tendency to think of slavery as a permanent sadistic camp." And that's what comes through in the movies, too.

WSWS: Right. The idea, and I think the 1619 Project very much promotes this, that slavery was created as a form of racial oppression, rather than a form of labor exploitation that ultimately became rationalized ideologically by racism.

Even when slavery existed, its form of exploitation was so conspicuous, and so brutal, that it obscured other forms of exploitation, including wage labor. But now it's 2019, and you have the *New York Times* arguing that every social ill that we have today is descended directly from slavery. As if wage labor exploitation hasn't happened, as if it's not happening at the *Times* itself. As if the great majority of African Americans today are not exploited today as wage laborers, alongside whites.

AR: Right. I've had this argument with the proponents of reparations. And my question for them all along has been, how can you imagine putting together a political alliance that would be broad enough so that you win on this issue? And if you can't imagine it, then what are you really doing? And their answer is, "Well, don't you think black people deserve something?" Well, a lot of people deserve a lot.

WSWS: I agree. The people behind the 1619 Project would of course deny they're advocating a race war. But if blacks and whites have immutable, intrinsic, and suprahistorical differences, that's the logic of the position.

AR: That's also the punchline of Afro-pessimism, that racism is ubiquitous. That everybody hates blacks or embraces antiblackness. It's everywhere and there's this global condition of whiteness.

WSWS: Hannah-Jones writes that antiblack racism is stamped in the national DNA.

AR: The only place that can lead, if it's impermeable, if it's immutable, is race war.

The "legacy of slavery" construct is also one I've hated for as long as I can remember because, in the first place, why would the legacy of slavery be more meaningful than the legacy of sharecropping and Jim Crow and the legacy of the Great Migration? Or even the New Deal and the CIO? But what's ideologically useful about the legacy of the slavery trope is that it can mean two seemingly quite different things. One is that it can be invoked as proof that blacks are inferior, because slavery has forged an indelible mark. Or it can be invoked as a cultural pathology argument. But it's a misunderstanding to assume that there's a sharp contrast between cultural arguments about inequality and biological arguments. They're basically the same.

If you go back to the highwater mark of race theory at the end of the nineteenth century and the beginning of the twentieth, you don't need to have a theory of biological heredity to make a deterministic claim. You can shed the need for complex biological argument and just say that the cultures are different, and the culture decrees these kinds of inadequacies.

WSWS: I have not tried to search out a historical linkage to this before, but it seems to me that going all the way back to the antebellum it has been the Democratic Party that has done the heavy lifting in promoting racial identity. Of course, there's a division of labor with the Republicans since the late 1960s and Nixon's so-called "Southern strategy." Not so long ago, people referred to Republican politicians using "dog whistles" for racism. With Trump it's become a bullhorn. But the *Times*' 1619 Project reflects the agenda of the Democratic Party today. They're trying to cobble together an electoral coalition based on identities.

AR: Absolutely. It's fascinating to watch Hillary Clinton in 2016 because I remember very well 1992, when the cutting edge of Clintonism was showing there was a new Democratic Party that was going to make Wall Street grateful. It wasn't a party that was going to coddle black and poor people. And Bill Clinton was very clear about that. That's what the Crime Bill and Welfare Reform were all about. To see the Clintons presenting themselves as the avatars of racial justice against Bernie Sanders in 2016 was really extraordinary.

WSWS: Thank you for speaking with us. Before we conclude, let me ask you what you are working on now.

AR: Well I've started doing a column every month in the *New Republic*, but I'm trying to finish a book that actually started at the beginning of the Obama era. I was approached by Verso to do a book on Obama and I said no, but I would consider doing a book on Obama-mania, by which I mean the phenomenon that people who should have known better got so excited about him.

WSWS: You had a really prescient essay on Obama way back in 1996, when he was an Illinois state senator. You referred to him as "a smooth Harvard lawyer with impeccable do-good credentials and vacuous-to-repressive neoliberal politics," and predicted he was the wave of the future.

AR: Yes, that essay was just an example of right place at the right time and just keeping your eyes open. I was living right there in that district. I've kind of joked that I was in the birthing room at the outset of his political career. But to really answer the Obama question requires something better and more elaborate. So, the book I'm working on is an account of the decline and transformation on the left in the US since World War II, and I've just started work on the last chapter.

WSWS: I look forward to reading it.

Richard Carwardine

Richard Carwardine

Richard Carwardine is Emeritus Rhodes Professor of American History at Corpus Christi College, Oxford University. Carwardine is author of *Evangelicals and Politics in Antebellum America*; *Abraham Lincoln and the Fourth Estate: The White House and the Press During the American Civil War*; and *Lincoln: A Life of Purpose and Power*, which was awarded the Lincoln Prize.

WSWS: Let me begin by asking you your reaction to the 1619 Project's lead essay, by Nikole Hannah-Jones, upon reading it.

Richard Carwardine: As well as the essay, I have read your interviews with James McPherson and James Oakes. I share their sense that, putting it politely, this is a tendentious and partial reading of American history.

I understand where this Project is coming from, politically and culturally. Of course, the economic well-being of the United States and the colonies that preceded it was constructed for over two-and-a-half centuries on the labor and sufferings of slaves; of course, like all entrenched wielders of power, the white political elite resisted efforts to yield up its privileges. But the idea that the 1619 Project's lead essay is a rounded history of America—with relations between the races so stark and unyielding—I find quite shocking. I am troubled that this is designed to make its way into classrooms as *the* true story of the United States, because, as I say, it is so partial. It is also wrong in some fundamentals.

Thomas Mackaman, "Oxford historian Richard Carwardine on the New York Times' 1619 Project," World Socialist Web Site, December 31, 2019.

I'm all for recovering and celebrating the history of those whose voices have been historically muted and I certainly understand the concern of historians in recent times, black and white, that the black contribution to the United States has not been fully recognized. But the idea that the central, fundamental story of the United States is one of white racism and that black protest and rejection of white superiority has been the essential, indispensable driving force for change—which I take to be the central message of that lead essay—seems to me to be a preposterous and one-dimensional reading of the American past.

WSWS: I agree with everything you've said. There was a long period in American historiography in which the contributions of African Americans were written out, and what prevailed was a basically false presentation in which the problems of slavery were obscured. But it seems the 1619 Project has simply put a minus sign where that earlier historiography, the Dunning School and so on, put a plus.

RC: Yes. As an undergraduate at Oxford in the 1960s I was aware of work that brought a fresh and deeper understanding of African American history. This was an era of breakthrough studies on slavery and antislavery, and "history from below" more widely, a development which chimed with so much of the best British radical and Marxist historiography. That was a stimulating time to be studying American history. As you say, African American historiography has been transformed since then. I am pleased, but not surprised, that some African American historians are stepping forward to challenge the narrative that appeared in the *New York Times*.

WSWS: Let me ask you about the treatment of Abraham Lincoln. Nikole Hannah-Jones homes in on two episodes: the meeting on colonization with leading African Americans in 1862, and the well-known quote from the Lincoln-Stephen Douglas debates in which Lincoln disavows social equality for blacks. Could you comment on these two episodes, their presentation by the *New York Times*, or situate them in the evolution of Lincoln's thinking as regards race and slavery?

RC: There is indeed an evolution, but first I'll make two broad points. One is that context is all. Illinois was in 1858 one of the most race-conscious states of the Union. Alexis de Tocqueville concluded that white hostility towards blacks was strongest in the northwestern states. The black laws of Illinois were amongst the fiercest in the country. Lincoln knew that he could not be elected if he were seen as a racial egalitarian. I'm not suggesting he *was* a racial egalitarian, but we should take into account the political context that prompted his clearly defensive statements, at Ottawa and Charleston, that he was not seeking black political and social equality. Those statements of his are very few in number, grudging, and at times, I think, even satirical—as when he says that blacks are not "equal ... in color."

When Lincoln addressed the issue of slavery in his speeches from 1854 to 1860, he was on strong ground: slavery was widely disliked, and the prospect of its spread was unwelcome to his political audience. But on the issue of race the Republicans were vulnerable. Their call for an ultimate end to slavery had to explain the consequence for black-white relations, and that of course made Lincoln extremely vulnerable to Stephen Douglas's racism, and his assault on Lincoln as the "lover of the black"—though he would have used a worse epithet, wouldn't he? So, in reality, Lincoln could only win an election in 1858 by making some concessions to the prevailing racial antipathies of whites. These two statements have understandably, and reasonably, attracted attention. They demonstrate that Lincoln, to secure a Republican victory that would advance the antislavery cause, fell short both of what blacks aspired to, and of what the small minority of white racial egalitarians endorsed.

It seems to me that what's really striking, however, is what Lincoln positively demands for blacks at this time. He embraces them within the Declaration of Independence's proposition that all men are created equal. By "all men" he means regardless of color, and that's where he gets into a tussle with Douglas. Douglas insisted the Declaration of Independence was never intended to apply to black people, and of course, Lincoln is emphatic that it does. So for me it's what Lincoln *claims* for black people that is striking, and not what he says he will deny them.

With the August 1862 episode, again, context is important. It's a very striking meeting and it's not Lincoln's finest hour. Both Nicolay and Hay, his secretaries, said that they thought that Lincoln was at his most emotionally on edge and mentally fraught in the summer of 1862, when the Peninsular campaign had ended in failure, when he had determined on the Emancipation Proclamation but was waiting for a military victory to bring it forward, and when there was increasing clamor for emancipation. Both secretaries said that they had never known Lincoln as nervy as he was then.

The point I'm making here is that at that time Lincoln was under even greater human strain than ever. He knew he was on the brink of taking the most dramatic, even revolutionary, action of any president. He's nervous. He can't see what all the consequences will be, but he knows the consequences of *not* issuing the Emancipation Proclamation. It will leave the Confederacy with the whip hand.

That startling episode of Lincoln's discussions with the five African Americans—the first blacks invited into the White House as equals—should be placed in this context. Buffeted from all sides during one of the Union's lowest points of the war, Lincoln lost the good humor that commonly lubricated his meetings with visitors. His message to them about the causes of the war, and the advantages of colonization and racial separation, has to be seen also in the context of the daunting prospective challenge of embracing four million former slaves fully into the American polity.

WSWS: Could you discuss the origins of the colonization idea?

RC: Promoting the migration of American free blacks to colonies in Africa took institutional form in the American Colonization Society in 1816. In the main, its early supporters were white benevolent paternalists who couldn't see a positive future for blacks in the United States because of the depth of white prejudice, but part of its appeal was to slaveowners who saw the advantage of ending the troublesome presence of free blacks in the United States. In time, it alienated pure abolitionists, who thought it a bromide, and slave-masters, who deemed it the thin end of an antislavery wedge; it won the support of a few black radicals, including Henry Highland Garnet, but most black leaders strongly opposed it.

Lincoln was one of the many who, before the war, supported voluntary colonization as a means towards gradual emancipation. During 1861 and 1862 his advocacy of colonization continued at the same time that he pressed schemes of compensated emancipation and, in September 1862, issued his preliminary emancipation proclamation. However, the final Emancipation Proclamation of January 1863 was silent on the issue, suggesting that Lincoln had been using it, at least in part, to quell the fears of whites. There is evidence that he continued to consider voluntary colonization as just one amongst a cluster of strategies to effect a route into a viable post-emancipation, postwar world of racial adjustment.

So that would be my way of looking at those two episodes, of 1858 and 1862. And then I would add that those are only two of the episodes that bear on the matter. I could choose other episodes which give a very different perspective.

WSWS: Could you elaborate on that?

RC: Where in Nikole Hannah-Jones's reading of Lincoln, and in her wider perspective, is the voice of the greatest of all African Americans, Frederick Douglass? He doesn't appear. Douglass was not uncritical of Lincoln: he famously said that the black race were only Lincoln's stepchildren. But he also came to extol Lincoln, too, as a white man who put him at his ease, treating him as an equal, with no thought of the "color of our skins," and showing he could conceive of a society in which blacks and whites lived together in a degree of harmony, that racial relationships in America were not irredeemably fixed by its seventeenth- and eighteenth-century past.

Douglass was absolutely stunned when Lincoln suggested in the summer of 1864 that he, Douglass, should organize a band of scouts to penetrate beyond Union lines into the rebel states to spread the news of emancipation among the slaves and encourage their flight. Lincoln proposed this when he thought he would lose the 1864 election and wanted to get as many slaves as possible into the Union lines before then.

WSWS: I had forgotten about that episode.

RC: It's there in David Blight's magnificent book on Frederick Douglass. There are many other examples of Lincoln's positive views of blacks. You could take his letter to James Conkling in September 1863. Lincoln was invited by Conkling, a Springfield colleague who asked him to go to Illinois to campaign for the fall elections. Lincoln felt he had to stay in Washington, but he wrote a letter for Conkling to read to the Springfield audience, which he knew would comprise those who condemned him for issuing the Emancipation Proclamation, sanctioning the use of black troops, and creating an interracial Army. He wanted this letter read to Illinois voters, but it was designed for a wider audience. Lincoln was very specific about how it should be delivered, telling Conkling to read it very slowly and clearly. He was outraged when the text was leaked beforehand. The letter is in part a paean to the bravery of the black soldiers. I consider it his greatest public letter, a powerful statement of how much he admires those African Americans who have sacrificially taken up arms for the Union.

I'd like to return to what you said about the evolution of Lincoln's thinking on race. In Indiana, and then in Illinois, the vast majority of African Americans that he encountered were uneducated and in menial jobs; they provided the basis for the black stereotypes of the tall tales and ludicrous stories of the time. But once Lincoln reached Washington he found an aspirational black middle class, and in Frederick Douglass he met someone whom he considered his intellectual equal. Add to this the tens and then hundreds of thousands of black sailors and soldiers fighting on behalf of the Union, and it's no wonder that by April 1865, he was now prepared to advocate for blacks the political benefits of citizenship, including voting rights. These he wanted to extend only to a minority of black Americans—the educated and those in arms—but still this was a step towards the integration of blacks in a multiracial America.

It's not too much to say that Lincoln was a civil rights martyr. John Wilkes Booth shot him soon after hearing him propose, in what would be his final speech, full citizenship—with voting rights—for very educated blacks and those who had fought for the Union. Booth declared: "That means nigger citizenship. Now, by God! I'll put him through."

WSWS: It's a powerful point.

RC: My concern with the 1619 Project is not that it highlights the often-cited Lincoln remarks of 1858 and the White House meeting of August 1862. They are part of the overall story. They are real, and are not to Lincoln's credit. But they are thoroughly uncontexted, historically deaf and blind to a broader reality. Which of us would want to be judged on the basis of two snapshots in our lives? If the essence of Lincoln is captured in these episodes, then why does Frederick Douglass, arguably the preeminent African American of all time, come to admire Lincoln as a great man and leader? Through his successive encounters with Lincoln, Douglass developed a growing respect and admiration for a president who sought to live up to a progressive reading of the principles of the Declaration of Independence—one, by the way, that is very much at odds with the reading of that document in the 1619 lead essay.

WSWS: I'm glad you've raised Frederick Douglass. I think there's been, from some quarters, this sort of knee-jerk reaction to any criticism of the 1619 Project, and some of this has been playing out on Twitter, where one person said, "You're trying to silence black voices." But one of the ironies is that there are very few historical black voices in the entire 1619 Project. As you say, Douglass isn't there. Neither is Martin Luther King, whose name appears only in a photo caption. To say nothing of wage labor, or any attempt to present the African American experience as having to do with masses of actually existing people. Instead, the focus is on white racism as this sort of suprahistorical force.

RC: You're exactly right.

WSWS: Let me ask one more question about Lincoln. Can you explain how you see Lincoln emerging in his own time? He's not just an individual. He's a product of a time and a place.

RC: Lincoln's age was the optimum time to extol, as he himself did, the American free labor system. Lincoln embodied the social fluidity and market expansion of his era, characterized by the widening of life-chances as individuals—particularly if white and male—freed themselves from hierarchies of deference and ascribed status. Rising from a humble, hard-scrabble farming background to professional respectability and the White House, Lincoln was the quintessential self-made man, honoring self-control, self-improvement, and industriousness. His personal experiences in the aspirational village of New Salem and the growing state capital of Springfield led him to believe that, at least in the white society of the free states, barriers to success were more likely to be personal than structural. In other words, he saw himself as a beneficiary of the opportunities that the American republic, which he deemed unique in world history, offered to its inhabitants—and, by emancipatory example, to the rest of the globe.

WSWS: And in such a society of social fluidity, then slavery becomes very conspicuous.

RC: Indeed, absolutely. Lincoln's hostility to slavery, I judge, has less to do with any emotional empathy with the slave and rather more with his profound sense of the injustice of denying to the slaves the product of their labor. "By the sweat of thy brow shalt thou eat bread," was a biblical text he often invoked in his speeches during the 1850s. So slavery is at odds with the morality, with the ethical principles, of free labor.

Lincoln, of course, doesn't live to see the changes in capitalist society and the advance of corporate America after the Civil War. His career and beliefs are shaped by the broadening economic opportunities of antebellum westward expansion, by the technical developments that go along with the transportation revolution. His career also runs in parallel with the emergence of mass democratic politics. Although women and most blacks were excluded, universal white male suffrage produced the first representative mass democracy in human history. Lincoln grows to his majority in that system. And he's not only one of its beneficiaries, but one of its authors, its inventors, one of its facilitators. He has a profound faith in democracy, in the capacity of informed individuals to consider rationally where their best interests, and those of their community, lie. He encourages and manages this system and its overturning of an older, deferential politics. Lincoln, then, has experience of a society where it is possible to rise above the social status of your birth, and to hold the same rights in politics and citizenship as any other man. That's why Marx and others so admired Lincoln, why Lincoln was the darling of overseas socialists, democrats, and radicals—particularly, those in Europe who had fought and lost in the revolutions of 1848.

WSWS: An element of the presentation of American history by the 1619 Project that has a sort of deceptive plausibility, is this idea that it is only a litany of white racism for black Americans, and part of that is the undeniable fact that Reconstruction fails, and is ultimately supplanted by Jim Crow segregation. In that connection, I wanted to ask you about Lincoln's conception of freedom for the freed slaves—and perhaps it was echoed in other figures from his time, for example Frederick Douglass. And that was that if you freed the slaves, turning four million people out from slavery, freedom would now present them with the possibilities that have been available to the society more broadly. And it seems to me that they were not able to fully comprehend the social problem that would emerge, that their overriding focus was on the political questions of reunification.

RC: The question of what Lincoln would have done if he had lived, in terms, say, of extending the principles and purposes of the Homestead Act to the freedmen, is unknowable. "Forty acres and a mule" was something that a very few politicians spoke of; classical economics didn't push in that direction.

I think Lincoln clearly understood that freedom was not compromised by the intervention of a significant federal government. He understood that the federal government could do things that other forces in American society couldn't do. That it was the biggest potential economic player: hence the tariff, the call for credit facilities, internal improvements. So freedom did not mean freedom from government. It meant freedom through government—the enhancing of opportunity through the government's taking on a role which no one else could. His understanding of freedom included access to a good education. His own limited education had not been a barrier, in the end, to his achievement. But it certainly was *despite* his lack of education, not because of it, that he got to be where he ended up. So education and opportunity in a growing economy was central to his understanding of freedom. Freedom to carve out your own economic and social destiny.

Had he lived he would have had to confront the question, to what extent, in order to create a genuinely level starting point, do you have to give land to the freedmen? He certainly hadn't got to that position when he died. But Lincoln's presidency is marked by his capacity to adapt. He becomes a practical emancipationist during the war. He had always hated slavery, but he never expected to be in a position to apply those principles. So, since he saw government as an agent of citizens' freedom, as a protector of their well-being, would he have come to see that land distribution was a central part of protecting those four million freedmen? We don't know.

WSWS: One of American history's fascinating counterfactuals. I think that a problem with the historiography on Reconstruction is that the great drama of American history before the Civil War through the Civil War draws the focus to the South. But I think it tends to overlook the fact that the Civil War birthed a new society also in the North, and that the world that produced Lincoln and Douglass and Thaddeus Stevens is in its last days.

A centerpiece of your scholarship has been the role of religion in the antebellum. Could you discuss this work?

RC: The drive towards immediate emancipation among the abolitionists of the early nineteenth century, and particularly during the 1820s and 1830s, owes much to evangelical Protestant fervor. I should say, as an aside in the light of Hannah-Jones's 1619 essay, that, although there were a number of important and brave black abolitionists, taken as a whole, the abolitionist movement of the 1820s and 1830s was largely white—as it unavoidably had to be, given black numbers, status, and resources—in its membership, its sources of funding, and its agencies of agitation and propaganda.

These white reformers were moved by a powerful sense of the equal humanity of blacks, by the idea of a single Creation, and by the doctrine of disinterested benevolence, the outworking of faith through charitable action. Hence, for example, the setting up of Oberlin College, radical and biracial. This urgent thrust towards immediate emancipation surely poses a problem for those who see racial hostility as the ineradicable DNA of white America. So, too, do the targets of the antiabolitionist mobs in the 1830s. White advocates of emancipation and abolition were prepared to court martyrdom: this was the fate of Elijah Lovejoy in Alton, Illinois. The 1619 approach reads such biracial progressivism out of the country's history.

My interest in religion developed through studying slavery and antislavery. My first book dealt with trans-Atlantic religion in the nineteenth century, and in particular, the considerable impact of American revivalists in British churches, especially those of nonconformist traditions. Oberlin's Charles

Finney, for example, the premier revivalist of his day, made two trips to Britain, and his lectures circulated widely; they were even translated into Welsh. The Atlantic acted less to divide than to act as a religious bridge and market.

As a graduate student at Berkeley, I met Bill Gienapp; we became lifelong friends. Bill, drawing on the lessons of his study of the early Republican Party, urged me to carry my interest in popular religion into the political sphere. This was the genesis of my book *Evangelicals and Politics in Antebellum America.* I'm not a religious determinist, but I do see the power of different forms of religious identity, and of religious imperatives, as integral to the cultural side of politics, and to electoral mobilization. These elements, come the Civil War, help explain the sacrificial willingness to suffer on both sides.

One of the many attractive aspects of David Blight's book on Frederick Douglass is its focus on Douglass as a "prophet of freedom." There is a prevailing providentialism amongst Americans of this era: a strong sense that they are operating under God, that God intervenes in human history, and that one has to read the times in the light of God's Word. It goes some way to understanding the sources of the sacrificial imperative that I've mentioned.

WSWS: Could you explain Lincoln's attitude on religion?

RC: Lincoln had much the same troubled attitude toward the evangelicals as Jefferson. He was unimpressed by Peter Cartwright's Methodistic revivalism, as well as his Democratic politics.

WSWS: I'm thinking of the Second Inaugural, which is a wonderful speech, in which he refers to both the North and the South praying to the same God. And maybe this is one of these moments where Lincoln is being ironic?

RC: Mark Noll rightly says that the most profound theological statement of the Civil War was when Lincoln noted that both sides pray to the same God, that God cannot be on the side of both—and then reflects that "it is quite possible that God's purpose is something different from the purpose of either party." This is what he writes in a private document, "Memorandum on the Divine Will," dating from 1863 or 1864. It's significant that he now sees the Almighty as a God who mysteriously intervenes in human history, as opposed to the distant creator God, the God of reason, that he himself invoked as a young man. That was the God of Tom Paine, the clockmaker God who sets the universe in motion and then retreats, leaving the machinery to run itself.

WSWS: An autobiographical question. What inspired your interest as a young man, I believe from Wales, in the American sectional crisis, the Civil War, and Abraham Lincoln—an interest that has become an entire career?

RC: You'll not be surprised that I've often been asked that!

I grew up in a mining valley in southeast Wales. Coal mining is inevitably part of the family's past. My great-grandmother was a first cousin of the mother of John L. Lewis, the Welsh American miners' leader. His grave is just a stone's throw from Lincoln's tomb in Springfield. My father, son of a miner, was a high school history teacher. I enjoyed history above all other subjects in my pre-university years, but I didn't meet US history until my final year as an Oxford undergraduate in 1967–68. Don Fehrenbacher was, that year, the visiting Harmsworth Professor. Alongside Oxford's amateur, but gifted, Americanists, he taught the course "Slavery and Secession," which Allan Nevins had designed when he had been the Harmsworth Professor some years earlier.

That was a life-changing experience. It drew me into that complex of moral, economic, and political issues through a mountain of compelling primary sources, including Lincoln's speeches, and a rich historiography, including some of the great books on American history, not least Fehrenbacher's *Prelude to Greatness*, Kenneth Stampp's *Peculiar Institution*, David Potter's *Lincoln and His Party in the Secession Crisis*, and James Randall's multivolume life of Lincoln. I was hooked. When I got a permanent post at the University of Sheffield in 1971, to teach "US History 1776–1877," I devised courses on the opposition to slavery and on the coming of the Civil War, so Lincoln was a salient figure in my teaching. My research interests, however, as I've explained, lay in evangelical Protestantism and the intersection of religion and politics in antebellum America. I had no plan to become a Lincolnian until I was asked by the publisher Longman to write a short analytical study of Lincoln, his politics, and his use of power. That was in 1987, but I didn't start work on the book until the mid-1990s. By then Longman had been taken over by Pearson and they wanted a longer study. I was happy with that!

WSWS: Are you working on any new research?

RC: My current project is a study of the diverse American religious nationalisms before and during the Civil War. Religion was not, of course, the only element in shaping the identities on which American nationalism was constructed in the young republic: economic interest, race, ethnicity, and social class played vital roles, too. Religion, however, gave moral energy and conviction to the various ways in which Americans defined themselves individually and collectively. The United States' unique separation of church and state, the religious pluralism of the new nation, and the decentralised political framework of 1787 left the country's disparate religious traditions and communities free to champion competing and conflicting routes to national righteousness. As a dynamic but divided cultural force, American religion functioned both to advance and inhibit national integration, playing a critical role in the United States' evolution from the fragile republic of 1776 to the Union fractured by civil war. That conflict took on the character of a holy war, with North and South defining their nationality in religious terms. Both sides characterized the conflict as a providential struggle, and mobilized support on that basis. Confederates strove to prevent the "perversion of our holy religion"; Unionists declared that they contended against "proslavery atheism." The triumph of a Yankee Protestant understanding of national righteousness in 1865 would prove neither complete nor unquestioned: Confederate religious nationalism survived and even flourished after Appomattox.

Clayborne Carson

Clayborne Carson

Clayborne Carson is the Martin Luther King, Jr., Centennial Professor of History at Stanford University and Ronnie Lott Founding Director of the Martin Luther King, Jr., Research and Education Institute. His *In Struggle: SNCC and the Black Awakening of the 1960s* was awarded the Frederick Jackson Turner Award. Carson is editor of *The Autobiography of Martin Luther King, Jr.*, and was senior academic adviser to the documentary *Eyes on the Prize.*

WSWS: Could you start by telling us something about your background? Because as I understand it, you're not only a leading scholar of Martin Luther King Jr. and the civil rights movement, but are yourself a veteran of that movement?

Clayborne Carson: Yes, I was at the March on Washington [in 1963] and I knew Stokely Carmichael for most of his adult life. I was much more closely connected to the Student Non-Violent Coordinating Committee (SNCC) than to King. My first book was on SNCC. So, I kind of come at this from the point of view of grassroots movements being the heart of the movement, rather than King being this charismatic leader at the top.

WSWS: I'd like to ask you something that we've been asking all the historians with whom we've been speaking. Were you approached by the authors of the 1619 Project as it was being prepared, or prior to its publication?

Thomas Mackaman, "An interview with historian Clayborne Carson on the New York Times' 1619 Project," World Socialist Web Site, January 15, 2020.

CC: No, no I wasn't, which is strange, because if you go to our website, we have a lot of educational materials for schools. So, I wasn't approached as a historian, but I'm also an educator engaged in online teaching, trying, as much as possible, to get free material in the hands of students. I would have loved to work with the *New York Times*, with all of their clout and resources, to make a change in terms of how American history is taught in the schools.[1]

I just think that part of the problem of this whole project is that they did not really approach this as a collaborative activity involving historians, educators, and journalists. It seems quite obvious that the number of people involved in the actual process was quite limited.

WSWS: It also seems that it was written to a preconceived determination, and that historians who might have a somewhat different take were avoided. It's also not clear to whom they did speak. The editor in chief, Jake Silverstein, in his reply to the five historians, said that they spoke to a group of African American scholars, but they didn't say who was in that group.

CC: Yes, and that was a little bit strange. If I were called in to have a meeting at the *New York Times* and they told me they'd like to do this project to make people more aware of the deep roots of African American history within American history and the importance of 1619, I would have said fine, that sounds wonderful, how can I help? I can understand, however, why some scholars would be reluctant because of the work that should go into something like this. I was very much involved in *Eyes on the Prize*, for example.

WSWS: Right, you were the senior academic adviser for *Eyes on the Prize*?

CC: I was one of four. That was a three-year commitment. We met regularly for three years to produce that series. There was a lot of research, the selection of whom to interview. We had what we called "the school," and at every stage the filmmakers would come in with footage, and we would critique it: "Well, why didn't you interview this person? Why didn't you ask that question?" It was an interactive process for three years to get that on the air. On 1619, I'm just not sure on a lot of the factual background of this, and maybe you're trying to figure that out, too.

WSWS: *Eyes on the Prize* is a real achievement, and the immense amount of work that went into it is clear. With 1619, you think about the orientation of this project to school children, and its problems become all the more glaring.

---

1. For educational resources from the Martin Luther King Institute: https://kinginstitute. stanford.edu/information-teachers

And that it didn't talk to eminent historians might be more pardonable if it were not also claiming to be imposing an entirely new narrative on American history, and a new curriculum in the schools. What you say about *Eyes on the Prize* is interesting. You get the impression that the 1619 Project was pulled together quickly.

CC: Yes, that's what I would compare it to. Henry Hampton was the guiding force behind *Eyes on the Prize*. One of the things that happened was that the scholars got together before the filmmakers arrived. So, from the very beginning, that's why we called it a school. The filmmakers came in, and we had a number of discussions right at the start of the process, before any filming was done.

One result of those early discussions was to answer the question, do you tell this as a story about King? Or do you tell it the way most of us wanted it told, that King was important, but he was the *result* of a movement, not the *cause* of the movement? The bus boycott in Montgomery would have happened even if King had never been born. It was already a successful movement before he became the leader of it. Similarly, with the sit-ins, and the Freedom Rides, and the voting rights campaign. In all of these cases, King was the beneficiary of movements he didn't start. That's not to deny the importance of Martin Luther King. I've spent the last thirty years researching him. But it does put his contribution in context.

WSWS: King's ninety-first birthday is coming up. He was born a little more than a half century after the Civil War, and it's been a little more than a half century since his assassination. You've explained that he was the product of a movement, not its creator, but I wanted to ask you more about what went into his formation as a leader. I don't know if that question is better approached by considering King's historical antecedents, or by assessing just what the civil rights movement was.

CC: The course I've taught for many years at Stanford is not called "The Civil Rights Movement." I avoid that term. Because when did it begin, and when did it end? There's no date that you can give me that clarifies this. Was it the founding of the NAACP in 1909? Did it end in 1965 or 1968? What's going on with the suppression of the Voting Rights Act right now?

The term I prefer is the modern African American freedom struggle. Then you can say that that struggle has been going on since the beginning of the African presence in America, and is still going on today. But we can choose to look at a certain period when it was possible to build a mass movement and when there were major civil rights reforms. That doesn't mean that the movement started then. It just means that for a very brief period of time it was successful. It was able to get major changes and end the legal system in the 1960s. And that was an enormous achievement.

WSWS: And we're speaking of a mass movement, are we not, when we're talking about the 1960s?

CC: It becomes mass in certain places at that time, particularly in the South. That's the difference between then and now. There was a mass movement that was directed against legalized segregation in the South. And after that there was this recognition that a lot of these problems were not limited to the South. You had a massive movement in Chicago, in New York, in Los Angeles, where I was. So, if we see this in terms of continuity, rather than saying "back in Civil Rights Days," it just gives you a more honest picture.

It's just like saying the antislavery movement had certain periods where it achieved major victories. But the antislavery movement was going on from the Stono Rebellion of the early eighteenth century. The antislavery movement was going on from the time there were enough slaves here to mobilize a movement. So, you have rebellion, and you have freedom struggles. If your focus is on when and how do freedom struggles occur throughout history, then that's an important topic to take up. What are the circumstances that led to them?

That kind of gets back to the 1619 Project. A lot of their focus seems to be the founding of the United States as a nation. The way I would look at that, is that at that time, for a variety of reasons, you have a predominant group, white men, beginning to articulate a human rights ideal. We can study why that happened when it happened. It had to do with the Enlightenment, the spread of literacy, the rise of working-class movements. All of these factors led people to start talking in terms of human rights. It was both an intellectual movement from the top down and a freedom struggle from the bottom up. People begin to speak in terms of rights: that I, we, have rights that other people should respect. The emergence of that is important.

And it does affect African Americans. We know that from Benjamin Banneker and lots of other black people who realized that white people were talking about rights, and said, "Well, we have rights too." That's an important development in history, and an approach to history that doesn't say we should privilege only the rights talk of white people. There's always a dialogue between that and oppressed people. You have to tell the story from the top down, that intellectuals began to articulate the notion of rights. But simultaneously, non-elites are doing that—working-class people, black people, colonized people.

There were three nations that came out of the spread of literacy and Enlightenment ideals. Usually the focus is on the United States and France. But Haiti came out of that as well. That often gets overlooked.

WSWS: I agree with you. I think one of the things that is missing in the lead essay by Nikole Hannah-Jones is any appreciation of the power of the contradiction that was introduced in 1776 with the proclamation of human equality, and also the impact of the Revolution itself. I thought in our interview with Gordon Wood he took that question up very effectively, pointing out that slavery became very conspicuous as a result of the Revolution. Also disregarded is the Afro-Caribbean historian Eric Williams, who analyzed the impact of the American Revolution on the demise of slavery. Instead, the Revolution is presented as a conspiracy to perpetuate slavery.

CC: Yes, and it's wonderful to concentrate on that contradiction because that to me explains Frederick Douglass, it explains King. What all of these people were united on was to expose that contradiction—and we should always keep exposing it—the contradiction between the self-image of the United States as a free and democratic country and the reality that it's not. If you are a black leader, your job is to expose that contradiction. If you go through a list of all the great orations in African American history, nearly all of them focus on that. They want to expose that and use that contradiction.

WSWS: I'm glad you mentioned Douglass and King. Richard Carwardine, in our interview with him, said that he was struck by the absence of Douglass, whose name does not appear in the lead essay or anywhere else. The same is true of King, whose name appears only once, in a photo caption. The civil rights movement is barely mentioned. Black power and Malcolm X are absent. The list of what's left out is astonishing—no A. Philip Randolph, no Harlem Renaissance. But I wanted to ask you about the absence of King, and any significant attention to the civil rights movement, and what you make of that.

CC: I think that's the saddest part of this, that the response of the *New York Times* is simply to defend their project. Rather than to say, "We welcome the critique, let's work with you to see what we can do." Obviously, this would have been better done a year ago, two years ago, but it's never too late. And particularly if the purpose of this is to have an impact on the way young people are educated. I'm very concerned about that.

I call our education program The Liberation Curriculum. I see it as a way of encouraging people to see themselves as rights bearers and right declarers. One way of looking at the founding of this country is to understand the audacity of a few hundred white male elites getting together and declaring a country—and declaring it a country based on the notion of human rights.

Obviously, they were being hypocritical, but it's also audacious. And that's what rights are all about. It is the history of people saying, "I declare that I have the right to determine my destiny, and we collectively have the right to determine our destiny." That's the history of every movement, every freedom movement in the history of the world. At some point you have to get to that point where you have to say that, publicly, and fight for it. At various points women have done that. Just in our lifetime gay people have done that, and raised what would have been astounding to people fifty years ago or one hundred years ago.

So, the question is how do you move someone from acquiescence in their own oppression to that audacious statement of, "We have the right to determine our own future? We have the right to participate in the decisions that affect our lives"? In a way, if they can do that, that simple declaration is a statement of freedom. Of course, backing it up with something other than a declaration is kind of necessary! To have the power to *make* someone listen.

WSWS: The American Revolution was a revolution that drew on masses of people, ultimately, and so too the Civil War, which going all the way back to the Progressive historians has been called "The Second American Revolution." And in terms of mass movements, the freedom struggle, as you call it, is certainly among the most important in American history. You raise an important point, the decisive question of why some things happen *when* they happen. So, one hundred years after the Civil War this mass movement of very oppressed people takes place in the American South, and then, as you said, it also grips the big cities. Why does it happen when it happens? Why in the 1960s?

CC: I would argue that freedom struggles are always going on. All you have to do is look for them carefully and you will see that at the grassroots level they are always going on. But the question is when can they develop power? Well a lot of that is changes that, by nature, are gradual.

Among the most important changes leading to the articulation of rights was the spread of literacy. As people became more literate it became harder to dominate them. Literacy in the African American tradition, from Frederick Douglass learning to read, to Malcolm X being in jail and learning to read the dictionary—literacy is itself a freedom. One of the commonalities of oppressed people is that they get all of their information through people who dominate them.

For most of human history, people never got more than twenty miles from where they were born. They knew very little of the world. There was no way of overcoming that until you could get to the point where you could read. That was often purposeful. Dominant people wanted to control information. You don't want people working for you to know that they can walk twenty miles and find better conditions. Of course, you can also mystify them by religion and say, there's this sacred book. You can't read it, but I can interpret it for you, and tell you what your role in society is. So, literacy is huge.

So is mobility. Just think of the impact on the whole notion of labor when workers in Europe began to move from place to place building the cathedrals. They learned by moving to a new place that conditions could be better. That's why there was a huge movement to put up gates at the outskirts of Paris and other cities, because they knew that once you got in the city you could negotiate with whoever wants your labor. So, literacy, mobility. But the commonality of it is just being able to not be enslaved by ignorance.

I remember doing an interview with one of the young people who launched the sit-ins, I think it was David Richmond[2] And he said to me, one of the important experiences was just visiting the North. He came back to the South and asked himself, "Why am I putting up with this?" The whole world is not like this. So, mobility, literacy, being able to expand your frame of reference.

WSWS: Those are important points. I suppose it's not accidental that the civil rights movement—and you've problematized that term for me, so I should say in its 1950s and 1960s iteration—emerges in cities in the South, in Birmingham and Montgomery.

CC: Exactly. And it emerges among college students. That is another important factor. Of course, there's no commonality in education itself. It can be education to continue slavery, or it can be education to liberate yourself. That's why I call our material a liberation curriculum. That is, how do you educate people to imagine that a better world is possible than the one you are a part of? And once you've done that for enough people, you have a lot of discontent that can be mobilized.

---

2. Richmond (1941–1990) was one of the "Greensboro Four," who staged a sit-in at Woolworth's "Whites Only" lunch counter in downtown Greensboro, North Carolina in 1960—eds.

One of the things that strikes me is that so much of any oppressive world is built on mystification. Just think of how many people assume that corporations are something that was not invented. Haven't we always had them? So, you have this entire legal structure that maintains wealth, and not only just maintains it, but mystifies it. We can't know how this happened that—what is it now, one hundred people? Or five hundred people?—Have $6 trillion worth of wealth? How is that even conceivable? That level of concentration didn't even exist in the Gilded Age.

WSWS: Let me ask you a little bit more about King, and what went into his formation. I suppose the common knowledge, so to speak, is that it's Baptism and Gandhi.

CC: Both Gandhi and King were Enlightenment figures in the same way Toussaint L'Ouverture was. They are seeing the possibilities in this movement, that in their time, is dominated by white males. What they did in their most profound speeches and writings—for Gandhi it's in his writings, and for King it's more in his speeches—is to say, why should it be limited to that? If there is this notion, this ideal, that every human being has certain rights that other human beings should respect, and if a couple hundred white men can go into a room in Philadelphia and create a nation, why can't we declare we want another kind of nation? That we want a different kind of society? And the only thing that's really stopping that is our own imagination.

King does this in his most famous speeches, starting with Montgomery. You have this movement that is a bus boycott. We want to sit wherever we want on a bus. So that's a very concrete right, and Rosa Parks asserted that. Then they organize a boycott. And King is asked to be the leader of it. He gives his first speech, and what does he do? He says, you may think what you're doing is fighting for a seat at the front of the bus, but I'm here to tell you that you're fighting for human rights, you're fighting for the Declaration of Independence, the Sermon on the Mount. In his first speech he lays it all out: This is not about a seat at the front of the bus. It's about much more than that. Use your imagination.

He was very good at doing that. When I saw him at the March on Washington, it was the same thing. Most of us were there for the Kennedy Civil Rights Bill. We hadn't seen it and didn't even know what it was. And what he does in that speech is he doesn't even mention the pending legislation. He goes back to human rights, to that ideal expressed in the Declaration of Independence, back to those kinds of things, just like Frederick Douglass would have done. It's about your own liberation. It's not about the right to sit at the lunch counter. And that's what becomes inspiring.

Because, quite frankly, those are people for whom the *immediate* goal is not worth the sacrifice. Just think of all those people walking through the rain in Montgomery trying to get to their jobs for 381 days. It's about something more than that. It's about our own liberation.

WSWS: Why was it that the historian C. Vann Woodward's *Strange Career of Jim Crow* was considered a "bible" of the movement? I believe that King paraphrased from it extensively at the end of the Selma to Montgomery march. King said in a portion of that speech, "And as the noted historian, C. Vann Woodward ... clearly points out, the segregation of the races was really a political stratagem employed by the emerging Bourbon interests in the South to keep the Southern masses divided and Southern labor the cheapest in the land."[3]

CC: My understanding is that one of the reasons why Woodward called it *The Strange Career of Jim Crow* is the point that segregation is something artificially imposed rather than the natural course of Southern history. He was saying that segregation was not seen as an essential part of white domination in the South. The slaves weren't segregated from the master—they were dominated. But it's precisely when slavery ended that you needed this public manifestation of the separation of the races.

There was a generalization, which had some truth to it before the civil rights reforms, that in the South white people don't care how close black people get as long as they don't get too high; but in the North, people don't care how high black people get as long as they don't get too close. We associate the system with the overall system of white domination, but it was simply one expression of it that became more and more common in the late nineteenth century, in response to challenges to white political domination.

WSWS: King was, by the standards of African American leaders today, very left in his politics, opposing the Vietnam War and launching his interracial Poor People's Campaign in the final years before his assassination. Is it correct that he understood himself as a social democrat?

---

3. Martin Luther King Jr. Address at the Conclusion of the Selma to Montgomery March, March 25, 1965, https://kinginstitute.stanford.edu/king-papers/documents/address-conclusion-selma-montgomery-march

CC: Well, I edited a book called *The Autobiography of Martin Luther King*. You might look at that. It's not like a secret. On their first date King told Coretta he was a socialist.

Coretta was at the Progressive Party Convention in 1948. She was an acquaintance of Paul Robeson. One of the things I'm writing about is her relationship to King. When they are dating back in 1952, she sends him a copy of Edward Bellamy's *Looking Backward* and King writes her about how impressed he is by Bellamy's ideas. So, King says something along the lines of, that's what he's going to base his ministry on and that he looks forward to the day when there will be a nationalization of industry. This is 1952.

WSWS: Right at the height of the McCarthyite Red Scare.

CC: Exactly.

WSWS: And you knew Coretta Scott King? Because I think, in general, the media portrayal of her is a grieving widow, but an intellectual non-entity.

CC: Have you ever heard of Women's International Strike for Peace? In 1962 she goes to a peace conference in Geneva, and this is followed by the first major women's march in Washington, which she participates in. By the time the Vietnam War becomes more intense, she's already taken a stand, and long before Martin did. I think that she's way underestimated, in terms of her impact. She has her own FBI file, by the way. She was investigated by the FBI from the 1950s on. They were very worried about Women's International Strike for Peace because most of the women around the world who supported it were socialists, communists.

WSWS: And King's opposition to the Vietnam War, which seems relevant given the US war drive against Iran?

CC: Next week we plan to play a recording, a new recording, of his Riverside Speech. We were able to find a recording that was better than that which was available. It was at Riverside Church but for some reason it wasn't the one circulated. It was recorded from his microphone, so it doesn't have any of the background noise. It's very interesting to listen to it today.[4]

---

4. King delivered his "Riverside Speech," also called "Beyond Vietnam," on April 4, 1967, at Riverside Church in New York. King referred to the war as "madness" that created "a hell for the poor," and called the American forces "strange liberators." Three days later the *New York Times* issued an editorial condemning King ("Dr. King's Error," April 7, 1967) for "slander" against US military practices in the war and for broaching the connection between the cost of the war and the depletion of social reform programs.

Dolores Janiewski

Dolores Janiewski

Dolores Janiewski is Associate Professor in the School of History, Philosophy, Political Science, and International Relations at Victoria University of Wellington, New Zealand. She is the author of *Sisterhood Denied: Race, Gender, and Class in a New South Community* and *Subversive Sisterhood: Black Women and Unions in the Southern Tobacco Industry*.

WSWS: What is your overall response to the 1619 Project and particularly the way it leaves out the class struggle in the United States?

Dolores Janiewski: That's been one of the submerged things in American thinking for a terribly long time. Identity politics in the recent period has buried class under race and gender, and so forth. I was an intersectional person before the word got invented, because I was writing about race, gender, and class in the 1970s.

I went through the two main articles in the 1619 Project, and what I was immediately struck by from the beginning is it leaves out indigenous people. It starts with slavery in 1619. Hannah-Jones only has one or two paragraphs about the Indians getting removed from Georgia. But in the course I've just been teaching, in 1512, the leader of the Taino people in the Caribbean was burned at the stake for leading an indigenous rebellion against the Spanish.

Part of the way capitalism develops in North America is about dispossession. That's also true in the British Isles, dispossessing the Highlanders, dispossessing the Irish. The first plantations are actually in Ireland. The British take

Tom Peters and John Braddock, "An interview with historian Dolores Janiewski on the New York Times' 1619 Project," World Socialist Web Site, December 23, 2019.

over and deprive the peasants of the land. It's a much more complicated story than reducing it down to slavery being the engine of capitalism.

WSWS: Slavery is also narrowed down. Hannah-Jones claims that slavery has always existed, but in the US it's special.

DJ: Yes, it's an exceptionalist, US original sin story. She ignores slavery in Cuba, Brazil, other places. And if you want to talk about original sin, America has many original sins, one of them is the dispossession of the indigenous people.

WSWS: She uses the expression that slavery is part of America's DNA.

DJ: It's somewhat of an ahistorical concept. A lot of the colonizing in America was because those people were driven off the land in Europe. They're indentured servants. Two-thirds of the people who crossed the Atlantic in the first two hundred years are unfree. Some of them are indentured and some of them are slaves.

A really good book by Edmund Morgan called *American Slavery, American Freedom*, which Hannah-Jones doesn't seem to look at, is about how, in the first period, they don't have permanent slavery. So those people coming in 1619 are, in some sense, treated like indentureds. Eventually they can become free along with the indentured white people, and then they become problems. The poor people, black and white, share common interests.

By the late 1600s, the wealthy Virginia planters start passing laws to distinguish between black and white, and they create permanent slavery for the African that will be inherited by the children. They make race a privilege: a sign of freedom versus slavery. They change the laws to break up those alliances between poor whites and poor blacks. And they treat women differently: white women are assumed not to have to work in the field as part of that new set of laws, and black women are assumed as laborers.

Slavery isn't a fully developed system from 1619; it evolves. Likewise, Indians were initially seen as whites, and then, by the 1850s, they're seen as "redskins." So, race is an evolving system developed by people with an economic stake in evolving it.

WSWS: Hannah-Jones says that after the Civil War, "White southerners of all economic classes ... experienced substantial improvement in their lives even as they forced black people back into a quasi-slavery."[1] What do you make of these statements about this period?

---

1. The *New York Times Magazine*, August 18, 2019, p. 21.

DJ: Well, it's a pretty broad generalization. If you're talking about economics, the Southern income is half of the national average at 1900. The South doesn't really recover from the destruction of the Civil War. In the 1930s, poverty in the South is one of the major problems for Roosevelt. So, it's not true that every white person's life improved. In some sense, poverty helped to entrench the racial system over time, because you had one thing that made you better: being white. It wasn't that you were economically, necessarily, better off. The ideology of white skin privilege was part of the system, but it doesn't mean in material fact that was actually the case.

WSWS: Can you talk about the development of unions and class conflict in the early twentieth century in the South? Were there attempts to integrate black and white workers' struggles?

DJ: In terms of unions, there were attempts in the 1890s that didn't last very long, and then in about 1919–1920 another effort, and that was largely destroyed. I looked at textile executives' papers at the University of North Carolina, and they were using various methods, including the Ku Klux Klan, industrial spies, and things like that against the workers.

Then in the 1930s, because of the New Deal, you start having CIO unions in the textile industry, and I interviewed several union stalwarts from that time. The textile industry was organized on a racially segregated basis and there's almost no place for black labor except unpacking bales of cotton and other forms of "outside" work in the factory yard. Tobacco is a more stratified labor system. I went on a tour of a cigarette factory when I was doing my thesis, and you could still see the hierarchy. The black people were pushing the brooms and the white women were doing the cigarette machines, and the white men were the machinists. So, there was a racial and gender hierarchy. Black women did the preparation of the leaf, the dustiest and dirtiest job.

The tobacco industry was organized on a segregated basis by the AFL; they had a black local and a white local. But in Winston-Salem, there was a CIO tobacco workers' union. The CIO was much more progressive on racial matters, and there was a leftist organizer, a Communist. He decided, after serving in World War II, that he was going to organize in the factories. They organized a much more progressive union with black workers, but they had trouble getting white workers. Then he gets redbaited and loses all capacity to have any job, and eventually he sets up a nursery in Greensboro, North Carolina.

WSWS: So, the employers saw the unity of black and white workers as a real threat?

DJ: Yes, divide and rule is a common technique. Different industries did it in various ways. The steel industry hired lots of different ethnic groups so they couldn't speak the same language. That was quite useful. There's a picture of Uncle Sam, after the great steel strike of 1919, saying "go back to work!" in about twelve languages.

In North Carolina there was an attempt at organizing black and white farmers in the 1890s, under the Farmers Alliance. They formed a Fusion ticket and they won the state government. It was a Republican-Populist alliance. Blacks and whites were working together, but blacks were mostly in the Republican Party and whites were mostly in the Populist Party.

In response to that, in 1898, the Democrats start whipping up calls for a "white man's government." There was a black newspaper in Wilmington, North Carolina, and it had an editorial suggesting that white women weren't always so hostile to black men, and that created this big outrage, you know, "How dare he, how dare he!" The white newspapers kept talking about the editor besmirching the morality of white women.

They also had guns, and threatened any African American who'd actually tried to vote in the 1898 election. The Republicans and Populists managed to win the election and then a mob marches on the black newspaper in Wilmington, and on the black community, and we don't know how many people get killed. That overturns that city government.

So, blacks had some political rights up until 1898. It's not the full story that after the Civil War everything collapses. But it was pretty systematic from 1890 onwards. In different states there are these ways of driving blacks out of the political system, starting with Mississippi in 1890. But in North Carolina it takes this major upheaval in 1898. Then, in 1900 they passed a constitutional amendment that you cannot vote if you're illiterate unless your grandfather could vote in 1867. Then you have segregation and all the rest.

There were still people who were critical of it and opposing it. Then, in the 1930s, the Communists and others in the CIO wanted to prevent workers being divided on racial matters.

WSWS: The *Times* doesn't talk about the CIO.

DJ: They're sort of running roughshod over a lot of history in a few paragraphs. It's not an in-depth analysis.

WSWS: Writing about the beginning of the civil rights struggle, Hannah-Jones says, "For the most part, black Americans fought back alone."[2]

DJ: Well, of course that isn't completely the truth. The tobacco workers union was involved in organizing in South Carolina in 1945 and the song that they're singing as they march on their picket line is "We Shall Overcome," which is then taken to a labor history training center called Highlander, and it becomes the song of the civil rights movement. A lot of the labor activists become civil rights activists. There is an interaction between them. Bob Korstad has written about how these two movements merged in a book called *Civil Rights Unionism*.

There were Communists in the 1930s defending the rights of blacks in one way or another, but there were also relatively progressive whites, Christians, and people criticising racism. So, it's not just blacks alone.

The NAACP [National Association for the Advancement of Colored People] was founded by a group of progressive whites and blacks in the North. In North Carolina in the late Reconstruction era, Albion Tourgée, a white progressive from the South, tried to organize poor whites and blacks for the Republican Party in 1868, helped write a nonracial state constitution, then became a judge and had poor whites and blacks as his allies. Then, systematically, the Klan lynched a poor white activist, lynched some of the blacks he knew, and then tried to assassinate Tourgée. Ultimately, he's forced out of North Carolina in 1878. He then wrote an antilynching column, he tried to challenge segregation in the Supreme Court, then he helped to create the predecessor to the NAACP.

There are probably about twenty thousand blacks who are killed and five thousand whites who are killed in this Reconstruction period by the Klan and those kinds of groups. It's like death squads in Latin America; you go after activists and organizers using terror. White activists were seen as race traitors.

WSWS: Did any trade unionists who attempted an integrated struggle have any success?

DJ: There was a short period. You can look at Bob Korstad's book on what happened with his father's organizing in Winston-Salem. That union was fairly progressive. But the other union, the AFL affiliate, started raiding, because of the Taft-Hartley Act of 1947. Those unions that don't sign affidavits and get rid of their communists are no longer protected by the labor law. So, there are

2. Ibid., p. 24.

times when there are efforts. But the use of race and anticommunism together are very effective.

WSWS: That's an interesting connection that you make, that the segregationists used anticommunism as a weapon.

DJ: Because communists had been progressive on the race question, and anyone who's interested in racial equality is by definition a subversive. This goes back to the Red Scare of 1919, when you have the first Communist parties and the Bolsheviks have just had the revolution, and those people like A. Philip Randolph and Chandler Owen are editing a socialist paper in Harlem. They get targeted. There's a New York State Senate committee investigating communism in 1919–20 and they target those people in the North.

Randolph goes on to help form the Brotherhood of Sleeping Car Porters union. He's the one in 1941 who organizes for a march on Washington and he tells Roosevelt: "Unless you desegregate the war plants, we'll march," and Roosevelt issues an order to desegregate war plants in the North. So, the war allows blacks to go into the automobile industry and others; that is very important in terms of wages.

The NAACP has about eight thousand members before the war. After the war they get 400,000 members and they start the legal battle that leads to the *Brown v. Board of Education* decision. Veterans came home determined to fight against segregation. The war itself, and Nazi Germany, made racism look somewhat suspect, and so you have a period where a lot of Americans are embarrassed that in a big part of their country, blacks can't vote. So, in the 1950s and '60s, there are some kinds of changes. Tobacco workers I interviewed who came back from the war were very determined to fight segregation.

There was a big union presence in the 1963 March on Washington, which in some sense was repeating what Randolph threatened to do. King, when he's killed in Memphis, he's there to support organizing garbage workers. The UAW [United Auto Workers], one of the CIO unions, helped to organize the March on Washington in 1963.

WSWS: The 1619 Project jumps over Martin Luther King. He's just absent.

DJ: There's a lot of absences in there.

WSWS: To them it is simply blacks versus whites.

DJ: They're imposing identity politics all the way back. And in certain times, people don't even think in terms of categories of white and black. They have to be taught that skin color is significant. Racial identity politics is real in terms of what it does to you, but also unreal because it has no actual scientific basis, although some people keep trying to reinvent it over and over again. Saying racism is in America's "DNA," I don't think Hannah-Jones really meant it, I think that's just a metaphor. But still, it's using a genetic explanation for this stuff, which isn't necessarily true.

* * * * *

Dolores Janiewski also described some of her personal experiences growing up during the civil rights struggle.

DJ: My family were the town liberals in Okeechobee, Florida, and my mother would talk about poor whites, the ones who didn't have shoes and had never left the county. She was a great teacher and she would take kids to the ocean, which was thirty-six miles away; they'd never seen the ocean. She was a New Deal liberal, French Canadian, relatively enlightened in racial and class terms; she organized a teachers union and tried to integrate the schools and make sure black teachers didn't lose their jobs. She took it upon herself to do those kinds of things. She created a stir one day when she called the black principal "mister." That was a no-no, to give a black man a title of respect. She was an oppositionist and she was trying to educate us.

My sister and I tore down Klan posters in the park, I think when I was twelve, around 1960 or thereabouts. It said, "Be a Man, Join the Klan." There was a post office box address, so I wrote a letter to the Klan to denounce them, saying, "You're not men!" The deputy sheriff was supposed to be head of the Klan, which was very typical in the South. I kept looking out the front door to see if there was a burning cross.

The Klan threatened to bomb the high school where my mother was working together with black teachers. We were doing a literacy project with black children and we were forced to move to the Episcopal church. Then we were accused of stealing hymn books, so we were forced to move to the black part of town. I took some black children into the local public library and the librarian was not pleased with me. But I thought they deserved to go there.

When I went to Tallahassee, to Florida State University, we did Freedom Schools: setting up schools for black children to teach real history. We went to the black university too. That was one of our subversive activities.

It was a pretty repressive regime in much of the South, and violent too. Those three civil rights workers who were killed—James Chaney, Andrew

Goodman, and Michael Schwerner—part of why they were killed was because it was two white guys with a black guy.

WSWS: Were there connections and overlaps between the antiwar movement and the civil rights movement?

DJ: Certainly. The fact that African Americans were a large share of those who were fighting and dying in Vietnam, Martin Luther King made that connection when he came out against the war in 1967. He talked about how the US was spending $200,000 or $300,000 for every enemy killed, and about $50 for every poor person. That was when he was starting to organize the Poor People's Campaign. So certainly, there were people who were making the connection. Cassius Clay, before he became Muhammad Ali, said, "The Viet Cong never called me 'nigger.'"

In Southern states, at universities like Duke University in North Carolina, where I did my PhD, there were progressive whites who held vigils against the war. They were called the Southern Organizing Committee, which was linked to the SDS [Students for a Democratic Society].

Part III

Polemics

An Analysis of the *New York Times'* Reply to Five Historians

On December 20, 2019, the *New York Times* replied to a letter signed by five prominent historians requesting that the *Times* correct the historical falsifications upon which the 1619 Project, launched in August 2019, is based.

This is the *Times'* first public response to the interviews of four of the letter's signatories, Victoria Bynum, James McPherson, James Oakes, and Gordon Wood, on the World Socialist Web Site. The fifth signatory, Sean Wilentz, published a separate critique of the 1619 Project in the *New York Review of Books*.

The historians are among the most widely read and respected authorities on US history. Together, they have dedicated a combined 250 years to analyzing the American Revolution, the Civil War, and Reconstruction.

The five signatories assert their "strong reservations about important aspects of the 1619 Project," and state they "are dismayed at some of the factual errors in the project and the closed process behind it." The scholars continue:

> These errors, which concern major events, cannot be described as interpretation or "framing." They are matters of verifiable fact, which are the foundation of both honest scholarship and honest journalism. They suggest a displacement of historical understanding by ideology. Dismissal of objections on racial grounds—that they are the objections of only "white historians"—has affirmed that displacement.

The signatories focus on the central falsification:

David North and Eric London, "The 1619 Project and the falsification of history: An analysis of the New York Times' reply to five historians," World Socialist Web Site, December 28, 2019.

The Times asserts that the founders declared the colonies' independence of Britain "in order to ensure slavery would continue." This is not true. If supportable, the allegation would be astounding—yet every statement offered by the project to validate it is false.

The signatories state:

> Still other material is misleading. The project criticizes Abraham Lincoln's views on racial equality but ignores his conviction that the Declaration of Independence proclaimed universal equality, for blacks as well as whites, a view he upheld repeatedly against powerful white supremacists who opposed him. The project also ignores Lincoln's agreement with Frederick Douglass that the Constitution was, in Douglass's words, "a GLORIOUS LIBERTY DOCUMENT." Instead, the project asserts that the United States was founded on racial slavery, an argument rejected by a majority of abolitionists and proclaimed by champions of slavery like John C. Calhoun.

Further, the historians raise troubling questions about how the *Times* produced the project, writing:

> The process remains opaque. The names of only some of the historians involved have been released, and the extent of their involvement as "consultants" and fact checkers remains vague. The selective transparency deepens our concern.

The signatories conclude:

> We ask that The Times, according to its own high standards of accuracy and truth, issue prominent corrections of all the errors and distortions presented in The 1619 Project. We also ask for the removal of these mistakes from any materials destined for use in schools, as well as in all further publications, including books bearing the name of The New York Times. We ask finally that The Times reveal fully the process through which the historical materials were and continue to be assembled, checked and authenticated.[1]

---

1. The historians' letter is contained within the *New York Times'* response. The *New York Times Magazine*, December 20, 2019. Accessed on 12/9/2020: https://www.nytimes.com/2019/12/20/magazine/we-respond-to-the-historians-who-critiqued-the-1619-project.html

The *New York Times Magazine* editor in chief, Jake Silverstein, rejected the historians' objections, and refuses to correct the mistakes or explain the process leading to the publication of the 1619 Project essays.

"We are familiar," writes Silverstein, "with the objections of the letter writers, as four of them have been interviewed in recent months by the World Socialist Web Site."

He continues:

> The project was intended to address the marginalization of African-American history in the telling of our national story and examine the legacy of slavery in contemporary American life. We are not ourselves historians, it is true. We are journalists, trained to look at current events and situations and ask the question: Why is this the way it is?[2]

Silverstein's response to questions raised by the historians about the background of the 1619 Project is evasive and disingenuous. The 1619 Project is not merely a journalistic endeavor. It was launched by the *Times* with the explicitly declared intention of fundamentally changing the teaching and understanding of the history of the United States. The introduction to the project states that its purpose is to "reframe the country's history, understanding 1619 as our true founding, and placing the consequences of slavery and the contributions of black Americans at the very center of the story we tell ourselves about who we are."[3]

The articles published in the *New York Times Magazine* are only the first salvos of a broader campaign involving the expenditure of immense financial and editorial resources. The *Times* is planning the publication of a series of books and other printed material. It is developing curricula that are already being taught to millions of schoolchildren in history and social studies classes.

Eradicating the distinction between historiography and journalism, the *New York Times* violates the professional standards and ethics of both fields. When challenged on its numerous factual errors, the paucity of its source material, and the ignoring of the scholarly literature, the *Times* excuses itself by arguing that its authors do not claim to be historians. But when it is pointed out

2. Ibid.
3. This phrase initially appeared on the *New York Times Magazine* website of the 1619 Project on August 18, 2019. It is no longer available. The magazine's editor, Jake Silverstein, defended the change on October 16, 2020 in the *New York Times Magazine*. https://www.nytimes.com/2020/10/16/magazine/criticism-1619-project.html

that the authors have failed to present accurately, as is expected of competent journalists, the conflicting arguments in the debate over America's founding, the *Times* proclaims that it is writing a new history.

Historians and journalists serve different functions. Journalism lives in the present, observing, assessing, and commenting on what is happening. Of course, the best journalism is informed by a knowledge of history. But it operates with a perspective, and with an array of source material, entirely different from that required for the writing of history.

The preoccupation of journalists is with events and controversies of their own time. Historians strive to understand, reconstruct, and explain the conditions and events of another time, different in many ways from their own. The subjects of their work are generally not among the living and cannot be interviewed. An anachronistic approach to history—that is, one which judges the dramatis personae of another historical period on the basis of modern-day standards which were not known, let alone actionable, in the times in which they lived—is among the worst of all intellectual errors, exceeded only by getting the facts plainly and obviously wrong. The *New York Times'* 1619 Project can serve as a future case study for both an anachronistic approach to history and a deplorable indifference to factual accuracy.

To the extent that there is a method to the 1619 Project, it is pragmatic in the most vulgar sense of the word. The writers rummage carelessly through the past, cherry-picking incidents to concoct a narrative that conforms to their preconceived racialist viewpoint. They explain historical events in terms of what the authors claim, often incorrectly, to have been the immediate motives of the actors. Of what Friedrich Engels referred to as the "motive behind the motives"—that is, the objective economic, technological, and social forces and processes operating independently of the consciousness of individuals—there is barely a word. The protracted political and ideological evolution of the conflict between the colonists and the British Empire is ignored.

Based on what is written in the 1619 Project essays, readers would have no idea whatever of the profound influence exerted by the Enlightenment on the leaders of the Revolution, or that there existed a complex connection between Britain's conflict with the colonies and the global politics of the second half of the eighteenth century.

The *Times* justifies its racial approach by claiming that slavery and the experience of African Americans are subjects long neglected by historians. In fact, the slave system—its origins, changing economic role in pre- and post-revolutionary North America, and its social, political, and cultural significance over a period spanning several centuries—has been the subject of voluminous research. The essays that introduce the 1619 Project evince no familiarity with the massive body of work produced by generations of historians. The 1619 Project essays are not footnoted, nor are the readers provided with a bibliography.

Ignoring the historiography of the Revolution and Civil War, the 1619 Project presents as settled issues that have been subject to decades of intense and rigorous scholarly debate. There is a substantial body of literature on the points the project addresses: in particular, the interaction between the Revolution and slavery, the influence of slaveowners on the drafting of the Constitution, and, in the Civil War era, Lincoln's changing attitudes on race and abolition.

Had the *Times'* editors approached the 1619 Project as serious journalists, they would have had a particular obligation, at the very least, to take notice of and reference the disputes of the recent past—disputes that were open and ongoing, even as Hannah-Jones and her coauthors were preparing their essays for publication. Many of these disputes were covered in the *Times* before the newspaper committed itself in recent years to racial politics.

In 2015, the *Times* published an article written by Sean Wilentz in its opinion section in which the historian opposed "the myth that the United States was founded on racial slavery." Sean Wilentz described this myth as "one of the most destructive falsehoods in all of American history." The *Times* did not challenge Sean Wilentz' views at the time. But it failed to consult Sean Wilentz in the preparation of the 1619 Project essays. This was not an accidental mistake, but a conscious decision to exclude from the project all countervailing arguments.[4]

The five signatories asked the *Times* to explain the "closed process" by which the project was compiled. They noted that the *Times* bypassed experts, disregarded "matters of verifiable fact, which are the foundation of both honest scholarship and honest journalism," and displaced "historical understanding by ideology."[5]

Silverstein answers with disingenuous generalities. He states that the *Times* "consulted with numerous scholars of African American history

---

4. Sean Wilentz, "Constitutionally, Slavery Is No National Institution," September 16, 2015, *New York Times*. Accessed on 12/09/2020: https://www.nytimes.com/2015/09/16/opinion/constitutionally-slavery-is-no-national-institution.html.
5. The *New York Times Magazine*, December 20, 2019. https://www.nytimes.com/2019/12/20/magazine/we-respond-to-the-historians-who-critiqued-the-1619-project.html

and related fields, in a group meeting at The Times as well as in a series of individual conversations." He does not explain how individuals were selected to participate in the "group meeting" or in the "individual conversations." It is evident from Silverstein's vague reply that the *Times* made no attempt to include, in either the "group meeting" or "individual conversations,"[6] historians who represented a variety of interpretative tendencies. Clearly, the *Times* was not interested in listening to what historians who disagreed with the predetermined line of the 1619 Project had to say.

In view of their exclusion from the discussions from which the 1619 Project emerged, it is appropriate to recall what the *Times* once wrote about the work of professors Wood and McPherson. The *Times* praised Gordon Wood's *The Creation of The American Republic, 1776–1787* when it was originally published in 1969 as "one of the half dozen most important books ever written about the American Revolution." Forty years later, in the November 27, 2009, edition of the *Times*, reviewer Jay Winik had this to say of the author of *Empire of Liberty,* a history of the United States from 1789 to 1815:

> A final word about Gordon S. Wood himself. Who better to un-tangle this extraordinary but frequently overlooked story than a distinguished Pulitzer Prize winner and an author of several clas-sic works about the Revolutionary era? On every page of this book, Wood's subtlety and erudition show. Grand in scope and a landmark achievement of scholarship, "Empire of Liberty" is a tour de force, the culmination of a lifetime of brilliant thinking and writing.[7]

As it turned out, this was not the *Times'* "final word" on the work of Gor-don Wood. In a lengthy essay published in the July 22, 2011, issue of the *New York Times Book Review,* Wood was lauded by David Hackett Fisher as *the* "His-torian of the American Revolution." The reviewer described Wood's singular contribution to the understanding of the founding of the United States and the society that emerged from the Revolution:

> He went deep into primary materials and made an open-minded effort to understand the language and thought of 18th-century

---

6. Ibid.
7. Jay Winik, "A New Nation," *New York Times*, November 27, 2009. https://www.nytimes.com/2009/11/29/books/review/Winik-t.html.

Americans in their own terms. After 10 years of research he reported his results, first in a short essay reprinted in this collection, then in the 1969 book "The Creation of the American Republic, 1776–1787." Leading his readers into the sources, Wood demonstrated that Americans in those years invented "not simply new forms of government, but an entirely new conception of politics." They rejected ancient and medieval ideas of a polity as a set of orders or estates. In their place they created a model of a state that existed to represent individual interests, and to protect individual rights.[8]

Nor was the *Times* sparing in its appreciation of the work of James McPherson. In 1988, the *Times*' reviewer, in an enthusiastic essay that appeared on the front page of its Sunday book review section, gave the following appraisal of McPherson's history of the Civil War period, *Battle Cry of Freedom*:

> The Civil War is the most worked-over topic in United States history, one of the most written about in the history of the world. It is therefore a particular pleasure to report that "Battle Cry of Freedom" … is the best one-volume treatment of its subject I have ever come across. It may actually be the best ever published.[9]

In the light of what the *Times* has written about the scholarly work of professors Wood and McPherson, their exclusion from discussions on the framing and content of the 1619 Project was clearly a conscious decision, arrived at in bad faith.

Professors Wood, McPherson, Oakes, Bynum, and Sean Wilentz challenge the essential claim upon which the 1619 Project's condemnation of the American Revolution is grounded. The historians assert unequivocally that it is "not true," as the *Times* asserts, that "the founders declared the colonies' independence of Britain 'in order to ensure slavery would continue.'" They call the allegation "astounding," adding, "every statement offered by the project to validate it is false."

Silverstein responds:

---

8. David Hackett Fischer, "Gordon S. Wood, Historian of the American Revolution," *New York Times*, July 22, 2011. https://www.nytimes.com/2011/07/24/books/review/the-idea-of-america-by-gordon-s-wood-book-review.html.

9. Hugh Brogan, "The Bloodiest of Wars," February 14, 1988, *New York Times*. https://archive.nytimes.com/www.nytimes.com/books/99/04/25/specials/mcpherson-battle.html.

I think it would be useful for readers to hear why we believe that Hannah-Jones's claim that "one of the primary reasons the colonists decided to declare their independence from Britain was because they wanted to protect the institution of slavery" is grounded in the historical record.[10]

Defending the claim that "uneasiness among slaveholders in the colonies about growing antislavery sentiment in Britain and increasing imperial regulation helped motivate the Revolution," Silverstein argues that "large numbers of the enslaved came to see the struggle as one between freedom and continued subjugation."[11]

This assertion rests on one episode in the Revolution, the issuing of the Dunmore Proclamation in 1775, which, writes Silverstein, "offered freedom to any enslaved person who fled his plantation and joined the British Army." He cites one sentence from a recent book by historian Jill Lepore, *These Truths: A History of the United States*, in which she writes: "Not the taxes and the tea, not the shots at Lexington and Concord, not the siege of Boston; rather, it was this act, Dunmore's offer of freedom to slaves, that tipped the scales in favor of American independence." Declaring, on this narrow foundation, the world-historical significance of the Dunmore Proclamation, Silverstein writes: "And yet how many contemporary Americans have ever even heard of it? Enslaved people at the time certainly knew about it. During the Revolution, thousands sought freedom by taking refuge with British forces."[12]

Professor Jill Lepore is a thoughtful writer, but the importance that she assigns to the Dunmore Proclamation is supported with only one statement by Edward Rutledge, a delegate from South Carolina to the Continental Congress. Moreover, Lepore proceeds to undermine her appraisal of the impact of the Proclamation, as she goes on to state in the very same chapter of her book:

> Aside from Dunmore's proclamation of freedom to slaves, the strongest impetus for independence came from brooding and tireless Thomas Paine, who'd immigrated to Philadelphia from England in 1774. In January 1776, Paine published an anonymous pamphlet called *Common Sense*, forty-seven pages

---

10. *The New York Times Magazine*, December 20, 2019. https://www.nytimes.com/2019/12/20/magazine/we-respond-to-the-historians-who-critiqued-the-1619-project.html
11. Ibid.
12. Ibid.

of brisk political argument. "As it is my design to make those that can scarcely read understand," Paine explained, "I shall therefore avoid every literary ornament and put it in language as plain as the alphabet." Members of Congress might have been philosophers, reading Locke and Montesquieu. But ordinary Americans read the Bible, *Poor Richard's Almanack*, and Thomas Paine.

Paine wrote with fury, and he wrote with flash. "The cause of America is in a great measure the cause of all mankind," he announced. "'Tis not the affair of a city, a country, a province, or a kingdom, but of a continent—of at least one eighth part of the habitable globe. 'Tis not the concern of a day, a year, or an age; posterity are virtually involved in the contest, and will be more or less affected, even to the end of time."[13]

Professor Lepore is caught in an evident contradiction. If, as her reference to Dunmore suggests, American independence was instigated by a threat to the permanence of slavery, how is this reconciled with her admission that "the strongest impetus for independence" was generated by Tom Paine's *Common Sense*, which made the case for the liberation of all mankind? As is typical of his slapdash journalistic method, Silverstein seizes on one ill-considered passage by Professor Lepore, but ignores her more carefully considered appreciation of the ideological motivations of the American Revolution.

Let us now investigate the Dunmore Proclamation. It is not a newly discovered issue: the Dunmore Proclamation has long drawn the attention of historians. Much has been written on it, with Benjamin Quarles' 1958 article in the *William and Mary Quarterly*, "Lord Dunmore as Liberator," among the most cited.[14] Only recently have racial-nationalist historians attempted to endow Dunmore's act with a progressive character. This falsification of history has far-reaching consequences. *The conclusion that must follow from the* Times' *glorification of the Dunmore Proclamation is that the defeat of the colonists by the British would have been the preferable outcome of the war; for the British were waging a war of social liberation against the efforts of the colonists to perpetuate slavery.*

---

13. Jill Lepore, *These Truths: A History of the United States* (New York: W. W. Norton, 2018), pp. 94–95.

14. Benjamin Quarles, "Lord Dunmore as Liberator," *The William and Mary Quarterly*, 3rd Ser., Vol. 15, No. 4.

The Dunmore Proclamation was issued in November 1775 by John Murray, Fourth Earl of Dunmore (1730–1809), who was appointed governor of New York and then of Virginia by King George III.

The presentation of the Dunmore Proclamation as the critical trigger event of the revolution ignores the chronology of the American rebellion. The Dunmore Proclamation was issued a decade after the Stamp Act (passed by the British Parliament on March 22, 1765), nearly five years after the Boston Massacre (March 5, 1770), two years after the Boston Tea Party (December 16, 1773), over a year after the convening of the First Continental Congress (September 5, 1774), seven months after military hostilities began with the Battles of Lexington and Concord and the initiation of the Siege of Boston (April 19, 1775), six months after the Battle of Fort Ticonderoga (May 10, 1775) and five months after the Battle of Bunker Hill (June 17, 1775). Even in the Southern states, the revolutionary movement was already far advanced by the time Dunmore issued his order.

Lord Dunmore was a representative of the British aristocracy. As a fifteen-year-old in 1745, Dunmore had participated with his father in the reactionary Jacobite revolt to restore the Stuart "Bonnie Prince Charlie" to the throne.[15] Eventually, the Dunmore family overcame the political difficulties created by this ill-advised allegiance. He ascended to the position of governor of Virginia upon the death of Norborne Berkeley, Fourth Baron of Botetourt. Upon becoming governor, Dunmore launched a vicious war to conquer territory in the Ohio River Valley primarily from the Shawnee Indians, a population of mound builders who had lived in the region for over 1,500 years.[16]

Dunmore led an expedition through parts of modern Pennsylvania and West Virginia, subdued the Shawnee, and opened up the valley for settlement. Soon after concluding the expedition in late 1774, Dunmore turned his attention to the growing revolutionary mood among the colonists.

As governor, Dunmore had refused to sign a bill closing the slave trade to Virginia. But confronted with the threat of rebellion, Dunmore saw the need for a tactical initiative. He wrote to Lord Dartmouth on March 1, 1775, that he hoped freeing the colonists' slaves would "reduce the refractory people of

---

15. James Corbett David, *Dunmore's New World: The Extraordinary Life of a Royal Governor in Revolutionary America—with Jacobites, Counterfeiters, Land Schemes, Shipwrecks, Scalping, Indian Politics, Runaway Slaves, and Two Illegal Royal Weddings* (University of Virginia Press, 2013), p. 20.

16. Eric Hinderaker and Peter C. Mancall, *At the Edge of Empire: The Backcountry British in North America* (Johns Hopkins University Press, 2003), p. 159.

this colony to obedience."[17] He acted in November 1775, issuing a proclamation that applied only to adult male slaves belonging to owners who actively opposed the crown. The "divide-and-conquer" maneuver was a well-practiced ruse of the British to crush dissent.

Dunmore was acting on behalf of a British monarchy that was building a global empire based on the exploitation, enslavement, pillaging, and military subjugation of the peoples of the world. The Irish, the Indians, and the Chinese were being subjected to brutal oppression that would last hundreds of years. Well into the twentieth century, the crimes of British imperialism are recalled by the Amritsar Massacre, the gassing of Iraq, the suppression of the Mau Mau uprising in Kenya, and countless other acts of colonial and imperialist brutality.

As Sylvia Frey wrote in her 1983 article "Between Slavery and Freedom: Virginia Blacks in the American Revolution":

> Dunmore was no champion of emancipation. A slaveowner himself, he persistently invited slave defections without, however, freeing his own slaves or unleashing the black violence feared by the horror-stricken proprietor class. ...
>
> The narrow limits of the policy were, moreover, purposely and unashamedly designed to accommodate the army's time-honored practice of taking spoils of war. Military expediency joined to the practice of despoiling the enemy produced a policy of ambivalence that both contradicted and invalidated even their limited and selective offer of freedom.[18]

While there is evidence that thousands of slaves escaped to join the British forces in the hope of securing freedom, the British treated these runaways with such extreme brutality that many runaways soon fled the British. Loyalist forces returned slaves whose owners switched their support to the crown, subjecting the slaves to brutal punishment as captured fugitives.

The British armed a small minority of the runaways, but the vast majority were made to perform dangerous and brutal labor with virtually no pay and little food. There is evidence that many were ultimately sold off into the West Indian slave trade. Frey notes that of the eight hundred who escaped

---

17. Sylvia R. Frey, *Water from the Rock: Black Resistance in a Revolutionary Age* (Princeton: Princeton University Press, 1991), p. 56.
18. Sylvia R. Frey, "Between Slavery and Freedom: Virginia Blacks in the American Revolution," *Journal of Southern History*, Vol. 49, No. 3 (August 1983), pp. 387–88.

to Dunmore's forces, most died of disease by 1776 due to lack of food, clothing, and shelter. Of course, these slaves cannot be blamed for seeking freedom with the British. However, they were tossed aside when the imperial ploy to maintain control of the colonies fell through. One critical episode—the evacuation of Dunmore's forces from the British lord's headquarters at Gwynne's Island—testifies to the tragic fate of slaves who had been misled by Britain's cynical promises:

> When finally routed by American forces the British vessels slipped their cables and fled Gwynne's Island, abandoning cannon, cattle, horses, furniture, tents for seven to eight hundred men, and several hundred sick, dying and dead blacks. ... Although the total number of the dead cannot be ascertained, one American officer counted 130 graves, "or rather holes," as he put it. In the seven-week occupation of Gwynne's Island, American sources estimated that five hundred of Dunmore's people died, most of them blacks. Twenty years later, "the shocking remembrance of thousands of miserable negroes who had perished there with hunger and disease" still remained.[19]

Nor can the reference to the Dunmore Proclamation explain the increasingly vocal abolitionist sentiments in the North. In 1775, the first abolitionist society in the world was founded in Pennsylvania, while Vermont, Massachusetts, New Hampshire, Connecticut, and Rhode Island banned slavery between 1777 and 1784. Four years after the conclusion of the Revolutionary War, Congress banned slavery in the Northwest Territories with the passage of the Northwest Ordinance in 1787.

In contrast, Lord Dunmore left the colonies to become royal governor of Bermuda from 1787 to 1796, where he enforced a brutal slave system and personally owned a significant number of slaves.

The *Times* also does not mention the established fact that thousands of freed blacks and slaves served in the racially integrated Continental Army after January 1, 1777, when the ban on black conscription was lifted. Baron Von Closen, a German officer serving in the French Royal Deux-Ponts, estimated that up to a quarter of the Revolutionary army was black. In 1783, the Virginia legislature passed an Emancipation Act granting freedom to all slaves who had

---

19. Ibid., p. 391.

"faithfully served agreeable to the terms of their enlistment, and have thereby of course contributed towards the establishment of American liberty."[20]

If Dunmore's Proclamation triggered the American Revolution, how does the *Times* account for the century and a half of antecedent colonial history, which culminated in the development of a popular political movement against oligarchy, aristocracy, and monarchic rule?

Franklin, Washington, the Adamses (both Samuel and John), Jefferson, Paine, and many others were the greatest representatives of an extraordinary generation of revolutionaries. They did not hold identical views on many subjects, including the eventual fate of slavery. But the argument that any of the principal leaders of the Revolution, let alone their mass following among the colonial population, were fighting to defend slavery against the threat of a British-led emancipation movement is historically and politically preposterous. It can be legitimately said that the Founders did not know or agree among themselves on how to end slavery, but none of them initiated and led the Revolution in order to save it.

The leaders of the American Revolution were confronted with the complex challenge of simultaneously waging a war against the world's most powerful military and maintaining the unity of thirteen colonies that previously did not consider themselves part of the same nation.

Karl Marx wrote in the *Eighteenth Brumaire of Louis Bonaparte*: "Men make their own history, but they do not make it just as they please; they do not make it under circumstances chosen by themselves, but under circumstances directly encountered, given and transmitted from the past. The tradition of all the dead generations weighs like a nightmare on the brain of the living."[21]

The American rebellion against British rule was a bourgeois-democratic revolution. It was in the nature of such revolutions to promise more than they could deliver. There is no question that compromises were made to secure the unity of the colonies in the struggle against Britain and, later, to achieve agreement on a constitution for the new United States of America. Historians may find fault, if they wish, with the morals of those who made these compromises. But they must still provide an accurate account of the historical context and political constraints which led to the decisions of the Founders. No such analysis is provided by the authors of the 1619 Project. Everything is explained in

---

20. George Washington Williams, *History of the Negro Race in America from 1619 to 1880* (Putnam Press, 1882), p. 410.

21. Karl Marx, "The Eighteenth Brumaire of Louis Bonaparte," *Marx & Engels Collected Works*, Vol. 11 (London: Lawrence & Wishart, 2010), p. 103.

terms of the alleged racial hatreds of "white" people. That is the one constant in the 1619 Project narrative, which it applies to its discussion of the entirety of American history—from the seventeenth to twenty-first century.

The Founders compromised with the slaveholding Southern colonies in order to establish and maintain national unity. But this does not alter the fact that the American Revolution was a monumental event that changed the course of world history. The objective event was greater than the fault-ridden mortals who found themselves in the leadership of the Revolution. Professor Jonathan Israel explains in *The Expanding Blaze: How the American Revolution Ignited the World, 1775–1848*:

> The American Revolution, preceding the great French Revolution of 1789–99, was the first and one of the most momentous upheavals of a whole series of revolutionary events gripping the Atlantic world during the three-quarters of a century from 1775 to 1848–49. Like the French Revolution, these were all profoundly affected by, and impacted on, America in ways rarely examined and discussed in broad context. ...
>
> Its political and institutional innovations grounded a wholly new kind of republic embodying a diametrically opposed social vision built on shared liberty and equal civil rights. The Revolution commenced the demolition of the early modern hierarchical world of kings, aristocracy, serfdom, slavery, and mercantilist colonial empires, initiating its slow, complex refashioning into the basic format of modernity.[22]

An anachronistic approach to the Revolution—that is, interpreting an event in a manner that is inconsistent with, or not relevant to, the general historical conditions prevailing at the time of its occurrence—works against an understanding of the event and the subsequent development of American and world history. As Wood writes in *The Radicalism of the American Revolution*, the democratic principles of the revolution called into question the previously unquestionable:

> Americans now recognized that slavery in a republic of workers was an aberration, "a peculiar institution," and that if any Americans were to retain it, as Southern Americans eventually did, they

---

22. Jonathan Israel, *The Expanding Blaze: How the American Revolution Ignited the World, 1775–1848* (Princeton: Princeton University Press, 2017), pp. 1–2.

would have to explain and justify it in new racial and anthro-pological ways that their former monarchical society had never needed. The Revolution in effect set in motion ideological and social forces that doomed the institution of slavery in the North and led inexorably to the Civil War.[23]

The *Times'* racialist presentation also undercuts a *genuine* understanding of the historical roots of the growth of anti-black racism in the South. The historian John Shy wrote:

> By 1783, Southern slave owners, previously content to run a sys-tem more flexible and less harsh in practice than it appeared in the statute books, realized as never before how fragile and vulner-able the system actually was, and how little they could depend on the cowardice, ignorance, and gratitude of their slaves. Troubled by the agitation, even within themselves, created against slavery by the rhetorical justification of the Revolution, slaveowners set about giving legal and institutional expression to a new level of anxiety about the system. New rules governing slavery and a new articulation of racist attitudes may have been one of the most im-portant, enduring, and paradoxical legacies of the Revolutionary War.[24]

The period separating the end of the Revolutionary War from the begin-ning of the Civil War was just seventy-eight years—equal to the distance be-tween 1941, when Franklin Roosevelt was president, and today. In this brief timespan, an economic mode of production based on slavery, which had ex-isted for thousands of years, was abolished through mass social struggle. Such profound transformations have their roots in objective processes, decades, if not centuries, in the making, of which even the events' leaders could not have been fully conscious. But that does not undermine the Revolution's lasting historic significance, nor does the fact that the participants did not hold con-temporary views on questions of race and identity.

Defending Hannah-Jones against the historians' claim that her portrayal of Lincoln as a racist was "misleading," Silverstein responds:

---

23. Gordon Wood, *The Radicalism of the American Revolution* (New York: Vintage Books, 1993), pp. 186–87.
24. John Shy, *A People Numerous and Armed: Reflections on the Military Struggle for American Independence* (Ann Arbor: University of Michigan Press, 1990), p. 257.

> She provides an important historical lesson by simply reminding the public, which tends to view Lincoln as a saint, that for much of his career, he believed that a necessary prerequisite for freedom would be a plan to encourage the four million formerly enslaved people to leave the country. ...
>
> The story of abolition becomes more complicated, and more instructive, when readers understand that even the Great Emancipator was ambivalent about full black citizenship.[25]

It is undoubtedly true that Lincoln is the most revered of American presidents, but this is not because he has been the subject of endless and uncritical eulogies by historians. The contradictions in Lincoln's political evolution and views have been the subject of innumerable books. Professor Oakes, one of the five historians who signed the letter to the *Times*, is certainly not an uncritical admirer of Lincoln. He evaluates the president in the context of the political conditions of his time. An article published by the *Times* on February 12, 2013, reporting the awarding of the Lincoln Prize to Oakes for his book *Freedom National: The Destruction of Slavery in the United States, 1861–1865*, cites a passage in which the historian sums up his view of the president:

> There's too much hyperbole in the way we talk about Lincoln. He was neither the Great Emancipator who bestrode his times and brought his people out of the darkness, nor was he in any way a reluctant emancipator held back by some visceral commitment to white supremacy. In the evolution of wartime antislavery policy, Lincoln was neither quicker nor slower than Republican legislators. Instead they seemed to move in tandem.[26]

One of the central conceits of the 1619 Project is that it is advancing a daring, highly original, and long overdue reevaluation of the Civil War and the role of Abraham Lincoln. Hannah-Jones was not "simply reminding the public" that Lincoln supported colonization, as Silverstein dishonestly claims. In her opening essay she asserts that Lincoln was a racist who viewed "black people [as] the obstacle to national unity."[27]

---

25. *The New York Times Magazine*, December 20, 2019. https://www.nytimes.com/2019/12/20/magazine/we-respond-to-the-historians-who-critiqued-the-1619-project.html
26. James Oakes, *Freedom National: The Destruction of Slavery in the United States, 1861–1865* (New York: W. W. Norton, 2013), p. xviii.
27. *The New York Times Magazine*, August 18, 2019, p. 21.

Silverstein's claim that support for colonization in the 1840s and 1850s marks Lincoln as a racist is based on an anachronistic and moralistic appraisal that strips the issue out of its historical context.

From the aftermath of the Revolution to the run-up to the outbreak of the Civil War, colonization defined the mainstream position of opponents of slavery. Prominent colonization proponents like Whig Party leader Henry Clay "considered slavery's end an important element in unifying and modernizing the nation."[28] Clay believed that "the two races could not exist together in equality and in harmony" and that "for the good of the black race, the immediate abolition of slavery, with its expected sinister results, was not practical, and another option must be found."[29]

Abolitionism developed both out of and in opposition to the limitations and racist roots of the colonization perspective. Lincoln, like most Whigs, supported colonization well into the 1850s. But amid the breakdown of the Compromise of 1850 and the breakout of militia warfare in the Kansas-Nebraska Territories, the Whig Party was destroyed by its inability to tackle the question of slavery head-on, with its Southern members largely supporting the pro-slavery Democratic Party and its Northern, antislavery members—including Lincoln—becoming Republicans in the mid-1850s. The significance of Lincoln's decision in 1862 to issue the Emancipation Proclamation was a radical break from the perspective that had dominated antislavery politics for the prior half century.

Ironically, it was among sections of the black nationalist movement in the twentieth century that proposals for colonization—advocating that African Americans move "back to Africa" to establish their own societies in countries like Liberia—found renewed popularity. As Clay biographer James C. Klotter notes, "The Pan-African movement of Marcus Garvey and others in the next century could recognize much of their rhetoric in the words of the ACS [American Colonization Society] a hundred years earlier."[30] Both viewed the harmony of blacks and whites as impossible—a position which shares much in common with Hannah-Jones's emphasis on the unbridgeable, unique historical "experiences" of blacks and whites.

Much of what Nikole Hannah-Jones writes in her introductory essay to the 1619 Project is indistinguishable from the anti-Lincolnism that was fairly

---

28. James C. Klotter, *Henry Clay: The Man Who Would Be President* (Oxford: Oxford University Press, 2018), p. 200.
29. Ibid., p. 198.
30. Ibid., p. 200.

common among black nationalist writers in the 1960s. In fact, the entire framework of the 1619 Project and, in particular, its evaluation of Abraham Lincoln, is to be found in a 1968 essay in *Ebony*, a magazine focused on African
American culture. Written by the racial-nationalist historian Lerone Bennett
Jr. (1928–2018), its title asked, "Was Abe Lincoln A White Supremacist?" The
author answered his question in the affirmative. Bennett wrote:

> Over the years, the Mythology of the Great Emancipator has be-
> come part of the mental landscape of America. Generations of
> schoolchildren have memorized its cadences. Poets, politicians,
> and long-suffering blacks have wept over its imagery and drama.
>   No other American story is so enduring. No other American
> story is so comforting. No other American story is so false. ...
>   Abraham Lincoln is not the light, because he is in
> fact standing in the light, hiding our way; because a real
> emancipation proclamation has become a matter of national
> survival and *because no one has ever issued such a document in this
> country* — because, finally, lies enslave and because the truth is
> always seemly and proper, it has become urgently necessary to
> reevaluate the Lincoln mythology.[31]

Bennett continued to add—with increasing levels of vituperation,
superficiality and dishonesty—to his indictment of Lincoln over the next
three decades, culminating in his 1999 book, *Forced into Glory: Abraham
Lincoln's White Dream*. In this work Bennett denounced "White Americans
who have worked night and day for more than 140 years to perpetuate the
memory of a White separatist who wanted to deport all African Americans
and who provides, moreover, the greatest example in all history of the wisdom
of standing idly by in a great national crisis like slavery or apartheid or the
Third Reich."[32]

If the editors and scribes of the 1619 Project had spent more time researching their subject, they might have discovered an essay in the February 11, 1968,
edition of the *New York Times Magazine*, a lengthy reply to Lerone Bennett Jr.
written by editorial member Herbert Mitgang. The essay's title asked the question: "Was Lincoln Just a Honkie?" Mitgang summarized Bennett's indict-

---

31. Lerone Bennett Jr., "Was Abe Lincoln A White Supremacist?" *Ebony Magazine*, February
1968, Vol. 23 No. 4, pp. 35–36. Google Books.
32. Lerone Bennett Jr., *Forced into Glory: Abraham Lincoln's White Dream* (Chicago: Johnson
Publishing Company, 2007), p. 25.

ment, which anticipated all the arguments that would be made by Hannah-Jones a half century later:

> The main points stated about Lincoln are that he was a firm believer in white supremacy; that he was not opposed to slavery; that even his opposition to the extension of slavery was late and hypocritical; that he grew during the war—but not much, because he really was not a humanitarian; that the Emancipation Proclamation was a political stratagem to buy time and forestall a real act to free the slaves; that Lincoln intended Reconstruction to be strictly for white people.[33]

Mitgang presented a detailed refutation of Bennett's arguments, reconstructing the evolution of Lincoln's views on slavery from the 1840s to the end of his life. Mitgang did not glorify Lincoln, but he forcefully argued that the sixteenth American president came to play a monumentally progressive role in the history of the United States. His words serve as a condemnation of the actions of his successors in the editorial offices of the *Times*. Mitgang wrote:

> To brand Lincoln a white supremacist is to call the Emancipation Proclamation, the constitutional amendments against slavery and for freedom, and the defeat of the Confederacy and its inhuman "institution" anti-Negro acts. To judge a President by selective quotations, and apply these a century later as a means of clouding contemporary yearnings, is historical mischief and sad.[34]

Bennett's name does not appear in Hannah-Jones's essay, nor is his article and later book referenced. One cannot avoid the conclusion that the *Times* considered it ill-advised to associate the 1619 Project with Bennett's writings, which have been largely discredited among historians. But the influence of his writings on the 1619 Project is obvious. Hannah-Jones herself stated, in an interview published in the *Daily Press* on November 8, 2019, that reading Bennett's *Before the Mayflower: A History of the Negro in America, 1619–1962* while still a high school student in Iowa deeply affected her. "I just remember being struck that we have grown up knowing about the Mayflower and 1620

---

33. Herbert Mitgang, "Was Lincoln Just a Honkie?" The *New York Times Magazine*, February 11, 1968, p. 35.
34. Ibid.

but had never heard of the White Lion [the name of the ship that transported the Africans to the English colonies in 1619]."[35]

Hannah-Jones's devotion to the work of Lerone Bennett may help explain why James McPherson was not consulted by the editors of the 1619 Project. McPherson wrote a critical review of Bennett's *Forced into Glory*, which was published in the August 27, 2000, edition of the *New York Times*. He tore Bennett's misrepresentation of the Emancipation Proclamation to pieces. McPherson concluded his review of *Forced Into Glory* with the following observation: "Bennett fails to appreciate the acuity and empathy that enabled Lincoln to transcend his prejudices and to preside over the greatest social revolution in American history, the liberation of four million slaves."[36]

The editors of the *Times* are less bombastic than Bennett, but they are not more accurate. Silverstein's claim that Lincoln was "ambivalent about full black citizenship" discounts the fact that the Fourteenth Amendment, which guaranteed the right of citizenship to freed slaves, could not have become reality without both the Emancipation Proclamation and Union victory in the war. The Thirteenth, Fourteenth, and Fifteenth Amendments were collectively called the Civil War Amendments because they enshrined in constitutional law what the war had accomplished through political and military deeds.

In calling attention to the influence of Bennett's writings on the 1619 Project, one proviso must be made. Bennett did acknowledge the critical role of abolitionists such as Wendell Phillips in advancing the struggle for emancipation and African American equality. That is ignored by Hannah-Jones, who claims that in the fight for democracy African Americans fought "alone."

The *Times* claims its racialist narrative is justified because "it is difficult to argue that equality has ever been truly achieved for black Americans." In fact, equality *could never* and never *has been achieved* for the great majority of the population in capitalist America. But before examining the question of contemporary inequality in the United States, one is obligated to call attention to the fact that Hannah-Jones and the 1619 Project as a whole display indiffer-

---

35. Lisa Vernon Sparks, "'1619 Project' reporter details series about 400th anniversary of Africans' arrival to Virginia colonies," *Daily Press*, November 8, 2019. https://www.dailypress.com/news/education/dp-nw-hampton-nyt-the-1619-project-jones-20191108-uxvztdkjzng6ffciohfw3tbqqy-story.html

36. James M. McPherson, "Lincoln the Devil," The *New York Times*, August 27, 2000. https://archive.nytimes.com/www.nytimes.com/books/00/08/27/reviews/000827.27mcphert.html

ence to the oppression and suffering of all other, i.e., non-African American, inhabitants of the American continent.

The existence of chattel slavery was one of the greatest crimes committed on the guilty soil of the United States. But the blood drawn by the slaveowners' lashes was, to some significant extent, as Lincoln so memorably declared in his Second Inaugural, paid for with the blood of the several hundred thousand soldiers who perished in the Civil War of 1861–1865. But there was no such retribution for the genocidal wars waged against the original inhabitants of the American continent. Their fate receives no mention in the 1619 Project.

What of the extreme brutality confronting the waves of Irish immigrants fleeing famine? Or of the Italians who were viciously stereotyped, abused, and, during the Red Scare of the early 1920s, deported? One wonders if Hannah-Jones has ever heard of Sacco and Vanzetti. Or of the exploitation of Chinese "coolie" labor. And what of the internment of the Japanese Americans? What of the Jewish immigrants, who faced decades of vicious anti-Semitic prejudice in "Christian" America? Not a word about these elements of the harsh "immigrant experience" is to be found in the 1619 Project essays. And the entire vast subject of the American labor movement, with its violent struggles and innumerable martyrs, is not mentioned.

All of the many instances of oppression should be documented and remembered. Each victim of injustice, in whatever form, has a legitimate claim on the conscience of mankind. But sympathy, in and of itself, is inadequate. It is necessary that the real causes of the crimes be understood. For this, a moralistic and anachronistic attitude toward history is not only inadequate. It is a barrier to identifying and, ultimately, removing the objective causes of the many forms of oppression and exploitation that developed within the United States in the aftermath of both the Revolution of 1775–83 and the Civil War of 1861–65.

For all the magnificent principles and ideals proclaimed by the two great revolutions that erupted on the American continent between 1775 and 1865, these events were, in the final analysis, bourgeois revolutions. There existed, inevitably, a gap between the ideals they proclaimed and their real socioeconomic and political purpose.

The Revolution of 1775–83 paved the way for the vast expansion of capitalism on the North American continent and the development of a new form of capitalist nation-state. After the still-maturing North American bourgeoisie threw off the shackles of colonial rule, the class tensions within the new society developed rapidly.

As the Revolution broke down the old aristocratic system, Gordon Wood notes, "growing opportunities for wealth turned social mobility into a scramble" and "expectations of raising one's standard of living—if only to buy new consumer goods—seeped deeper and deeper into the society and had profound effects on the consciousness of ordinary people. Instead of creating a new order of benevolence and selflessness, enlightened republicanism was breeding social competitiveness and individualism; and there seemed no easy way of stopping it." The Revolution, Wood writes, "was the source of its own contradictions."[37]

These contradictions found expression in the Constitution itself, drafted by erstwhile revolutionary politicians who now held state power. The new ruling class confronted the dangers of popular plebeian democracy in the rebellion of poor farmers in Shays' Rebellion of 1786–87 and would soon confront it again in the Whiskey Rebellion of the early 1790s.

Wood explains, "The federal Constitution of 1787 was in part a response to these popular social developments, an attempt to mitigate their effects by new institutional arrangements."[38] While the Constitution sought to establish a strong federal state, so powerful were the democratic aspirations of the masses of people, unleashed by the Revolution itself, that the Bill of Rights emerged as a compromise to protect the people against the government. For the past two hundred years, the Bill of Rights has provided the framework for all discussion of social change, reform, and even revolution.

The *Times*, as we have already noted, states that "it is difficult to argue that equality has ever been truly achieved for black Americans." The implicit claim that inequality—socioeconomic and political—is the exclusive fate of African Americans is a stunning demonstration of the blindness and self-absorption that characterizes the outlook of the editors and writers of the 1619 Project.

The *Times*' racialist attack on the American Revolution and Civil War takes place under conditions of growing opposition to social inequality in the United States. After decades of their suppression, mass demonstrations and strikes by workers are emerging as powerful manifestations of social opposition. Significantly, the mass demonstrations and strikes of 2019 involved in every case the unified action of the working class. There is not a single example of unified action by workers being disrupted by differences related to race, nationality, ethnicity, religion, gender, or sexual orientation. The protests were not the actions of different "identities," but rather of a social class.

---

37. Wood, *The Radicalism of the American Revolution* pp. 229–230.
38. Ibid., p. 230.

The movement of the working class in the United States is part of a global process. In 2019, people of all races and many nationalities participated in mass demonstrations and protests demanding equality and democratic rights. Though the skin pigmentation of the people of Chile, Lebanon, Iraq, France, Haiti, Sudan, and Hong Kong differ, the demands of the masses of people are similar.

Inevitably, the emergence of the mass working-class movement is finding its political reflection in a renewed interest in socialism as an alternative to capitalism. Of course, popular understanding of socialism and how it is to be achieved is still very limited. But the process of political radicalization will gather speed as the mass movement grows and social conflict becomes increasingly intense. The ruling class, supremely sensitive to any intellectual, cultural, and political tendency that threatens its wealth and power, is alarmed by the incipient spread of socialistic sentiments and ideas. President Trump proclaims that socialism will not be allowed to come to power in the United States.

Trump gives expression to the ruling class's fear of socialism in an obscene and fascistic language that is consistent with his political persona and objectives. He relentlessly scapegoats immigrants as a means of disorienting and misdirecting the social anger generated by economic hardship experienced by broad sections of the working class, i.e., the overwhelming majority of the population.

Democrats employ a different, and certainly more politically sophisticated, strategy, which is no less directed toward fomenting divisions in the working class. It is based on the relentless promotion of various forms of "identity" politics.

Over the course of the last three decades, the Democratic Party has become more closely identified with finance capital, even winning a majority of the votes of affluent Americans in the 2016 and 2018 elections. The Democrats' obsessive focus on race and identity is aimed at undermining the development of class consciousness. To the extent that the Democratic Party retains an electoral base among African American workers, it seeks to root this not on an appeal to their economic interests, but rather to their racial identity.

Support for this political stratagem is particularly pronounced among affluent African Americans who have benefited from various forms of racially grounded affirmative action programs, which have provided access to positions that make possible the accumulation of substantial wealth. In his brief reference to inequality, Silverstein refers only to the disparity between black and white household income. It should be noted that the figures he provides to accentuate this disparity are distorted by the inclusion of megamillionaires and billionaires in the calculation of white household income. Significantly, Silverstein avoids any reference to the extreme growth of social inequality *within* the African American population. From 2007 to 2015, the share of the total wealth among African Americans owned by the richest 1 percent of African Americans soared from 19 percent to over 40 percent.[39]

The politics of racial identity have flourished under conditions where the wealthiest African Americans are separating themselves from the vast majority of black workers, the poorest 60 percent of whom own negative wealth. Meanwhile, white people who belong to the working class—those who the *Times* alleges benefit from "privilege"—are dying at unprecedented rates from diseases of social despair, including alcoholism, suicide, and opioid overdose.

It is not our contention that every editor and writer involved in the 1619 Project is engaged in deliberate deception or is merely chasing career opportunities. As always, many individual factors and motivations are at work. Some are merely ill-informed. There are some who may sincerely feel they are making amends for the history of racial discrimination in the United States. And there are those, to be blunt, who welcome the opportunity to profit handsomely off of speaking fees, book contracts, corporate promotions, and all manner of revenues generated by diverse forms of pseudo-intellectual huckstering. Hannah-Jones's acceptance of the sponsorship of Shell Oil, which is implicated in the murderous oppression of the Ogoni people in Nigeria, is a deplorable example of the latter.

The falsification of history invariably serves very real, even if unstated, contemporary political interests. The racial narrative is intended to replace one that is based on the analysis of objectively existing social and class interests. The *New York Times*, as a corporate entity and, more importantly, a powerful voice of the ruling class and its state, has a very real political agenda, which is closely coordinated with the Democratic Party. Silverstein never explains why the *Times* now adopts, as the basis of an essential change in the teaching of American history, the race-based narrative of Lerone Bennett Jr., which it explicitly and forcefully rejected fifty years ago. Nor does he explain why the *Times* rejects the criticisms of Gordon Wood and James McPherson, whom it

---

39. Eric London, "Identity politics and the growth of inequality within racial minorities," World Socialist Web Site, October 7, 2017. https://www.wsws.org/en/articles/2017/10/07/pers-o07.html.

was describing less than a decade ago as the leading authorities in the fields of Revolutionary- and Civil War-era studies.

Clearly, it is not the historical events that have changed. But the political imperatives and social interests that determine the editorial policy of the *New York Times* have. That alone is a good reason why the writing of history and the determination of historical curricula that is intended to guide the teaching of youth should not be determined by the corporate management of newspapers. The justification of the domestic and global interests of American capitalism, the relentless quest for corporate profitability, the effort to suppress the class struggle, and the justification of staggering levels of social inequality are not compatible with the pursuit of historical truth.

Whatever the *Times* believes to be the advantages of pursuing a racial narrative to secure an electoral majority for the Democratic Party, this is a politically dangerous and utterly reactionary strategy, with potentially catastrophic consequences.

Those who argue for a history of "black America" are legitimizing a history of "white America" as well. They are assisting the racist politicians of the fascistic right. The creation of different "racial narratives" is aimed at presenting the races as "intrinsically different" from one another, to borrow a phrase from Democratic politician Stacey Abrams. Past efforts to expose the lie of racial differences are being undermined. When the advocates of race-based politics claim that "white privilege" is based on the real interests of "white people," they are opposing—in violation of reason, science, and the counsel of history—the unity of the working class in the struggle against capitalism, authoritarianism, and the growing threat of war.

During the past several months, since the publication in September 2019 of its initial critique of the 1619 Project, the Socialist Equality Party and the World Socialist Web Site have been asked by journalists representing bourgeois publications to explain why we oppose the *New York Times*' initiative. These questions, which generally arise from genuine curiosity rather than political malice, reflect the extent to which the "left" is identified with "identity politics." In response, we explain that the exaltation of such politics has nothing in common with the theory, principles, and political program of the socialist movement. The historical slogan of the socialist movement is "Workers of the World, Unite!" not "Races of the World, Divide!"

The falsification and repudiation of the enduring principles and aims of past revolutions deprive the contemporary revolutionary movement of an essential historical orientation. The dismissive, cynical, and even nihilistic attitude toward the struggles of the past undermines an appreciation of the enduring value of their real advances, however limited and contradictory, toward the ultimate achievement of true democracy, universal prosperity, and genuine human equality, which are the real aim of the socialist movement.

As Marxists, we understand and have settled accounts with the limitations of the *bourgeois-democratic* revolutions of the eighteenth and nineteenth centuries. We know very well the difference between ideological rationalizations and historically determined realities. But those who are not inspired by the world-historical and universal ideals proclaimed by Jefferson's immortal Declaration and Lincoln's Gettysburg Address are neither socialists nor revolutionaries. Those who glibly surrender positions won through the shedding of blood in the past will never conquer new ones. Particularly in a period of global class struggle, the underlying revolutionary principles that made the struggles of 1776 "the cause of all mankind" acquire renewed and accentuated significance.

The uncompromising defense of the progressive heritage of the first two American revolutions is necessary for resisting intellectual retrogression and political reaction, educating the working class, and, on that basis, building a powerful American and international socialist movement.

Historian Gordon Wood Responds to the *New York Times'* Defense of the 1619 Project

Historian Gordon Wood, author of the 1993 Pulitzer Prize-winning book The Radicalism of the American Revolution *and the 1970 Bancroft Prize-winning* The Creation of the American Republic 1776–1787, *was one of five signatories to write a letter to the editor of the* New York Times Magazine, *asking the* Times *to correct "factual errors" in the 1619 Project which evinced "a displacement of historical understanding by ideology." Professor Wood is the leading historian of the American Revolution.*

The other signatories were historians Victoria Bynum, James McPherson, Sean Wilentz, and James Oakes. The Times *responded on December 20, 2019 in a letter by* New York Times Magazine *editor in chief Jake Silverstein, and refused to make any corrections. Wood then wrote the following response. The* Times *declined to publish it.*

21 Dec. 2019

Dear Mr. Silverstein,

I have read your response to our letter concerning the 1619 Project. I have no quarrel with the idea behind the project. Demonstrating the importance of slavery in the history of our country is essential and commendable. But that necessary and worthy goal will be seriously harmed if the facts in the project turn out to be wrong and the interpretations of events are deemed to be perverse and distorted. In the long run the project will lose its credibility, standing, and persuasiveness with the nation as a whole. I fear that it will eventually

Gordon Wood, "Historian Gordon Wood responds to the *New York Times'* defense of the 1619 Project," World Socialist Web Site, December 24, 2019.

hurt the cause rather than help it. We all want justice, but not at the expense of truth.

I have spent my career studying the American Revolution and cannot accept the view that "one of the primary reasons the colonists decided to declare their independence from Britain was because they wanted to protect the institution of slavery." I don't know of any colonist who said that they wanted independence in order to preserve their slaves. No colonist expressed alarm that the mother country was out to abolish slavery in 1776. If Southerners were concerned about losing their slaves, why didn't they make efforts to ally with the slaveholding planters in the British West Indies? Perhaps some Southern slaveholders were alarmed by news of the Somerset decision, but we don't have any evidence of that. Besides, that decision was not known in the colonies until the fall of 1772 and by that date the colonists were well along in their drive to independence. Remember, it all started in 1765 with the Stamp Act. The same is true of Dunmore's proclamation of 1775. It may have tipped the scales for some hesitant Virginia planters, but by then the revolutionary movement was already well along in Virginia.

There is no evidence in 1776 of a rising movement to abolish the Atlantic slave trade, as the 1619 Project erroneously asserts, nor is there any evidence the British government was eager to do so. But even if either were the case, ending the Atlantic slave trade would have been welcomed by the Virginia planters, who already had more slaves than they needed. Indeed, the Virginians in the years following independence took the lead in moving to abolish the despicable international slave trade.

How could slavery be worth preserving for someone like John Adams, who hated slavery and owned no slaves? If anyone in the Continental Congress was responsible for the Declaration of Independence, it was Adams. And much of our countrymen now know that from seeing the film of the musical "1776." Ignoring his and other Northerners' roles in the decision for independence can only undermine the credibility of your project with the general public. Far from preserving slavery, the North saw the Revolution as an opportunity to abolish the institution. The first anti-slave movements in the history of the world, supported by whites as well as blacks, took place in the Northern states in the years immediately following 1776.

I could go on with many more objections, some of which I mentioned in my interview with the World Socialist Web Site. But for now this may be enough to justify some correction and modification of the project. Again, let me emphasize my wholehearted support of the goal of the project to demonstrate accurately and truthfully to all Americans the importance of slavery in our history.

If you are willing to publish this letter, you may.

Sincerely,
Gordon S. Wood

A Historian's Critique of the 1619 Project

Historian Victoria Bynum, author of The Free State of Jones: Mississippi's Longest Civil War *and Distinguished Professor Emeritus of History at Texas State University, wrote the following reply to the* New York Times' *1619 Project. Bynum came under attack by the 1619 Project's proponents for her October 2019 interview in the World Socialist Web Site.*

"White privilege," "wealthy elites," "mansplainers," "old white people," "ivory tower elites." These are just a few of the epithets hurled at me and the four historians I joined in protesting the flawed and inaccurate history presented in the *New York Times'* 1619 Project. A quick pass through Twitter reveals that some historians are "ashamed of," even "heartbroken by," our letter to the *Times* editor. One historian chastised us for criticizing the 1619 Project at a time when our "republic" is so dangerously divided! Really, historians? Is it no longer our right or responsibility to critique works of history, at least not when they're about a long, ugly episode of our nation's history? Does history not have to be accurate if the subjects were truly victims, as enslaved Americans surely were? But I digress.

On August 18, 2019, the *New York Times* released its highly-touted 1619 Project, featuring historical essays and original literary works aimed at "reframing" American history with a new founding date—1619, the year that twenty or more Africans were brought to Virginia—to replace 1776, the year the Declaration of Independence was signed. The project offers slavery and its lega-

Victoria Bynum, "A historian's critique of the 1619 Project," World Socialist Web Site, December 22, 2019.

cies to contemporary American society as the nation's central defining features. *New York Times* journalist and project director Nikole Hannah-Jones provides the project's "intellectual framework," which posits slavery as the dominant feature of North American settlement, and the American Revolution as a duplicitous movement designed to protect slavery from its abolition by the British Empire. Hannah-Jones urges that we remember Presidents Thomas Jefferson and Abraham Lincoln first and foremost for their racism rather than their ideals of nationhood. Her assertions on these topics were forcefully critiqued by historians Gordon Wood, James McPherson, and James Oakes in interviews with the World Socialist Web Site (WSWS), and by Sean Wilentz in the *New York Times Review of Books* (NYTR). My own criticisms, in an interview with the WSWS, centered on the project's historical treatment of class and race. I elaborate here on those remarks.

After reframing the meaning of the American Revolution, Hannah-Jones moves on to the Civil War and Reconstruction, barely touching on American abolitionism and ignoring the free soil movement, though both were seeds of the antislavery Republican Party. In discussing the nation's wrenching effort to reconstruct itself after the Civil War, she asserts that "blacks worked for the most part ... alone" to free themselves and push for full rights of citizenship through passage of the Reconstruction Amendments. Rightly emphasizing the vigilante white violence that immediately followed the victories of a Republican-dominated Congress, she ignores important exceptions, including the Southern white "Scalawags," many of whom were nonslaveholders who fought against the Confederacy in the war and participated with blacks and Northern Republicans in passing the Reconstruction Amendments.

To be sure, Southern whites were among the most conservative members of the Republican Party. Nonetheless, important legislation was passed with their participation, enabling the United States by 1868 to begin building a more racially just, democratic society before white supremacist Democrats derailed Reconstruction. Furthermore, not only does Hannah-Jones ignore the Scalawags, but also Matthew Desmond, in his essay on capitalism and slavery, ignores nonslaveholding propertied farmers, the largest class of whites in the antebellum South, and from which many Southern Republicans emerged.

Likewise, the 1619 Project ignores late nineteenth and twentieth century interracial efforts to combat the power of corporations by an emergent industrial working class. Instead of studying the methods by which industry destroyed such efforts by fomenting racism, the project continues to argue that blacks struggled "almost alone" in a world where an undifferentiated class of whites controlled the levers of power. Thus, some of our nation's greatest historical moments of interracial class solidarity, the labor struggles shared by working class people across the color line, are erased. For example, the Populist Movement is barely mentioned, the early twentieth century Socialist Movement, not at all. And, although Jesse Jackson's rousing Rainbow Coalition speech at the Democratic Convention of 1984 is remembered favorably by one project author, the small farmers, poor people, and working mothers that Jackson included alongside African Americans, Arab Americans, Hispanic Americans, and gay and lesbian people are ignored.

Multiracial communities are also passed over by the 1619 Project. Yet, race-mixing among Africans, Europeans, and American Indians early on presented British colonists with a dilemma—how to maintain the image of race-based slavery while increasing their labor force by enslaving people of partially white ancestry. The essentialist one drop rule, based on a theory of hypodescent, eventually provided the solution. Simply put, African blood was decreed so powerful (or polluting) that a mere fraction of African ancestry was enough to render a person "black," no matter how white that person's appearance. Hannah-Jones herself recognizes the fallacy of "race" when she writes that "enslavement and subjugation became the natural station of people who had *any discernible drop of 'black' blood*" (italics mine). The 1619 Project makes no attempt, however, to explore connections between race mixing and the class history of the United States. But make no mistake. The Southern slaveholding class knew that the one drop rule was a game of semantics. Slavery was first and foremost a closed labor system. Racism provided the rationale. Between 1855 and 1860, prominent pro-slavery author George Fitzhugh had no difficulty urging the United States to merge its systems of class and race by enslaving lower-class whites as well as people of color.

The 1619 Project claims to be a long overdue contribution to understanding slavery and racism over the course of four hundred years of American history. It includes literary works of poetry, fiction, and memory that are revelatory and moving. They and many of the short research pieces evoke sadness, outrage, and anger. But they are not well served by the larger project, which sweeps over vast chunks of innovative and ground breaking historiography to tell a story of relentless white-on-black violence and exploitation that offers no hope of reconciliation for the nation. The project's great flaw is its lack of solid grounding in the history of European colonization, the American Revolution, the American Civil War, and racial and class relations throughout.

History is a profession that takes years of training. In his response to our letter to the *New York Times*, editor Jake Silverstein admits that, although the *Times* consulted with scholars, and although Nikole Hannah-Jones "has consistently used history to inform her journalism.".... the newspaper "did not assemble a formal panel [of historians] for this project." Perhaps this explains why a number of 1619 Project defenders, including Hannah-Jones, implicitly deny the need for training by claiming there is no such thing as objective history anyway. Too often, the assumption that journalists make good historians leaves us fighting over dueling narratives about the past based on political agendas of the present.

A Reply to the *American Historical Review*'s Defense of the 1619 Project

On January 23, 2020, Alex Lichtenstein, editor of the *American Historical Review* (AHR), posted an online statement defending the *New York Times Magazine*'s 1619 Project against criticism from the World Socialist Web Site and several eminent historians. The editorial, "From the Editor's Desk: 1619 and All That," will appear in the forthcoming issue of the leading journal among American academic historians.

The fact that the 1619 Project is now being editorially defended in the AHR, despite the withering criticisms of highly respected professional historians, is a very troubling development. It reveals the extent to which racialist mythology, which has provided the "theoretical" foundation of middle-class identity politics, has been accepted, and even embraced, by a substantial section of the academic community as a legitimate basis for the teaching of American history.

Published by the *Times* in August 2019, the 1619 Project essays are presented as the basis of a new curriculum, to be provided to the nation's underfunded public schools, free of charge, by the corporate-endowed Pulitzer Center on Crisis Reporting. The 1619 Project, according to its architect Nikole Hannah-Jones, aims to "reframe" all of American history as a story of "anti-black racism" rooted in a "national DNA," which, it claims, emerged out of the allegedly unique American "original sin" of slavery.[1]

Thomas Mackaman and David North, "A reply to the American Historical Review's defense of the 1619 Project," World Socialist Web Site, January 31, 2020.

1. Nikole Hannah-Jones, *New York Times Magazine*, August 18, 2019, pp. 14–26.

In his effort to defend the 1619 Project, Lichtenstein argues not as a conscientious historian, but as a lawyer defending what he knows to be a weak case. He is disingenuous to the point of dishonesty in his effort to dismiss the extent of the revision and falsification of history advanced by the 1619 Project. The differences, he claims, are merely a matter of emphasis or nuance.

The arguments advanced by Hannah-Jones are: a) that the establishment of the United States was a counterrevolution, whose primary purpose was the protection of slavery against the danger posed by a British-led emancipation movement; b) that Lincoln was a racist and that the Civil War therefore was unrelated to the fight to abolish slavery; c) that African Americans have fought alone in the face of relentless racism based on the universally popular doctrine of white supremacy; d) racism and slavery are the essential elements of American exceptionalism; and, therefore (and most important of all); e) all of American history is to be understood as the struggle between the white and black races. The driving forces of American history are not objective socioeconomic processes that give rise to class conflict, but, rather, eternal and suprahistorical racial hatreds.

What is involved in the 1619 Project controversy is not a case of semantic differences that can be reconciled by a mere rephrasing of arguments. Two absolutely irreconcilable positions are being advanced, which cannot even be described as conflicting "interpretations." A racialist narrative, which is what the 1619 Project advances, is by its very nature incompatible with empirical research and scientific methodology. It counterposes to genuine historical research a reactionary racial myth.

Lichtenstein's essay abounds with contradictions, errors, outright falsifications, and cynical posturing. He begins by relating a recent visit to New York City's Green-Wood Cemetery, where he was "struck" by the inscription on the Civil War Soldiers' Monument noting that 148,000 residents fought "in aid of the war for the preservation of the Union and the Constitution." Lichtenstein is unmoved by the fact that nearly one-fifth of the entire population of America's largest city fought in the Civil War—with all of the death and tragedy that such an astonishing statistic entailed. Instead, he is troubled by what he finds missing from the monument's inscription: "Not a word about slavery or emancipation, let alone black military service." This omission, Lichtenstein implies, proves that the Union soldiers who fought and died in the Civil War were indifferent to slavery.

However, the connection between the defense of the Union and the abolition of slavery, lost on the editor of the AHR, was understood by all contemporaries. Why, one wonders, does Lichtenstein suppose the South seceded from the Union in 1861? What does he suppose Lincoln was speaking about on November 19, 1863, at the dedication of the national cemetery at Gettysburg, when he explained to a grieving nation that the meaning of the war was a "new birth of freedom"? Or in his Second Inaugural Address, weeks before the end of the war and his own assassination at the hands of white supremacist John Wilkes Booth, when he stated:

> One eighth of the whole population were colored slaves, not distributed generally over the Union, but localized in the Southern part of it. These slaves constituted a peculiar and powerful interest. *All knew that this interest was somehow the cause of the war.* To strengthen, perpetuate, and extend this interest was the object for which the insurgents would rend the Union, even by war; while the government claimed no right to do more than to restrict the territorial enlargement of it [emphasis added].[2]

Lichtenstein's cynical disparagement of the cemetery monument would be uninteresting except for its centrality to his aim—to lend weight to central premises of the 1619 Project: that race is the axis of American history, that African Americans fought for freedom alone, and that the two seminal events of American history—the Revolution and Civil War—were either opposed or unrelated to the liberation of the slaves.

Lichtenstein claims that the 1619 Project's "reframing" is a mere "rhetorical move ... that impressed upon a wider public an interpretive framework that many historians probably already accept." In other words—and here he approvingly quotes from *New York Times Magazine* editor Jake Silverstein—"slavery and racism lie at the root of 'nearly everything that has truly made America exceptional.'"[3]

The editor of the AHR palms off as "widely accepted" what is actually a disputed and untenable generalization: that "slavery and racism lie at the root of 'nearly everything that has truly made America exceptional.'" This, as a matter of historical fact, cannot be true, as neither slavery nor racism is unique to America. Both have existed in innumerable societies, from the ancient world to modern times.

---

2. Abraham Lincoln, Second Inaugural Address, April 10, 1865. https://www.ourdocuments. gov/doc.php?doc=38
3. Alex Lichtenstein, "1619 and All That," The *American Historical Review*. Accessed on 12/12/20: https://academic.oup.com/ahr/article/125/1/xv/5714757

In fact, what makes American slavery truly "unique" was not that it existed, but that it gave rise to the most powerful and intransigent antislavery movement the world has ever known, and that it was destroyed in a great civil war during four years of fighting, in which approximately as many Americans perished as in all other US wars combined. This, in turn, led to the enactment of constitutional amendments that, at least in law, established the equality of the former slaves.

The version of North American history advanced by the 1619 Project, and defended by Lichtenstein, has not only to negate 1776, but to cancel 1492.

It is no small matter that the authors and editors of the *Times* manage to ignore all that occurred in the 127 years that preceded the arrival of Africans in Virginia. The "uniqueness" of American history, indeed, that of the entire New World, is entirely bound up with the emergence of capitalism as a new economic world system. All the brutalities of the New World, beginning with the long and horrible process of the extermination of the aboriginal population, developed out of this process. As Marx observed, in the period of primitive accumulation, capital emerged "dripping from head to foot, from every pore, with blood and dirt." [4]

However, the horrors of slavery and the dispossession of the indigenous populations, what Bernard Bailyn has aptly characterized as the "barbarous years" in colonial history, intersected with other economic, social, and political processes that also contributed to American "uniqueness."

The societies of the thirteen colonies were characterized by the absence of a feudal past, a distinct feature of American development that has been the subject of prolonged and significant discussion among serious historians. Also "unique" was the profound influence of the English Civil War of the seventeenth century and the Enlightenment philosophy of the eighteenth, whose revolutionary defense of liberty and revolutionary ideas reached deep into the colonial population—indeed, even to the slaves themselves, as Professor Clayborne Carson pointed out in his interview with the World Socialist Web Site. All of these "unique" aspects of the colonies intersected with the imperial crisis of the mid-to-late eighteenth century, the Seven Years' War (1756–63), and the global conflict between France and Britain, setting the stage for the confrontation that erupted in 1775. The victory of the colonial rebellion stunned the world and sounded the tocsin for revolutions in France and Haiti.

---

4. Karl Marx, "Capital Volume 1," *Marx & Engels Collected Works*, Vol. 35 (London: Lawrence & Wishart, 1996), pp. 739, 748.

But Lichtenstein cynically dismisses the world-historical significance of the American Revolution. "The first republic and its Constitution, so revered, lasted about as long as the USSR, a mere seventy-four years, before dissolving into the bloodiest conflict of the nineteenth century," he sneers. "For my part, I always considered this a pretty weak foundation on which to erect unconditional veneration."[5]

Serious historians do not "venerate" events. They attempt to understand and explain them, and to trace back their roots in the past as well as their consequences. The latter is particularly important in the study of the American Revolution, for if it had achieved *only* the preconditions for the destruction of slavery within a "mere seventy-four years"—and it in fact achieved far more than that—it would still rank as one of the most consequential political events in history. To compound the confusion, the Civil War, which Lichtenstein also minimizes, is made exclusively dependent on the "black freedom struggle," implying that the latter's development was unconnected with the American Revolution and the political conflicts within the United States that unfolded between 1787 and 1861.

Lichtenstein writes that he is "perplexed" by criticism of the 1619 Project. But then he proceeds to provide a concise summary of the critique developed by the World Socialist Web Site:

> As good Marxists, the adherents of the Fourth International denounced the project for its "idealism," that is to say, its tendency to reduce historical causation to a "supra-historical emotional impulse." By mischaracterizing anti-black racism as an irreducible element built into the "DNA" of the nation and its white citizens, the Trotskyists declared, the 1619 Project is ahistorical and "irrationalist." This idealist fallacy requires that racism "must persist independently of any change in political and economic conditions," naturally the very thing that any materialist historian would want to attend to. "The invocation of white racism," they proclaim, "takes the place of any concrete examination of the economic, political and social history of the country." Perhaps even worse, "the 1619 Project says nothing about the event that had the greatest impact on the social

---

5. Lichtenstein, https://academic.oup.com/ahr/article/125/1/xv/5714757

condition of African-Americans—the Russian Revolution of 1917." (Well, OK, I was with them up to that point.)[6]

Taking Lichtenstein at his word—i.e., that, except for its estimation of the significance of the 1917 October Revolution, he was "with" the WSWS—he contradicts his defense of the 1619 Project. Because the WSWS's position is diametrically opposed to that of the *Times*, to the extent Lichtenstein acknowledges the legitimacy, and even correctness of its critique, he is discrediting the 1619 Project.

Lichtenstein goes on to concede the high quality of the WSWS's discussions with leading scholars. "Frankly, I wish the *AHR* had published these interviews, and I hope they get wide circulation," he writes. But Lichtenstein proceeds to insinuate that the historians were tricked into speaking, imagining the interviewed scholars "trying to avoid saying what the Trotskyists would like them to say," and even resisting "the Trotskyists' bait."

Lichtenstein claims that "it is safe to say that [James McPherson] would not sign on to the Marxist version of the Civil War preferred by the ICFI—'the greatest expropriation of private property in world history, not equaled until the Russian Revolution in 1917.'" Sadly for Lichtenstein, this point is made explicitly by Professor McPherson in *Abraham Lincoln and the Second American Revolution*, with which the editor of the AHR is evidently unfamiliar. McPherson wrote:

> The abolition of slavery represented a confiscation of about three billion dollars of property—the equivalent as a proportion of national wealth to about three *trillion* dollars in 1990. In effect, the government in 1865 confiscated the principal form of property in one-third of the country, without compensation. That was without parallel in American history. ... When such a massive confiscation of property takes place as a consequence of violent internal upheaval on the scale of the American Civil War, it is quite properly called revolutionary.[7]

Lichtenstein takes gratuitous and insulting jabs against his colleagues throughout. He accuses Professor Gordon Wood, who has dedicated his life to the study of the American Revolution, of being motivated by egotistical

---

6. Ibid.

7. James McPherson, *Abraham Lincoln and the Second American Revolution* (Oxford: Oxford University Press, 1992), pp. 17–18.

concerns. Wood, he baldly asserts, "seems affronted mostly by the failure of the 1619 Project to solicit his advice." He contends that Professor Victoria Bynum, author of the landmark *The Free State of Jones*, is "best known for her attention to *glimmers* of anti-slavery *sentiment* among Southern whites" (emphasis added), as if the fact that a substantial proportion of white Southerners *took up arms* against the Confederacy, helping to ensure its defeat, is a trivial matter. As for James Oakes, Lichtenstein claims that the two-time Lincoln Prize-winner "doesn't really direct much fire at the 1619 Project." This is simply not so. In his interview with the WSWS, Oakes issued a scathing critique of the 1619 Project. As for Sean Wilentz of Princeton, Lichtenstein dismisses him out of hand for leading the aforementioned historians in writing "a far less enlightening" letter to the *Times* criticizing the 1619 Project than the "spirited rebuttal" that came in reply from *New York Times Magazine* editor Jake Silverstein. In fact, Silverstein's reply, like Lichtenstein's own editorial, was a simple evasion that failed to approach the content of the historians' criticisms, much less their more substantial interviews with the WSWS.

In a manner unfitting the office of AHR editor, Lichtenstein scoffs at all of these eminent historians—with multiple Bancroft, Lincoln, Pulitzer, and National Book Award prizes among them—as a "motley crew," and "Sean Wilentz and the gang of four." He then attributes to them positions they have never taken, claiming that they were aggrieved by the *Times* "practicing history without a license" and consulting "with the *wrong* historians" (emphasis in the original).

A nasty and cynical gibe. The objection of the historians interviewed by the WSWS to the 1619 Project is not that its authors are "practicing history without a license," but that they are concocting a historical narrative without facts.

Lichtenstein, who has chosen to adapt himself to the pressures exerted by identity politics, finds it difficult to believe that there are historians—with spines less flexible than his own—who conduct work as principled scholars and are not afraid to engage in discussions of history with Marxists. As Bynum has stated in an open letter replying to Lichtenstein:

> I entirely agree with Marxist scholars, however, that neither race nor gender can be understood apart from the class systems in which they are experienced. In this regard, I may care a bit more deeply than my fellow letter signers about what *is not,* as well as

what *is*, in the 1619 Project. For, as you suggest, the Project does ignore "class and class conflict." It is for just that reason that my concerns are more closely aligned with the WSWS than you have surmised.

Perhaps it's not surprising that racial essentialism forms the basis of much of the public reaction against historians critical of 1619, since the same essentialism underlies the Project itself. My understanding of class deeply informs my analysis of race, both of which I addressed in my interview with the WSWS, and my essay, "A Historian Critiques the 1619 Project," published on my blog, Renegade South, and by the WSWS. In both the interview and the essay, I dismissed pseudoscientific theories about separate races and argued that such beliefs predispose one to embrace a theory of hypodescent (i.e., the "one-drop-rule" of race), which posits certain ancestral "bloodlines" as more powerful than others.[8]

Lichtenstein is certainly aware that Hannah-Jones and her backers on Twitter have engaged in the most shameless race-baiting of these historians, as well as the WSWS, for daring to criticize the *New York Times*. In a disgrace to the AHR, Lichtenstein alludes to this approvingly, writing that, "as many critics hastened to note, all of these historians are white," before quickly adding that, "in principle, of course, that should do nothing to invalidate their views." Then why state it? His unmistakable insinuation—that speaking to "white" historians was a "choice on the part of the Trotskyist left"—is that one's understanding of history is determined by one's race.

In fact, Lichtenstein's claim is itself another lie. He simply chose to disregard the WSWS interviews with Clayborne Carson, editor of the papers of Martin Luther King Jr., and leading political scientist Adolph Reed Jr.

Curiously, Lichtenstein chastises the WSWS specifically for not reaching out to Barbara Fields, a leading scholar of slavery and the Civil War at Columbia University, who is also African American. As a matter of fact, though we have been unable as yet to arrange an interview, Professor Fields has sent us a letter via email which provides a succinct assessment of the 1619 Project:

---

8. Victoria Bynum, "My Response to Alex Lichtenstein Regarding the 1619 Project," World Socialist Web Site. https://www.wsws.org/en/articles/2020/01/31/resp-j31.html

I could hardly miss the hype of The 1619 Project, particularly since I am a print subscriber to the NYT. Although I have saved the issue (knowing that some of my students will have seen it, most likely online, and will have been seduced by its tendentious and ignorant history), I'm afraid I have not troubled to read the issue all the way through. The pre-launch publicity warned me of racecraft in the offing. And once I had the issue in hand, the first few bars disinclined me to waste my time on the rest of the operetta. Not that I would have expected anything more of the Times. Ask their writers to take the time to read Edmund Morgan or David Brion Davis or Eugene Genovese or Eric Williams or any of the explosion of rich literature about slavery in the United States and the hemisphere published over the past century? What an idea! And the packaged history they have assembled fits well with neo-liberal politics.

Having race-baited, mocked, and attributed to his colleagues positions that they did not in fact take, Lichtenstein retreats to his position that, after all, there is really nothing at stake in the *Times'* racialist presentation of the two American revolutions. He allows that Hannah-Jones's statement that the Revolution was waged to defend slavery "admittedly ... overstates" the case. He then imagines that the entire project might be acceptable if a few words were changed, softening Hannah-Jones's monocausal explanation for 1776 with qualifiers such as "one of the primary reasons" that "*some* of the Patriots" revolted was to defend slavery. He concludes, "While Hannah-Jones may be guilty of overstatement, this is more a matter of emphasis than it is of a correct or incorrect interpretation."

This is pure sophistry. To claim that the differences are merely over a somewhat careless wording is at once a conscious distortion and absurd. The claim that the colonials separated in order to preserve slavery is the very heart of the entire 1619 Project. In fact, Hannah-Jones has been on a lecture tour making the argument even more stridently than she did in her essay. In the curriculum being sent to the schools—a matter Lichtenstein also distorts—children are being asked to "rewrite" the Declaration of Independence in light of the lead essay's claims.

Lichtenstein uses the same tactic in relationship to Hannah-Jones's distortion of Lincoln, which she clearly borrowed, unattributed, from the late black nationalist historian Lerone Bennett Jr. Like Bennett, the 1619 Project rips from their context two episodes in order to present Lincoln as a racist—from one of his debates with the archracist Stephen Douglas, and another his meeting with five black leaders in the summer of 1862 on colonization. The contexts of these episodes were ably discussed by Oxford historian Richard Carwardine and Oakes in their interviews. As Carwardine explained, many more quotes could be mustered to defend the opposite conclusion: that Lincoln believed the concept of equality in the Declaration of Independence extended to blacks. But to Lichtenstein, the 1619 Project's tendentiously selective quotation "is a matter of emphasis and nuance."

Drawn into the 1619 Project's tangled web, Lichtenstein extends the falsification of Lincoln to Frederick Douglass—a figure who, like Martin Luther King Jr., is not mentioned in the entire magazine that purports to offer a new version of American race relations. The AHR editor points to Douglass's 1876 oration on Lincoln and homes in on partial statements in which the black abolitionist said that Lincoln "shared the prejudices of his white fellow-countrymen against the negro" and "was pre-eminently the white man's President, entirely devoted to the welfare of white men."[9] Astonishingly, Lichtenstein concludes this section by equating Douglass, the towering figure of abolitionism, to Hannah-Jones!

Yet the bulk of Douglass's magnificent speech was a brilliant exposition of Lincoln as a historical figure in which, among other things, Douglass said: "The name of Abraham Lincoln was near and dear to our hearts in the darkest and most perilous hours of the Republic. We were no more ashamed of him when shrouded in clouds of darkness, of doubt, and defeat than when we saw him crowned with victory, honour, and glory. Our faith in him was often taxed and strained to the uttermost, but it never failed."[10] Elsewhere, in his autobiography, Douglass said of Lincoln:

> In all my interviews with Mr. Lincoln I was impressed with his entire freedom from popular prejudice against the colored race. He was the first great man that I talked with in the United States freely, who in no single instance reminded me of the difference between himself and myself, of the difference of color, and I thought that all the more remarkable because he came from a State where there were black laws.[11]

---

9. *The Life and Times of Frederick Douglass*, Google Books, pp. 372, 376.
10. Ibid., p. 373.
11. *Narrative of the Life of Frederick Douglass*, Google Books, pp. 234–235.

Douglass's speech on Lincoln came in 1876, at the end of Reconstruction and its promise of full racial equality. Yet this was still two decades before the full implementation of Jim Crow segregation, which the 1619 Project's racialist narrative suggests demonstrates the immutability of "anti-black racism." On the contrary, the oppression of the African American population after the Civil War exemplified, in the most profound and tragic manner, the inability of a bourgeois revolution that had led to the unfettered and explosive development of capitalism to realize Lincoln's promise of "a new birth of freedom."

Here again, however, the African American population was hardly "alone," as the 1619 Project claims. In answering this claim, it is necessary to call attention to other facets of the American experience that are totally absent from the race-based narrative of the 1619 Project.

Beginning during the Civil War, and intensifying over the next three decades, the American military waged a ruthless war against the Indians of the American West, culminating in the conversion of their communal lands to private property under the Dawes Act of 1887 and the murderous rampage against the Sioux at Wounded Knee in 1890. The Indians, whose cultures could not be reconciled to capitalist notions of private property, occupied land demanded by the robber barons for the railroads and for the plunder of its mineral wealth.

And then there is the fact that in the half century separating the end of the Civil War with the beginning of World War I, millions upon millions of immigrants poured in from Europe and Asia—Irish, German, Italian, Jewish, Polish, Chinese, Japanese, and many others. Lichtenstein writes that "the African American experience must be considered central to every aspect of American history." This is the sort of vast generalization that can mean almost anything. But would it be less true to state that "the immigrant experience must be considered central to every aspect of American history"? It should be noted, in this connection, that the primary targets of immigration exclusion in the 1920s, and the central target of the revived Ku Klux Klan, were European immigrants. The exclusion of the Chinese and Japanese came earlier still, in 1882 and 1907, respectively.

In this half century, the American working class faced enormous difficulties in unifying over racial and national barriers. Nonetheless, workers—immigrant and native-born, white and black—fought innumerable bloody battles against factory owners and their hired gunmen and allies in the police departments and state militias. The class struggle in the United States was vicious. Hundreds of thousands died on the job, and many more died from poor living conditions, realities brought to an international audience by Upton Sinclair's *The Jungle* as well as other works of American realist literature. Many hundreds of workers died in labor massacres, from assassinations, and behind bars, in the precise same decades that hundreds of Southern blacks were lynched, typically, as Ida Wells established, on false allegations of assaults against women.

None of this is to minimize the experience of African Americans, who have been, with the single exception of the American Indians, the most oppressed part of the American population. However, notwithstanding its specific origins and characteristics, the struggle of African Americans to overcome the legacy of slavery and achieve the democratic rights guaranteed by the Constitution becomes inextricably connected with the broader mass struggle of the American working class against capitalist exploitation.

Lichtenstein pretends that there is nothing at stake in this debate. Yet the imposition on history of a racialist narrative must have contemporary political consequences. It was clear from the outset that the effort of the *New York Times* to utilize the 1619 Project as the basis of new educational curricula has definite political aims. These have become undeniable in light of the many public statements made by Hannah-Jones, including a boast made in Chicago in October that should stop historians in their tracks: "I'm making a moral argument. My method is guilt."[12]

The 1619 Project is, first of all, intended to bolster the Democratic Party's efforts to utilize racial identity, and the concept that blacks and whites have historically opposed interests, as a central electoral strategy. Ironically, this is a reworking of the political method that was employed by white supremacists in the South to maintain the dominance of the Democratic Party well into the 1960s, and which was later taken over by the Republicans in Richard Nixon's "Southern strategy."

Second, and still more fundamentally, it is aimed at undermining the growth of interracial class solidarity at a time of growing popular opposition, within the American and *international* working class, to massive social inequality. A historical interpretation that focuses on the centrality of economic forces and class conflict leads to demands for, at the very least, the curtailment of corporate power and an equitable redistribution of wealth. But the race-based interpretation advanced by the 1619 Project, reflecting

---

12. "Disputed NY Times '1619 Project' Already Shaping Schoolkids' Minds on Race—RealClearInvestigations." January 31, 2020. Accessed January 5, 2021. https://www.realclearinvestigations.com/articles/2020/01/31/disputed_ny_times_1619_project_is_already_shaping_kids_minds_on_race_bias_122192.html

the social aspirations of the more affluent sections of the African American middle class, serves to bolster demands for reparation payments. This is not incidental to the Project's aims. Hannah-Jones has already announced that her forthcoming project will be a demand for racially based reparations.

The disrespect expressed by Lichtenstein and the 1619 Project defenders toward leading historians such as Wood, McPherson, Oakes, Carwardine, Bynum, and Sean Wilentz expresses the rejection of a progressive democratic tendency in American historiography. The historians who have stressed the world-historical and progressive character of the two American Revolutions (1775–83 and 1861–65) tended to legitimize, even if that was not their intention, the perspective of a third American, socialist, revolution.

The 1619 Project, which takes no notice of the class struggle in its mythological narrative, advances a perspective that is, both in its theoretical foundations and political perspective, deeply reactionary. Lichtenstein knows this to be the case. He writes, at the conclusion of his essay, it is not his intention to "defend unconditionally what appears in the 1619 Project." The editor admits to feeling "frustration" with the exaggerated claims of the journalists behind the 1619 Project. "And, as the Trotskyists point out," Lichtenstein writes, "Marxists may find the substitution of 'race' for class relations disconcerting."

Coming at the conclusion of a lengthy defense of the 1619 Project, Lichtenstein's admission of reservations testifies not only to the unprincipled character of his essay but also to the degraded state of those sections of the academic community who have been drawn to racialist theories of history.

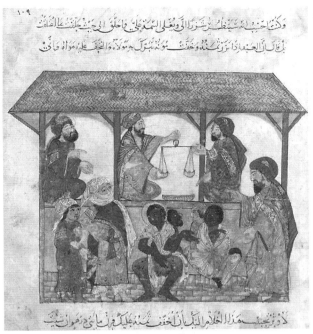

A thirteenth century Arab illustration depicting a dispute over the sale of African slaves in Yemen from the manuscript *Maqamat al-Hariri*. The origins of slavery reached back to the ancient world.

Source: Zabid Bibliothèque nationale de France, Département des Manuscrits, Division orientale.

Slavery was not simply imposed by "whites" on "blacks." A lithograph from around 1880 depicting Africans marching other Africans into slavery. Slaves were often captured in war or simply kidnapped.

Source: Wellcome Collection. Attribution 4.0 International (CC BY 4.0).

A map depicting the trade routes of Eastern European slaves taken into slavery in the Mediterranean and Middle East in the Middle Ages. The words "slave" and "Slav" have a common origin.

Source: Marturano, Aldo. 2008. "I secoli degli schiavi slavi," Centro Studi La Runa Archivio di storia, letteratura, tradizione, filosofia.

"Stowage of the British slave ship Brookes under the regulated slave trade act of 1788." During the three centuries of the slave trade from Africa to the Americas, hundreds of thousands died during the "middle passage" crossing of the Atlantic. The illustration was created by British abolitionists in 1788, indicating the emergence of antislavery sentiment after the American Revolution.

Source: Library of Congress Rare Book and Special Collections Division, Washington D.C.

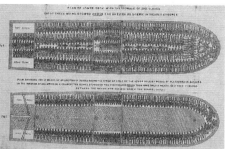

Lithograph of slaves working on a sugar plantation in Suriname, ca. 1840–1860. The British North American colonies received fewer than one in ten of the 12 million slaves taken from Africa during the four hundred years of the trans-Atlantic slave trade.

Source: Collectie Stichting Nationaal Museum van Wereldculturen.

An advertisement for the sale of indentured servants, *Virginia Gazette*, May 19, 1774. Indentured servants, like slaves, could be bought and sold and subjected to corporal punishment. Many were convict laborers forced into servitude. Unlike slaves, their children did not inherit their status.

Source: Smithsonian Institute.

During the Stamp Act crisis of 1765, a broadside by the Sons of Liberty called for patriots to gather for the forced resignation of a royal stamp distributor. By 1765 the "imperial crisis" was well underway—seven years before the Somerset ruling of 1772 that held slavery was not legal in England. The 1619 Project points to Somerset to argue that the American Revolution was waged to defend slavery.

Source: Massachusetts Historical Society.

Portrait of John Murray, Fourth Earl of Dunmore, 1765, by Joshua Reynolds. The royal governor's martial law order of November 7, 1775, known as the Dunmore Proclamation, offered emancipation to slaves and servants who would take up arms against their masters in rebellion. It exempted Loyalist slave-owners, many of whom would follow Dunmore to his final post as royal governor of the Bahamas. Slavery continued in the British Caribbean until 1833.

Source: National Galleries of Scotland.

Thomas Jefferson in 1786, age forty-three, portrait by Mather Brown. Jefferson articulated the revolutionary and egalitarian impulses of the war for independence in the Declaration of Independence. He authored the Northwest Ordinance banning slavery in what was to become the Midwest and was president when the US joined Britain in making illegal the trans-Atlantic slave trade. Yet he was not able to separate himself from the institution of slavery.

Source: National Portrait Gallery.

Benjamin Franklin in 1778, portrait by Joseph Siffrein Duplessis. In 1775 in Philadelphia, the first year of the American Revolution, the first antislavery meeting in world history took place; this led to the formation of the Pennsylvania Abolition Society. Franklin became its president in 1785.

Source: National Portrait Gallery.

The Storming of the Bastille, July 14, 1789. The American Revolution contributed decisively to the French Revolution of 1789. Jefferson was present as the American ambassador to France and consulted with Lafayette in the drafting of The Rights of Man and Citizen. The two "republican" revolutions initiated modern world history.

Source: Museum of the History of France.

The invention of the cotton gin in 1793 upset all predictions about the demise of slavery. It enabled a massive development of slavery and plantation agriculture—and with it the wealth and power of the Southern slaveowners. This image, called the *First cotton-gin*, was drawn by William L. Sheppard and appeared in *Harper's* weekly in 1869.

Source: Library of Congress's Prints and Photographs Division.

An 1853 map of the Erie Canal system. While cotton drew the South deeper into slavery, in the North the rapid development of canals and railroads expanded the reach of the emerging capitalist economy far into the interior and promoted "free labor," a middle class of farmers and shopkeepers, and factory owners and wage earners.

Source: Annual report of the New York State Engineer and Surveyor (C. Van Benthuysen, Albany, 1860).

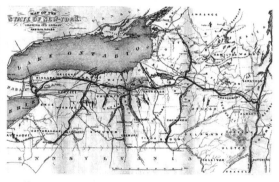

Wood engraving of the proslavery riot in Alton, Illinois, on November 7, 1837, in which abolitionist Elijah P. Lovejoy was murdered. The 1619 Project minimizes the role of white abolitionists in the fight against slavery.

Source: Illinois State Historic Preservation Office.

An 1856 map showing the free states in red and the slave states in black. Territorial expansion—achieved at the expense of the American Indians and Mexico—persistently raised the question of slavery during the sectional crisis between North and South.

Source: "Reynolds's political map of the United States, designed to exhibit the comparative area of the free and slave states and the territory open to slavery or freedom by the repeal of the Missouri Compromise." William C. Reynolds, 1856. Geography and Map Division, Library of Congress.

A Harvest of Death, 1863 photo by Timothy H. O'Sullivan. Union dead on the Gettysburg battlefield. Some 650,000 soldiers died in the war that destroyed chattel slavery.

Source: Library of Congress Prints and Photographs Division.

The burning of Union Depot in Pittsburgh during the Great Railway Strike of 1877. The rail strike swept the country the same year that Reconstruction came to an end, announcing that the class struggle between wage earners and capitalists had taken center stage in American history.

Source: Harper's Weekly, Saturday, August 11, 1877.

Karl Marx had understood that the Civil War would usher in a new era of class struggle. Just as "the American War of Independence initiated a new era of ascendancy for the middle class," Marx had written Lincoln in congratulation on his 1864 election, "so the American Anti-slavery War will do for the working classes." Later, Marx observed that "a new life immediately arose from the death of slavery. The first fruit of the American Civil War was the eight hours' agitation, which ran from the Atlantic to the Pacific, from New England to California with the seven-league boots of the locomotive."

Abraham Lincoln photographed in 1865. Because of Lincoln's antislavery convictions, his election in 1860 precipitated Southern secession and the Civil War. Lincoln issued the Emancipation Proclamation and saw through passage of the Thirteenth Amendment abolishing slavery. He was assassinated by white supremacist John Wilkes Booth on April 15, 1865, six days after Lee's surrender at Appomattox. The 1619 Project presents Lincoln as a racist who viewed blacks as an "obstacle to national unity."

Source: Library of Congress.

Frederick Douglass photographed in 1856. "War for the destruction of liberty must be met with war for the destruction of slavery," Douglass said early in the war. Douglass and Lincoln came to admire each other. Douglass is not mentioned in the 1619 Project.

Source: National Portrait Gallery, Smithsonian Institution.

Newton Knight led the Free State of Jones, a Unionist enclave in Mississippi and the subject of historian Victoria Bynum's book of the same name. Many poor and yeoman Southern whites opposed the Confederacy, forcing it to engage in "hidden civil wars" against areas like Jones County, Mississippi, and eastern Tennessee, western North Carolina, northern Georgia, and western Virginia, which broke away to form its own state in 1861. Several slave states did not join the Confederacy— Missouri, Kentucky, Maryland, and Delaware.

Source: Herman Welborn Collection, posted on Mississippi History Now.

C. Vann Woodward (1908–1999), historian of the American South. His book, *Strange Career of Jim Crow,* argued that the imposition of Jim Crow segregation was a response of the Southern ruling elite to the threat posed by the Populist movement of poor farmers, white and black. Martin Luther King Jr. called it "the bible" of the civil rights movement.

Source: Yale University.

Eugene V. Debs (1855–1926) delivering his Canton, Ohio, speech opposing US entry into World War I, for which he was jailed by the Wilson administration. Debs, the founding figure of American socialism, refused to speak before racially segregated audiences.

James P. Cannon (1890–1974), founder of the Trotskyist movement in the United States. "American capitalism took hundreds of thousands of Negroes from the South [and] succeeded in transforming them and their sons into one of the most militant and reliable detachments of the great victorious steel strike of 1946. This same capitalism took tens of thousands and hundreds of thousands of prejudiced hillbillies from the South [who] learned to exchange the insignia of the KKK for the union button of the CIO, and to turn the Klansman's fiery cross into a bonfire to warm pickets at the factory gate."

Claude McKay (1889–1948) in 1920. The young poet, like many African American intellectuals and artists, was inspired by the Russian Revolution. "For American Negroes the indisputable and outstanding fact of the Russian Revolution," McKay explained in 1921, "is that a mere handful of Jews, much less in ratio to the number of Negroes in the American population, have attained, through the Revolution, all the political and social rights denied them under the regime of the Czar."

Jacob Lawrence's 1941 Migration Series: In 1910, roughly 90 percent of the African American population lived in the former slave states. The "Great Migration" of millions from country to city in the North and West transformed them into an important section of the polyglot American working class.

Source: National Public Radio, courtesy of the Phillips Collection.

Autoworkers at shift change at a Detroit Ford Motor Company factory in 1948.

Source: Walter P. Reuther Library, Archives of Labor and Urban Affairs, Wayne State University.

Martin Luther King Jr., arrested for "loitering" in Birmingham, Alabama, in 1958. "We can't solve our problems now until there is a radical redistribution of economic and political power. ... We are engaged in a class struggle ... dealing with the problem of the gulf between the haves and the have nots." Like Frederick Douglass, the civil rights leader is not mentioned in the 1619 Project.

Part IV

Historical Commentary

Hands off the Monuments to Washington, Jefferson, Lincoln, and Grant!

In recent weeks, participants in demonstrations against police violence in the United States have demanded the removal of monuments to Confederate leaders who waged an insurrection to defend slavery during the American Civil War of 1861–65.

But the justifiable demand for the removal of monuments to these defenders of racial inequality has been unfairly accompanied by attacks against memorials to those who led the American Revolution, which, in upholding the principle of equality, for the first time placed a question mark on the institution of slavery, and the Civil War that ended slavery.

On June 14, 2020, a statue of Thomas Jefferson, the author of the Declaration of Independence, was torn down in Portland, Oregon, followed four days later by a statue of George Washington, who led the forces that defeated the British during the American Revolution. On June 19, protesters in San Francisco knocked over a statue of Ulysses S. Grant, who commanded the Union Army to victory in the Civil War and suppressed the Ku Klux Klan during Reconstruction.

Now, a social media campaign has been launched for the removal of the famous Emancipation Memorial statue in Washington D.C., which depicts Abraham Lincoln standing above a kneeling slave who has been freed. The statue, erected in 1876, was in fact paid for by freed slaves. Frederick Douglass gave the oration at its dedication.

Thomas Mackaman and Niles Niemuth, "Hands off the monuments to Washington, Jefferson, Lincoln and Grant!," World Socialist Web Site, June 22, 2020.

No one can object to the removal of monuments to the leaders of the Confederacy, who dedicated their lives to the rejection of the thesis that "all men are created equal." These figures sought to "wring their bread from the sweat of other men's faces," in the words of Lincoln's Second Inaugural Address. The monuments to the leaders of the seceded states were erected in a period of political reaction following the end of Reconstruction, with the aim of legitimizing the Confederacy as part of the "lost cause" school of historiography, which denied the revolutionary character of the American Civil War.

But the removal of monuments to the leaders of America's revolutionary and civil wars has no justification. These men led great social struggles against the very forces of reaction that justified racial oppression as an incarnation of the fundamental inequality of human beings.

It is entirely possible that those who participated in the desecration of monuments to the leaders of the two American revolutions were not conscious of what they were doing. If that is the case, then the blame must be placed on those who incited these actions. In the months preceding these events, the *Times*, speaking for dominant sections of the Democratic political establishment, launched an effort to discredit both the American Revolution and the Civil War.

In the *New York Times*' 1619 Project, the American Revolution was presented as a war to defend slavery and Abraham Lincoln was cast as a garden variety racist.

Historical clarification of some of the major historical figures involved is necessary.

Thomas Jefferson was the author of what is arguably the most famous revolutionary sentence in world history: "We hold these truths to be self-evident, that all men are created equal." That declaration has been inscribed on the banner of every fight for equality ever since 1776. When Jefferson formulated it, he was crystalizing a new way of thinking based on the principle of natural human equality. The rest of the preamble to the Declaration of Independence spells out in searing language the natural right of people to revolution.

The American Revolution delivered a powerful impulse in that direction, which led to the French Revolution of 1789 and the greatest slave revolt in history, the Haitian Revolution of 1791, in which slaves liberated themselves and threw off French colonial domination.

George Washington was the commander of the Continental Army in the American Revolution (1775–83), in which the thirteen colonies asserted their independence from their British colonial masters. Washington, in a decision that electrified the world, left behind his military post and returned to private life, helping to institute in practice the separation of the civilian from military power in the republic.

Abraham Lincoln must rank as one of the greatest figures of modern history. The leader of the North, or the Union, in the Civil War, his historical purpose was revealed over the course of that war to be the destruction of what contemporaries called "the Slave Power." Lincoln saw that struggle through to a victory in April of 1865, only days before he was martyred to the cause of human liberty. The world grieved at his death. This was so in both the North and South, and especially among the freed slaves. "The world only discovered him a hero after he had fallen a martyr," Marx wrote.

Ulysses S. Grant was a hero of the Civil War whose stature was second only to that of Lincoln. Prior to his ascension to lead the entire military effort in 1864, the cause of the Union was hampered by generals who opposed the emancipatory impulse of the Civil War.

Grant and his trusted friend General William Tecumseh Sherman recognized that to defeat the South required a war for the destruction of slavery, root and branch. "I can't spare this man. He fights," Lincoln said of Grant. As president in the White House (1869–77), Grant was overwhelmed by the force of capitalism unleashed by the Civil War, but he defended the freed slaves and suppressed the Ku Klux Klan (KKK). After he retired from the presidency in 1877, Grant toured Europe, where throngs of workers attended his public events and speeches.

The attacks on the monuments to these men were instigated in an increasingly frenzied attempt by the Democratic Party and the *New York Times* to racialize American history, to create a narrative in which the history of mankind is reduced to the history of racial struggle. This campaign has produced a pollution of democratic consciousness, which meshes entirely with the reactionary political interests driving it.

It is worth noting that the one institution seemingly immune from this purge is the Democratic Party, which served as the political wing of the Confederacy and, subsequently, the Ku Klux Klan.

This filthy historical legacy is matched only by the Democratic Party's contemporary record in supporting wars that, as a matter of fact, primarily targeted nonwhites. Democrats supported the invasion of Iraq and Afghanistan, and under President Barack Obama, destroyed Libya and Syria. The *New York Times* was a leading champion and propagandist for all of these wars.

The *Times* and the Democratic Party seek to confuse and disorient the democratic sentiments of masses of people entering into political struggle against the capitalist system and its repressive forces within the state because they know that the growing multiracial, multinational, and multiethnic movement of the working class will take place in direct opposition to their own politics.

There are many people involved in the taking down of these statues who do not understand the political implications of what they are doing. However, ignorance is not an excuse. Actions have an objective significance. Those who attack the American Revolution assist contemporary reaction.

The Second Assassination of Abraham Lincoln

One month after the killing of George Floyd, the mass multiracial demonstrations against police violence are in danger of being hijacked and misdirected by reactionary political forces who are attempting to promote racial divisions, sabotage the unity of working people and youth, and undermine the development of the class struggle against capitalism. This campaign is now concentrated on desecrating and destroying the statues of figures who led the American Revolution and the Civil War.

It is difficult to find words that adequately express the sense of revulsion produced by the monstrous attacks on memorials that honor the memory of Abraham Lincoln, the United States' greatest president, who led the country during the Second American Revolution that destroyed the Slave Power and emancipated millions of enslaved African Americans.

On the evening of April 14, 1865, less than a week after the surrender of the main Confederate army, which brought the four-year Civil War to an end, Lincoln was shot in the head by the proslavery actor John Wilkes Booth. Nine hours later, at 7:22 on the morning of April 15, Lincoln died of the wound inflicted by the assassin. Standing beside Lincoln's deathbed, Secretary of War Edwin Stanton famously declared, "Now he belongs to the ages."

Lincoln's martyrdom produced an outpouring of grief throughout the United States and the world. The working class recognized that it had lost a great champion of democracy and human equality. Karl Marx, writing on behalf of the International Working Men's Association, wrote in the days

Niles Niemuth and David North, "Racial-communalist politics and the second assassination of Abraham Lincoln," World Socialist Web Site, June 25, 2020.

after Lincoln's assassination that he was "one of the rare men who succeed in becoming great without ceasing to be good."[1]

Abraham Lincoln was an extraordinarily complex man, whose life and politics reflected the contradictions of his time. He could not, as he once stated, "escape history." Determined to save the Union, he was driven by the logic of the bloody civil war to resort to revolutionary measures. In the course of the brutal struggle, Lincoln gave expression to the revolutionary-democratic aspirations that inspired hundreds of thousands of Americans to fight and sacrifice their lives for a "new birth of freedom."

Every period of political upsurge in the United States has drawn inspiration from Lincoln's life. Since its opening in 1922, the Lincoln Memorial in Washington D.C. has been the site of some of the most important moments in the struggle against racial oppression and for equality. In 1939, when Hitler's Nazis were on the march in Europe and fascism had many sympathizers among the American ruling elite, the famous African American contralto Marian Anderson was denied the right to sing at Constitution Hall. So instead she sang on the steps of the Lincoln Memorial before a crowd of 75,000.

In 1963, at the March on Washington, Martin Luther King Jr. stood at the same location as he delivered his "I Have a Dream" speech, calling for equality and racial integration before a crowd of 250,000. Later in that decade, tens of thousands of youth protesting the Vietnam War assembled at the monument.

It is not coincidental that the working-class upsurge of the 1930s was associated with many great artistic depictions of Lincoln, including the films *Young Mr. Lincoln* (1939) and *Abe Lincoln in Illinois* (1940). Aaron Copland's beloved orchestral-narrative masterpiece, *Lincoln Portrait* (1942), concludes with the declaration that the sixteenth president of the United States "is everlasting in the memory of his countrymen."

But now, 155 years after the tragedy at Ford's Theatre, Lincoln is the subject of a second assassination. This one must not succeed.

Eleanor Holmes Norton, Washington D.C.'s nonvoting delegate to Congress, said she will introduce a bill to remove the famous Emancipation Monument from the Lincoln Park in Washington, D.C. The race-fixated protesters have declared their intention to tear down the monument, which was paid for by former slaves and movingly dedicated by black abolitionist Frederick Douglass in 1876.

---

1. Karl Marx, *Marx & Engels, Letters to Americans 1848–1895* (International Publishers, New York, 1953) p. 72.

"The designers of the Emancipation Statue in Lincoln Park in DC didn't take into account the views of African Americans," Norton stated in a tweet. Democrats assert that the statue demeans "the black community" because it depicts Lincoln freeing a slave crouched in a runner's pose, which the sculptor intended to symbolize the liberation of the Civil War.

Norton's reactionary effort is being supported by Democratic Party officials in Boston, who will hold hearings in the coming weeks to entertain demands for the removal of a replica of the Emancipation Memorial in that city.

Lincoln is not the only leader of the anti-Confederate forces to be targeted. In San Francisco last week, a statue of Ulysses S. Grant, the great general of the victorious Union Army and later president of the United States, was torn down.

An even filthier example of the racialist campaign is the desecration of the Boston monument honoring the legendary 54th Massachusetts Volunteer Infantry Regiment. The 54th Massachusetts, led by abolitionist Robert Gould Shaw, was the second all-black regiment organized in the Civil War. Protesters object to the fact that the 54th, famously depicted in the film *Glory* (1989), was commanded by a white officer, Shaw. Holland Cotter, the *New York Times'* co-chief art critic, slandered the monument as a "white supremacist" visual for its depiction of Shaw leading his African American battalion.

Another Union monument, a statue of abolitionist Hans Christian Heg (1829–63), was pulled down Tuesday night in Madison, Wisconsin. The statue was beheaded before being thrown into a nearby lake. A Norwegian immigrant, Heg led the Fifteenth Wisconsin Regiment, known as the Scandinavian Regiment, against the Confederacy. Prior to the war, Heg, a member of the Free Soil Party, fiercely opposed slavery and headed an anti-slave-catcher militia in Wisconsin. He was killed at the age of 33 at the Battle of Chickamauga in September 1863.

The Socialist Equality Party rejects all the lame liberal excuses and justifications that are offered to legitimize the desecration of these memorials. Actions, whatever the motivations ascribed to them, have objective significance and very real political consequences.

The assault on Lincoln monuments and other memorials honoring the leaders of the American Revolution and Civil War are political provocations aimed at whipping up racial animosities. Such provocations are well-known forms of communalist politics, which resemble the burning down of Muslim mosques by Hindu fanatics or Hindu temples by Muslim fanatics. Here in the United States, the statues are being attacked as examples of "white" rule.

The attacks on the statues are the outcome of a campaign by the two capitalist parties and various reactionary elements in the upper-middle class to racialize and communalize American politics. The growing intensity of this campaign is a response to the upsurge of working-class militancy, which is seen as a threat to capitalism. Far from welcoming the interracial unity displayed in the demonstrations against police brutality, the ruling elites and most affluent sections of the middle class are terrified by its political implications.

In the promotion of racial politics, there is a division of labor between the Democratic and Republican parties. Trump and the Republicans pitch their appeal to the most politically disoriented elements in American society, manipulating their economic insecurities in a manner intended to incite racial antagonism and deflect social anger away from the capitalist system.

The Democratic Party employs another variant of communalist politics, evaluating and explaining all social problems and conflicts in racial terms. Whatever the particular issue may be—poverty, police brutality, unemployment, low wages, deaths caused by the pandemic—it is almost exclusively defined in racial terms. In this racialized fantasy world, "whites" are endowed with an innate "privilege" that exempts them from all hardship.

This grotesque distortion of present-day reality requires a no less grotesque distortion of the past. For contemporary America to be portrayed as a land of relentless racial warfare, it is necessary to create a historical narrative in the same terms. In place of the class struggle, the entire history of the United States is presented as the story of perpetual racial conflict.

Even before the outbreak of the pandemic, efforts to create racial foundations for contemporary communalist politics were well underway. The *New York Times*, the principal voice of corporate and financial patrons of the Democratic Party, concocted the insidious 1619 Project, the central purpose of which was to promote a racial narrative. The main argument of this project, unveiled in August 2019, was that the American Revolution was undertaken to protect North American slavery and that the Civil War, led by the racist Abraham Lincoln, had nothing to do with the ending of slavery. The slaves, so the new story went, liberated themselves.

The purpose of lies about history, as Trotsky explained, is to conceal real social contradictions. In this case, the contradictions are those embedded in the staggering levels of social inequality produced by capitalism. These contradictions can be resolved on a progressive basis only through the methods of class struggle, in which the working class fights consciously to put an end to capitalism and replaces it with socialism. Efforts to divert and sabotage that struggle by dissolving class identity into the miasma of racial identity lead inexorably in the direction of fascism.

Through the promotion of a racial version of communalism, all factions of the ruling class seek to divide the working class so as to better exploit it and ward off the threat of revolution. It is no coincidence that when American society is straining under the weight of the COVID-19 pandemic, which has killed more than 120,000 people and sparked an economic crisis on the scale of the Great Depression, the Democrats are ever more ferociously seeking to make race the fundamental issue.

The alternative to the politics of racial communalism is the socialist politics of working-class unity.

July 4, 1776 in World History

Today marks the 244th anniversary of the public proclamation of the Declaration of Independence, on July 4, 1776, which established the United States of America. By the time the Declaration was issued, the American colonists—and especially those of Massachusetts—had already been at war with the immensely powerful military forces of Great Britain for fifteen months. Though the final decision for independence had not yet been taken, the drafting of a Declaration was assigned on June 11 by the Continental Congress, assembled in Philadelphia, to a Committee of Five. It consisted of Benjamin Franklin of Pennsylvania, John Adams of Massachusetts, Thomas Jefferson of Virginia, Robert Livingston of New York, and Roger Sherman of Connecticut.

After agreeing on an outline of the document, the Committee decided that the first draft should be written by the thirty-three-year-old Thomas Jefferson, whose exceptional intellect and remarkable literary gifts were already widely recognized. On June 28, he completed his draft, which was then reviewed by members of the Congress. Various changes were made in the course of the editing process. The most substantial change was the removal of Jefferson's indictment of Great Britain for having imposed slavery on the colonies. On July 2, 1776, the Continental Congress adopted a resolution that authorized the break with Great Britain. Two days later, on July 4, it approved the final draft of the Declaration of Independence.

David North, "The two American Revolutions in world history," World Socialist Web Site, July 4, 2020.

The immediate political consequence of the document—the formal break with Britain and the initiation of a full-scale war to secure the independence of the United States—was, in itself, sufficient to impart to the Declaration immense and enduring historical significance. But it is not only the direct political impact of the document but, rather, the principles it proclaimed that determined the world-historical stature of the Declaration.

The document begins with the words, "When in the Course of human events it becomes necessary for one people to dissolve the political bands which have connected them with another." What these words meant was that governments, and the political and social relations upon which they were based and which they defended, were not timeless and unalterable. They were the creation of men, not God. This assertion exploded the essential justification, sanctified by religion, for monarchy, aristocracy, i.e., for all forms of political power based on obscurantist veneration of bloodlines. What was created by man could be changed by man.

The Declaration then proceeded to a remarkable assertion: "We hold these truths to be self-evident, that all men are created equal, that they are endowed by their Creator with certain unalienable Rights, that among these are Life, Liberty and the pursuit of Happiness."

In a strictly empirical sense, there was nothing "self-evident"—that is, so obviously true that it hardly required further argument—about any of these "truths." Reality, as it was to be observed in every part of the world, including the colonies, contradicted what the Declaration claimed to be "self-evident."

In the world of the late eighteenth century, most human beings were treated like beasts of burden, if not worse. Where in the world did existing conditions substantiate the claim that all of humanity had been "created equal"? The monarchies and aristocracies were based on the unchallengeable legitimacy of inherent inequality. The place of people in society, even where there had been a slow erosion of feudal relations, was a manifestation of a divine design.

Where was "Life," for the great mass of people, honored and protected? In advanced Britain, children as young as six could be hanged for pickpocketing a wealthy person's handkerchief. The great mass of people lived in wretched poverty, enforced by strict relations of feudal and semifeudal hierarchy. There was little "Happiness" in the lives of the general population, let alone for the millions throughout the world and in the Americas who were enslaved and hardly considered to be human.

The "truths" invoked by Jefferson were not "self-evident" in a crudely empirical sense. They were, rather, "truths" that were obtained through the application of scientific thought, i.e., Reason, as it had developed under the influence of the physicist Isaac Newton, materialist thinkers such as John Locke, and the great French philosophes of the Enlightenment, to the study of history and human society. It was the application of Reason that determined what was, and was not, politically legitimate. It was science, not the irrational and unsubstantiated invocations of a divine order, that determined what must be. It was in this profound sense that the equality of man and the "unalienable Rights" to "Life, Liberty and the Pursuit of Happiness" were "self-evident."

Jefferson and his comrades in arms were well aware that empirically existing political and social conditions did not conform to the "self-evident Truths" asserted in the Declaration. From this fact, the following conclusion was drawn: Governments derive their "just powers from the consent of the governed." Therefore, "whenever any Form of Government becomes destructive of these ends, it is the Right of the People to alter or to abolish it, and to institute new Government, laying its foundation on such principles and organizing its powers in such form, as to them shall seem most likely to effect their Safety and Happiness."

Thus, the Declaration of Independence proclaimed revolution to be a legitimate and even necessary means of removing from power governments that had become oppressive and injurious to the "Happiness" of the people. Jefferson adhered to this principle and displayed not the slightest squeamishness when the masses of France, inspired by American Revolution, took bloody vengeance against King Louis XVI and the aristocracy. Louis, declared Jefferson, ought to be punished "like other criminals." Rather than witness the defeat of the French Revolution, Jefferson wrote to a friend: "I would have seen half the earth desolated. Were there but an Adam and an Eve left in every country, and left free, it would be better than as it is now." He expressed unmitigated joy at the prospect of the revolution's victory, which would "bring at length kings, nobles and priests to the scaffolds which they have been so long deluging with human blood."

It is, of course, an undeniable historical fact that Jefferson's personal ownership of slaves and his compromises with slavery represent the great irony and even tragedy of his life. They were the expression in his personal biography of the existing social conditions and contradictions of the world into which he was born—a world in which slavery, serfdom, and numerous forms of indentured servitude flourished and whose legitimacy was hardly questioned. No doubt, the moralizing philistines of academia will continue to condemn Jefferson. But their condemnations do not alter by one iota the revolutionary impact of the Declaration of Independence.

The American Revolution of 1775–83 did not solve the problem of slavery. This is not because the solution was blocked by Jefferson or other revolutionary leaders, like Washington, who owned slaves. The incomplete character of the first stage of the American *bourgeois-democratic revolution* was determined by the existing objective conditions—and not simply those that existed in North America. Mankind, as Marx was later to explain, "inevitably sets itself only such tasks as it is able to solve, since closer examination will always show that the problem itself arises only when the material conditions for its solution are already present or at least in the course of formation."[1] The conditions for a decisive settlement with slavery did not yet exist. That still required several decades of industrial development and the emergence of an economically powerful capitalist class in the North. Moreover, that class had to develop a democratic political movement capable of mobilizing masses and sustaining a long and bitter civil war.

This essential social and economic process unfolded rapidly in the decades that followed the American Revolution. The capitalist development of the North became increasingly incompatible with the political domination of the United States by the Southern Slave Power. This objective incompatibility found its ideological expression in the ever more intense awareness that the ideals of human equality proclaimed in the Declaration of Independence could not be reconciled with the horrifying reality of slavery.

However, it must be stressed that the process of historical causation that led up to the Civil War was not driven in a one-sided manner by socioeconomic factors, with the ideological conflicts a mere reflection of the former. The influence exerted by the principles articulated in the Declaration played an immense, almost independent, role in influencing mass political consciousness in the North and preparing it for an intransigent struggle against the Slave Power.

Abraham Lincoln's intellectual and political development epitomized the influence exerted by Thomas Jefferson and the Declaration that he authored. Again and again, in numerous speeches, Lincoln invoked the political legacy of Jefferson. For example, in a letter written in 1859, Lincoln stated:

---

1. Karl Marx, *A Contribution to the Critique of Political Economy* (New York: International Publishers, 1970), p. 21.

All honor to Jefferson—to the man who, in the concrete pressure of a struggle for national independence by a single people, had the coolness, forecast, and capacity to introduce into a merely revolutionary document, an abstract truth, applicable to all men and all times, and so to embalm it there, that to-day and in all coming days, it shall be a rebuke and a stumbling-block to the very harbingers of re-appearing tyranny and oppression.[2]

Following his election to the presidency in 1860, and on his way to Washington to assume the presidency, Lincoln declared, in an impromptu speech in Philadelphia on February 22, 1861, "I have never had a feeling politically that did not spring from the sentiments embodied in the Declaration of Independence."

He continued:

It [the Revolution] was not the mere matter of the separation of the colonies from the mother land; but something in that Declaration giving liberty, not alone to the people of this country, but hope to the world for all future time. It was that which gave promise that in due time the weights should be lifted from the shoulders of all men, and that all should have an equal chance. This is the sentiment embodied in that Declaration of Independence.[3]

Jefferson was the author of the great revolutionary manifesto that provided the ideological inspiration for the Civil War. Under Lincoln's leadership, the Union armies—which ultimately mobilized and armed tens of thousands of slaves in struggle against the Confederacy—destroyed slavery.

Of course, the United States that emerged from the Civil War soon betrayed the promises of democracy and equality that Lincoln had made. The "new birth of freedom" gave way to the imperatives of modern capitalism. A new form of social struggle, between an emerging working class and an industrial bourgeoisie, came to dominate the political and social landscape. In this new class struggle, the Northern bourgeoisie saw the benefit of an alliance with the remnants of the old slaveowning class. Reconstruction was brought to an

---

2. Abraham Lincoln, Letter to Henry L. Pierce, April 8, 1859,
http://www.abrahamlincolnonline.org/lincoln/speeches/pierce.htm
3. Abraham Lincoln, Speech in Independence Hall, Philadelphia, February 22, 1861, *Collected Works of Abraham Lincoln*, Vol. 4,
https://quod.lib.umich.edu/l/lincoln/lincoln4/1:376?rgn=div1;view=fulltext

end. Racism was incited and utilized as a potent weapon against the unity of the working class.

Intransigent opposition to this specific form of political reaction became a central task of the working class in the fight for socialism. Only through the establishment of workers power, the ending of capitalism, and the building of a socialist society on a world scale can the scourge of racism and all forms of social oppression be overcome. And in this fight, the words and deeds of both Jefferson and Lincoln will continue to inspire. All that was historically progressive in their lifework lives on in the modern socialist movement.

Lincoln and the Tragedy of the Dakota 38

On October 11, 2020, protesters in Portland, Oregon, tore down a statue of Abraham Lincoln, leaving the phrase "Dakota 38" spray-painted at its base. The attack took place during a protest called the Indigenous Peoples Day of Rage Against Colonialism, organized in opposition to the nationally observed Columbus Day holiday on October 12.

"Dakota 38" is a reference to the Dakota War of 1862, which resulted in the execution of thirty-eight Dakota Sioux Native American men for launching an uprising in Minnesota during the Civil War. This is the largest mass execution in US history. It was also the largest act of executive clemency in US history. Though the Civil War was raging and the fate of the nation hung in the balance in the autumn of 1862, Lincoln personally reviewed the case and reversed the death sentences of 265 other Sioux men. He suffered bitter political recriminations as a result.

The executions took place during a war which would abolish chattel slavery at the cost of more lives than all other American wars combined. For leading the revolutionary struggle to emancipate four million slaves, Lincoln would ultimately pay with his life on April 15, 1865, just six days after Confederate General Robert E. Lee's surrender at Appomattox.

Ripped from this historical context, the tragic events that took place in Minnesota 158 years ago are manipulated to portray Lincoln as a racist no different from those who called for the extermination of the Native populations. This is part of a larger campaign, spearheaded by the *New York Times'* 1619

Renae Cassimeda, "Lincoln, the Dakota 38 and the racialist falsification of history," World Socialist Web Site, November 9, 2020.

Project, to undermine the democratic and egalitarian legacy of America's first two revolutions.

Another Lincoln statue has been targeted for removal on the same grounds as in Portland. On September 29, the University of Wisconsin-Madison student government voted to unanimously approve a resolution to remove a historic Lincoln statue from a main common area on the campus, arguing that it serves as a remnant "of this school's history of white supremacy."

In an email to *The College Fix*, Robyn George, chair of the Associated Students of Madison (ASM) Legislative Affairs Committee, argued Lincoln should not be memorialized on account of the "good things he's done for America, such as passing the 13th amendment, [when] in fact, Lincoln ordered the largest execution on American soil: 38 Dakota peoples." ASM's Diverse Engagement Coordinator Chrystal Zhao told the outlet that Lincoln is a "representation of ethnic cleansing of indigenous folks" and claimed that seeing his figure on campus makes students "feel uncomfortable."

Significantly, no social demands were put forward by the October 11 protesters or by the ASM. They make no reference to jobs, hospitals, housing, or health care for Native peoples, the most oppressed section of the American population.

The WSWS condemns the destruction of the Lincoln statue in Portland and the broader attack on the sixteenth president, and rejects the distorted narrative put forward by the petty-bourgeois promoters of identity politics. As always, the best answer to the racialist falsification of history comes from a review of the actual historical record.

Leading up to the outbreak of conflict in southwestern Minnesota, tensions had been rising for years due to injustices inflicted on the Dakota by the national and state governments, as well as by land speculators and business interests that sought to rob them of their ancestral lands.

An estimated 150,000 American settlers had moved into Dakota territory over the course of the decade before the Civil War. Treaties passed between the Dakota Sioux and the US government forced the Native Americans to relinquish nine-tenths of their land. By 1858, the same year Minnesota was admitted to the US as a state, over seven thousand Dakota Sioux were confined to a tiny reservation on a narrow strip of land along the Minnesota River. They were no longer able to fully support themselves in their traditional manner via hunting and agriculture, and were dependent on goods, services, and annuity payments promised in treaties with the federal government. The Dakota depended on these payments for their survival, but corrupt federal agents and traders would often cheat them out of their money.

The fall harvest in 1861 was poor due to an infestation of cutworms, and the following winter was severe. By late spring, many Native Americans were starving and forced to sustain themselves on roots. When they assembled to receive their annuity payments, the goods and money were late. Reservation traders claimed half of the annuity for payment of goods previously given to the Dakota, even though Dakota Chief Wabasha had never agreed to this transfer of funds. There was promise of a successful fall harvest of corn and vegetables, but rumors circulated that there would be no annuities at all that year.

On August 4, Dakota broke into the Yellow Medicine Upper Agency settlement warehouse to get food, and a small group of Minnesota Militia, threatening the use of cannon, fought off the starved and desperate group. Additionally, agents and traders at the Redwood Lower Agency settlement refused to allow Dakota to purchase food on credit, even though they faced starvation. Andrew Myrick, a trader at the Lower Agency, famously expressed the attitude of many American settlers in the region at the time, remarking, "So far as I'm concerned, let them eat grass." The callous statement ignited fury among the Mdewakantonwan band of Dakota, who received their annuities from the Lower Agency traders.

On August 17, four Dakota men returning from a hunting expedition killed five white settlers in Acton, Minnesota. Upon hearing news of the killings, Dakota leaders met to discuss the situation and decided to go on the offensive.

The next morning, on August 18, a group of Dakota men led by Taoyateduta (Little Crow), a leader of a Mdewakantonwan band of Dakota, attacked the Lower Agency settlement. The uprising was encouraged by the absence of fighting-age men among the settlers. About one-eighth of Minnesota's entire population of 180,000 fought in the Civil War, higher than any other Union state.

A six-week period of fighting ensued in Minnesota and resulted in the bloodiest conflict between Native American and American settlers since the colonial period. The fighting affected tens of thousands of civilians and non-combatants. Over a hundred settlers, mostly women and children, were captured by the Dakota. Terrified by the outbreak of violence, an estimated twenty thousand farmers picked up their families, deserted their crops, and fled to St. Paul. Well over six hundred white settlers, an estimated two hundred soldiers, and as many as three hundred Dakota died in the conflict.

Confronted with the combined force of the US military and citizen militia, and facing diminished support for the war among their own ranks as well as from neighboring tribes, the Dakota surrendered on September 23 after a bloody defeat at the Battle of Wood Lake. American troops rounded up thousands of Dakota soldiers as well as hundreds of men, women, and children who had nothing to do with the conflict. Soldiers burned crops, destroyed homes, and placed the Dakota Sioux into barbaric internment camps.

Approximately 1,500 Dakota men, women, and children were taken into custody. Almost immediately, the military carried out show trials to condemn hundreds of them to death.

From September 28 until November 5, nearly four hundred Dakota men were tried by a five-man military commission. Prior to Lincoln's final decision in the matter, the majority of the 392 who were convicted—303 Dakota men—were sentenced to death.

In his 2013 study "I Could not Afford to Hang Men for Votes—Lincoln the Lawyer, Humanitarian Concerns, and the Dakota Pardons," legal historian Paul Finkelman, who was then a professor at Albany Law School and is now the president of Gratz College in greater Philadelphia, notes that the Dakota trials were in violation of the traditional rules of war, as combatants were put on trial and sentenced to death on the theory that they had not been involved in a legitimate war, but rather had participated in some illegal violent activity.

Finkelman writes: "The military tribunal essentially held that there was no meaningful distinction between those who committed what might be regarded as war crimes and those who were merely soldiers or fellow travelers in Little Crow's make-shift army. ... The standard of guilt was quite simple: anyone who fired a rifle in any form of combat was considered guilty and subject to the death penalty."[1]

The Dakota trials denied counsel for the defendants and were carried out with vengeance and haste by a military commission, appointed by General Henry Hastings Sibley and comprised of white Minnesota residents who tried the Dakota as murderers instead of belligerents engaged in a legitimately declared war. Finkelman explains, "General Sibley clearly had no real sense of due process or fair trials, as he reviewed the trials that lasted a few minutes and sentenced men to death for non-capital offences on the basis of virtually no

---

1. Paul Finkelman, "I Could not Afford to Hang Men for Votes—Lincoln the Lawyer, Humanitarian Concerns, and the Dakota Pardons," *William Mitchell Law Review: 2013*, Vol. 39: Iss. 2, Article 2. pp. 405–449. http://open.mitchellhamline.edu/wmlr/vol39/iss2/2

evidence."[2] In response to the bloody conflict, the Minnesotans demanded a mass execution.

Trials had been underway for two weeks before Lincoln received news of the planned executions. On October 14, US General John Pope, then head of the newly established War Department of the Northwest, sent a report on the ongoing trials and planned executions to Lincoln, which was read aloud during a cabinet meeting in Washington D.C. Lincoln and his cabinet were deeply disturbed by the news and swiftly moved to prevent any precipitous action in Minnesota.

Secretary of the Navy Gideon Welles noted in his diary, "I was disgusted with the whole thing; the tone and opinions of the dispatch are discreditable ... what may have been the provocation we are not told."[3] Welles suspected that the atrocities inflicted on the Dakota were part of a larger plan to remove all Native Americans from the state. His inclination would prove correct in the years following the trials.

The detailed account of the Dakota War trials and executions presented by Finkelman provides insight into the extreme care taken by Lincoln in his examination of the trial transcripts. By October 17, General Pope wrote to General Sibley, then head of the Second District War Department in Minnesota, that "the President directs that no executions be made without his sanction."[4]

The trials ended November 5. On November 10, directly after General Pope had forwarded the names of the condemned men, Lincoln immediately ordered all evidence be sent directly to him, requesting "the full and complete record of their convictions" and "a careful statement" indicating "the more guilty and influential culprits."

For nearly a month, even as the Civil War raged, Lincoln and his aides painstakingly reviewed the trial transcripts. They discovered a lack of incriminating evidence against most of the accused. The commissioners who had handed down the mass sentences were the very military officials who fought in the war against the Dakota. Under these circumstances, an objective and unbiased verdict was impossible.

University of Minnesota law professor Carol Chomsky notes in her often-cited 1990 study, "The United States-Dakota War Trials: A Study in Military Injustice," that Lincoln faced immense pressure to rubber-stamp the mass exe-

---

2. Ibid., p. 429.
3. Entry of October 14, 1862, *Diary of Gideon Welles*, Vol. 1 (New York: W. W. Norton & Company, 1960), p. 171.
4. Finkelman, p. 407.

cution of all 303 Dakota men.[5] Multiple reports forwarded to Lincoln warned if there were not executions, gangs of settlers would carry out mass murder of not only the 303 defendants, but of women and children. In response to reports that Lincoln might not carry out the full order, the *Stillwater Messenger* demanded blood. Its November 11 headline screamed: "DEATH TO THE BARBARIANS! Is the sentiment of our people."[6]

Minnesota Governor Alexander Ramsey and military officers involved in the conflict threatened the outbreak of mob rule if the executions did not take place. "I hope the execution of every Sioux Indian condemned by the military court will be at once ordered," Ramsey declared. "It would be wrong upon principle and policy to refuse this. Private revenge would on all this border take the place of official judgment on these Indians."[7]

When forwarding the trial transcripts to Lincoln, General Pope also included a call for all the executions to be approved. The letter from Pope, Chomsky explains, "warned [Lincoln] that the people of Minnesota, perhaps combined with some of the soldiers, would take matters into their own hands and kill 'all the Indians—old men, women, and children,' if the President did not allow all the 303 executions to go forward. If the President proved reluctant to decide, he suggested the condemned be turned over to the state government."[8]

Republican Minnesota Senator Morton Wilkinson and representatives Cyrus Aldrich and William Windom wrote to Lincoln reciting stories of rapes and mutilation "well known to our people" and protesting any decision to pardon or reprieve the Dakota. If Lincoln did not permit the executions, they said, "the outraged people of Minnesota would dispose of these wretches without law. These two peoples cannot live together. We do not wish to see mob law inaugurated in Minnesota, as it certainly will be, if you force the people to it."[9]

---

5. Carol Chomsky, "The United States-Dakota War Trials: A Study in Military Injustice," *Stanford Law Review*, November 1990, Vol. 43, No. 1, pp. 13–97. https://www.jstor.org/stable/1228993

6. *Stillwater Messenger*, November 11, 1862, quoted in Chomsky, p. 27.

7. Letter from Gov. Alexander Ramsey to Pres. Abraham Lincoln (November 10, 1862), quoted in Chomsky, p. 29.

8. Letter from Maj. Gen. John Pope to Pres. Abraham Lincoln (November 12, 1862), Abraham Lincoln Papers, Minnesota Historical Society, quoted in ibid.

9. Letter from Sen. Morton Wilkinson, Rep. Cyrus Aldrich, and Rep. William Windom to Pres. Abraham Lincoln (November 1862), reprinted in S. Exec. Doc. No. 7, 37th Cong., 3d sess. 2, 3, (1862), quoted in Chomsky, pp. 29–30.

Even the US Senate—controlled by Republicans—passed a resolution introduced by Senator Wilkinson in early December demanding that Lincoln carry out the executions.

Reverend Henry Whipple, a Minnesota Episcopal clergyman sympathetic to the plight of the Dakota, visited the president in the White House as the conflict was raging in September, and painted a picture of the brutality faced by the tribe. Lincoln reportedly responded that his encounter with Whipple had shaken him to his core, noting that the Reverend "talked to me about the rascality of this Indian business until I felt it down to my boots."[10]

After careful consideration of the case, Lincoln decided to commute the sentences of 265 Dakota and to not overturn the executions ordered by the military tribunal of thirty-nine, writing their names out in various phonetical interpretations to ensure there would be no mistakes. Additionally, recognizing the real threat of vigilante violence in Minnesota, Lincoln ordered that the remaining prisoners be held, "subject to further orders, taking care that they neither escape, nor are subjected to any unlawful violence."[11]

In a letter to the Senate dated December 11, 1862, outlining his decision on the matter, Lincoln wrote, "Anxious to not act with so much clemency as to encourage another outbreak on the one hand, nor with so much severity as to be real cruelty on the other, I caused a careful examination of the records of trials to be made, in view of first ordering the execution of such as had been proved guilty of violating females."[12] Lincoln said that only two Dakota men could be proven to have violated women. He then explained that he attempted to distinguish those who participated in "massacres" from those participating in "battles," which considerably reduced the number of death sentences. One additional Dakota man would be commuted days prior to the December 26 executions, based on additional evidence, bringing the number of those executed to thirty-eight.

In the seminal book *Bury My Heart at Wounded Knee*, Dee Brown notes that information was released later that two of the men hanged were not on Lincoln's list, and many had maintained their innocence until the very end. One of those was a young Dakota, Rdainyanka, who was the son-in-law of Chief Wabasha, who had encouraged their surrender, promising that it would

---

10. Finkelman, p. 436.
11. Letter from Pres. Abraham Lincoln to Brig. Gen. Henry Sibley (December 6, 1862), quoted in Chomsky, p. 33.
12. S. Exec. Doc. No. 7, 37th Cong., 3d sess. 1 (1862). quoted in ibid.

ensure no future loss of life. In a final letter to his father-in-law Chief Wabasha, Rdainyanka wrote:

> Wabasha—You have deceived me, you told me that if we followed the advice of General Sibley and gave ourselves up to the whites all would be well; no innocent man would be injured. I have not killed, wounded, or injured a white man or any white persons. I have not participated in the plunder of their property; and yet today I am set apart for execution. ... When my children are grown up, let them know that their father died because he followed the advice of his chief and without having the blood of a white man to answer for to the Great Spirit.[13]

Lincoln's distinction between the Dakota's participation in "battles" versus "massacres" also uprooted the entire public narrative about the wars against the Native peoples and acknowledged, through the framework of the laws of war, the legitimacy of the Dakota's cause.

In this context, his decision to consider the Native American defendants as "people" who had the right to the presumption of innocence exemplifies a far more humane approach than that of the political parties, courts, settlers, and land speculators who by and large had, at every turn throughout American history, supported the removal of Native Americans from their land without any consideration for their rights.

The line of presidents that preceded Lincoln, dating back to Andrew Jackson, supported as state policy something that today would be defined as ethnic cleansing. This policy would reemerge with a vengeance with the explosive growth of American capitalism after the Civil War. Lincoln's approach proved to be only a pause in this chain of dispossession and violence.

His own personal experiences with Native Americans provide insight into Lincoln's careful decision concerning the Dakota.

Lincoln came of age in a climate of tremendous prejudice against Native Americans. He was himself from the backwoods of the trans-Appalachian frontier, having been born in Kentucky and moved to southern Indiana in 1816, then to the Illinois frontier in 1830. The uncertainty and danger of living in the backwoods and in close proximity to Native Americans was ever present.

This was most certainly the case for Lincoln's family, as his grandfather, Abraham Lincoln Sr., was killed by a small group of Shawnee Native Americans

---

13. Dee Brown, *Bury My Heart at Wounded Knee, An Indian History of the American West* (New York: Henry Holt and Company Inc., 1970), p. 61.

during a raid on their farm in Kentucky in 1786. Lincoln's father, Thomas, was eight years old when he witnessed his father's murder and his older brother Mordecai shooting a Native American dead. The event would have a profound impact on the family.

In writing to a relative in 1863, Lincoln wrote that of all the stories relative to his ancestry, "the story of my grandfather's death and of uncle Mordecai, then fourteen years old, killing one of the Indians is the legend more strongly than all others imprinted among my mind and memory."[14]

At just twenty-three years old, Lincoln enlisted in the Illinois militia to fight in the Black Hawk War of 1832. He was made the commander of his unit, and though prepared to fight the Sauk tribe, he was able to ensure that his company never engaged in combat. He witnessed the war's atrocities as well as the resulting removal of the Sauk from northwest Illinois to a reservation in Iowa.

Lincoln encountered the aftermath of battles and therefore saw with his own eyes the brutal style of warfare with the Sauk. After the American defeats at Stillman's Run and the Second Battle at Kellogg's Grove, Lincoln and his company were given the somber and gruesome task of gathering and burying the dead. Near Ottawa, Illinois, Lincoln and his unit also encountered the bloody result of a massacre in which soldiers, women, and children had been mutilated and killed.

Toward the end of the war, Lincoln's company buried a cadre of scouts that had been attacked. Lincoln recalled: "I remember just how those men looked ... as we rode up the little hill where their camp was. The red light of the morning sun was streaming upon them as they lay, heads toward us, on the ground, and every man had a round, red spot on the top of his head, about as big as a dollar, where the redskins had taken his scalp. It was frightful, but it was grotesque, and the red sunlight seemed to paint everything all over."[15] Despite his horrific experiences during the Black Hawk War, Lincoln recognized the complexity of relations with the Native Americans and maintained an appreciation for their cultures and individual humanity.

---

14. Abraham Lincoln, *Collected Works of Abraham Lincoln*, Vol. 2, Roy P. Basler, editor; Marion Dolores Pratt and Lloyd A. Dunlap, assistant editors (The Abraham Lincoln Association, Springfield, Illinois), p. 218.   http://name.umdl.umich.edu/lincoln2 The quoted text is from a letter written by Abraham Lincoln to his relative, Jesse Lincoln, on April 1, 1854, while in Springfield, Illinois.

15. Francis F. Browne, *The Everyday Life of Abraham Lincoln* (Chicago: Browne & Howell, 1913), p. 67.

On one occasion during the Black Hawk War, Lincoln's unit was camped in Henderson County, Illinois, when an old man from the Potawatomi tribe arrived and presented a letter of introduction and safe passage from US Secretary of War Lewis Cass. Lincoln's men took the man to be a spy and were set to kill him.

William G. Greene, Illinois militiaman and close friend to Lincoln, remembered the encounter: "Mr. Lincoln in the goodness & kindness and humanity & justice of his nature stood—got between the Indian and the outraged men—saying—'Men this must not be done—he must not be shot and killed by us.' Some of the men remarked—'The Indian is a damned Spy.' Still Lincoln stood between the Indian and the vengeance of the outraged soldiers—brave, good & true."[16] The company threatened to attack Lincoln, but backed down after he challenged them to choose their weapons and fight him.

By 1862 it was clear that the Civil War would be long and bloody. As the year was ending, Union casualties exceeded 100,000, the national debt was accumulating, and many—even within Lincoln's own party—began to refer to the war as "Lincoln's War" and called for a truce with the South even if it meant the continuation of slavery.

The Battle of Shiloh in April 1862 stunned the nation. It resulted in 13,000 casualties, of whom 1,750 were killed, in a few days of fighting. In the summer of 1862, General George B. McClellan failed in his bid to capture Richmond, Virginia, the capital of the Confederacy. The Union army was humiliated at the Second Battle of Bull Run in Virginia in late August, even as the Sioux uprising was taking place in Minnesota, suffering another fourteen thousand casualties. Then, in September, Confederate General Robert E. Lee launched his Maryland campaign, invading the North and threatening Washington D.C. itself.

The Lincoln administration was thrown into crisis. The longer the war went on, the more the Democratic Party in the North, which backed peace with the Confederacy, gained support.

It was in this context that the Dakota War broke out. Assumptions of conspiracy were common. The *New York Times* wrote that "the Indians are in league with the rebels," reporting that the outbreak of violence in Minnesota was the product of Confederate manipulation across the entire frontier. Mil-

---

16. William G. Greene to William H. Herndon (interview), May 30, 1865, Douglas L. Wilson and Rodney O. Davis, eds., *Herndon's Informants: Letters, Interviews, and Statements about Abraham Lincoln* (Urbana: University of Illinois Press, 1998), pp. 18–19.

itary commanders warned that thousands of Native Americans would rise up in arms and deliver the West to the Confederacy. In October 1861 the Confederate government had formally recognized a faction of the Cherokee as a separate nation in Oklahoma. Lincoln wrote that "the relations of the government with the Indian tribes have been greatly disturbed by the insurrection."

As the Dakota War was raging, Lincoln implemented a pivotal change. On September 22, five days after the Union Army stopped Lee's invasion of Maryland at Antietam—still the bloodiest day in American history—Lincoln issued the preliminary emancipation proclamation, proclaiming "as an act of justice" and "military necessity" the freedom of slaves in all states or portion of states in rebellion against the US effective January 1, 1863. From this point forward, Lincoln would wage an uncompromising and increasingly violent struggle against the Confederacy to restore the Union and wipe slavery off the map for good.

The Dakota trials took place on the eve of the national elections of 1862, which became a referendum on Lincoln's war policy. Democrats, who ran an openly racist campaign against Lincoln and the "Black Republicans," won a twenty-seven-seat swing in the House of Representatives on a peace platform. Republicans lost control of state legislatures in the critical states of Ohio, Pennsylvania, Illinois, and New York due to war weariness and opposition to the Emancipation Proclamation. Lincoln needed the support of settlers in Republican strongholds like Minnesota.

On December 11, the same day Lincoln announced his decision to the Senate regarding the Dakota executions, Union forces under General Ambrose Burnside were engaged in a bitter four-day conflict with Confederate troops under General Lee at Fredericksburg, resulting in another crushing defeat for the Union on December 15. It was the largest battle fought during the Civil War to that point, with an estimated two hundred thousand soldiers present, and would result in 12,000 Union and 5,400 Confederate casualties, dealing a devastating blow to Union confidence in the war. When Lincoln heard of the outcome, he is reported to have said, "If there is a worse place than Hell, then I am in it."[17]

In this historical context, Lincoln exhibited a level of humanity in the Dakota case that few others in his situation would have been capable of.

If he had been guided by short-term political calculations, Lincoln would have had every reason to simply allow the military tribunal's order to execute

---

17. Carl Sandburg, *Abraham Lincoln: The War Years* (New York: Harcourt, Brace & Co., 1939), Vol. 1, p. 630.

all 303 Dakota men to take place. Lincoln was aware of the backwardness and racism that existed toward Native Americans, just as he was of racism toward blacks. Yet he did not make concessions to these tendencies, even within his own party. Lincoln's larger strategy involved elevating the consciousness of the population. His aim throughout the war was to tactfully mitigate the powerful racist tendencies that did exist and that were an objective block on his war policies.

In view of these facts, we join fully in Marx's assessment, written in the name of the International Working Men's Association on news of Lincoln's assassination, that he was "one of the rare men who succeed in becoming great, without ceasing to be good."[18]

Those who denounce Lincoln for the execution of the thirty-eight Dakota men, ordered and carried out by the Minnesota military tribunal, do so on the grounds of moral absolutes abstracted from history and the class struggle.

It is the same sort of approach to the past that Engels criticized long ago: "Its conception of history, as far as it has one at all, is therefore essentially pragmatic; it judges everything according to the motives of the action; it divides men who act in history into noble and ignoble and then finds that as a rule the noble are defrauded and the ignoble are victorious."[19]

The moralistic attack on Lincoln is in reality an attack on the great struggle he led: the Civil War, the Second American Revolution. To Marxists, the instinctive class hatred of the petty bourgeoisie for history's revolutions is nothing new. The moralizers also wag their fingers at the English Civil War, the Enlightenment, the American Revolution, the French Revolution, and, most of all, the Russian Revolution.

In his 1938 essay *Their Morals and Ours*, Leon Trotsky argued against those who, under the banner of morality, equated the October Revolution with Stalinism, and associated the actions of Trotsky and Lenin with the crimes of the Stalinist bureaucracy. Such arguments were used to discredit the Russian Revolution of 1917. Trotsky referenced the American Civil War and Lincoln, and in so doing, stressed that historical events and figures cannot be judged solely on the basis of bourgeois morality:

> We leave to some Emil Ludwig or his ilk the drawing of Abra-
> ham Lincoln's portrait with rosy little wings. Lincoln's signifi-

---

18. "Address from the Working Men's International Association to President Johnson." *The Bee-Hive Newspaper* (United Kingdom), No. 188, May 20, 1865.
19. Friedrich Engels, "Ludwig Feuerbach and the End of Classical German Philosophy," *Marx & Engels Collected Works*, Vol. 26, p. 388.

cance lies in his not hesitating before the most severe means, once they were found to be necessary, in achieving a great historic aim posed by the development of a young nation. The question lies not even in which of the warring camps caused or itself suffered the greatest number of victims. History has different yardsticks for the cruelty of the Northerners and the cruelty of the Southerners in the Civil War. A slave-owner who through cunning and violence shackles a slave in chains, and a slave who through cunning and violence breaks the chains—let not the contemptible eunuchs tell us that they are equals before a court of morality![20]

The events in Minnesota took place in the immediate context of the Civil War and the revolutionary fight against the powerful slaveholding oligarchy that ruled the South. Lincoln, as the leader of this revolutionary struggle, had to subordinate all other questions to the war, which hung on a knife's edge in the fall and winter of 1862. It is to Lincoln's credit that even in this desperate scenario he did not concede to the bloodlust of the Minnesota politicians and military officers.

The Dakota people were entirely justified in opposing the seizure of land by Minnesota settlers. They faced dispossession and as a result of their defeat they were largely driven out of the state. The immense crimes committed against the Dakota and all other Native populations of North America, a history that stretches back to colonial times, can never be washed away.

Yet this historical tragedy cannot be understood through the lens of petty-bourgeois moralizing. It is bound up with the emergence of capitalism. The indigenous peoples could not be reconciled to the private ownership of land, and so they were dispossessed. When they fought back, they faced savage reprisals again and again.

The history of capitalist oppression of Native Americans continues to the present. The toppling of the Lincoln statue in Portland does nothing to benefit Native Americans, who are the most impoverished and oppressed segment of the American population. They face the shortest life expectancy, highest rates of substance abuse, domestic violence, and joblessness in the country, as well as a general lack of access to health care and basic necessities on the reservations.

A reckoning for the crimes of the past can only come through the fight for socialism in a struggle against capitalism and its many political apologists. This

---

20. Leon Trotsky, *Their Morals and Ours* (New York: Pathfinder Press, 1973), pp. 43–44.

requires an unflinching defense of America's revolutionary heritage, including Abraham Lincoln.

Martin Luther King Jr. and
the Fight for Social Equality

On January 20, 2020, the United States observed Martin Luther King Jr. Day, a holiday commemorating the birth of the civil rights leader.

Since its inception in the 1980s, the holiday has aimed to turn King into a harmless icon of social conciliation, while obscuring his radical criticisms of American capitalism and militarism. But now, in 2020, this has been joined by a new thrust. King's conception of a mass democratic movement for civil rights based on the unified action of all the oppressed sections of the population is being replaced with an essentially racialist narrative that presents all of American history in terms of a struggle between whites and blacks. This racial narrative requires the marginalization of King's historical role.

This is exhibited starkly in the *New York Times'* 1619 Project, whose "reframing" of the history of American race relations makes no mention of King. This is not an oversight on the part of a project that proclaims itself as nothing less than a new curriculum for school children. The core of King's politics—the struggle for equality—runs counter to the aims of contemporary liberalism, which is predicated on a fight for privileges among the upper-middle class.

King, a Baptist minister and theologian, emerged as the most prominent leader and voice of the mass civil rights struggle for racial equality that emerged in the period after World War II—from the Montgomery, Alabama, bus boycott in 1955 against Jim Crow segregation until 1968, when King was assassinated in Memphis, Tennessee, while supporting striking sanitation workers.

Thomas Mackaman and Niles Niemuth, "Martin Luther King, Jr. and the fight for social equality," World Socialist Web Site, January 23, 2020.

King was born in Atlanta, Georgia, in 1929, during a period that scholars have called "the nadir" of American race relations. In the Jim Crow South, beginning in the 1890s, a raft of laws stripped the right to vote from the vast majority of blacks. All public space was segregated by law or custom—schools and colleges; buses, trains, streetcars; water fountains and bathrooms; diners and movie theaters. Interracial marriage was illegal, and even casual interactions between whites and blacks, for example, on city sidewalks, were to play out in a custom designed to humiliate and degrade blacks.

The Democratic Party ruled the Jim Crow South unchallenged. Behind it stood the ever-present threat of state-sanctioned racist violence. By one count, mobs and bands of killers lynched more than four thousand blacks in the South from the 1870s through the 1940s.

Yet racism was not an end in and of itself. As C. Vann Woodward long ago established in *The Strange Career of Jim Crow* (1955), it was imposed as a direct response to the Populist movement of poor farmers, which, in the 1880s, had raised the specter of interracial unity among the oppressed. That Woodward's book was upheld as "the historical Bible" of the civil rights movement reflected that movement's agreement with its key finding, that, as King put it, "racial segregation as a way of life did not come about as a natural result of hatred between the races"—the position advanced by the 1619 Project—but "was really a political stratagem employed by the emerging Bourbon interests in the South to keep the Southern masses divided and Southern labor the cheapest in the land."[1]

The Populist movement collapsed a few decades before King's birth. Its inability to overcome the Southern oligarchy resulted from its social composition among isolated rural farmers, an undifferentiated and rapidly declining section of the population. Yet its achievements were extraordinary. Shaking the two-party system to its foundations, Populism's challenge to capitalism ultimately fed into the emergence of American socialism.

While King looked to Populism for inspiration, it was ultimately a far more profound transformation, arising from the powerful development of American capitalism, that provided the basis for the civil rights movement: the development of the working class.

In 1900, after the defeat of the Populist movement, 90 percent of African Americans lived in the South, most in conditions of rural isolation. In the

---

1. Martin Luther King Jr., Address at the Conclusion of the Selma to Montgomery March, March 25, 1965, https://kinginstitute.stanford.edu/king-papers/documents/address-conclusion-selma-montgomery-march

1920s, over 1.5 million blacks left the South for Northern cities, bound for wage work. Many more moved to cities in the South—including Atlanta, where King was born, as well as Alabama's industrial cities of Birmingham and Montgomery, which birthed the modern civil rights movement. By 1960, only 15 percent of African Americans remained on farms, a dramatic social transformation which historians now term the Great Migration.

In the cities, the black migrants faced new forms of racism and, as in East St. Louis in 1917 and Chicago in 1919, occasional paroxysms of vicious violence, typically overseen by their historical antagonists in the Democratic Party. Yet it is undeniable that this vast movement—from country to city, from farm to factory, and from South to North and West—was an intensely liberating development. Its impact on American culture can only be called exhilarating.

The arrival in the cities of this brutally oppressed people, a mere half century separated from chattel slavery, germinated the cultural and intellectual florescence associated with the Harlem Renaissance, the first mass African American political organizations and trade unions, as well as the great forms of popular music including ragtime, rhythm and blues, jazz, and rock and roll.

The Great Migration raised African American workers as a critical section of the working class. But the fusing of that class across racial and national lines was no mean task under conditions in which capitalist employers knew well that they could pit workers—white, black, immigrant—against each other in wage competition. The American Federation of Labor (AFL), among the most provincial and reactionary labor organizations on the planet, fed into these divisions. Most of its unions imposed racial exclusions against blacks and agitated against immigrants. Reformist socialists who oriented to the AFL, such as Victor Berger of Milwaukee, also excluded blacks from their conception of the working class.

Under these conditions—the emergence of a powerful industrial working class, but one hamstrung by outmoded forms of organization—the Russian Revolution of 1917 hit with meteoric impact. Among the black intellectuals inspired by the Bolsheviks were Claude McKay, Jean Toomer, Langston Hughes, Paul Robeson, and A. Philip Randolph, who cofounded the socialist magazine *The Messenger* in 1917 and went on to head the largest predominantly black trade union, the Brotherhood of Sleeping Car Porters.

These intellectuals immediately drew comparisons to the situation of Jews under the seemingly eternal Romanov dynasty. "For American Negroes the indisputable and outstanding fact of the Russian Revolution," McKay explained in 1921, "is that a mere handful of Jews, much less in ratio to the number of

Negroes in the American population, have attained, through the Revolution, all the political and social rights that were denied to them under the regime of the Czar."[2]

In the North, socialists took the lead in the fight for the great industrial unions in auto, meatpacking, rubber, and steel, insisting that blacks be accepted on equal footing with all others. Even in the Deep South, socialists fought under the banner of the Russian Revolution in the 1920s and 1930s, winning the allegiance of militant workers, black and white, in such places as Alabama, where the defense of the Scottsboro Boys, nine African American youth falsely accused of rape, won the support of workers the world over. It is difficult to overstate the heroism of these workers who braved the wrath of the "Southern lawmen" as well as the Ku Klux Klan.

The Stalinists of the Communist Party, along with the supposedly left Congress of Industrial Organizations (CIO) bureaucracy, betrayed these workers in the name of their alliance with the Democratic Party, whose Southern wing remained in the hands of the white supremacist oligarchy. Nonetheless, socialism remained the *bête noire* of the Jim Crow politicians, who saw in every stirring of the Southern workers the work of "outside agitators" and "communists." And, despite the best efforts of reactionary red-baiters, socialism continued to influence a layer of Southern intellectuals and leaders.

King was neither a Marxist nor a revolutionary. But his socialist sympathies, and those of his wife, Coretta Scott King, were well known. He agitated for a significant economic restructuring of American society, albeit without calling for the overthrow of the capitalist system. Even though he cautiously adapted his politics to the pressures of the red-baiting environment of the United States in the 1950s, King spoke a language utterly incompatible with the racial narrative of contemporary right-wing, affluent, petty-bourgeois nationalists.

Communism "should challenge us first to be more concerned about social justice," King noted in a sermon first delivered in 1953. "However much is wrong with Communism we must admit that it arose as a protest against the hardships of the underprivileged. The Communist Manifesto which was published in 1847 by Marx and Engels emphasizes throughout how the middle class has exploited the lower class. Communism emphasizes a classless society. Along with this goes a strong attempt to eliminate racial prejudice. Commu-

2. Letter from Claude McKay, *The Crisis*, Vol. 22 No. 3, July 1, 1921. Accessed 12/11/20: https://modjourn.org/issue/bdr513738/

nism seeks to transcend the superficialities of race and color, and you are able to join the Communist party whatever the color of your skin or the quality of the blood in your veins."[3]

King eloquently articulated the democratic sentiments of Americans of all races and ethnicities striving to tear down all the artificial barriers erected by the ruling class in a conscious effort to divide the working class.

In a 1965 sermon, King explained that the "majestic words" of the Declaration of Independence penned by Thomas Jefferson, that "all men are created equal," were the cornerstone of the civil rights movement. He did not see that document, which gave expression to the Enlightenment principles which animated the American Revolution, as a cynical ploy or a lie—as 1619 Project figurehead Nikole Hannah-Jones imagines it—but an as yet unfulfilled promise, "lifted to cosmic proportions," and one the civil rights movement was fighting to make a reality.

He and many others who were part of the mass movement in the 1950s and 1960s understood very well that no lasting progress could be made without the unity of the working class and recognized that under capitalism workers were being oppressed regardless of the color of their skin.

Writing in 1958, King noted that two summers of work in a factory as a teenager had exposed him to "economic injustice firsthand, and [I] realized that the poor white was exploited just as much as the Negro. Through these early experiences I grew up deeply conscious of the varieties of injustice in our society."[4]

Whether or not King's assassination was more than the work of the small-time hood James Earl Ray, it is a documented fact that, from the early 1960s on, the FBI under J. Edgar Hoover aimed to destroy the civil rights leader through a campaign of dirty tricks, media leaks, intense surveillance, and even encouraging King to kill himself. "Yet somehow," historian William Chafe writes, "King emerged from the ordeal a stronger, more resolute, more courageous leader."[5]

King responded to the attack from the FBI in 1967 by launching his interracial Poor People's campaign, an initiative seeking economic justice for all

3. Martin Luther King Jr., "Communism's Challenge to Christianity," August 9, 1953, https://kinginstitute.stanford.edu/king-papers/documents/communisms-challenge-christianity
4. "My Pilgrimage to Nonviolence," September 1, 1958, https://kinginstitute.stanford.edu/king-papers/documents/my-pilgrimage-nonviolence
5. William H. Chafe, *The Unfinished Journey: America Since World War II* (Oxford: Oxford University Press, 1985) p. 353.

impoverished Americans. He also became among the most outspoken critics of the American onslaught in Vietnam, memorably denouncing the United States government as the "greatest purveyor of violence today" in his 1967 Riverside Church speech.

He had become convinced, King told his staff the same year, "that we can't solve our problems now until there is a radical redistribution of economic and political power." It was time, he said, "to raise certain basic questions about the whole society. ... We are engaged in a class struggle ... dealing with the problem of the gulf between the haves and the have nots."[6]

King's recognition of the necessity of interracial struggle and the contributions that whites had made to the civil rights movement informed King's criticism of the racial separatism espoused by the Black Power movement, which he rightly asserted in 1966 "was born from the wombs of despair and disappointment."[7]

King's turn to the left caused alarm among conservative civil rights leaders. To them, King responded—in words that echo with the same force against the lavishly funded "race experts" of today—"What you're saying may get you a foundation grant but it won't get you into the Kingdom of Truth."[8]

The logic of these positions, indeed his entire life's work, placed King on a collision course with the Democratic Party—the same party that ruled over the Jim Crow South and the big-city political machines in the North, and had led the United States into Vietnam. Even if his political limitations caused him to delay this reckoning to the end, his life's work had a real impact on the lives of millions.

Now, the universal Enlightenment principles King fought for and defended are under vicious assault. It is striking that in the 1619 Project, the *Times*' initiative to write the "true" history of America as rooted in slavery and racism, King's contribution to the fight for equality is totally ignored. This doesn't represent a different interpretation of facts or a mere oversight, but an outright historical falsification.

The *Times* is seeking to impose a new "narrative" on US history in which antiblack racism is presented as an immutable feature of "America's DNA."

---

6. No single source contains the full text of King's report to SCLC staff in May, 1967. A partial is available here: https://kairoscenter.org/wp-content/uploads/2014/11/King-quotes-2-page. pdf. And a partial is available in David Goldfield, *Black, White, and Southern: Race Relations and Southern Culture 1940 to the Present* (Louisiana State University Press, 1990), p. 213.

7. Martin Luther King Jr., November 14, 1966, quoted in "Black Power," https://kinginstitute. stanford.edu/encyclopedia/black-power

8. Cited in Cornel West, ed., *The Radical King* (Boston: Beacon Press, 2015), p. ix.

This, Hannah-Jones argues, emerged out of the "original sin" of chattel slavery, itself a function not of labor exploitation, but of white racism against blacks.

Promoted by the Pulitzer Center for Crisis Reporting, which is heavily endowed by corporations and billionaires, the 1619 Project proposes itself as a new curriculum for public education. Crumbling schools and hungry children from Chicago to Buffalo are being given lesson plans that argue the American Revolution and Civil War were conspiracies to perpetuate white racism, and that all manner of contemporary social problems—lack of health care, obesity, traffic jams, etc.—are the direct outcomes of slavery.

Following other eminent historians interviewed by the World Socialist Web Site, Stanford Professor Clayborne Carson, director of the Martin Luther King Jr. Research and Education Institute, criticized the 1619 Project from the standpoint of its treatment of history, its dismissal of the American Revolution, and the obscure and rapid process through which it was produced. He went further, however, making powerful observations about King and the civil rights movement he came to lead—two subjects almost entirely absent from the 1619 Project.

Carson noted that the ideals of the American Revolution and the Enlightenment played a key role in the civil rights movement and King's own role as a political leader. "One way of looking at the founding of this country is to understand the audacity of a few hundred white male elites getting together and declaring a country—and declaring it a country based on the notion of human rights," Carson explained.

"Obviously, they were being hypocritical, but it's also audacious. And that's what rights are all about," he noted. "It is the history of people saying, 'I declare that I have the right to determine my destiny, and we collectively have the right to determine our destiny.' That's the history of every movement, every freedom movement in the history of the world. At some point you have to get to that point where you have to say that, publicly, and fight for it."

It is these principles and this perspective which are being explicitly rejected by the *New York Times* as upper-middle-class layers marshal various forms of identity politics to jockey for a greater share of the massive amounts of wealth which have been piled up in the coffers of the top one percent. In this struggle for privilege and wealth, the political principles which King stood for can find no place, and therefore he too must be excised from the historical narrative.

Bernard Bailyn, Historian of American Colonial and Revolutionary Periods, 1922–2020

Bernard Bailyn, an influential and significant historian of the American colonial period, passed away August 7, 2020, at his home in Belmont, Massachusetts. The cause of death was heart failure. He was ninety-seven.

Bailyn's writing spanned seventy years. His first book, *The New England Merchants in the Seventeenth Century*, was published in 1955. His last book, *Illuminating History: A Retrospective of Seven Decades*, appeared last year.

In the course of his long academic career, all of it spent at Harvard University, Bailyn published dozens of books and articles. Bailyn guided the dissertations of many historians, several of whom themselves have made extraordinary contributions to knowledge of the colonial and revolutionary periods, foremost among them Gordon S. Wood of Brown University. Bailyn's most famous study, published in 1967, is *The Ideological Origins of the American Revolution*, which demonstrated the extraordinary breadth of the political debate that ruptured the colonies' relationship with Great Britain. It won both the Bancroft and Pulitzer prizes for history.

Bailyn brought to his work enormous technical skills, vast erudition, and the capacity to imagine the past as a time profoundly different from one's own, in which the actors lived, thought, and struggled in the context of a historically conditioned situation. Bailyn valued historians, as he explained it, who "sought to understand the past in its own terms: to relocate events, the meaning

Thomas Mackaman, "Bernard Bailyn, historian of American colonial and revolutionary periods, 1922–2020," World Socialist Web Site, August 13, 2020.

261

of documents, the motivations of historical actors in their original historical sockets."[1]

Bailyn captured the drama of historical actors moving toward ends unknown to them, an approach that imbued his writing with a literary quality. History, he wrote, imposed "limitations within which everyone involved was obliged to act; the inescapable boundaries of action; the blindness of the actors—in a word, the tragedy of the event."[2] And further, "the essence and drama of history lie precisely in the active and continuous relationship between the underlying conditions that set the boundaries of human existence and the everyday problems with which people consciously struggle."[3]

Wood, in a tribute to his mentor, noted that "George Eliot or Thomas Hardy or Henry James could not have described better what they were doing in their tragic novels."[4]

This outlook brought Bailyn into conflict with anachronism in history writing throughout his career. When *The Ideological Origins of the American Revolution* was published, it challenged the conservative "consensus school" of American history, sometimes called "Whig history," that dominated the 1950s and which saw the revolutionary period as unfolding to a predetermined, liberal, end. It also put him at odds with an ostensibly "left" history—falsely identified with Marxism—that interpreted the eighteenth-century politics of the revolutionaries as nothing more than hypocritical rationalizations for economic interests. This school of thought was associated above all with the progressive historian Charles Beard.

The Ideological Origins, through an analysis of hundreds of revolutionary pamphlets, revealed the broad scope and the intensity of the political crisis of the late colonial period—a crisis Bailyn saw as essentially a challenge to traditional, aristocratic, and English authority taking place at the very fringe of the European world. The colonists' conspiratorial view that the British Parliament sought to strip them of their free-born liberties as Englishmen, so prevalent in

---

1. Bernard Bailyn, *History and the Creative Imagination* (St. Louis: Washington University Press, 1985), p. 13.
2. Bernard Bailyn, *The Ordeal of Thomas Hutchinson* (Cambridge: Cambridge University Press, 1974), p. ix.
3. Bernard Bailyn, Speech at the American Historical Association, 1981, https://www.historians.org/about-aha-and-membership/aha-history-and-archives/presidential-addresses/bernard-bailyn
4. Gordon Wood, "The Creative Imagination of Bernard Bailyn," in James A. Henretta, Michael G. Kammen, and Stanley Nider Katz, *The Transformation of Early American History: Society, Authority, and Ideology* (New York: Random House, 1991), p. 45.

the documentary evidence, could not simply be dismissed as propaganda, as many historians had done. The ideological worldview at the disposal of the colonists, largely derived from English radical sources, lagged behind the actual social conditions of the colonies, but this did not make their thinking unreal.

As Bailyn explains in the important chapter "The Contagion of Liberty," the politics soon swept over all forms of authority, challenging existing established order in government, churches, and even plantations. Contrary to both the consensus and progressive historians, Bailyn therefore perceived that the American Revolution was a radical event.

Bailyn's work can certainly be criticized for its underestimation of the significance of class forces in the revolutionary period. Commenting on Bailyn's work in a letter to this writer, Gordon Wood observed, "He didn't like any suggestion of a class conflict." Nevertheless, Bailyn told the American Historical Association in his 1981 presidential address, "We are all Marxists in the sense of assuming that history is profoundly shaped by underlying economic or 'material' configurations and by people's responses to them."[5]

Bailyn was born to a middle-class Jewish family in Hartford, Connecticut. His wife, Lotte, was of German-speaking background, connected to emigrants who had fled Nazi Germany. In one of the few biographical comments he made in his academic work, he spoke of how these exiles from Hitler, often talented artists and intellectuals, were "the least parochial" people he ever knew and viewed the United States as a "far outer Anglo-American periphery." This clearly contributed to Bailyn's own view of the British North American colonies, which he constantly presented as a sort of border rim that ran European cultural and intellectual life to its very edges.

Lotte Bailyn survives her husband. A longtime professor of management at MIT and herself a prolific author, Lotte assisted her husband in one of his early books, *Massachusetts Shipping, 1697–1714: A Statistical Study*. Published in 1959, it was one of the first historical studies to use computer technology to compile data.

Bailyn's education was interrupted by World War II, during which he was assigned to the Signal Corps and trained to fluency in German, having already studied French. He entered Harvard graduate school in 1946, where Oscar Handlin, one of the first Jewish professors at the leading Ivy League university, was his mentor and later his colleague. Whatever challenges he may have

---

5. Bailyn, Speech to the American Historical Association, 1981, https://www.historians.org/about-aha-and-membership/aha-history-and-archives/presidential-addresses/bernard-bailyn

himself faced in this environment, notorious for its anti-Semitism, Harvard offered Bailyn one of the most sought-after tenure-track jobs in America in 1953, though he was a relatively young and unknown scholar.

Bailyn appears to have said very little about the political environment at the time. But anticommunism had exacted a terrible price among writers and artists, and on the American intellectual environment as a whole. It was in this shadow of McCarthyism that the conservative consensus school of American history held sway, a trend in historical writing sometimes associated with Bailyn's contemprorary, Edmund S. Morgan of Yale University. Bailyn thus emerged as a major intellectual figure in the late 1950s, in the immediate aftermath of the McCarthy period but before the emergence of the New Left on the campuses just a decade later.

In the years immediately after the publication of *The Ideological Origins of the American Revolution*, entire new academic fields emerged: critical revisionist studies of political, diplomatic, and labor history, as well as African American history, women's history, Native American history, and many more. The new fields criticized what the late Howard Zinn called "establishment history" and brought forward the social history of the oppressed, who had often left behind little or no written record. This yielded fresh and significant results, and, for the colonial period, considerably widened the lens.

Yet the New Left historians tended to dismiss the American Revolution as an elite conspiracy—a position, ironically, that was first made by the Loyalists and the Tories during the imperial crisis—and began to label Bailyn as a consensus, or purely intellectual, historian.

By the 1990s, when Bailyn retired from the classroom, college history departments were becoming bogged down in the miasma created by the cross-pollination of identity politics with postmodernism, a philosophical tendency that rejects narrative in history and even the very effort to establish a factual or objective approach to the study of the past. At that point, the weaknesses and political confusion of the New Left-inspired history, there from the start, emerged as a destructive force aimed not at the revision of history but at its destruction.

These reactionary intellectual tendencies for many years appeared to be confined largely to the campuses and the university presses. And even though new identity-politics-dominated academic history was richly fed, itself becoming a new establishment, Bailyn continued to win national prizes and awards, and appreciations regularly appeared in the major publications of American liberalism, including the *New York Times*.

This is no longer the case. The *Times* obituary to Bailyn, while it acknowledged the undeniable influence of his early career, insinuated that his recent work—his four-decades long study of immigration to the colonies entitled *The Peopling of British North America*—was outmoded. In line with its relentless promotion of racial conflict as the axis of American history, which is coupled with the libelous claim that white historians are incapable of understanding the historical role and contribution of nonwhites, the *Times* made sure to devote a portion of the obituary to the "strong criticism from fellow historians for what they saw as inadequate or dismissive treatment of nonwhite people." There is no merit to this criticism. It is a smear aimed to make the *Times* readership believe that Bailyn's work is no longer relevant, and that he was a racist.[6]

The last year of Bailyn's life witnessed the publication of the *Times*' promotion of a racialist falsification of history, the 1619 Project. In a blunt, though unintended, admission of the intellectually fraudulent character of this operation, Nikole Hannah-Jones—the public face of the project—recently tweeted that "the 1619 Project is not a history." It is, rather, "about who gets to control the national narrative, and, therefore, the nation's shared memory of itself." This retrograde conception obliterates the distinction between history and myth, and legitimizes lies in the interests of a race-centered political agenda.

The 1619 Project's central claim—that the American Revolution was a counterrevolution to defend slavery—rests on a series of falsehoods and distortions, up to and including basic errors of chronological order. This flagrant distortion of the past contradicts Bailyn's career. The aged historian was not consulted for the project, nor, it is clear enough, were his major books. His work, with its precision of fact and its appreciation of the colonial world as it existed, was of no use to the *Times*' exercise in historical falsification.

The effort to brush aside Bailyn will not succeed. The resurgence of social struggles in the United States will generate a renewed interest in the democratic ideals that inspired the great revolutionaries of the eighteenth century. In this intellectually healthier environment, the work left behind by Bernard Bailyn will be respected for its honesty and objectivity.

---

6. Renwick McLean and Jennifer Schuessler, "Bernard Bailyn, Eminent Historian of Early America, Dies at 97," The *New York Times*, August 7, 2020, sec. Books. https://www.nytimes.com/2020/08/07/books/bernard-bailyn-dead.html.

Part V

The Crisis of
the *New York Times*' 1619 Project

Race Theory and the Holocaust

On the evening of November 18, 2019, *New York Times* staff writer and 1619 Project director Nikole Hannah-Jones addressed an audience at New York University (NYU) on the subject of the *Times'* initiative marking the four-hundredth anniversary of the landing of the first African slaves in Virginia. NYU President Andrew Hamilton introduced the event, stating that the 1619 Project had the trademarks of "the best pieces of journalism." The event was moderated by Fordham professor and MSNBC commentator Christina Greer.

There was not a single statement made by Hannah-Jones that evening on historical issues that withstands serious examination.

She presented her personal opinions—and, in the absence of historically informed substance, that is all they were—on the "undemocratic" character of the American Revolution and Constitution. The white working class opposes social programs because of a conscious desire to "punish black people," she claimed, adding that "whiteness" is in the best interest of white people: "So we hear again and again, why are poor white people voting against their interests? Well, it's assuming that whiteness isn't in your best interest. And it is. And they know that. And so we cannot rid ourselves of that."

Hannah-Jones never explained what this "best interest" actually is. The assumption underlying her ungrounded assertion is that racial self-identification is a self-supporting interest *in itself*—indeed, the supreme interest that overwhelmed all others.

Eric London and David North, "Nikole Hannah-Jones, race theory and the Holocaust," World Socialist Web Site, November 26, 2019.

The intellectually bankrupt, historically false, and politically reactionary character of Hannah-Jones's race-fixated conceptions found its most disturbing and chilling expression when she turned to the subject of the anti-Semitism and genocide carried out by the Nazi regime in Germany. Hannah-Jones stated:

> I've thought a lot about this. I'm reading this book now comparing what Nazi Germany did after the Holocaust to the American South or America. And one thing you realize is Germany, though they didn't initially want to, dealt with a cleansing of everything that had to do with Nazism and in some ways had a reckoning of what the country did. But that's also because there's really no Jewish people left in Germany, so it's easy to feel that way when you don't have to daily look at the people who you committed these atrocities to, versus in the United States where we are a constant reminder.[1]

It is hard to know where to begin with Hannah-Jones's head-spinning combination of ignorance, historical falsification, and antiscientific race theory. Failing to work through the implications of her opinions, Hannah-Jones came dangerously close to endorsing the conception that genocide, by ending the daily encounter of Germans and Jews, was a solution to inherent racism. Hannah-Jones does not, of course, support genocide. However, she argues that once the Nazis killed the Jews, it eliminated the source of the underlying racial problem and, therefore, anti-Semitism disappeared in Germany. In the United States, on the other hand, racism has persisted because whites still have to look at and interact with blacks. There is nothing in this twisted narrative with which a Nazi would disagree.

But it is a narrative that has nothing to do with real history. As a preliminary matter, Hannah-Jones's assertion that there was "a reckoning of what the country did" is a grotesque distortion of postwar German politics. It is a well-established fact that the vast majority of Nazi officials were never held to account for their crimes. Many leading Nazis, including individuals who played a major role in the extermination of the Jews, led successful political, corporate, and academic careers after 1945.

With the complicity of the United States, the denazification program initially implemented after Germany's surrender was abandoned so that it would

---

1. Nikole Hannah-Jones, lecture at New York University, November 18, 2019.

not interfere with the Cold War against the Soviet Union. The new federal government, established in 1949 under the leadership of Chancellor Konrad Adenauer, provided a safe haven for countless Nazis.

Adenauer's principal adviser, Hans Globke, had played a central role in drafting the anti-Jewish laws of the Nazi regime. The new head of the secret police of West Germany, Reinhard Gehlen, had been been in charge of intelligence operations of the German Nazi army on the Eastern Front during World War II. And from 1966 to 1969, a former Nazi, Kurt Kiesinger, was the country's chancellor. The fight for a reckoning with the legacy of Nazism began in earnest only in the late 1960s, as a consequence of the political radicalization of German students and youth.

Hannah-Jones spoke flippantly about the Holocaust, tossing off her half-baked impressions about a crime of staggering dimensions. Condemnation of the vicious racism and oppression of African Americans in the American South (and throughout the United States) does not require, let alone justify, facile comparisons to the Holocaust. In the span of six years, the Nazis mobilized the industrial power of an advanced twentieth-century economy to systematically exterminate European Jewry with bullets and poison gas. The Nazis murdered six million Jews, killing up to 90 percent of the total Jewish population in each of the countries they invaded.

Hannah-Jones's explanation of the Holocaust and the alleged absence of anti-Semitism in present-day Germany proceeded entirely from racialist premises. The mass murder of the Jews, she implied, was the outcome of an inherent racial conflict between Germans and Jews. She accepts the fundamental framework of Nazi racial theory: that German Jews constituted a race and not a religious community, that Jewish existence and interests were organically antagonistic to those of Germans, that hostility to "the other" was inherent within both groups, and that violent conflict between the races was inevitable.

This explanation of the Holocaust is based not on a study of objective facts and social forces, but on racialist mythology. German anti-Semites did not hate Jews because they could see them. The growth of anti-Semitism, as a political movement in the late nineteenth and early twentieth centuries, arose not out of inherent racial differences between Jews and Germans (or, for that matter, the French). There is no such thing as a Jewish or Aryan race. Politically motivated anti-Semitic movements were products of growing class antagonisms within capitalist society in the late nineteenth and early twentieth centuries and efforts by the ruling elites to break up the growth of the socialist movement and the class struggle.

The main function of political anti-Semitism, as it developed in Germany, Austria-Hungary, France, and other European countries, was to deflect growing social anger against capitalism in a reactionary direction, to eliminate the class struggle from politics and replace it with a mythologized struggle between the races. The concept of inherent "racial" differences between Germans and Jews, where none existed, was developed as a pseudoscientific mythology—supported by the grotesque falsification of evolutionary theory known as social Darwinism (i.e., "the survival of the fittest")—to obscure the real economic, political, and class structure of society.

It took a great deal of work by reactionary intellectuals in the nineteenth century to lay the theoretical foundations for the growth of anti-Semitic movements. The Hungarian Marxist philosopher Georg Lukács explained in *The Destruction of Reason* how the racial theorists of the late nineteenth century sought to substitute "race for class in sociology." Lukács wrote, "This reversal of the relation between politics and economics was connected with the central issue in Social Darwinism, namely the endeavour to grasp biologically, and thus do away with, every social distinction, class stratification, and class struggle."[2]

It was not the case, as Hannah-Jones claimed, that the Nazis came to power due to a groundswell of anti-Semitism that arose organically from the masses of non-Jewish Germans.

In 1933, Jewish people comprised only 1 percent of the German population, approximately 600,000 out of 60 million. Jewish people, particularly in the urban centers, had played an important role in the cultural and professional life of the country. In many parts of the country, and particularly in the rural areas, anti-Semitism flourished despite the fact that the local population had little contact with or interaction with Jews. Contrary to Ms. Hannah-Jones's opinion, seeing Jews was not a necessary precondition for hating them. Particularly among peasants and small businessmen, frustrated resentment of economic oppression was directed toward anger against "Jewish capitalists." It was not without reason that anti-Semitism was referred to as "the socialism of fools."

In any event, anti-Semitism was not the main factor that brought the Nazis to power. In *The Logic of Evil: The Social Origins of the Nazi Party, 1925–1933*, historian William Brustein writes: "Hitler was astute enough as a politician

---

2. Georg Lukács, *The Destruction of Reason* (London: Merlin Press, 1980), p. 692.

to realize that his rabid anti-Semitism lacked drawing power among the German masses. Indeed, it appears that increasingly the Nazi Party relegated anti-Semitism to a role as backdrop to other more materialistic appeals."[3]

The Nazis generally toned down anti-Semitic rhetoric in the run-up to elections, and, as Brustein notes, "As difficult as it may be for many of us to believe, Nazi anti-Semitism, though a driving force in the foundation of the Nazi Party, hardly explains the NSDAP's spectacular rise to power."[4]

It is also false to claim that the absence of Jewish people in present-day Germany has led to a decline in anti-Semitism.

First of all, Hannah-Jones is wrong when she states there are "no Jewish people left" in Germany. In fact, there are an estimated eighty thousand Jewish people living in Germany today. And they play, despite this small number, a significant role in the intellectual and cultural life of the country.

As for her claim that the absence of Jewish people has allowed Germany to "cleanse everything that had to do with Nazism," a neo-Nazi party, the Alternative für Deutschland (AfD), is presently the third-largest party in the federal parliament. Attacks on Jews in Germany are increasing, of which last month's assault on a synagogue in Halle is only the most publicized example. Israel's *Haaretz* newspaper recently posted an opinion article titled, "The German Jews Who Think Now Is the Time to Leave, Before It's Too Late—Again," which warns of the contemporary existence of "thousands of armed extremists and an ascending political far right."

The resurgence of German fascism is rooted in political interests, especially the efforts of the ruling elites to legitimize the reestablishment of militarism and an aggressive imperialist foreign policy. In this process, right-wing academics are attempting to revise history and downplay the crimes of Hitler's regime.

Hannah-Jones's race-based explanation of German history and politics is fundamentally of the same character as her presentation of American history. Hannah-Jones and the *New York Times'* 1619 Project are utilizing racial mythology to divert class antagonisms into racial division. Whether this is Hannah-Jones's intention, or if she even understands the implications of her arguments, is really beside the point.

Racism in the United States has always served as an ideological justification for brutal forms of economic exploitation, first under slavery and then

---

3. William Brustein, *The Logic of Evil: The Social Origin of the Nazi Party, 1925–1933* (New Haven: Yale University Press, 1996), p. 58.

4. Ibid., p. 60.

particularly through the policies of post-Civil War Jim Crow segregation. The development of racial myths about the supposed supremacy of white people became a critical mechanism for blocking the threat of a racially unified movement of whites and blacks, first against slavery and then against the capitalist system.

Then, as now, race theory is the mechanism by which the ruling class justifies a strategy to divide and weaken the working class, shrouding its aims with lies about intrinsic differences between the races, "whiteness," "blackness," and other such nonsense.

Almost as distressing as Hannah-Jones's remarks was the response of the affluent audience. The president of NYU, Andrew Hamilton, offered no objection to her ignorant remarks. Nor—with the exception of a speaker from the Socialist Equality Party, whose microphone was cut off—was there any critical response to Hannah-Jones's racialist interpretation of history and ignorant comments on the Holocaust.

Nikole Hannah-Jones, Shell Oil, and Mass Killings in Africa

On Wednesday, December 11, 2019, Nikole Hannah-Jones, lead author of the *New York Times'* 1619 Project, delivered a speech in Houston to inaugurate the Emancipation Park Conservancy's lecture series depicting the "Black Experience."

The appearance was part of a nationwide lecture tour in which Hannah-Jones is promoting the 1619 Project's "reframing" of the history of the United States as an unending racial struggle of whites against African Americans. The American Revolution of 1775 to 1783 and the Civil War of 1861 to 1865, according to Hannah-Jones, were sham events, unrelated to the struggle for equality and the eventual destruction of slavery. George Washington, Thomas Jefferson, and Abraham Lincoln were racist hypocrites dedicated to the defense of white supremacy.

Hannah-Jones's appearance in Texas was sponsored by the Houston-based Shell Oil Company. This is the US subsidiary of the oil and gas corporate giant Royal Dutch Shell, which is confronting international public outrage over its involvement in massive human rights abuses in the African country of Nigeria. The focus of protests has been Shell's collaboration with the Nigerian government in the suppression of the Ogoni ethnic group. The company currently faces multiple court cases over its complicity in the murder of thousands, including the Nigerian dictatorship's hanging in 1995 of the well-known Ogoni writer and environmental activist Ken Saro-Wiwa.

Trévon Austin, Bill Van Auken, and David North, "Nikole Hannah-Jones, Shell Oil and mass killings in Africa," World Socialist Web Site, December 18, 2019.

275

Hannah-Jones is unsparing in her condemnation of the moral failings of the democratic revolutionaries of the eighteenth and nineteenth centuries. She can barely contain her contempt for those who failed to leap out of the historical epoch in which they lived and embrace the rhetoric of twenty-first-century middle-class identity politics. But the unforgiving code of ethics she imposes upon the historic figures of the past does not seem to apply to herself. Her own personal moral compass does not seem to be in working order.

Shell's history in Africa has long made it an international pariah. In the 1980s, it was described as "the worst corporate collaborator" of apartheid South Africa, systematically violating sanctions to provide oil that fueled the racist regime's repressive apparatus. It also carried out mining operations in the country, including at its Rietspruit coal mine, where striking workers were beaten and forced back to work at gunpoint. Its support for apartheid provoked an international boycott movement against the oil giant.

Just two years ago, Amnesty International released an 89-page report titled "A Criminal Enterprise? Shell's Involvement in Human Rights Violations in Nigeria in the 1990s." The report explained:

> In November 1995, the Nigerian state arbitrarily executed nine men after a blatantly unfair trial. The executions led to global condemnation. The United States and the European Union imposed sanctions on Nigeria, and the Commonwealth group of nations suspended the country's membership. Officially accused of involvement in murder, the men had in fact been put on trial for confronting the Anglo-Dutch oil giant, Shell, over its devastating impact on the Ogoniland region of Nigeria's oil-producing Niger Delta.
>
> The executions were the culmination of a brutal campaign by Nigeria's military to silence the protests of the Movement for the Survival of the Ogoni People (MOSOP), led by author and activist Ken Saro-Wiwa, one of the men executed. MOSOP said that others had grown rich on the oil that was pumped from under their soil, while pollution from oil spills and gas flaring had, *"led to the complete degradation of the Ogoni environment, turning our homeland into an ecological disaster."* In January 1993, MOSOP declared that Shell was no longer welcome to operate in Ogoniland. The military's subsequent campaign directly led to widespread and serious human rights violations, including the unlawful killing of hundreds of Ogonis, as well as torture and

other ill-treatment, including rape, and the destruction of homes and livelihoods. Many of these violations also amounted to criminal offences.[1]

Shell's exploitation of oil in Nigeria goes back to the period of British colonial rule. After independence, it became the most important economic actor in the country, with immense power over its government. Shell's operations centered in Ogoniland, located in the southernmost part of the country, along the Gulf of Guinea. Fifty years of exploitation and Shell's continuous oil spills have left the region an ecological disaster, with its soil no longer viable for agriculture and its ground water massively contaminated with carcinogens. The Ogoni people saw their livelihoods destroyed, while they received nothing from the billions of dollars that Shell extracted from the region.

In the early 1990s, under the leadership of Saro-Wiwa, MOSOP emerged to challenge the destruction of the region by Shell and the Nigerian government.

As the protests grew, Shell called upon the government to provide "security protection" for its facilities, while the company offered "logistical" support in deploying heavily armed police and troops against the Ogoni people, providing them with transportation, salaries, and even weapons. In some cases, those sent in to "murder, rape, and torture" wore uniforms bearing the Shell logo.

Over the course of these operations, it is estimated that twenty-seven Ogoni villages were raided, leading to the deaths of as many as 2,000 people and the forced displacement of 80,000 more. Rape was employed as a weapon to intimidate the population and prisoners were routinely tortured.

In May 1994, Saro-Wiwa and other prominent leaders of MOSOP were arrested for killings of which they were patently innocent. After imprisonment and torture, he and eight others were brought to a kangaroo court organized by the military dictatorship of General Sani Abacha, found guilty, and sentenced to hang.

In his final words to the sham tribunal that convicted him, Saro-Wiwa said that Shell itself would face its own day in court.

In a moving testimonial to his father published in the *Guardian* on November 10, 2015, Ken Wiwa, Saro-Wiwa's son, wrote:

---

1. Amnesty International, "A Criminal Enterprise? Shell's Involvement in Human Rights Violations in Nigeria in the 1990s," 2017, p. 5. https://www.amnesty.org/download/Documents/AFR4473932017ENGLISH.PDF

Twenty years ago today my father and eight other Ogoni men were woken from their sleep and hanged in a prison yard in southern Nigeria. When the news filtered out, shock and outrage reverberated around the world, and everyone from the Queen to Bill Clinton and Nelson Mandela condemned the executions. ...

That it was a kangaroo court is no longer in dispute. The trial and execution were consistent with the way Nigeria's military regimes summarily dealt with people they regarded as a threat to their authority. A UN fact-finding mission led by eminent jurists vigorously condemned the process, and John Major, Britain's prime minister, described the trial as "fraudulent", the convictions as a "bad verdict", and the executions as "judicial murder". ...

If my father were alive today he would be dismayed that Ogoniland still looks like the devastated region that spurred him to action. There is little evidence to show that it sits on one of the world's richest deposits of oil and gas.[2]

The *New York Times*—which has promoted the 1619 Project and selected Hannah-Jones as its principal mouthpiece—is thoroughly familiar with this history, having published numerous articles on the life and death of Saro-Wiwa. In an editorial written in the aftermath of his execution, the *Times* noted that, after the MOSOP leader's conviction, Shell issued a statement that "it is not for a commercial organization to interfere with the legal processes of a sovereign state." Clearly worried about the oil giant's reputation, the *Times* concluded tepidly, "Summary executions, fraudulent trials and brutal suppression of dissent are not practices a responsible corporation can ignore."[3] Shell was not ignoring anything; it was entirely complicit in these crimes.

The crimes committed by Shell in Ogoniland did not occur in the eighteenth, nineteenth, or even the early decades of the twentieth centuries. This is a contemporary event and an ongoing crime. Shell is now on trial at a court in The Hague, charged with complicity in murder, rape, and burning down villages by the Nigerian regime. The plaintiffs are the widows of four of the

---

2. Ken Wiwa, The *Guardian*, November 10, 2015, accessed 12/8/2020:   https://www.theguardian.com/commentisfree/2015/nov/10/ken-saro-wiwa-father-nigeria-ogoniland-oil-pollution

3. The *New York Times*, December 3, 1995, "Shell Game in Nigeria," accessed 12/8/2020: https://www.nytimes.com/1995/12/03/opinion/shell-game-in-nigeria.html

nine Ogoni leaders who were hanged after being falsely convicted by the dictatorship's sham tribunal. Shell fought an earlier attempt to try the company in the US all the way to the Supreme Court, where the case was thrown out on jurisdictional grounds.

A report by the *Guardian* published on February 12, 2019, quoted Mark Dummett, a researcher at Amnesty International, who stated that the widows of the executed Ogoni leaders "believe that their husbands would still be alive today were it not for the brazen self-interest of Shell." The trial, Dummett continued, "is an historic moment which has huge significance for people everywhere who have been harmed by the greed and recklessness of global corporations."[4]

The oil giant is facing a second criminal prosecution in the Netherlands on charges of bribery and corruption for its part in handing out $1.1 billion that went into the pockets of Nigerian politicians and middlemen to secure lucrative offshore drilling rights.

Meanwhile, another lawsuit brought by Ogoni villagers and Friends of the Earth Netherlands over the environmental devastation of the Niger Delta region has been fought by the company for the past decade, with two of the plaintiffs dying in the meantime.

In November, 2019, *Jacobin* magazine conducted an interview with two academic experts on conditions in Ogoniland, Roy Doron and Toyin Falola, who stated that Shell and other oil companies devote far more time to "public relations aimed at Western audiences and allaying investor guilt than actually making a difference to the communities impacted by years of oil spills, gas flaring, and systemic land dispossession."[5]

Shell used Hannah-Jones, who was only too willing to be used, as part of its public relations operation aimed at diverting attention from the company's crimes as they face fresh exposure. Sponsoring an appearance by Hannah-Jones allows Shell to posture as an intrepid corporate fighter against racism. Moreover, the 1619 Project's obsessive focus on race conceals the essential economic interests that underlie the business practices of Shell.

Shell executives obviously sponsored the event in the expectation that endorsement of the 1619 Project would counteract the impact of ongoing law-

---

4. The *Guardian*, "Ogoni widows testify at The Hague over Shell's alleged complicity in killings," accessed 12/8/2020: https://www.theguardian.com/global-development/2019/feb/12/ogoni-widows-testify-the-hague-shell-alleged-complicity-killings

5. *Jacobin*, "The Nigerian Activist Whose Death Shamed Shell," accessed 12/8/2020: https://www.jacobinmag.com/2019/11/ken-saro-wiwa-nigeria-environment-oil-companies-ogoni

suits, and they could not have been disappointed by the results of their investment. Everything went exactly as planned. Shell basked in a moment of public adulation as the event moderator, Melanie Lawson, a local media personality, prefaced her introduction of Hannah-Jones with a shout-out:

> I want to take a moment first to recognize tonight's presenting sponsor. And you might know this name, it's a giant in our community, Shell Oil. And if someone is here from Shell Oil, will you please stand or wave or all of the above? Do we have some Shell folks? There we go.

The audience responded with an ovation, in which Hannah-Jones joined. Lawson continued:

> Yeah, don't be shy about this. Shell people, stand up so we can thank you. We appreciate you. We know this event would not be possible without your very generous donation and we appreciate your continued support of Emancipation Park Conservancy.[6]

It should not come as a surprise that Lawson did not ask the audience to stand and observe a minute of silence to honor the memories of Saro-Wiwa and other victims of Shell's criminal activity.

The event in Houston underscores the fraudulence and class character of the 1619 Project. Hannah-Jones's appearance on a platform paid for by Shell Oil makes her politically and morally complicit in the oppression of the Ogoni people. Her staggering hypocrisy and moral blindness is not merely a personal characteristic. It is typical of an ultraegotistical, self-absorbed, and affluent petty-bourgeois social stratum, determined to make as much money as possible, regardless of where it is coming from.

It is not at all clear how Hannah-Jones's racialist interpretation of history, which claims that North American slavery and all subsequent forms of discrimination in the United States stem from white people's allegedly inbred and intractable hatred of African Americans, would serve to explain her own apparent indifference to the crimes of Shell Oil against modern-day Africans. Moreover, Hannah-Jones's association with Shell is of an entirely voluntary character. Jefferson and Lincoln were born and lived in a historical situation in which slavery was a major element of the economic structure of the North American and world economy. What objective historical factors have *compelled* Hannah-Jones to associate herself with, and profit from, collaboration with Shell Oil?

---

6. Hannah-Jones lecture in Houston, December 11, 2019.

What excuse does she have, other than personal self-interest, for appearing on a platform provided by Shell Oil?

Having promoted herself as the avenging angel of American history, Hannah-Jones is obligated to reveal all the facts related to her participation at an event sponsored by Shell. Did she receive any form of remuneration for her appearance in Houston? Why is she serving the publicity needs of a corporation branded as a "criminal enterprise," complicit in the "murder, rape, and torture" of African men, women, and children?

An Embarrassing Pulitzer Prize
for Personal Commentary

There are occasions when an award is a humiliation. Such is the case with Nikole Hannah-Jones's Pulitzer Prize for the lead essay to the *New York Times'* 1619 Project, won in the category of Commentary—that is, opinion-writing.

The Pulitzer Prize in the prestigious category of History went to Professor W. Caleb McDaniel of Rice University for *Sweet Taste of Liberty: A True Story of Slavery and Restitution in America.*

The Commentary prize is a major comedown for the *New York Times*, which staked to this racialist "reframing" of American history immense editorial resources, untold millions of dollars, and its credibility as the self-proclaimed "newspaper of record." The Pulitzer Prize committee took no specific notice of the 1619 Project itself. Given the cost of the 1619 Project, winning the prize for Commentary is akin to a Hollywood multi-million-dollar blockbuster winning the Oscar for nothing more than best makeup.

The Pulitzer went only to Hannah-Jones, and not to the *Times* or the 1619 Project, which was released on August 13, 2019, amid an unprecedented publicity blitz, to coincide with the four hundredth anniversary of the arrival of the first slaves in colonial Virginia. The initial glossy magazine was over one hundred pages long and included ten essays, a photo essay, and poems and fiction by sixteen more writers. It has been followed by podcasts, a lecture tour, school lesson plans, and even a commercial run during the Academy Awards. The 1619 Project was a massive institutional enterprise. But what the *New York*

Thomas Mackaman and David North, "Hannah-Jones receives Pulitzer Prize for personal commentary, not historical writing," World Socialist Web Site, May 9, 2020.

Times wound up with was nothing more than an individual award for Commentary. This is certainly the most expensive consolation prize in the history of the Pulitzers.

In a departure for the Commentary Award, Hannah-Jones won only for her *single* essay titled, "Our democracy's founding ideals were false when they were written. Black Americans have fought to make them true." One cannot help but suspect that the *Times* brought considerable pressure to bear to eke out this minimal recognition of the 1619 Project's existence. Hannah-Jones beat out finalists considered for a whole year's work. Her competitors were Sally Jenkins, a sturdy sports writer for the *Washington Post*, and Steve Lopez of the *Los Angeles Times* for his series of columns on homelessness in America's second-largest city.

The Pulitzer board cited Hannah-Jones for her "sweeping, deeply reported and *personal* essay" (emphasis added). The word choice is revealing and damning. The board did not evaluate her essay, which defined the content of the 1619 Project, as rising to the level of a history. This is not an insignificant judgment. In the realm of scholarly work, the profound difference between the writing of a historical work and the spinning out of opinions is of a fundamental character. As Hegel, among the greatest of all philosophers of history, once wrote, "What can be more useless than to learn a string of bald opinions, and what more unimportant?" While a reporter's "personal" thoughts about history may prompt a "public conversation," as the Pulitzer citation acknowledges, they do not provide the basis for the overturning of documented history, much less a new curriculum for the schools.

The "public conversation" to which the Pulitzer citation refers was set into motion by the World Socialist Web Site, which published in the first week of September 2019 a comprehensive rebuttal of the 1619 Project. The WSWS followed this with a series of interviews with leading historians who subjected the *Times*' unprecedented and extravagant foray into history to a withering critique: Victoria Bynum, James McPherson, James Oakes, Gordon Wood, Adolph Reed Jr., Dolores Janiewski, Richard Carwardine, and Clayborne Carson.

The central argument advanced in the essays and interviews was that the 1619 Project was a travesty of history. The WSWS exposure of the 1619 Project's shoddy research, numerous factual errors, and outright falsifications attracted a huge audience and was the subject of discussion in numerous publications.

The *Times* responded desperately, lashing out at its critics. As Carson, the editor of the Martin Luther King papers, pointed out, "the saddest part of this [is] that the response of the *New York Times* is simply to defend their project."

On December 20, 2019, *New York Times Magazine* editor Jake Silverstein asserted that the 1619 Project had proved the astounding fact, hitherto suppressed by historians, that all of the American experience, present and past, is the ineradicable spawn of "slavery and the anti-black racism it required," including America's "economic might, its industrial power, its electoral system, its diet and popular music, the inequities of its public health and education, its astonishing penchant for violence, its income inequality, the example it sets for the world as a land of freedom and equality, its slang, its legal system and the endemic racial fears and hatreds that continue to plague it to this day. The seeds of all that were planted long before our official birth date, in 1776, when the men known as our founders formally declared independence from Britain."[1]

The 1619 Project's central claims ran roughshod over virtually every field of historical research. Slavery was transformed into an exceptionally American "original sin" and a vehicle for the transmission of racism, not a global system of labor exploitation with ancient roots. The American Revolution was reduced to a conspiracy of white founders defending slavery against the enlightened British aristocracy.

According to Hannah-Jones and the *Times*, the Civil War was not about the destruction of slavery, but was rather a war between racist brothers, an interpretation first developed by Jim Crow historians more than a century ago. There was no interracial abolitionist movement and no labor movement whatsoever. Despite claims about putting "black people at the very center," there were no black people as historical actors to be found, only victim-symbols of white oppression. There was no Frederick Douglass, no Martin Luther King Jr., no Harlem Renaissance, no Great Migration. Racism itself was transformed into a suprahistorical and biological impulse that, as Hannah-Jones wrote, "runs in the very DNA of this country." In this new narrative there was no room whatsoever for American Indians, indentured servants, immigrants, farmers, or wage workers.

Moreover, Hannah-Jones and the 1619 Project loudly and crudely insisted that *only* African Americans could intuitively grasp this history. In rolling out its special edition, the *Times* boasted, "Almost every contributor in the

---

1. Jake Silverstein, "Why We Published the 1619 Project," The *New York Times Magazine*, December 20, 2019, https://www.nytimes.com/interactive/2019/12/20/magazine/1619-intro.html

magazine and special section—writers, photographers and artists—is black, a nonnegotiable aspect of the project that helps underscore its thesis." Hannah-Jones claimed on Twitter that "white historians" could never sufficiently rid themselves of racism to understand African American history, and therefore could be disregarded.

The Pulitzer board was not unmindful of the fact that among the "white historians" that Hannah-Jones and the *Times* denounced were previous Pulitzer winners Gordon Wood and James McPherson—the leading historians of the American Revolution and Civil War, respectively. These two scholars have dedicated their lives to the study of America's twin revolutions. As a young historian in his twenties, decades before the publication of his Pulitzer Prize-winning *Battle Cry of Freedom*, McPherson wrote a significant study of the movement against slavery, *The Struggle for Equality: Abolitionists and the Negro in the Civil War and Reconstruction*.

The exclusion of the 1619 Project from the History category leaves the integrity of the Pulitzer selection criteria and the prestige of the earlier awards to Wood and McPherson unmolested.

When Wood and McPherson joined Sean Wilentz and two other eminent historians interviewed by the WSWS, Victoria Bynum and James Oakes, in writing a letter to the *Times* pointing to egregious errors of fact in the 1619 Project, Silverstein published a scornful and dismissive letter insisting that the project had "consulted with numerous scholars of African American history and related fields" and that the whole effort had been "carefully reviewed [by] subject-area experts."

However, in early March, one of the 1619 Project's own "subject-area experts," Professor Leslie Harris of Northwestern University, revealed that her objections to the 1619 Project's pivotal argument—that the American Revolution was waged to defend slavery against imminent British emancipation—had been disregarded. The patently false claim that the American Revolution was a counterrevolution to defend slavery was the essential foundation of Hannah-Jones's thesis that the "true founding" of the United States was not 1776, but 1619. Silverstein offered a modest wording change to "correct" this "mistake," but what remained of the credibility of the lavishly funded enterprise had been reduced to rubble.

It is worth contrasting the Pulitzer board's language for the prizes in History and Commentary. While it cited Hannah-Jones for her "personal" essay, it called McDaniel's *Sweet Taste of Liberty* "a *masterfully researched* meditation on reparations based on the remarkable story of a 19th century woman who survived kidnapping and re-enslavement to sue her captor" (emphasis added).

McDaniel's book is an impressive example of historical research, involving voluminous reading in the existing literature, as well as the discovery of documents relating to the struggle of a former slave contending with powerful historical forces. It includes in its notes numerous citations of the works of McPherson and upholds the revolutionary significance of the Civil War. Like McPherson, McDaniel, at Rice University in Texas, happens to be a "white historian." We are compelled to note this otherwise irrelevant detail because, according to the reactionary nationalist ideology of Hannah-Jones and the race-obsessed editors of the *Times*, McDaniel should not have been able to fathom "the nuances of what it means to be a black person in America." The historian's award-winning work discredits this racialist prejudice. Evidently, the three academics who decided to award Professor McDaniel the Pulitzer for History were not influenced by the sort of zoological criteria espoused by Hannah-Jones and the *Times*.

The *Times*' own muted response to Hannah-Jones's prize in Commentary is revealing, and stands in stark juxtaposition to the shameless self-promotion, "Pulitzer buzz," and arrogant denunciation of critics that accompanied the 1619 Project's first months. One can imagine the crowing that would have followed a Pulitzer for the *New York Times* in the History category. Instead, the *Times*' noticeably low-key coverage of the 2020 Pulitzer selections refers to the prize won by its heavily promoted reporter-celebrity in a short paragraph about 225 words into the article.

The 1619 Project was never about history or even serious journalism. From its inception, in the leaked words of *Times*' executive editor Dean Baquet, it was an "ambitious and expansive" *campaign*, under conditions of mounting opposition in the working class, to make race "*the* American story" (emphasis added). This effort has fared badly. The contrast between the boastful claims made by the *Times* and the actual content of the 1619 Project recalls the ancient epigram:

> What could he produce to match his opening promise?
> Mountains will labour: what's born? A ridiculous mouse![2]

---

2. "The Mountain in Labour" is one of Aesop's Fables.

New York Times Ignored Objections Raised by 1619 Project Fact-Checker

A fact-checker for the 1619 Project has revealed that the *New York Times* ignored her objection to the project's claim that the American Revolution was a counterrevolution waged to defend slavery.

In the article, published March 6, 2020, on Politico ("I Helped Fact-Check the 1619 Project. The *Times* Ignored Me"), Professor Leslie M. Harris of Northwestern University explains that weeks before the August 2019 publication of the project, she was approached by a *Times* research editor to verify historical statements, among them the following:

> One critical reason that the colonists declared their independence from Britain was because they wanted to protect the institution of slavery in the colonies, which had produced tremendous wealth. At the time there were growing calls to abolish slavery throughout the British Empire, which would have badly damaged the economies of colonies in both North and South.[1]

Harris wrote that she "vigorously disputed the claim," writing in Politico that, "although slavery was certainly an issue in the American Revolution, the protection of slavery was not one of the main reasons the 13 Colonies went to war." Harris also disputed a second tenet of the project—its implication that

Eric London and Thomas Mackaman, "New York Times ignored objections raised by 1619 Project fact-checker," World Socialist Web Site, March 9, 2020.

1. Leslie M. Harris, Politico, March 6, 2020, https://www.politico.com/news/magazine/2020/03/06/1619-project-new-york-times-mistake-122248

during the colonial period, slavery was the same as it was in 1860, at the time of the Southern secession that led to the Civil War. This position underlies the Project's claim that slavery was, beginning in 1619, a fully formed expression of white racism. Both errors appeared in spite of Harris's "vigorous" objections, which included providing "references to specific examples." The Northwestern historian, an expert in antebellum slavery, "never heard back ... about how the information would be used."[2]

Harris begins her article by describing how she learned that her objections were disregarded—when she appeared on Georgia Public Radio together with Nikole Hannah-Jones. Harris said she "listened in stunned silence as" the lead essayist and 1619 Project figurehead "repeated an idea that I had vigorously argued against with her fact-checker: that the patriots fought the American Revolution in large part to preserve slavery in North America."[3]

Harris provides a summation of the historical evidence, exposing the claim regarding the 1619 Project's claim that the American Revolution was a slaveholders' revolt. She writes:

> Slavery in the Colonies faced no immediate threat from Great Britain, so colonists wouldn't have needed to secede to protect it. It's true that in 1772, the famous Somerset case ended slavery in England and Wales, but it had no impact on Britain's Caribbean colonies, where the vast majority of black people enslaved by the British labored and died, or in the North American Colonies. It took 60 more years for the British government to finally end slavery in its Caribbean colonies. ...
>
> Far from being fought to preserve slavery, the Revolutionary War became a primary disrupter of slavery in the North American Colonies. Lord Dunmore's Proclamation, a British military strategy designed to unsettle the Southern Colonies by inviting enslaved people to flee to British lines, propelled hundreds of enslaved people off plantations and turned some Southerners to the patriot side. It also led most of the 13 Colonies to arm and employ free and enslaved black people, with the promise of freedom to those who served in their armies.[4]

---

2. Ibid.
3. Ibid.
4. Ibid.

Harris's revelation that the *Times* disregarded her is all the more damning because, in the remainder of her article, she solidarizes herself with the project, and expresses concern that its recklessness with facts will discredit it.

It seems not to have occurred to Harris that the project's thesis—that "anti-black racism" residing in a "national DNA" as an immutable, suprahistorical force—*necessitates* the falsification of history, and not only of the origins of slavery in the Atlantic world and the Revolution, but of the entire course of American and world history. The falsification continues in Hannah-Jones's tendentious selection of quotations from Lincoln, and in her writing out—in spite of claims about putting black Americans at "the very center" of a new history—figures such as Frederick Douglass, Martin Luther King Jr., and A. Philip Randolph, as well as the abolitionist, civil rights, and labor movements, the Harlem Renaissance, and so much more.

Harris's revelations discredit *Times* magazine editor Jake Silverstein's dismissive January 4, 2020, reply to five eminent historians, who objected to the 1619 Project's claim that the colonists launched the American Revolution to defend slavery. Silverstein claimed that "during the fact-checking process, our researchers carefully reviewed all the articles in the issue with subject-area experts." Silverstein concealed the fact that a *Times* fact-checker had raised serious objections to one of the project's principal claims.[5]

Silverstein has not commented on Professor Harris's exposure of his dishonest method, which discredits his and Hannah-Jones's pompous and fraudulent claim that the project represents a breakthrough in the study of American history.

On March 6, the same day as the publications of Harris's exposure, the *Times* hosted a public event at its plush TimesCenter hall in Manhattan. Titled "The 1619 Project—Slavery and the American Revolution: A Historical Dialogue," the meeting promoted the falsification of history to which Harris had objected, i.e., that the American Revolution was a counterrevolutionary slaveowners' revolt. Neither Silverstein nor Hannah-Jones, who jointly introduced the evening, mentioned the article by Professor Harris. Nor did any of the five historians on stage: Karin Wulf, Gerald Horne, Alan Taylor, Annette Gordon-Reed, and Eliga Gould.

The event was an intellectual travesty. Advertised as a discussion among "historians with a range of views" on the 1619 Project's claims about slavery and

---

5. The *New York Times Magazine*, December 20, 2019, https://www.nytimes.com/2019/12/20/magazine/we-respond-to-the-historians-who-critiqued-the-1619-project.html

the American Revolution, the discussion was orchestrated to *exclude* critics and lend a veneer of academic credibility to the 1619 Project.

Wulf moderated the event in such a way as to distort and evade the actual content of criticism of the project. Prior to the meeting, historian Thomas Mackaman, whose interviews with leading historians critical of the 1619 Project have been widely read, sent an email to Wulf requesting that he be allowed to speak. This request was denied.

Near the end of the meeting, a few minutes were given over to respond to carefully vetted questions submitted via email.

Jake Silverstein Slithers Away from the Central 1619 Fabrication

Last Wednesday, March 11, 2020, editor in chief of the *New York Times Magazine* Jake Silverstein announced that the 1619 Project would slightly amend its claim that the American Revolution was a racist endeavor undertaken to fight plans by the British Empire to end slavery.

In "An Update to the 1619 Project," Silverstein claimed that a modification to the project's lead essay by Nikole Hannah-Jones would serve as a "clarification to a passage" whose "original language could be read to suggest that protecting slavery was a primary motivation for all of the colonists."[1]

Silverstein's "update" is nothing more than a cynical face-saving exercise necessitated by the revelation that the 1619 Project disregarded its own fact-checkers. On March 6, Professor Leslie Harris of Northwestern University published an exposé on Politico entitled "I Helped Fact-Check the 1619 Project. The *Times* Ignored Me." Harris wrote that she "vigorously disputed" the claim that the American Revolution had been waged to defend slavery. She explained:

> Slavery in the Colonies faced no immediate threat from Great Britain, so colonists wouldn't have needed to secede to protect it. It's true that in 1772, the famous Somerset case ended slavery in England and Wales, but it had no impact on Britain's Caribbean

---

Thomas Mackaman, "New York Times Magazine editor Jake Silverstein attempts to slither away from central 1619 Project fabrication," World Socialist Web Site, March 16, 2020.

1. Jake Silverstien, "An Update to The 1619 Project, The *New York Times Magazine*, March 11, 2020, https://www.nytimes.com/2020/03/11/magazine/an-update-to-the-1619-project. html

colonies, where the vast majority of black people enslaved by the British labored and died, or in the North American Colonies. It took 60 more years for the British government to finally end slavery in its Caribbean colonies.[2]

In his update, Silverstein does not apologize to the five eminent historians who sent a letter sent in December 2019 to the *Times,* specifically objecting to the claim that the Revolution was undertaken in defense of slavery. Historians Victoria Bynum, James McPherson, James Oakes, Sean Wilentz, and Gordon Wood asked that this assertion be corrected, along with several other egregious errors and distortions in the 1619 Project.

In an arrogant reply published in the December 29 issue of the *New York Times Magazine*, Silverstein dismissed the historians' letter. He claimed dishonestly that the entire Project was carefully vetted: "Finally, during the fact-checking process, our researchers carefully reviewed all the articles in the issue with subject-area experts," and that "we don't believe that the request for corrections to The 1619 Project is warranted."[3]

Silverstein's belated effort in damage control does not withdraw the 1619 Project's assertion that 1776 was a "lie" and a "founding mythology." The *Times* editor is attempting to palm off a minor change in wording as a sufficient correction of a historically untenable rendering of the American Revolution. Hannah-Jones's passage now reads, with the changed phrase in italics:

> Conveniently left out of our founding mythology is the fact that one of the primary reasons *some of* the colonists decided to declare their independence from Britain was because they wanted to protect the institution of slavery. By 1776, Britain had grown deeply conflicted over its role in the barbaric institution that had reshaped the Western Hemisphere.[4]

This passage is still false. Protecting slavery could not have been a significant cause of the American Revolution, because, far from posing a threat to

---

2. Leslie M. Harris, Politico, https://www.politico.com/news/magazine/2020/03/06/1619-project-new-york-times-mistake-122248

3. The *New York Times Magazine*, December 20, 2019, https://www.nytimes.com/2019/12/20/magazine/we-respond-to-the-historians-who-critiqued-the-1619-project.html.
The article also includes the letter from the historians.

4. Online edition of Nikole Hannah-Jones's essay in the *New York Times*, August 14, 2019. https://www.nytimes.com/interactive/2019/08/14/magazine/black-history-american-democracy.html

slavery, the British Empire controlled the slave trade and profited immensely from its commerce in people, as well as from its Caribbean plantations which remained loyal during the war for independence.

Yet in his March 11, 2020, article, Silverstein reiterates the initial error and compounds it with new layers of confusion. He writes, "We stand behind the basic point, which is that among the various motivations that drove the patriots *toward* independence was a concern that the British *would seek or were already seeking* to disrupt in various ways the entrenched system of American slavery" (emphasis added).[5]

There is no evidence for any of this. The chain of events that led "toward" independence had already emerged with the Stamp Act Crisis of 1765, seven years before the Somerset ruling. "The British" did not seek to disrupt "American slavery" until Lord Dunmore's proclamation of 1775—issued after the war of independence had begun—offered emancipation to slaves and indentured servants who took up arms against masters *already in rebellion*. The proclamation in fact explicitly *preserved* slavery among loyal British subjects, many of whom would live out their days under Dunmore in his final post as royal governor of the slave-rich Bahamas.

Silverstein claims that the 1619 Project is rooted in scholarship of "the past 40 years or so" that, he says, reveals "that the patriots represented a truly diverse coalition animated by a variety of interests, which varied by region, class, age, religion and a host of other factors" as opposed to those who "assume unanimity on the part of the colonists, as many previous interpretive histories of the patriot cause did."[6] This is a strawman. No serious scholar—going back a century to Charles Beard—has ever denied that there were various interests at stake in the Revolution and that wide layers of the colonial population were drawn into struggle, in a war that killed more Americans as a share of the population than any other outside of the Civil War, and that lasted longer than any until the current imperialist wars in Afghanistan and Iraq (both of which the *Times* has relentlessly supported).

In fact, it is the *Times* that has portrayed the American Revolution as an episode of "unanimity on the part of the colonists." The 1619 Project presents the revolution as a simple conspiracy of white Founding Fathers waged to preserve slavery and create a sham democracy. The crowning achievements of this conspiracy, in Hannah-Jones's telling, were the Declaration of Independence

---

5. The *New York Times Magazine*, March 11, 2020, https://www.nytimes.com/2020/03/11/magazine/an-update-to-the-1619-project.html
6. Ibid.

and the Constitution. On this question, Silverstein, Hannah-Jones, and the historians they cite—Lerone Bennett Jr., Gerald Horne, Woody Holton, and David Waldstreicher—find themselves in alignment with John C. Calhoun and the other fire-eating defenders of slavery in the late antebellum. Though these historians draw a minus sign where fire-eaters drew a plus sign, all agree that the Declaration of Independence and the Constitution founded a slavocracy, not a bourgeois democracy.

They disregard Frederick Douglass and other abolitionists who found in the Constitution the legal machinery for slavery's ultimate destruction and in the Declaration their "sacred scripture," in the words of the great scholar of American slavery, the late David Brion Davis. Indeed, what is most glaring about the 1619 Project's falsification is that it disregards the fact that the American Revolution ultimately led to the destruction of slavery. Just "four score and seven years later," as Lincoln counted the years backward from Gettysburg in 1863, an institution that had existed since the ancient world, and in the new world for 350 years, was destroyed.

Silverstein's article made no comment on the many other factual errors and distortions comprising the 1619 Project that have been exposed by the World Socialist Web Site and leading historians. These include:

- Its presentation of slavery as a uniquely American "original sin," fully formed—legally and racially—from the very beginning in 1619 just like it was at the time of the Civil War. Professor Harris reports that she also objected in her fact-checking to this error, but no change has been made.

- Its tendentious selection of quotes from Lincoln, designed to make him appear to be a racist, clearly taken from Bennett's discredited biography of Lincoln, *Forced into Glory*.

- Its assertion that black Americans fought back "for the most part ... alone" to make America a democracy. This disregards the hundreds of thousands of Americans who died in the Civil War, as well as the clearly interracial character of the abolitionist, civil rights, and labor movements.

- Its false claim to place black Americans at "the very center" of American history when, in fact, the project includes no black Americans as historical actors. Those who do appear are mere symbols, the playthings of the true historical actor, "anti-black racism" which is ineradicably rooted in a "national DNA."

- Neither Frederick Douglass nor Martin Luther King are even mentioned.

- Its argument that all manner of social problems in contemporary America—from lack of health care to obesity to traffic congestion—are the direct outcomes of the "original sin" of slavery, and therefore are functions of racial identity, not capitalist exploitation.

None of this is a matter of semantics. Silverstein's latest foray only adds a new layer of dishonesty to the sordid 1619 Project affair. Were he serious about valuing criticism, as he claims, Silverstein might have written the following:

> We thank the historians who have brought to our attention the many errors in the 1619 Project. We are compelled to acknowledge and correct these errors. We have written to schools that have already received copies of material from the Project asking that they return them, and that they withhold them from students until the errors and distortions, and the processes that led to them, can be corrected. We profoundly apologize to the historians whose scholarship and professionalism we maligned. The *Times* will seek their assistance in preparing a revised edition of the 1619 Project. Finally, as painful as it is to do, we recommend to our readers that they study the essays and interviews criticizing the 1619 Project published in the World Socialist Web Site.

We will not hold our breath waiting for such a statement.

The *Times* Decides that 1619 Was Not the Year of America's "True Founding"

The *New York Times*, without announcement or explanation, has abandoned the central claim of the 1619 Project: that 1619, the year the first slaves were brought to colonial Virginia—and not 1776—was the "true founding" of the United States.

The initial introduction to the project, when it was rolled out in August 2019, stated that:

> The 1619 Project is a major initiative from the New York Times observing the 400th anniversary of the beginning of American slavery. It aims to reframe the country's history, *understanding 1619 as our true founding*, and placing the consequences of slavery and the contributions of black Americans at the very center of the story we tell ourselves about who we are [emphasis added].[1]

The revised text now reads:

> The 1619 Project is an ongoing initiative from The New York Times Magazine that began in August 2019, the 400th anniversary of the beginning of American slavery. It aims to reframe the

---

Thomas Mackaman and David North, "The New York Times and Nikole Hannah-Jones abandon key claims of the 1619 Project," World Socialist Web Site, September 22, 2020.

1. This paragraph no longer appears on the *New York Times*' website. It became the subject of controversy addressed by Phillip W. Magness in Quillette: https://quillette.com/2020/09/19/down-the-1619-projects-memory-hole/, and Bret Stephens of the *New York Times*: https://www.nytimes.com/2020/10/09/opinion/nyt-1619-project-criticisms.html. Jake Silverstein addressed the controversy in his reply to Stephens: https://www.nytimes.com/2020/10/16/magazine/criticism-1619-project.html

country's history by placing the consequences of slavery and the contributions of black Americans at the very center of our national narrative.[2]

A similar change was made from the print version of the 1619 Project, which has been sent out to millions of school children in all fifty states. The original version read:

> In August of 1619, a ship appeared on this horizon, near Point Comfort, a coastal port in the British colony of Virginia. It carried more than 20 enslaved Africans, who were sold to the colonists. *America was not yet America, but this was the moment it began.* No aspect of the country that would be formed here has been untouched by the 250 years of slavery that followed [emphasis added].[3]

The website version has deleted the key claim. It now reads:

> In August of 1619, a ship appeared on this horizon, near Point Comfort, a coastal port in the English colony of Virginia. It carried more than 20 enslaved Africans, who were sold to the colonists. No aspect of the country that would be formed here has been untouched by the years of slavery that followed.[4]

It is not entirely clear when the *Times* deleted its "true founding" claim, but an examination of old cached versions of the 1619 Project text indicates that it probably took place on December 18, 2019.

These deletions are not mere wording changes. The "true founding" claim was the core element of the project's assertion that all of American history is rooted in and defined by white racial hatred of blacks. According to this narrative, trumpeted by Project creator Nikole Hannah-Jones, the American Revolution was a preemptive racial counterrevolution waged by white people in North America to defend slavery against British plans to abolish it. The fact that there is no historical evidence to support this claim did not deter the *Times* and Hannah-Jones from declaring that the historical identification of 1776

---

2. The *New York Times Magazine*, August 14, 2019, https://www.nytimes.com/interactive/2019/08/14/magazine/1619-america-slavery.html
3. The *New York Times Magazine*, August 18, 2019, front cover.
4. The *New York Times Magazine*, https://www.nytimes.com/interactive/2019/08/14/magazine/1619-america-slavery.html

with the creation of a new nation is a myth, as is the claim that the Civil War was a progressive struggle aimed at the destruction of slavery. According to the *New York Times* and Hannah-Jones, the fight against slavery and all forms of oppression were struggles that black Americans always waged alone.

The *Times*' "disappearing," with a few secret keystrokes, of its central argument, without any explanation or announcement, is a stunning act of intellectual dishonesty and outright fraud. When it launched the 1619 Project in August 2019, the *Times* proclaimed that its aim was to radically change what and how students were taught about American history. With the aim of creating a new syllabus based on the 1619 Project, hundreds of thousands of copies of the original version of the narrative, as published in the *New York Times Magazine*, were printed and distributed to schools, museums, and libraries all across the United States. A very large number of schools declared that they would align their curricula in accordance with the narrative supplied by the *Times*.

The deletion of the claim that 1619 was the "true founding" came to light this past Friday, September 18, 2020. Ms. Hannah-Jones was interviewed on CNN and asked to respond to Donald Trump's denunciation, from the standpoint of a fascist, of the 1619 Project. Hannah-Jones declared that the "true founding" contention was "of course" not true. She went further, making the astonishing, and demonstrably false, claim that the *Times* had never made such an argument.

The exchange went as follows:

> CNN: Trump's executive order speaks to a misconception that I know that you have tried to address about what the 1619 Project is, that it is not an effort to rewrite history about when this nation was founded.

> Hannah-Jones: Of course, we know that 1776 was the founding of this country. The Project does not argue that 1776 was not the founding of the country.[5]

This is, of course, an outright lie. Hannah-Jones has repeatedly made the "true founding" claim in innumerable tweets, interviews, and lectures. These are attested to in news articles and video clips readily available on the internet. Her own Twitter account included her image against a backdrop consisting of the year 1619, with the year 1776 crossed out next to it.

---

5. Brianna Keilar, CNN Twitter feed. Accessed on 1/18/2021, https://twitter.com/CNN/status/1307029623943831552

Ms. Hannah-Jones, caught in one lie, doubles down with new and even bigger lies. The *Times* journalist-celebrity not only denies her project's central argument. In self-contradictory fashion, she also says that the "true founding" claim was just a bit of a rhetorical flourish. She told CNN that the 1619 Project was merely an effort to move the study of slavery to the forefront of American history.

If, as Hannah-Jones now claims, all the *Times* had sought to do was draw more attention to the history of chattel slavery in the years it existed in British North America (1619–1776) and the United States (1776–1865), there would never have been a controversy. Neither the World Socialist Web Site nor the scholars it interviewed—James McPherson, Gordon Wood, Victoria Bynum, James Oakes, Clayborne Carson, Richard Carwardine, Dolores Janiewski, and Adolph Reed Jr.—ever disputed the importance of slavery in the historical development of the United States. Tens of thousands of books and scholarly articles have been devoted to the study of slavery and its impact on the historical development of the United States.

In its initial reply to the 1619 Project, published in early September 2019, the WSWS explained:

> American slavery is a monumental subject with vast and endur-ing historical and political significance. The events of 1619 are part of that history. But what occurred at Port Comfort is one episode in the global history of slavery, which extends back into the ancient world, and of the origins and development of the world capitalist system.

The WSWS rebuttal of the *Times* provided an account of the emergence of chattel slavery in the Western Hemisphere, its central role in the formation of capitalism, and its revolutionary destruction in the Civil War. Hannah-Jones responded to the WSWS intervention by denouncing its writers as "anti-black racists" on Twitter.

When Wood, McPherson, Bynum, and Oakes, joined by Sean Wilentz of Princeton, wrote an open letter to the *Times* in December 2019 requesting specific corrections to clear errors of fact, they stressed that their objection was not over whether or not slavery was important. The five historians expressed their dismay "at some of the factual errors in the project and the closed process behind it."

New York Times Magazine editor Jake Silverstein published a haughty and dismissive reply, in which he flatly rejected their criticisms:

Though we respect the work of the signatories, appreciate that they are motivated by scholarly concern and applaud the efforts they have made in their own writings to illuminate the nation's past, we disagree with their claim that our project contains significant factual errors and is driven by ideology rather than historical understanding. While we welcome criticism, we don't believe that the request for corrections to The 1619 Project is warranted.[6]

Silverstein's disgraceful letter appeared on December 20, 2019. At that point, he knew that the *Times'* 1619 Project was fatally flawed and that the newspaper had surreptitiously made a fundamental change in the online text of the article to which the distinguished historians had objected. Silverstein's behavior demonstrated a complete lack of professional ethics and intellectual integrity.

The *Times* is now obligated to issue a public statement acknowledging its distortion of history and the dishonest attempt to cover up its error. It should issue a public apology to professors Gordon Wood, James McPherson, Sean Wilentz, Victoria Bynum, James Oakes, and all other scholars it sought to discredit for having criticized the 1619 Project. To be perfectly blunt, Mr. Silverstein and his confederates in the editorial board of the *Times* should be dismissed from their posts.

Furthermore, the Pulitzer Prize given to Hannah-Jones this spring in the field of commentary for her lead essay, in which the false claims about the "true founding" and the American Revolution were made, should be rescinded.

The 1619 Project was never about historical clarification. As the WSWS warned in September 2019, the "1619 Project is one component of a deliberate effort to inject racial politics into the heart of the 2020 elections and foment divisions among the working class." As revealed in a leaked meeting with *Times* staff, executive editor Dean Baquet believed that it would be helpful to the Democratic Party to shift focus after the failed anti-Russia campaign. Baquet said:

Race and understanding of race should be a part of how we cover the American story. ... One reason we all signed off on the 1619 Project and made it so ambitious and expansive was to teach our readers to think a little bit more like that. Race in the

6. The *New York Times Magazine*, December 20, 2019, https://www.nytimes.com/2019/12/20/magazine/we-respond-to-the-historians-who-critiqued-the-1619-project.html

next year—and I think this is, to be frank, what I would hope you come away from this discussion with—race in the next year is going to be a huge part of the American story. [7]

The fraud perpetrated by the *Times* has already had serious political consequences. As the WSWS warned, the 1619 Project has been an enormous gift to Donald Trump. On September 17, Constitution Day, Trump delivered a speech at the National Archives Museum in which he obscenely postured as a defender of the Declaration of Independence and Constitution against the "radical left," specifically naming the 1619 Project. In his typically menacing fashion, Trump warned that he would "restore patriotic education" and that "our youth will be taught to love America."

It was in response to Trump's attacks that Hannah-Jones appeared on CNN. She noted that Trump is trying "to bring the 1619 Project into the culture wars." She went on, "He clearly is running on a nationalistic campaign that's trying to stoke racial divisions, and he sees it as a tool in that arsenal."

True enough. But Hannah-Jones is one of the key "stokers" of racial divisions. It was the *New York Times* that brought "the 1619 Project into the culture wars," viciously attacking all critics of a historical narrative that makes racial hatred the driving force of American history.

The falsification of history always serves the interests of reactionary political forces. By repudiating and denigrating the American Revolution and Civil War, the *New York Times* has provided an opportunity for Trump to fraudulently posture as a defender of the great democratic legacy of America's revolutions in the interests of his neofascist politics.

---

7. Ashley Feinberg, "The New York Times Unites vs. Twitter," Slate, August 15, 2019, https://slate.com/news-and-politics/2019/08/new-york-times-meeting-transcript.html

Factional Warfare Erupts at the *Times*

On October 11, 2020, *New York Times* publisher A. G. Sulzberger issued a statement to newspaper staff defending the newspaper's 1619 Project. Sulzberger called the project, a series of essays published in August 2019 to coincide with the four hundredth anniversary of the arrival of the first slaves in colonial Virginia, "a journalistic triumph" that "sparked a national conversation." He praised Project creator Nikole Hannah-Jones as a "brilliant and principled journalist" and said the 1619 Project is one of his "proudest accomplishments" as publisher. Having been dragged into a "conversation" that has imposed heavy costs on his newspaper's purse and reputation, Sulzberger's praise of Hannah-Jones is as sincere as a kiss on the lips from a mob boss.[1]

New York Times Magazine editor Jake Silverstein, who publicly tweeted Sulzberger's statement on Sunday evening, had posted a remarkably similar comment on Twitter a day earlier. This was followed on Monday by a formal statement from *Times* executive editor Dean Baquet, published on the New York Times Company website.

Like Sulzberger, Silverstein said he was "proud" of the 1619 Project. He called Hannah-Jones a "national treasure," a phrase normally used to describe parks like Yellowstone and the Grand Canyon. Baquet went even further. He hailed the 1619 Project as "one of the most important pieces of journalism The

Thomas Mackaman and David North, "Factional warfare erupts in New York Times over the 1619 Project," World Socialist Web Site, October 15, 2020.

1. Sulzberger's statement to staff was published in a tweet by Jake Silverstein. Accessed on 12/17/2020: https://twitter.com/jakesilverstein/status/1315467130494742528

Times has produced," thus placing it on the same level as the newspaper's publication of the Pentagon Papers in 1971. Baquet added that he continues to "reject" criticism of its failures, lauding the 1619 Project as "principled, rigorous and groundbreaking journalism."[2]

The gentlemen doth protest too much. There is clearly an air of desperation about this orchestrated, top-level public relations campaign. Such statements are made when necks are on the line and heads about to roll.

The immediate trigger for Sulzberger's memorandum was a Friday column written by *Times* opinion writer Bret Stephens, "The 1619 Chronicles." Stephens is one of the *Times'* leading columnists. An anti-Trump conservative, he pointed to the absurdity of many of the project's historical claims as well as its disregard for basic journalistic principles. Stephens concluded that the 1619 Project was "a thesis in search of evidence."[3]

Stephens quoted at length from historian James McPherson's interview with the World Socialist Web Site, to which he provided a link. In early September 2019, the WSWS produced the first major exposure of the racialist falsifications of the 1619 Project, a few weeks after its rollout amid an unprecedented media blitz. The WSWS followed this with interviews with scholars who dismantled the 1619 Project's major claims—McPherson, Victoria Bynum, James Oakes, Gordon Wood, Dolores Janiewski, Adolph Reed Jr., Richard Carwardine, and Clayborne Carson.

The Stephens column brought into the open the bitter conflict raging at the *Times* over its creation and promotion of the 1619 Project.

Sulzberger's statement claimed that Stephens' op-ed does not signify "an institutional shift" away from the project. But in the memo's second paragraph, Sulzberger rejected the demands of the project's backers that Stephens be censored and even fired. "I believe strongly in the right of Opinion to produce a piece, even when—maybe even especially when—we don't agree with it as an institution," Sulzberger wrote.[4]

The factional warfare within the *Times* included a Twitter attack improperly issued in the name of the Times Guild, a reporters union affiliated with the Communications Workers of America (CWA). The Guild tweeted: "It says a

2. "A Note from Dean Baquet on The 1619 Project," October 13, 2020, https://www.nytco.com/press/a-note-from-dean-baquet-on-the-1619-project/

3. Bret Stephens, "The 1619 Chronicles," The *New York Times*, https://www.nytimes.com/2020/10/09/opinion/nyt-1619-project-criticisms.html

4. Jake Silverstein, Twitter, October 11, 2020, accessed January 5, 2021: https://twitter.com/jakesilverstein/status/1315467130494742528/photo/1

lot about an organization when it breaks it's [sic] own rules and goes after one of it's [sic] own. The act, like the article, reeks."

The Guild later deleted the tweet after a "furor" erupted among *Times* staff against this transparent demand for managerial censorship of a fellow journalist—to say nothing of its mangling of the English language. The Guild declared that whoever issued the attack on Stephens had done so without permission.

It has not yet been revealed who authored the since-deleted tweet. One likely suspect is Hannah-Jones herself, who has become notorious for Twitter tirades against anyone who dares challenge her. The *Washington Post* reported on Tuesday that Hannah-Jones was "livid" when she learned that Stephens' article would appear and sent emails to Stephens and *Times* opinion page editor Kathleen Kingsbury "prior to publication," apparently in a bid to block it.

Aimed at propping up the 1619 Project, the statements from Sulzberger, Baquet, and Silverstein have only added new layers of dishonesty. This has been the pattern from the beginning.

There is nothing for the *Times* to be proud of. The 1619 Project is a travesty of both history and journalism that has humiliated the *Times* and undermined its self-proclaimed status as "the newspaper of record." As for the "conversation" to which Sulzberger refers, this emerged over and against a vicious campaign waged by Hannah-Jones and Silverstein to shut down debate and smear opponents, including the World Socialist Web Site and the eminent historians whom it interviewed.

Hannah-Jones repeatedly attacked on Twitter anyone who exposed the false claims of the project. She denounced World Socialist Web Site writers as "anti-black racists." She rejected McPherson, a revered historian who has dedicated his life to the study of the Civil War era, as a "white historian" unqualified to write on "black history."

None of the immense body of scholarship on the subject of slavery left any discernible trace on Hannah-Jones's "framing essay," which is the centerpiece of the 1619 curriculum. Every one of her arguments can be found in the work of just one historian, the late black nationalist Lerone Bennett Jr., and his two best-known books, *Before the Mayflower: A History of Black America*, and his discredited *Forced into Glory: Abraham Lincoln's White Dream*.

To this day, the *Times* has not revealed its methods in producing the project. In fact, when the 1619 Project was published, it did not even bother to include a bibliography—though it immediately began sending the print version out to cash-strapped public schools.

Concerned about the educational implications of teaching children false history, four eminent historians interviewed by the WSWS—McPherson, Wood, Bynum, and Oakes—joined Sean Wilentz of Princeton University in December 2019 in writing a public letter to the *Times* asking for corrections of basic errors of fact in the 1619 Project. Silverstein wrote a condescending reply insinuating that the scholars were motivated by petty professional jealousies.

Silverstein's letter dismissing the historians appeared on December 20, 2019. It has now been revealed, by cached versions of the 1619 Project, that *only two days earlier*, on December 18, the *Times* had surreptitiously deleted from the original text (posted on the *Times'* website) its central claim, that the year 1619, and not 1776, represents the "true founding" of the United States. This alteration only came to light a little over a month ago, on September 18, 2020. Hannah-Jones immediately compounded the original deceit by declaring she had never made this "true founding" statement—though she had repeatedly done so. Hannah-Jones then deleted her entire Twitter feed, which included tens of thousands of tweets.

Now the *Times* treats the deletion of the 1619 Project's central thesis as a minor change. But back in December, in his letter rejecting the five historians, Silverstein did not reveal that a change had already been made to this pivotal claim that the historians had criticized. While hiding that inconvenient alteration, Silverstein did take the time to insist that "during the fact-checking process, our researchers carefully reviewed all the articles in the issue with subject-area experts."

This turned out to be yet another lie. On March 6, 2020, one of those fact-checkers—Northwestern University historian Leslie Harris—published an article in Politico revealing that she had "vigorously disputed" the project's claim that the American Revolution had been launched as a counterrevolution against British plans to free the slaves.[5]

It is not clear who the *Times'* other fact-checkers may have been, but the 1619 Project was replete with errors and distortions. To cite one example, Hannah-Jones's assertion that Lincoln viewed blacks as "an obstacle to national unity" had already been dismantled by numerous historians in response to its original author, Lerone Bennett Jr.—including in a book review of Bennett's *Forced into Glory* written by McPherson and published in the *Times* on August 27, 2000, titled "Lincoln the Devil."

---

5. Leslie M. Harris, Politico, March 6, 2020, https://www.politico.com/news/magazine/2020/03/06/1619-project-new-york-times-mistake-122248

Five days after Harris's criticism, on March 11, 2020, Silverstein authored a wording change—an "update," he called it—to the 1619 Project stating that only "some" of the colonists wished for independence "because they wanted to protect the institution of slavery." The "update" left the basic chronological and logical errors in place. Silverstein did not recall the hundreds of thousands of magazines already sent out to school children. Nor did he apologize to the historians he maligned in his December letter, even though they had pointed to this error, among many others.

In sum, Sulzberger's "national conversation," from the standpoint of the *Times*, has been nothing but a series of failed face-saving retreats and cover-ups.

Sulzberger's most basic lie is his claim that the 1619 Project ever had anything to do with history. From the beginning, it was aimed at concentrating national attention on racial divisions under conditions in which social inequality—that is, division along class lines—is reaching explosive levels. It was the culmination of a race-obsessed campaign in which, to cite one example, *Times* readers were told that the crisis in American public education is a result not of cash-starved schools, but of "white parents."

As Baquet put it in a leaked speech that he gave to *Times* staff last summer:

> Race and understanding of race should be a part of how we cover the American story. ... One reason we all signed off on the 1619 Project and made it so ambitious and expansive was to teach our readers to think a little bit more like that. Race in the next year—and I think this is, to be frank, what I would hope you come away from this discussion with—race in the next year is going to be a huge part of the American story.[6]

This has so far backfired. Working-class Americans, black as well as white, draw inspiration from the great and ineradicable achievements of the two American revolutions. They believe human equality is a principle to be fought for and made real, not a "founding myth," as the *Times* sneered. The lynch-mob style attacks on statues of Jefferson, Washington, Lincoln, and Grant, encouraged on Twitter by Hannah-Jones, anger and disgust them. Worse, the clear connection of these attacks to the 1619 Project has allowed Trump and his fascist supporters to posture as custodians of the democratic heritage of the American Revolution and the Civil War.

---

6. Ashley Feinberg, "The New York Times Unites vs. Twitter," Slate, August 15, 2019 https://slate.com/news-and-politics/2019/08/new-york-times-meeting-transcript.html

No amount of self-serving flattery by Sulzberger and his dishonest editors can disguise the fact that the 1619 Project and those responsible for its publication have been discredited.

It Is All Just a Metaphor: The *Times* Attempts Yet Another Desperate Defense

On October 16, 2020, *New York Times Magazine* editor Jake Silverstein issued a new defense of the 1619 Project in which he now argues that its best-known claim—that the year 1619 and not 1776 represents the "true founding" of the United States—was a metaphorical turn of phrase not intended to be read literally.[1] Further confusion is attributed to an editorial error arising from the difficulties of managing a "multiplatform" media operation. Published under the title, "On Recent Criticism of The 1619 Project," Silverstein's essay is a convoluted lawyer's argument that attempts to palm off historical falsification as merely minor matters of syntax, punctuation, and a somewhat careless use of metaphor.

When the 1619 Project was published in August 2019, to coincide with the four-hundredth anniversary of the arrival of the first African slaves in colonial Virginia, no historical claims were too grandiose for Silverstein and lead writer and project creator Nikole Hannah-Jones. The 1619 Project, the *Times* proclaimed, would "reframe" all of American history to show that the past and the present can only be understood through the prism of slavery and the "endemic" racial hatred of whites for blacks.

In supporting this larger claim, the 1619 Project asserted that the events of 1776 were, in essence, a preemptive counterrevolution aimed at thwarting a

Thomas Mackaman and David North, "It is all just a metaphor: The New York Times attempts yet another desperate defense of its discredited 1619 Project," World Socialist Web Site, October 23, 2020.

1. Jake Silverstein, "On Recent Criticism of The 1619 Project," The *New York Times Magazine*, October 16, 2020, https://www.nytimes.com/2020/10/16/magazine/criticism-1619-project.html

British plan to end slavery in North America. Then, in the aftermath of the separation from Britain, black Americans "fought back alone," the *Times* asserted, to "make America a democracy"—without the assistance of abolitionists, the Union Army, Abraham Lincoln, or any other white person, all of whom benefited from slavery and "white capitalism."

Furthermore, according to Hannah-Jones and the *Times*, "true" history had been suppressed by dishonest "white historians" hell-bent on maintaining their racist "founding myth" of 1776. After two centuries of a historical narrative centered on the false elevation of 1776, the 1619 Project declared that "it was finally time to tell our story truthfully."

In spite of Silverstein's deletion of the "true founding" claim and his other word changes, the *Times*' essential position remains the same: the American Revolution was a retrograde event, in which the defense of slavery was the critical motivation. Yet, to this day neither Silverstein nor any other defender of the 1619 Project has bothered to confront the obvious historical questions that this position raises in relationship to both American and world history:

If the American Revolution was a reactionary event, why was it hailed by contemporaries beyond the shores of the United States as the dawn of a new democratic age? Did the American Revolution play no role in the chain of events that produced the French and Haitian revolutions, as well as the Industrial Revolution, the working class, and socialism? Why was Tom Paine made an honorary citizen of the new French Republic? If the proclamation of human equality in the Declaration of Independence is only a "founding myth," and not a discovery whose revolutionary meaning tears through all subsequent history, how do we explain the fact that every progressive social movement has inscribed this maxim on its banner? How was it that the United States developed, within a generation, a mass antislavery movement, and within "four score and seven years" a great Civil War that destroyed slavery? Were all those who identified the American Revolution with the cause of freedom, Frederick Douglass and Martin Luther King included, merely dupes of the American founding fathers?

The most obvious error made by the 1619 Project—that the American Revolution was waged to stop British abolition of slavery—became indefensible after the *Times*' own fact checker, Leslie Harris of Northwestern University, felt compelled to admit that she had "vigorously" opposed it. Silverstein tried to manage this exposure of the *Times*' dishonest suppression of the fact-checker's objection with a clever "cut and paste" modification of Hannah-Jones's false claim. The original categorical denunciation of pre-1619 Project historiography had read:

> Conveniently left out of our founding mythology is the fact that *one of the primary reasons* the colonists decided to declare their independence from Britain was because *they* wanted to protect the institution of slavery. By 1776, Britain had grown deeply conflicted over its role in the barbaric institution that had reshaped the Western Hemisphere [emphasis added].[2]

Silverstein added two words so that the amended version now reads:

> Conveniently left out of our founding mythology is the fact that one of the primary reasons *some of* the colonists decided to declare their independence from Britain was because they wanted to protect the institution of slavery. By 1776, Britain had grown deeply conflicted over its role in the barbaric institution that had reshaped the Western Hemisphere [emphasis added].[3]

In the original version, the defense of slavery is presented as "one of the primary reasons" the colonists decided for separation from Britain. In the 1619 Project version 2.0, the concern over the fate of slavery motivates only "some of" the colonists—How many? Who? Where? Presto! Problem solved. Or so Silverstein thought. But the modified statement is still false. Far from being "conflicted" over slavery, until 1833 the British Empire maintained its own lucrative slave plantations in the Caribbean, to which Loyalist slaveowners fled, human property in tow of His Majesty's Navy.

As for the project's quietly deleted "true founding" thesis—which was emblazoned on the *Times* website and repeated again and again by Hannah-Jones on social media, in interviews, and during her national lecture tour—Silverstein now claims that this was the product of nothing more than a minor technical error, the sort of snafu that is an inevitable outcome of difficulties for modern-day editors, such as himself, in managing a "multiplatform" publication and "figuring out how to present the same journalism in all those different media." With all of these formats to tend to, the beleaguered editors of the *Times* just couldn't get the story straight! Silverstein does not seem to grasp that the criteria of objective truth do not change as one moves from printed

---

2. The *New York Times Magazine*, August 18, 2019, p. 18.
3. The *New York Times Magazine*, dated August 14, 2019, https://www.nytimes.com/interactive/2019/08/14/magazine/1619-america-slavery.html

newspaper to website, or from Facebook to Twitter. What is a lie in one format remains a lie in another.

In addition to chalking up the mistaken "true founding" claim to his far-flung editorial responsibilities, Silverstein attempts to defend Hannah-Jones by implying that readers failed to appreciate "the sense that this was a metaphor." He should have been more attentive, he says, to "online language [that] risked being read literally." This is among the most inspired of Silverstein's excuses. From here on in, whenever *Times* correspondents like Judith Miller are caught lying, its editors may claim that the journalists are writing in metaphors that are not to be read literally.

Silverstein cites the original, "metaphorical," version of the 1619 Project. This is the version that was sent out to school children. It read, with emphasis added:

> 1619 is not a year that most Americans know as a notable date in our country's history. Those who do are at most a tiny fraction of those who can tell you that 1776 is the year of our nation's birth. *What if, however, we were to tell you that this fact, which is taught in our schools and unanimously celebrated every Fourth of July, is wrong, and that the country's true birth date, the moment that its defining contradictions first came into the world, was in late August of 1619?*[4]

He then quotes the revision that has been made to the online publication only:

> 1619 is not a year that most Americans know as a notable date in our country's history. Those who do are at most a tiny fraction of those who can tell you that 1776 is the year of our nation's birth. *What if, however, we were to tell you that the moment that the country's defining contradictions first came into the world was in late August of 1619?*[5]

Perhaps Silverstein hopes his readers will carelessly jump over this scissors-and-glue work. He writes that the difference in the two passages is "to the wording and the length, not the facts." But actually, there to be read *literally* in

---

4. *The New York Times Magazine*, August 18, 2019, p. 4.

5. Jake Silverstein, "Why We Published The 1619 Project," *The New York Times Magazine*, December 20, 2019, https://www.nytimes.com/interactive/2019/12/20/magazine/1619-intro.html

black and white, the first passage refers specifically to an allegedly false "fact." If a metaphor is being employed in the original version, it is very well concealed.

Silverstein repeats Hannah-Jones's conceit that historians have ignored the African American experience. Such a claim exposes both Silverstein's and Hannah-Jones's ignorance of historical literature. The 1619 Project is as much a falsification of historiography as it is of history.

Since the 1930s, an enormous body of scholarship has developed on the periods of American history that the 1619 Project breezes through, as so many turnstiles in the unfolding history of white racism: the colonial era and the emergence of slavery; the American Revolution and the entrenchment of slavery in the antebellum South with the development of cotton production; the development of the "free labor North," antislavery politics and the destruction of slavery in the Civil War; the struggle for and ultimate failure of Reconstruction; and the replacement of slavery by sharecropping, Jim Crow segregation, industry, and wage labor. These vast subjects have attracted the attention of significant historians, and generated fascinating and intense debate among them and their students—W. E. B. Du Bois, Eric Williams, Kenneth Stampp, Stanley Elkins, C. Vann Woodward, Bernard Bailyn, Gordon Wood, Eugene Genovese, Don Fehrenbacher, David Potter, James McPherson, Herbert Gutman, David Montgomery, Eric Foner, David Brion Davis, Ira Berlin, Barbara Fields, and James Oakes, to name only a few.

This scholarship has been ignored by the 1619 Project. There is no evidence that Hannah-Jones's passing acquaintance with American history extends beyond her reading of two books by the black nationalist Lerone Bennett Jr., the longtime editor of *Ebony* magazine.

In an attempt to buttress the claim that the 1619 Project is finally bringing to light suppressed history, Silverstein cites a recent study of US history textbooks by the Southern Poverty Law Center that found popular history textbooks do not provide "comprehensive coverage of slavery and enslaved peoples." As if it aids his cause, he points to one of the study's key findings, that "only 8 percent of high school seniors were aware that slavery was the central cause of the Civil War."

No doubt it is true that American students know little about slavery and its centrality to the Civil War. But this speaks to a larger crisis of historical consciousness. The public schools, starved of funding, have shifted limited resources away from social studies and the arts to "practical" pursuits, a process pushed forward by Barack Obama, who said in office that "folks can make a lot more, potentially, with skilled manufacturing or the trades than they might with an art history degree." The same shifting of resources away from history has taken place at the universities. There were over 19 million Americans enrolled in college in 2017, but only 24,255 graduated with degrees in history—a 33 percent decline since 2001—while 381,000 degrees were awarded to business majors.

Under these conditions, is it really any wonder that high school seniors know little about the causes of the Civil War or even precisely when it took place? But what share of American high school and college graduates can explain the causes of either World War I or World War II, or even correctly identify the years during which these wars were fought? What percentage of American students could state with even approximate accuracy the years of the American involvement in Vietnam, let alone explain the reasons underlying its intervention?

The lack of knowledge is even greater when it comes to the subject that is virtually absent from public discussion in the United States: the history of the working masses and the class struggle that they have waged against American capitalism. This is a subject that involves the fate of the vast majority of the population, including the countless millions of impoverished immigrants who arrived on the shores of America and then fought to "raise the dignity of labor," to use an old phrase. This history finds not the slightest echo in the 1619 Project, which does not acknowledge the existence of class struggle in the United States.

There is plenty of oppression and suffering to go around in the history of what John Brown called "this guilty land." The United States has long been the country with the most powerful and ruthless capitalist class on the planet. Before that it was home to the richest and most powerful slaveowning class. But the explosive development of industrial capitalism in the aftermath of the Civil War gave rise to the most polyglot working class. Under these conditions the great challenge confronting the socialist movement has always been to unite workers across innumerable racial, national, ethnic, linguistic, religious, and regional barriers to confront their common antagonists.

The 1619 Project has been a case study in historical ignorance and dishonesty. Silverstein's latest exercise in self-justification continues the pattern of falsification and evasion. When the 1619 Project was criticized as poor journalism, Silverstein claimed it was history; and when it was criticized as bad history, he claimed it was mere journalism. Now, when it is proven that the 1619 Project's central thesis is false, Silverstein announces that the argument was merely metaphorical and not meant to be taken literally.

In the end, the *New York Times'* argument is a variation of a crooked politician's age-old evasion: "We know that you *think* you *know* what we said. But what you *read* is not what we *meant*."

Afterword:
Trump's 1776 Travesty

The *New York Times*' 1619 Project, published in 2019, was an attempt to reinterpret American history through the prism of race and racial struggle. It condemned the American Revolution as a struggle by whites to preserve slavery against the British Empire. It portrayed Abraham Lincoln, who signed the Emancipation Proclamation and led the North to victory in the Civil War, as a racist. Throughout American history, according to the 1619 Project, black people fought alone to redeem democracy.

The World Socialist Web Site played a leading role in rebutting the 1619 Project, publishing a comprehensive and detailed series of essays and interviews with distinguished historians of American history. These essays and interviews, which touched off a major national controversy, exposed the 1619 Project as a politically motivated falsification of history—and a gift to Donald Trump and the far right.

"By repudiating and denigrating the American Revolution and Civil War, the *New York Times* has provided an opportunity for Trump," the WSWS warned. Indeed, it was not long before Trump himself appeared before the television cameras to respond to the 1619 Project with demands to "restore patriotic education." In his typically menacing fashion, Trump declared that "our youth will be taught to love America."

This is the context for the Trump administration's last-minute "1776 Report," released on January 18, 2021, Martin Luther King Jr. Day.

Tom Carter, "The Trump administration's 1776 Report: The far right attempts to seize opening from the 1619 Project," World Socialist Web Site, January 30, 2021.

The 1776 Report[1] was prepared by a hand-picked commission of sixteen members that did not include a single professional historian. The committee's chair, Larry P. Arnn, is the president of the conservative Hillsdale College in southern Michigan. Arnn attracted controversy in 2013 with his inflammatory testimony before the Michigan legislature regarding accusations against his college of discriminatory admissions practices. "We didn't have enough dark ones, I guess, is what they meant," Arnn said.

Arnn's committee released the 1776 Report less than two weeks after Trump and sections of the Republican Party attempted to overturn the results of the 2020 elections by means of a violent coup, and two days before incoming President Joe Biden's inauguration on January 20, 2021. Predictably, the Biden administration promptly rescinded it.

The 1776 Report begins with what is weakest in the 1619 Project—namely the historical significance of the American Revolution and Civil War—and proceeds from there to the right wing's favorite issues and hated targets: guns, family, prayer, God, and law and order, on one side, and multiculturalism, Hollywood, colleges, and public education, on the other.

The document makes reference to the basic principles of the American Revolution, including "equality" (which the authors hasten to qualify), but insist that "principle is only one" of the factors "binding the American people together" which is "insufficient by itself."

The authors invoke a minor passage written by American revolutionary John Jay (1745–1829) in the *Federalist Papers*, which described the American revolutionaries as "a people descended from the same ancestors, speaking the same language, professing the same religion, attached to the same principles of government, very similar in their manners and customs ..." From this passage, the authors insist that "a republican people must share a large measure of commonality in manners, customs, language, and dedication to the common good."

This essentially fascistic insistence on the necessity of cultural and linguistic homogeneity was issued, unsurprisingly, under the auspices of the same administration that was behind the infamous "Muslim ban" and the deliberate abuse of the children of refugees by separating them from their parents. In this shabby attempt to find in the American Revolution a historical and theoretical

---

1. All citations are taken from the 1776 Report, available at: https://trumpwhitehouse. archives.gov/wp-content/uploads/2021/01/The-Presidents-Advisory-1776-Commission-Final-Report.pdf

justification for such policies, one catches a whiff of the stink of fascistic aides like Stephen Miller, Jared Kushner, and Stephen Bannon.

From there, the document seeks at every turn to weave religion into the historical narrative of the United States. The words "God" and "Christianity" appear repeatedly. In contrast to Thomas Jefferson, who insisted on a "wall of separation" between church and state, the authors of the 1776 Report insist that "religious faith is indispensable to the success of republican government."

Turning abruptly to American history after the Civil War, the Trump administration's report becomes what can only be described as deranged. Progressivism, associated with the era of reforms from 1896 to 1916, is equated by the authors with fascism, communism, and slavery as "challenges to America's principles."

According to the 1776 Report, the Progressive Era reforms created a "shadow government" of bureaucratic regulators that "today operates largely without checks and balances." The report claims that progressives were like fascist dictator Benito Mussolini because they sought to "centralize power under the management of so-called experts."

The implication of this tortured historical narrative is a demand for the wholesale reversal of more than a century of national reforms: a return to unlimited work hours, unchecked tyranny in the workplace, and the failed laissez-faire system of unbridled domination by the capitalist class that prevailed until the stock market crash of 1929.

One of the most significant and representative cases of the Progressive Era was the Supreme Court case of *Lochner v. New York* in 1905, which involved an attempt by the state of New York to limit the work week of bakery employees to sixty hours—an attempt the authors of the 1776 Report presumably would have opposed.

In its explicit rejection of "progressivism," the 1776 Report provides a glimpse of the ideas now wafting around far-right and libertarian circles in America. Speaking for the interests of the most rapacious sections of the financial oligarchy, those denouncing "progressivism" regard any attempts to mitigate or limit the power of the billionaires as impermissible "interference" by the government in the operations of the "free" market.

The document is full of contradictions. After having denounced the progressives' theory of a "living" Constitution—according to which each new generation can discover in the essential principles of the founding documents new implications for democratic rights—the authors claim to posture as defenders of the legacy of the civil rights movement, despite the fact that the resulting reforms were implemented as part of a legal framework that the same authors had equated with Mussolini only a few pages before.

The authors of the 1776 Report contrast the demands for racial preferences now put forward by the practitioners of identity politics with the universal demands for equality that were advanced by Martin Luther King Jr. during the civil rights struggles of the 1960s. But in the 1776 Report, this contrast appears only as an empty talking point, as the authors have no coherent explanation for why the civil rights struggles were necessary at all.

Indeed, the Trump administration stood in the tradition of all those forces in American society that resisted the struggle to dismantle the system of racial apartheid in the southern states. As grotesque as it is to see the Trump administration attempting to drape itself in the mantle of the civil rights struggles, this state of affairs was only made possible by the protracted shift to the right by all that remains of the "civil rights" establishment, exemplified by the 1619 Project itself.

From this bizarre account of American history in the twentieth century, the 1776 Report careens into hysterical anticommunism, equating socialism and communism with slavery and fascism. After a tirade culminating in a quotation of Ronald Reagan, the document concludes with a straight face that the theories behind fascism and communism "fail" because they "deny the existence of God."

Then the document concludes with a rant titled "national renewal," in which the authors emphasize the importance of family and prayer: "When families pray together, they acknowledge together the providence of the Almighty God who gave them their sacred liberty." The document proceeds to make a thinly veiled case for purging the schools, purging the universities, and purging Hollywood of unpatriotic sentiments, along the lines of Campus Watch.

All this has a distinctly fascistic hue. Americans must be taught to speak of America with "reverence and love," the report threatens, and must "stand up" to those who deny "her greatness." Schools must be purged of "any curriculum" or theories that "demean America's heritage, dishonor our heroes, or deny our principles." Given how America's "principles" were defined on the preceding pages, this amounts to a demand for purging everyone who disagrees with Trump and the Republicans.

The final passage of the document features a spirited harangue in favor of "reverence for the laws"—which comes across as almost comical in its context, having been issued in the aftermath of a violent attempt by Trump to overturn the results of the 2020 elections.

Indeed, at the same moment as the 1776 Report was being uploaded to a government website, Trump himself was issuing a barrage of last-minute pardons for convicted criminals who had served as political allies or pawns of his mafia-style family organization.

The historian James McPherson, who was interviewed by the World Socialist Web Site regarding the 1619 Project, commented drily in the Princeton student newspaper, *The Daily Princetonian*, "While I think the 1619 Project has problems, nevertheless, countering it the way the 1776 Report did—it exalted one idea or approach to American history, that it is a triumphant story—is not the answer to the shortcomings of the 1619 Project."[2]

In the final analysis, the 1776 Report can only be regarded as a hastily thrown together attempt by the Trump administration to capitalize on the shipwreck of the 1619 Project and claim the legacy of the two American revolutions for its own brand of fascistic "America First" nationalism.

But even as such, it is a weak effort. The full 1776 Report, without appendices, is only twenty pages, and about a quarter has been cut-and-pasted from other sources, according to analysis published by Politico.[3]

It is a remarkable fact that with all the libraries and museums at its disposal, with limitless resources and grants, with legions of federal employees at its beck and call—and with all the original documents in archives and glass cases—that this twenty-page fascistic hack job was all that the American government could muster in defense of the legacy of the American Revolution and Civil War.

This is not an accident, but expresses the complete historical and political bankruptcy of the more and more openly fascistic American right wing, which has now gathered defiantly around Trump even after the failed coup of January 6, 2021. The 1776 Report has only to be contrasted with the devastating critique of the 1619 Project from the left developed by the World Socialist Web Site over the preceding year and a half.

The authors of the 1619 Project and the 1776 Report have more in common than they may care to admit. Both replace class struggle in history with forms of nationalist mythmaking—right-wing black nationalism in the former, and far-right "America First" nationalism in the latter. Both falsify America's

---

2. James McPherson, *The Daily Princetonian*, available at: https://www.dailyprincetonian.com/article/2021/01/princeton-historians-trump-1776-commission-report-1619-project
3. Tina Nguyen, "A big chunk of Trump's 1776 report appears to be lifted from an author's prior work," https://www.politico.com/news/2021/01/19/trump-1776-report-plagiarism-460464

revolutionary history in service of the present-day political needs of factions of the ruling class—the 1619 Project for the Democratic Party and its satellites; the 1776 Report for Trump and the Republicans. Neither the 1619 Project nor the 1776 Report can tell much of the actual history of the United States—much less coherently articulate the democratic legacy of the American Revolution and Civil War.

Leon Trotsky's words in *Results and Prospects* apply to both efforts: "The bourgeoisie has shamefully betrayed all the traditions of its historical youth, and its present hirelings dishonor the graves of its ancestors and scoff at the ashes of its ideals."[4]

It was first and foremost the World Socialist Web Site, the organ of the international Trotskyist movement, that was able to articulate and provide a rallying point for the defense of what was historically progressive in American history. This is because the struggle to defend the progressive achievements of the past is inseparably connected with the international struggle to advance the cause of socialism today.

---

4. Leon Trotsky, *Results and Prospects* (Seattle: Red Letter Books, 2010), p. 61.

Works Cited

Bailyn, Bernard, *The Barbarous Years: The Peopling of British North America—The Conflict of Civilizations 1600–1675* (New York: Vintage Books, 2013)

Bailyn, Bernard, *History and the Creative Imagination* (St. Louis: Washington University Press, 1985)

Bailyn, Bernard, *The Ordeal of Thomas Hutchinson* (Cambridge: Cambridge University Press, 1974)

Bailyn, Bernard, Speech to the American Historical Association, 1981, https://www.historians.org/about-aha-and-membership/aha-history-and-archives/presidential-addresses/bernard-bailyn

Beckert, Sven and Seth Rockman, *Slavery's Capitalism: A New History of American Economic Development* (University of Pennsylvania Press, 2018)

Blumenthal, Sidney, *The Self-Made Man: The Political Life of Abraham Lincoln, Vol. 1, 1809–1849* (New York: Simon and Schuster, 2016)

Brinkley, Alan *The End of Reform: New Deal Liberalism in Recession and War* (New York: Alfred A. Knopf, 1995)

Brown, Dee, *Bury My Heart at Wounded Knee, An Indian History of the American West* (New York: Henry Holt and Company Inc., 1970)

Browne, Francis F., *The Everyday Life of Abraham Lincoln* (Chicago: Browne & Howell, 1913)

Brustein, William, *The Logic of Evil: The Social Origin of the Nazi Party, 1925–1933* (New Haven: Yale University Press, 1996)

Cannon, James P., "The Coming American Revolution," *James P. Cannon Writings and Speeches, 1945–47: The Struggle for Socialism in the "American Century"* (New York: Pathfinder Press, 1977)

Chafe, William H., *The Unfinished Journey: America Since World War II* (Oxford: Oxford University Press, 1985)

David, James Corbett, *Dunmore's New World: The Extraordinary Life of a Royal Governor in Revolutionary America—with Jacobites, Counterfeiters, Land Schemes, Shipwrecks, Scalping, Indian Politics, Runaway Slaves, and Two Illegal Royal Weddings* (University of Virginia Press, 2013)

Davis, David Brion, *From Homicide to Slavery: Studies in American Culture* (Oxford University Press, 1988)

Debs, Eugene V., "The Negro in the Class Struggle," http://www.marxists.org/archive/debs/works/1903/negro.htm [printed in *International Socialist Review*, Vol. 4, No. 5. November 1903]

Douglass, Frederick, *Narrative of the Life of Frederick Douglass*, Google Books.

Engels, Friedrich, "Ludwig Feuerbach and the Outcome of Classical German Philosophy," *Marx & Engels Collected Works*, Vol. 26 (London: Lawrence & Wishart, 2010)

Finkelman, Paul, "I Could not Afford to Hang Men for Votes—Lincoln the Lawyer, Humanitarian Concerns, and the Dakota Pardons," *William Mitchell Law Review*: 2013, Vol. 39

Frey, Sylvia R., "Between Slavery and Freedom: Virginia Blacks in the American Revolution," *Journal of Southern History*, Vol. 49, No. 3 (August 1983)

Frey, Sylvia R., *Water from the Rock: Black Resistance in a Revolutionary Age* (Princeton: Princeton University Press, 1991)

Gay, Peter, *The Enlightenment: The Science of Freedom* (New York and London: W. W. Norton, 1996)

Genovese, Eugene D., *In Red and Black: Marxian Explorations in Southern and Afro-American History* (New York: Random House, 1968)

Goldfield, David, *Black, White, and Southern: Race Relations and Southern Culture 1940 to the Present* (Louisiana State University Press, 1990)

Herndon, William H. and Jesse W. Weik, *Herndon's Life of Lincoln* (World Publishing Co., 1949)

Hinderaker, Eric and Peter C. Mancall, *At the Edge of Empire: The Backcountry British in North America* (Johns Hopkins University Press, 2003)

Hobsbawm, E. J., *Nations and Nationalism Since 1780: Program, Myth, Reality* (London: Cambridge University Press, 1991)

Hofstadter, Richard, *The American Political Tradition, and the Men Who Made It* (Vintage Books, New York, 1989)

Howe, Daniel Walker, *What Hath God Wrought: The Transformation of America, 1815–1848* (Oxford: Oxford University Press, 2007)

Israel, Jonathan, *The Expanding Blaze: How the American Revolution Ignited the World, 1775–1848* (Princeton: Princeton University Press, 2017)

King, Martin Luther Papers, https://kinginstitute.stanford.edu

King, Martin Luther Jr., *Why We Can't Wait* (Signet Classic), 2000

Klotter, James C. *Henry Clay: The Man Who Would Be President* (Oxford: Oxford University Press, 2018)

Leff, Laurel, *Buried by the Times: The Holocaust and America's Most Important Newspaper* (Cambridge: Cambridge University Press, 2005)

Lepore, Jill, *These Truths: A History of the United States* (New York: W. W. Norton, 2018)

Lincoln, Abraham, *Collected Works of Abraham Lincoln*, Vol. 2, Roy P. Basler, editor (The Abraham Lincoln Association, Springfield, Illinois)

Lincoln, Abraham, *Collected Works of Abraham Lincoln*, Vol. 4, Second Inaugural Address, April 10, 1865.

Lincoln, Abraham, Letter to Henry L. Pierce, April 8, 1859 http://www.abrahamlincolnonline.org/lincoln/speeches/pierce.htm

Lofft, Capel, *Reports*, Margrave's Argument. (14 May 1772)

Lovejoy, Paul E., *Transformations in Slavery* (Cambridge: Cambridge University Press, 2012)

Lukács, Georg, *The Destruction of Reason* (London: Merlin Press, 1980)

Marx, Karl, "Address from the Working Men's International Association to President Johnson." *The Bee-Hive Newspaper* (United Kingdom), No. 188, May 20, 1865

Marx, Karl, "Capital, Volume 1," *Marx & Engels Collected Works*, Vol. 35 (London: Lawrence & Wishart, 1996)

Marx, Karl, *A Contribution to the Critique of Political Economy* (New York: International Publishers, 1970)

Marx, Karl, "The Eighteenth Brumaire of Louis Bonaparte," *Marx & Engels Collected Works*, Vol. 11 (London: Lawrence & Wishart, 2010)

Marx, Karl, "To Abraham Lincoln, President of the United States," *Marx & Engels Collected Works*, Vol. 20 (New York: International Publishers, 1984)

Marx, Karl and Friedrich Engels, *Marx & Engels, Letters to Americans 1848–1895* (International Publishers, New York, 1953)

McPherson, James, *Abraham Lincoln and the Second American Revolution* (Oxford: Oxford University Press, 1992)

McPherson, James, *What They Fought For* (Baton Rouge: Louisiana State University Press, 1994)

Merritt, Keri Leigh, *Masterless Men: Poor Whites and Slavery in the Antebellum South* (Cambridge University Press, 2017)

Novick, Peter, *That Noble Dream: The "Objectivity Question" and the American Historical Profession* (Cambridge: Cambridge University Press, 1988)

Nwokeji, G. Ogo, *The Cambridge World History of Slavery, Vol. 3, AD 1420–AD 1804*, David Eltis and Stanley L. Engerman eds. (Cambridge: Cambridge University Press, 2011)

Oakes, James, *Freedom National: The Destruction of Slavery in the United States, 1861–1865* (New York: W. W. Norton, 2013)

Oakes, James, *The Scorpion's Sting: Antislavery and the Coming of the Civil War* (New York: W. W. Norton, 2014)

Polenberg, Richard, "The Declining Significance of Race: Blacks and Changing American Institutions," quoted in *One Nation Divisible: Class, Race and Ethnicity in the United States Since 1938* (Penguin, 1980)

Palmer, R. R., *The Age of Democratic Revolution: A Political History of Europe and America, 1760–1800* (Princeton: Princeton University Press, 1959)

Quarles, Benjamin, "Lord Dunmore as Liberator," *The William and Mary Quarterly*, 3rd Series., Vol. 15, No. 4.

Rosenthal, Caitlin, *Accounting for Slavery: Masters and Management* (Cambridge: Harvard University Press, 2018).

Sandburg, Carl, *Abraham Lincoln: The War Years,*, Vol. 1 (New York: Harcourt, Brace & Co., 1939)

Shy, John, *A People Numerous and Armed: Reflections on the Military Struggle for American Independence* (Ann Arbor: University of Michigan Press, 1990)

Trotsky, Leon, *History of the Russian Revolution* (London: Pluto Press, 1977)

Trotsky, Leon, *Results and Prospects* (Seattle: Red Letter Books, 2010)

Trotsky, Leon, *Their Morals and Ours* (New York: Pathfinder Press, 1973)

Trotsky, Leon, "What Is National Socialism?" https://www.marxists.org/archive/trotsky/germany/1933/330610.htm

Trump White House Archive, 1776 Commission Report, January 18, 2021, https://trumpwhitehouse.archives.gov/wp-content/uploads/2021/01/The-Presidents-Advisory-1776-Commission-Final-Report.pdf

Welles, Gideon, *Diary of Gideon Welles*, Vol. 1 (New York: W.W. Norton & Company, 1960)

West, Cornel, ed., *The Radical King* (Boston: Beacon Press, 2015)

White, Richard, *The Republic for Which It Stands: The United States during Reconstruction and the Gilded Age, 1865–1896* (Oxford University Press, 2017)

Williams, David, *Bitterly Divided: The South's Inner Civil War* (New York: The New Press, 2008)

Williams, Eric, *Capitalism and Slavery* (Chapel Hill: University of N. Carolina Press, 1944)

Williams, George Washington, *History of the Negro Race in America from 1619 to 1880* (Putnam Press, 1882)

Wilson, Douglas L. and Rodney O. Davis, eds., *Herndon's Informants: Letters, Interviews, and Statements about Abraham Lincoln* (Urbana: University of Illinois Press, 1998)

Wolin, Richard, *The Seduction of Unreason: The Intellectual Romance with Fascism, from Nietzsche to Postmodernism* (Princeton University Press, 2004)

Wood, Gordon, "The Creative Imagination of Bernard Bailyn," in James A. Henretta, Michael G. Kammen, and Stanley Nider Katz, *The Transformation of Early American History: Society, Authority, and Ideology* (New York: Random House, 1991)

Wood, Gordon, *The Radicalism of the American Revolution* (New York: Vintage Books, 1993)

Woodward, C. Vann, *The Strange Career of Jim Crow* (New York: Oxford University Press, 2002)

Index